THE
HENRY
WILLIAMSON
ANIMAL SAGA

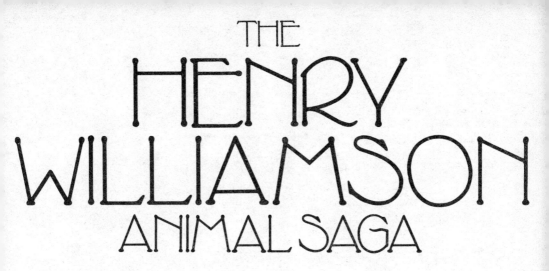

THE HENRY WILLIAMSON ANIMAL SAGA

TARKA THE OTTER
and other stories

BOOK CLUB ASSOCIATES
LONDON

Tarka the Otter *first published in 1927*
Salar the Salmon *first published in 1935*
The Epic of Brock the Badger *first published in 1926*
Chakchek the Peregrine *first published in 1923*

This edition first published in 1960
Fourth impression 1968
Fifth impression 1974
Sixth impression 1975
Seventh impression 1978

ISBN 0 356 01736 2

This edition published 1978 by Book Club Associates
by arrangement with Macdonald & Jane's

Printed and bound in Great Britain by
Richard Clay (The Chaucer Press) Ltd,
Bungay, Suffolk

FOREWORD

Within this volume are the four chief epics of the natural world of the first half of my life. They were written in the period, following the first World War, when I lived in North Devon and saw and heard many exciting things, the effect of which lies upon the following pages.

The subjects of my four stories are an otter, a salmon, a badger, and a peregrine falcon. The unity of place is preserved: the country covered by webbed paw, fin, clawed pad, and pinion lies between the Bristol Channel or Severn Sea on the north, and Dartmoor and its rivers on the south. The travels of the badger, by reason of his short legs, which tread rock and earth only, are the most confined. The otter, who often lets rapid water bear him, ranges farther; so does the salmon, who leaves the river for the ocean where much of his life is mysterious, although I tried to follow it with the imagination; while the peregrine falcon, a wanderer by name, ranges the winds above earth and sea when his need is upon him to find a wing-flicker like to his own.

The unity of spirit is that of the author, a young man in the time of the stories who saw his life, in conjunction with the wild, as a saga. Some details on the origin and creation of the literary work of recording what his senses perceived are given, but not too many, for these pages are not for his biography directly, but only indirectly in so far as they are the biographies of Tarka, Salar, Bloody Bill Brock, and Chakchek.

The author is grateful to Messrs Putnam & Co. for permission to include *Tarka the Otter* and the shorter biographies of Brock and Chakchek from their editions of *The Old Stag* and *The Peregrine's Saga*, all illustrated by Charles F. Tunnicliffe R.A.; and to Messrs Faber & Faber for *Salar the Salmon*, also illustrated by "Tunny", in those years, more than a quarter of a century ago, when we tramped together over the country of the Two Rivers.

Now to the book, for which four special pieces have been written, whereby the reader is led into the author's realm of river, sea, earth, and air.

Devon, 1959   H.W.

CONTENTS

TARKA THE OTTER

*His joyful water-life and death in the
Country of the Two Rivers*

THE GENTLEMAN'S RIVER

That was the name given to the Taw by the otter-hunters who walked its banks when I was a young man with an ambition to write the story of a wild otter. I was a stranger, and usually walked alone, but one day I dared to say to the Master, "Why, sir, is the Taw called the 'Gentleman's River'?"

Before this question, I had imagined that the Taw was so-named because some of the Hunt members were landed proprietors, each owning a few miles of water adjoining his property.

"Well, the inns along the Taw, unlike those of the Torridge, are so placed that we may refresh ourselves at luncheon."

The Master was dressed in white breeches, blue coat and worsted stockings, yellow waistcoat, white[1] pot hat, and heavy boots of the kind usually worn by labouring men. They were studded with brads on heels and sole for walking on the rocky beds of streams. He was a kindly man, carrying a six-foot ash-pole taller than himself, its many silver rings engraved with places and dates of otters killed, with zodiacal signs denoting male and female. Often one saw him leaning on his ash-pole, meditatively stroking drooping yellow moustaches.

There were salmon and sea-trout in the pools of the winding river, and as I followed behind the "field" I saw native brown trout making rings under the alders where hounds had splashed. Pheasants in the woods growing on the hillsides above the valley sometimes crowed to the huntsman's horn. Often we walked on the railway track, avoiding trains from Waterloo which, when crossing the river, thundered over the iron bridges built upon stone cutwaters against which were lodged tree-roots and branches brought down by floods.

[1] Mr. White was the London hatter for country gentlemen in Victorian days. The pot hat was a modification of that originally made by Mr. Bowler of Houndsditch for Lord Derby's gamekeepers; but was *grey* in colour.

Up the smaller valleys carved by tributary streams, called runners, were old pack-horse bridges of stone. Here the hounds came of a summer morning, travelling from their kennels in the town in an old van, out of which they tumbled, to be taken upstream by Tom the huntsman, until excited "tongues" and massed waving of tails (called sterns) marked the scent of an otter.

The Master's white hat, the solid tyres of his two-stroke engine'd Trojan, a metal-box-like motorcar without differential, dates the time of which I am writing. It was nearly forty years ago. Otter-hunting then was a pastime, an occasion for seasonal gatherings along the river banks of many who had known one another since childhood. In some of the inns by the bridges— I remember especially The Malt Scoop—we sat down to wonderful teas with bowls of cream, stewed fruit, cut-rounds, kitchen-made butter glistening with dew, and delicious sausage rolls, after the day's sport. Motorcars with chauffeurs and acetylene brass lamps raised clouds of dust taking us home through narrow lanes brushing our mudguards with ferns.

Every August there was a dance, with programmes embossed with an otter's mask in blue—the men wearing white kid gloves, tail-coats, tall wing collars and white ties with stiff starched shirts and patent leather pumps. We danced in the Assembly Rooms, the floor swung on hidden chains; or at one or another of the North Devon houses, now, alas, lived in no longer by their owner-families—Orleigh, Portledge, Tawstock, Moreton. . .

Not all the otters found and hunted in the waters of the Two Rivers were killed. Our local pack, the Cheriton, lost on an average two out of every three hunted otters. The Master never chased a gravid bitch. Hounds were whipped off—that is, called off by voice, horn, and whip-cracks in the air—when a bitch otter was seen to be in whelp, or when she returned again and again to the holt out of which she had been bolted, thus telling plainly to watching human eyes that she had cubs laid up within. I was glad when this happened; my sympathies were always with the hunted beast. At the same time I knew that otters were hunters more ferocious than their human antagonists.

After one long and pleasantly tiring drag up a valley along the Torridge I was returning on my motorbike, and had descended a steep lane to the river, to sit awhile on the parapet of a bridge built in mediaeval times at Taddiport. There I had the great fortune to watch several otters hunting salmon in the pool below. There is an account of how they manage to "beach" big fish in one of the chapters of *Salar the Salmon*, which I shall not anticipate here.

Otters in the West Country are not often hunted nowadays. The Cheriton is no more. Many of the small boys I used to watch eating plum cake and drinking lemonade while their parents munched sandwiches and drank ale among the farm labourers on the benches outside the inns of the Gentleman's River, have fallen in another war. Nowadays an otter's skin is worth £5 or £6, and otters are easily taken in gins laid on sunken posts at the edge of a pool. At least the otter-hunters saved them from a slow death by drowning, while swimming with a steel trap on one paw; and although this may seem possibly untrue to some, the otters were not previously preserved solely for hunting; but for themselves as part of the English scene.

It was during my third year in Devon, while living by myself in a thatched cottage rented for two shillings a week, that I began to write what I called *The Otter's Saga*. Soon I found that it was not an easy book to write. There was much to learn about the West Country. And the more I saw, the more I realised that very many passages already written imaginatively must be revised. By the time the book was completed three more years had passed, and the text had been rewritten seventeen times. As I became the more familiar with the country lying between Exmoor on the north, and Dartmoor on the south—a wild and beautiful terrain above steep valleys and clear streams running in their rocky beds below, where small trout darted before my descending shadow—the more I sought to wedge into my book, to impose a sharper seen reality upon its pages.

The later versions were written in what can only be described as anguish arising from a sense of insufficient knowledge. Looking at the manuscript today, with some of the botched typing done with minimum spacing, and scrawled all over in minute writing in ink, I recall that a time came when I could bear my doubts no longer: I must go on foot from scene to scene of actual country, making notes and starting afresh.

I was married then, and had a baby son who cried much, why, his mother and I and the doctor could not determine. Leaving the village one morning, with staff and knapsack, I climbed to the watershed of Taw and Torridge, to enter a region of mist and dead and dying heather. There I discovered Taw Head, where the smallest trickle cried faintly in the mossy channel of its granite bed, and crossed the bog by leaping and hopping from peat-hag to peat-hag, fearful of sinking into the black unknown, to where sister Torridge began her life. While curlews cried wildly above dragging clouds I made notes and a sketch of how little brother Taw, four inches in width from bank to bank, moved out of Cranmere tarn, to run bright at his beginning, while sister Torridge hardly stirred out of the silence and mystery of the peat. Soon the two parted, to run their different ways, each collecting tribute water from every smaller coombe and valley until they met again in the estuary below the monks' bridges of Barnstaple and Bideford, where their waters pound with salt waves on the grey pebble-ridge of Westward Ho!

I was embodying these notes and impressions in the seventeenth version of my manuscript one morning in March 1926 in our cottage at Georgeham, when my wife came to me with spotted cheeks and confused eyes. Never one to complain, she admitted she had a headache. I took her temperature—103 degrees—and asked her to go to bed. The doctor said she had cystitis, and must be kept warm, and fed on milky foods. The internal bleeding was painful, and her temperature rose to 104 degrees, and returned there, off and on for several days. The baby cried more than ever, and when at her husky request I weighed him on the kitchen scales, suspended in a napkin, he was under eight pounds—less than his weight at birth four weeks previously. I could hardly bear his wailing, which wrung a nervous weakness in myself, as some musical notes will ring delicate glass, and, if it has a flaw, may even shatter it. The doctor advised me to give the baby a bottle of hot water when he wailed at night, and leave him in an empty room to cry himself to sleep. I did this, but heard the cries despite two closed doors. When the paroxysms increased to periods when the baby seemed to throttle himself, I got up and, muttering some sort of comfort to his mother burning in silent pain beside me, went into the spare room we called Skullcracker—the doorway was only about five feet high—and taking the baby from the wicker cradle, gave him more hot water. He sucked for a few moments desperately, then began to scream again. What could I do, to save him such agony? The doctor had advised that he be not fed at night; but I felt he was starved. The direction of thought in those days, based on Dr. Truby King's ideas, was to get baby into regular habits almost from the moment of birth. So I gave him a bottle of condensed milk diluted with hot water. He sucked, he cried; he sucked, he screamed. So I nursed him downstairs in the kitchen through the night, and continued with my writing, one slow word after another.

His mother became thin in face and body, and in the mornings I had to steady her while she sat up in bed to wash him, a bowl of warm water on a towel on the bed-spread before her. The month of May passed, the apple-blossom was over, in the garden lettuces were hearting up. For a week or ten days I fed Loetitia on bread and butter with young lettuces and milk. This brought her temperature down to 100 degrees.

Meanwhile the final version of *Tarka* was being written slowly, every word being "chipped out of the breastbone". I began to write about 10 p.m. when things were quiet, and continued for three, four, sometimes five hours, while nursing the baby in the crook of my left arm. I sat at the white-enamelled iron table of Loetitia's pride—her Easiwork-fitted kitchen cabinet—with the napkins I had washed drying on a line across the ceiling. There was a Valor Perfection kerosene stove, warming the air. Of the book I had become a little weary, since it had been going on for nearly four years, and to small purpose. There was a feeling, persistent in despondency that no-one would read this matter-of-fact local record, its pages now so tightly packed with facts, most of them unexciting, even dull. Yet behind this superficial discouragement, some of it induced by an unfavourable opinion passed on an earlier typescript by a local squire, was a deeper feeling that it was the real stuff, for was it not true? My part as a writer seemed a small, entirely impersonal part: it was the Devon country-side that mattered, the trees, the rivers, the birds, the animals, the people.

The baby and I had some sort of routine by this time. When he cried I turned him over on my lap, tapping the small of his back to ease his chronic wind pain. "Windees, baby dear, windees?" I would inquire, looking at him. A sudden smile would come on his face; but soon, too soon, the mouth would droop, the lips quiver, the eyes become anguished, and his world would break. I felt helpless, he was so small and thin, my tears fell on his woollen jacket and on his face. Once he must have tasted salt, for he stopped crying and looked at me with surprise. He smiled, and we laughed together—such a joke, though what it was I do not know. But lest he use up all his energy I rested his soft warm head against my throat, he sighed, and fell asleep.

Then on with the book: Tarka travelling round the northern coast of Devon, by Wild Pear Beach near the bat-haunted silver-mines of Combe Martin, and along the shaley rocks of the Severn Sea. My neck ached and my eyes stung, and when I could not see properly in the light of the guttering candle, I went to sleep in Skullcracker, taking baby with me. Some-times his mother's voice came softly through the darkness that she would take him, for I must rest, she whispered. I gave baby to her, for I knew she did not sleep while we two were downstairs in the kitchen; she lay in the darkness, listening.

By now I was looking forward to the nightly vigil with my little friend. Welcome, too, was the light of the candle stuck in a battered Cromwellian candlestick of brass bought some years before in the Caledonian market in North London for one shilling and sixpence. It had become an adventure, writing with the aid of a solitary candle. The candlestick was hung with green waxicles, although each candle re-stuck every starting time upon the guttered stub of its predecessor, had been ordinary grey opaque paraffin wax. How came the drippings to be green? It took me some time to solve the mystery.

The candlestick was a hollow stem of latten, which is similar to brass, but contains more tin and less copper in the amalgam; it is a quieter, gentler metal. On its circular base the stem was cracked, and when a candle-stub, left overlong, became fluid, and the wick fell aslant and the flame flickered over the near-boiling grease, while I wrote on heedless of time and light because the surge was in me and I did not want to stop, then the heat of the metal rim melted the solid grease of previous drippings within the stalk; and, mixing with cuprous and stannic salts called verdigris, became green and seeped out of the crack just above the base. As night succeeded night, so that green coating of wax round the base became thicker.

Night after night I limited my stint of nursery writing to the life of one candle, and wrote on until the circling and lambent flame, wan at its life's end, curled away into darkness; then rising, I groped my way with the baby, my eyelids shut tight, to Skullcracker; to lie down with my cub on my chest, as a sort of hot-water bottle for him. For me, too; and some-times the bottle leaked, but our mutual warmth soon dried the slight discomfort.

One such night, or dawning, I noticed an absence of strong ammoniacal smell. It seems almost the confession of a simple-ton, but the idea did not occur to me for several weeks that his mother was not able to feed him properly. And was I feeding to him by bottle the right foods? I had tried several proprietary brands, all had been rejected. And had I fed to his mother enough proper food to make milk for him? Lettuces, bread and butter—white bread with the skin of the wheat berry ground away—and tea, with cheese and sometimes marmalade and an egg, were they too poor a nourishment? How obvious it was, after the idea had taken root!

Eventually, after some more trial foods, Savory and Moore's was suggested by an old lady. From the first bottle the baby ceased to wail; he put on weight, but not too much. He was now nearly six months old and weighed less than half his weight again at birth. And he seemed, in the years that were to come, to be the least secure child of the family, always a little anxious. Life with father when father depends on his feelings for imaginative writing (more exhausting than some people realise) to support a family is not always easy, for himself or for those around him; but for the moment, which was August 1926, all was apparently well, and baby appeared to be growing into a strong and happy child. When corn-harvest was on, mother and son were playing together on the "seasands".

The book, too, was finished. The new typescript was sent off to John Fortescue, historian of the British Army, and author of *The Story of a Red Deer*, a West Country classic. He was an old friend of my wife's family, and since he had been bred in Devon, where his forebears had lived since the fifteenth century, his verdict was awaited with mixed feelings. For while a remote part of me was sure about the spirit of the book, I had received adverse criticism from some otter-hunters who were not of the West Country, but seasonal visitors to what was called the Combined, or Joint, Week, when various packs came down to hunt the Cheriton water. One of these visitors, a wine and spirit merchant and former Cheriton M.O.H., wrote to demand what qualifications I, a stranger to Devon and not exactly a keen sportsman, possessed that I should presume to write about an otter, as I had in an article in *The Tatler*? My ears would burn, he went on to say, if I could have heard some of the comments of his fellow members of the Crowhurst, a Sussex pack.

To this letter I replied gently, admitting almost total ignorance compared with his great experience. A reply came in a different key: and from later correspondence I received some help, and to this day remain in his debt for the source of the final scene, when a dying otter in a tidal pool drowned the stallion hound of a pack which had hunted the otter to exhaustion during many hours. After the book was published, when I saw this gentleman again, he greeted me with enthusiasm, as one who knew more about otters than he did.

"People tell me that a sinking otter would never drown a hound, but I tell them that I saw the very thing happen in an Irish tidal river," he said to the author modestly receiving his congratulations.

Sir John Fortescue was kind enough to write an Introduction to the original edition of *Tarka*, and in a letter to me he said that the spirit of Exmoor which he had known since a boy was now revealed to him in a way that increased his own knowledge and feeling for his home. How was this possible, he asked. It was only later that I wondered if my sense of place, my feeling of being at home on Exmoor and in its elements could have been transmitted, genetically, through one line of my forebears which had lived below the moor at one place certainly as far back as the thirteenth century, according to published records; and, as Dr. W. G. Hoskins, a Devonian writer of first-class history and Fellow of All Souls, told me the other day, probably the family was at Knowestone in Saxon times. For it is established that some birds have an inherited sense of place, why not with the so-called mammals?

It is not evidence acceptable to any scientific laboratory mind, but I have also wondered about the name *Tarka*, which came suddenly to me, entirely without reflection. When the book was published I had some correspondence with a Professor at Nottingham University named Ernest Weekley, whose name was vaguely familiar to me. Then I recalled that a Mrs. Frieda Weekley had left her home to follow a young man called D. H. Lawrence, whose books were then read by the few, and the cause of anger and contempt among the many. Professor Weekley wrote that the names of some West Country rivers were possibly Celtic in origin, from the word *Ta*, water— such as Taw, Tor-ridge, Ta-mar, Teign, Ta-vy. The *a* was a diminutive, as in Wooda Bay near Lynton, and Forda, the little ford across the road winding down the valley from Georgeham (originally Ham, A-S *hame*).

So *Tarka*, "meaning wandering as water, or the little water wanderer", as the author had "invented" was not altogether fictitious.

One more point. The gravel ridge in the estuary of the Two Rivers is, today, generally called Middle Ridge. In the time of writing *Tarka*, old fishermen, and mast-and-yards men (deep-water sailors), called it variously—according to the beer they had drunk—The Shrarshook, or Sharshook—one of their number, a Captain Charles Hook, was caught on the ridge by the flowing tide at night, and swept away to drown.

Now it is time to go. Upon the river lie the last sunset hues. In colder air moving down from the moor the stony tongues of the water rise sudden loud under the oaks. . . .

THE FIRST YEAR

1

Twilight upon meadow and water, the eve-star shining above the hill, and Old Nog the heron crying *kra-a-ark!* as his slow dark wings carried him down to the estuary. A whiteness drifting above the sere reeds of the riverside, for the owl had flown from under the middle arch of the stone bridge that once carried the canal across the river.

Below Canal Bridge, on the right bank, grew twelve great trees, with roots awash. Thirteen had stood there—eleven oaks and two ash trees—but the oak nearest the North Star had never thriven, since first a pale green hook had pushed out of a swelled black acorn left by floods on the bank more than three centuries before. In its second year a bullock's hoof had crushed the seedling, breaking its two ruddy leaves, and the sapling grew up crooked. The cleft of its fork held the rains of two hundred years, until frost made a wedge of ice that split the trunk; another century's weather wore it hollow, while every flood took more earth and stones from under it. And one rainy night, when salmon and peal from the sea were swimming against the brown rushing water, the tree had suddenly groaned. Every root carried the groans of the moving trunk, and the voles ran in fear from their tunnels. It rocked until dawn; and when the wind left the land it gave a loud cry, scaring the white owl from its roost, and fell into the river as the sun was rising.

Now the water had dropped back, and dry sticks lodged on the branches marked the top of the flood. The river flowed slowly through the pool, a-glimmer with the clear green western sky. At the tail of the pool it quickened smoothly into paws of water, with star-streaming claws. The water murmured against the stones. Jets and rills ran fast and shallow to an island, on which grew a leaning willow tree. Down from here the river moved swift and polished. Alder and sallow grew on its banks. Round a bend it hastened, musical over many stretches of shillet; at the end of the bend it merged into a dull silence of deep saltwater, and its bright spirit was lost. The banks below were mud, channered by the sluices of guts draining the marsh. Every twelve hours the sea passed an arm under Halfpenny Bridge, a minute's heron-flight below, and the spring tides felt the banks as far as the bend. The water moved down again immediately, for the tide's-head had no rest.

The tree lay black in the glimmering salmon pool. Over the meadow a mist was moving, white and silent as the fringe of down on the owl's feathers. Since the fading of shadows it had been straying from the wood beyond the mill-leat, bearing in its breath the scents of the day, when bees had bended bluebell and primrose. Now the bees slept, and mice were running through the flowers. Over the old year's leaves the vapour moved, silent and wan, the wraith of waters once filling the ancient wide river-bed—men say that the sea's tides covered all this land, when the Roman galleys drifted up under the hills.

Earth trickled by the gap in the bank to the broken roots below. Voles were at work, clearing their tunnels, scraping new shafts and galleries, biting the rootlets which hindered them. An otter curled in the dry upper hollow of the fallen oak heard them, and uncurling, shook herself on four short legs. Through a woodpecker's hole above her she saw the starcluster of the Hunting Dogs as faint points of light. She was hungry. Since noon the otter had lain there, sometimes twitching in sleep.

The white owl alighted on the upright branch of the tree, and the otter heard the scratch of its talons as they gripped the bark. She looked from the opening, and the brush of her whiskers on the wood was heard by the bird, whose ear-holes, hidden by feathers, were as large as those of a cat. The owl was harkening, however, for the prick of the claws of mice on leaves, and when it heard these tiny noises, it stared until it saw movement, and with a skirling screech that made the mouse crouch in a fixity of terror, sailed to the ground and clutched it in a foot. The otter gave but a glance to the bird; she was using all her senses to find enemies.

She stood rigid. The hair on her back was raised. Her long tail was held straight. Only her nose moved as it worked at the scents brought by the mist from the wood. Mingled with flower odours, which were unpleasant to her, was the taint that had given her a sudden shock; causing her heart to beat quickly, for power of running and fighting if cornered: the taint most dreaded by the otters who wandered and hunted and played in the country of the Two Rivers—the scent of Deadlock, the great pied hound with the belving tongue, leader of the pack whose kills were notched on many hunting poles.

The otter had been hunted that morning. Deadlock had chopped at her pate, and his teeth had grooved a mark in her fur, as she ran over a stony shallow. The pack had been whipped off when the Master had seen that she was heavy with young, and she had swum away down the river, and hidden in the hollow of the water-lapped trunk.

The mist moved down with the river; her heart slowed; she forgot quickly. She put her head and shoulders under water, holding her breath, and steadying herself by pressing her tail, which was thick and strong and tapered from where her backbone ended, against the rough bark. She was listening and watching for fish. Not even the voles peeping from their holes again heard the otter as she slid into the water.

Her dark form came within the inverted cone of water-light wherein movement above was visible to a trout waving fins and tail behind a sunken bough. While the otter was swimming down to the rocky bed, she saw the glint of scales as the fish sped in zigzag course to its cave. The otter was six feet under the surface, and at this depth her eyes, set level with the short fur of the head, could detect any movement above her in the water lit by star-rays. She could see about four times her own length in front, but beyond all was obscure, for the surface reflected the dark bed of the river. Swimming above the weeds of the pool, she followed the way of the trout, searching every big boulder. She was way-wise in the salmon pool. In underwater pursuit her acute sense of smell was useless, for she could not breathe.

She peered around the rocks, and in every cave in the bank. She swam without haste, in a slow and easy motion, with kicks of her thick webbed hindfeet, and strokes of her tail which she used as a rudder to swing herself up or down or sideways. She found the fish under an ash-tree root, and as it tried to dart away over her head, she threw herself sideways and backwards and seized it in her teeth. By a bay in the bank, broken and beaten by the hooves of cattle going to drink, she ate her prey, holding it in her forepaws and cranching with her head on one side. She ate to the tail, which was left on a wad of drying mud cast from a hoof; and she was drinking a draught of water when a whistling cry came from under Canal Bridge. It had a thin, hard, musical quality, and carried far down the river. She answered gladly, for it was the call of the dog-otter with whom she had mated nearly nine weeks before. He had followed her down from the weir by the scent lying in her seal, or footprints, left on many scours, and on the otter-path across the meadowland of the river's bend. He swam in the deep water, hidden except for his nose, which pushed a ream on the surface placid in the windless night.

As she watched, the ream became a swirl. The otter on land heard the instant hiss of breath in the nostrils before they sank. Immediately she slipped into the river with the least ripple tracing where she had entered. The dog-otter had sniffed the scent of a fish.

Bubbles began to rise in the pool, making two chains with silver-pointed links, which moved steadily upstream. Twenty yards above the swirl, which lingered as the sway of constellations between black branches, a flat wide head fierce with whiskers looked up and went under again, the top of a back following in the down-going curve so smooth that the bubbles rising after it were just rocked. Time of breathing-in was less than half a second.

The bubbles, eking out of nostrils, ran over pate and neck and shook off between the shoulders, to rise in clusters the size of hawthorn peggles; the dog-otter was swimming with his forelegs tucked against his chest. Near the bridge the bubbles rose large as oak-apples; he was kicking four webs together, having sighted the fish. The bubbles ended in another swirl by a weed-fringed sterling, and a delicate swift water-arrow shot away between the two piers of the middle arch—the peal, or sea-trout, had gone down, passing three inches off the snapt jaws.

The river became silent again, save where it murmured by root and rock. Old Nog the heron alighted by a drain behind the sea-wall of the marsh two miles below Halfpenny Bridge, whither he had straightly flown. The white owl had just caught by an old straw rick its second mouse, which, like the first, caught five minutes before, was swallowed whole.

Where water clawed the stones at the tail of the pool the peal leapt to save itself from the bigger enemy ever trudging and peering behind it. It fell on the shillets, on its side, and flapped, once, then lay still, moving only its gills. Then the dog-otter was standing by it, holding up his nose to sniff the air as a thin, wavy, snarling cry rose out of the river. It was the bitch's yinny-yikker, or threat. She ran upon the fish, pulled it away from the dog, who was not hungry, and started to eat it.

While she was chawing the bones and flesh of the head the dog played with a stone, and only when she had turned away from the broken fish did he approach with a greeting, *tuck-a-tuck*, and lick her face. Her narrow lower jaw dropped in a wide yawn which showed the long canine teeth, curved backwards for holding fish, and kept white by the strength of bites. The yawn marked the end of a mood of anxiety. The dog had caught and eaten a peal on his journey, and was ready for sport and play, but the bitch did not follow him into the river. She felt the stir of her young, and turned away from the water.

She ran over the bullocks' drinking place and passed through willows to the meadow, seeking old dry grasses and mosses under the hawthorns growing by the mill-leat, and gathering them in her mouth with wool pulled from the over-arching blackberry brambles whose prickles had caught in the fleeces of sheep. She returned to the river bank and swam with her webbed hindfeet to the oak tree, climbed to the barky lip of the holt, and crawled within. Two yards inside she strewed her burden on the wood-dust, and departed by water for dry, sand-coloured reeds of the old summer's growth which she bit off, frequently pausing to listen. After several journeys she sought trout by cruising under water along the bank, and loach which she found by stirring up the sand and stones of the shallow whereon they lurked. The whistles of the dog were sometimes answered, but so anxious was she to finish making the couch in the hollow tree that she left off feeding while still hungry, and ran over the water-meadow to an inland pond for the floss of reed-maces which grew there. On the way she suprised a young rabbit, killing it with two bites behind the ear, and tearing the skin in her haste to feed. Later in the night a badger found the head and feet and skin as he lumbered after slugs and worms, and chewed them up.

The moon rose up two hours before the dawn, and the shaken light on the waters gladdened her, for she was young, and calling to the dog with a soft, flute-like whistle, she swam to the high arched bridge upriver and hid among the sticks and branches posited by the flood on the bow of the stone cutwater. Here he found her, and as he scrambled up she slipped into the river and swam under the arch to the lower end of the cut-water, meeting him nose-to-nose in a maze of bubbles, and swimming back under the arch. They played for half an hour, turning on their backs with sideway sweeps of rudders, and never touching, although their noses at each swirling encounter were but a few inches apart. It was an old game they played, and it gave them delight and made them hungry, so they went hunting for frogs and eels in a ditch which drained the water-meadow.

Here they disturbed Old Nog, who was overlooking one of his many fishing places along the valley. *Krark!* He flapped away before them, his long, thin, green toes scratching the water. The otters hunted the ditch until the moon paled of its gleam, when they went back to the river. They played for awhile, but jackdaws were beginning to talk in soft, deep, raven-like croaks in the wood, as they wakened and stretched wings and sought fleas. A lark was singing. The dog turned east, and ran along the otter-path used by otters long before the weir was made for the grist-mill below Leaning Willow Island. His holt was in the weir-pool. The bitch drifted lazily with spread limbs, over shallow and through pit, to the rippled water by the hollow tree, into which she crept. Cocks crew in the distant village as she was licking herself and when she was clean she turned in the couch and made a snug sleeping place, and resting chin on rudder, was asleep.

The rising sun silvered the mist lying low and dense on the meadow, where cattle stocd on unseen legs. Over the mist the white owl was flying, on broad soft wings. It wafted itself along, light as the mist; the sun showed the snowy feathers on breast and underwings, and lit the yellow-gold and grey of its back. It sailed under the middle arch of the bridge, and pulled itself by its talons into one of the spaces left in the stone-work by masons. Throughout the daylight it stood among the bones and skulls of mice, often blinking, and sometimes yawning. At dimmity it flew down the right bank of the river and perched on the same branch of the fallen oak and skirred to its mate, who roosted by day in a barn near the village.

It flew away; it fluttered down upon many mice in the fields; but the otter did not leave the holt. The instincts which had served her life so far were consumed in a strange and remote feeling that smouldered in her eyes. She lay on her side, in pain, and a little scared. The song of the river, hastening around Leaning Willow Island, stole into the holt and soothed her; the low whistles of her mate above the bridge were a comfort.

When the moon gleamed out of the clouds in the east, pale and wasted as a bird in snow, the occasional call of the dog ceased. She did not care, for now she needed no comfort. She listened for another cry, feeble and mewing, and whenever she heard it, she rounded her neck to caress with her tongue a head smaller than one of her own paws. All the next day and night, and the day after, she lay curled for the warming of three blind cubs;

29

and while the sunset was still over the hills, she slid into the water and roved along the left bank, looking in front and above her, now left, now right, now left again. A glint in the darkness! Her back looped as the hind legs were drawn under for the full thrust of webs, and bubbles wriggled off her back larger than oak-apples; she was only a little slower than when she had last chased a trout. Her rudder, about two-thirds as long as her body and two inches thick at the base, gave her such a power of swiftness in turning that she snatched the fish two feet above as it flashed over her head.

She ate it ravenously, half standing in shallow water, yinnying at shadows as she chawed and swallowed. After four hasty laps she went under again. She caught an eel, ate the lower part of it and returned to the holt. But she was still hungry and left them a second time, running up the bank to stand upright with the breeze drawing across her nostrils. Blackbirds in the wood were shrilling at tawny owls which had not yet hooted. The otter dropped on her forepads and ran to water again. The weight of her rudder dragging on a sandy scour enabled her to immerse noiselessly while running.

The eldest and biggest of the litter was a dog-cub, and when he drew his first breath he was less than five inches long from his nose to where his wee tail joined his backbone. His fur was soft and grey as the buds of the willow before they open at Eastertide. He was called Tarka, which was the name given to otters many years ago by men dwelling in hut-circles on the moor. It means Little Water Wanderer, or, Wandering as Water.

With his two sisters he mewed when hungry, seeking the warmth of his mother, who uncurled and held up a paw whenever tiny pads would stray in her fur, and tiny noses snuffle against her. She was careful that they should be clean, and many times in the nights and days of their blind helplessness she rolled on her back, ceasing her kind of purr to twist her head and lick them. And sometimes her short ears would stiffen as she started up, her eyes fierce with a tawny glow and the coarse hair of her neck bristling, having heard some danger sound. By day the dog was far away, sleeping in a holt by the weir-pool which had its rocky entrance underwater, but in the darkness his whistle would move the fierceness from her eyes, and she would lie down to sigh happily as her young struggled to draw life from her.

This was her first litter, and she was overjoyed when Tarka's lids ungummed, and his eyes peeped upon her, blue and wondering. He was then a month old. Before the coming of her cubs, her world had been a wilderness, but now her world was in the eyes of her firstborn. After a day of sight-seeing he began to play, tapping her nose with a paw and biting her whiskers. He kicked against the other cubs, growing lustily, and his eyes darkened, and he tried harder than ever to bite his mother's whiskers, which tickled him when he was being held between her paws and washed. Once, when he was milk-happy and had snarled his first snarl without frightening her into stopping the licking of his belly, he was so furious that he tried to bite off her head. She opened her mouth and panted, which is the way otters laugh among themselves, while he kicked and struggled, and she pretended to bite through his neck. Tarka was not afraid, and clawed her whiskers and struggled to be free. His mother released him very gently: on wobbly legs he returned to the assault of her head, but he snarled so much that he was sick; and when she had tidied him he fell asleep under her throat.

When his eyes had been opened a fortnight, Tarka knew so much that he could crawl as far as a yard from her, and stay away although in her anxiety she mewed to him to return. She was afraid of the daylight by the opening of the holt, but Tarka had no fear. He liked to stare at the waterflies dancing their sun-dance over the ripples. One morning as he was blinking away the brightness a bird about the size of a sparrow alighted on a twig over the hole. A sparrow in size, but not in colour! It may have been that the Quill Spirit had painted the bird with colours stolen from rock and leaf and sky and fern, and enriched them by its fervour, for the bird's feet were pinker than the rock-veins in the cleaves of Dartmoor, his wings were greener than opening buds of hawthorn, his neck and head were bluer than the autumn noonday sky, his breast was browner than bracken. He had a black beak nearly as long as his body. He was Halcyon the kingfisher. His feathers were now at their brightest, for his mate had just laid her seven glossy white eggs at the end of a tunnel in the bank.

Halcyon peered with a bright brown eye at Tarka who wanted the bird to play with. A wind ruffled one of the emerald feathers, and Halcyon crouched to peer into the water. Tarka mewed to him to come and be played with, and at the sound the bird gave a sudden piercing whistle and flew upriver, leaving Tarka creasing his nose as he blinked at the perching place, unable to understand why it was not there.

He went back to his mother and played the biting-game with her, after which he slept. When he awoke again, he saw one of his sisters playing with something and immediately wanted it. The cub was patting it with one paw, holding her head sideways; but as it did not run, she patted it with the other paw, while holding her head to that side. Tarka was slowly crawling towards it, meaning to take it for himself, when he noticed that it was looking at him. The look frightened him and he tissed at it. The other cub jumped back and tissed as well, and the noise awakened the youngest cub, who spat at her mother. The mother licked its face, yawned, and closed her eyes.

Again Tarka crawled towards the thing looking at him. He sniffed at it and crept away. He crept back to it, but the other cub tissed and so he returned to his mother. When next he went towards it, the look in its eyes had changed, and he boldly touched it with his nose and shifted it with a paw. It looked at him no longer, for it was only the skull of a field-vole, and light coming down the woodpecker's hole from above had put shadows into its empty eyes. Tarka moved it between his paws; some of its teeth dropped out and rattled inside the hollow. The sound pleased him. He played with the skull until he heard one of his sisters mewing in hunger, when he hurried back to his mother.

One evening, while the cubs were alone, Tarka was playing with his rattle when he saw a live vole, that had come into the holt through an opening by the roots. As the way was large enough for a rat to pass, he crept easily along the tunnel, up which the vole had fled in fright as soon as it smelled him. The tunnel ended at the broken roots, to which part of the earth that had nourished them still clung. Little green leaves were growing out of this earth, for the oaks' disaster had been as a blessing to many seeds of charlock which had been lying buried in the cold earth long before the acorn had sprouted.

Voles, which are the red mice of the fields, were squeaking among the roots as they hurried to their holes; for the explorer ran among them, crying the alarm that a great weasel was coming. Tarka did not know that his scent had filled them with terror; indeed, he did not know what a vole was. He had seen movement and gone to it, for he was always ready to play, and play was movement. The squeaks ceased.

All was quiet and he heard, for the first time, the jets and rills on the stones which made the ancient song of the river. He wanted to get nearer to the sounds and crawled along a root. When he was halfway along it, he saw that there was nothing on either side of him. He was alone on the root. He tried to turn back, but the claws of one hindfoot slipped and there he clung, curved across the wood, unable to go up or down. He mewed to his mother, but she did not come. His cries grew more and more plaintive as he became colder.

About five minutes afterwards a ream passed under the stone bridge and moved into deeper and quieter water where its raised lines were carried to the banks before being smoothed away by the flow. The angular wave pushed steadily down the river. The bitch was returning. She had caught and eaten six small trout and two eels during the uneasy half-hour she had been away. When nearly opposite the holt she turned across the current, and had almost reached it when she flung head and shoulders out of the water. While rising she was staring, sniffing the air, and listening; and before all the drops running off her whiskers had splashed, her head was under-water and her body doubling with the effort of thrusting four webs together. Then more drops splashed by the holt. A pebble rolled down the bank.

The bitch had heard Tarka's cries, and fear had shocked her into the swiftest movements. She was in the root-pit beside

33

Tarka while the stars were still shaking in the undulation of the old ream. He trembled with cold. A score of hearts under browny-red coats beat faster at the otter's chiding yikker as she picked up her cub by the neck and carried him to the shore. She swam with her head held high and carefully, lest the water should touch him. Afterwards, lying on the warm couch, she forgot her fright and closed her eyes in enjoyment of her young.

The next night Tarka crept along the root again, and fell in the same way. He was crawling around, when a strange-smelling animal leaned over him, wetting him with drops from its jowl. He tissed at it and tissed again when he heard the yinny-yikker of his mother and the snap of her teeth as the animal was driven away. Then something bit the back of his neck and lifted him up. With the cub dangling from her mouth, the bitch threatened the dog, who had followed her in curiosity to the holt. The dog tried to look into the tree on the following night, but the bitch dragged him down by the rudder, as though she would drown him. The dog thought this was fun, and ragrowstered with her under and on the water all the way to Leaning Willow Island, where she left him, remembering Tarka.

2

In mid-May the buds of the fallen oak began to open hopefully and to show their ruddy leaves. Seven small kingfishers perched on an alder branch outside the entrance of their tunnel, while the wind stirred the fledgling down between their feathers, and they waited for loach or beetle or shrimp or elver or troutling. At sunset seven beaks were laid on shoulders, sometimes to lift at a whistle shriller and louder than the whistle of their parents; but the night was to other hunters.

While the moon was full and bright the otters went to hunt the fish lying in the Tunnel Pool below Halfpenny Bridge— bass, grey mullet, and flukes, or flat-fish. The cubs were two months old and they had learned to squeeze through the inner opening of the holt and run along the root, in order to play on the grassy bank. One night as they were playing rough-and-tumble round the base of an ash tree, they heard their mother's whistle. This cry was not as piercing as the dog's call to his mate, but like wet fingers drawn down a pane of glass. Immediately Tarka stopped biting the tail of his younger sister, and the third cub ceased to gnaw his neck. As fast as they could they ran across the root and into the holt. The bitch was waiting for them, with a trout in her mouth. Tarka sniffed at it as she was breaking it up, then turned away, for he did not like the smell of it. The cubs struggled for their own food, so the bitch lay down and fed them with her milk until she grew tired of them. Shaking them off, she went away with the dog, who had swum upriver with her.

When next she returned, she brought two skinned frogs, which she had caught in the reed-grown, marshy bed of the old canal. She dropped them in the holt and slid back into the river, heedless of the cubs' cries. Tarka licked a frog and liked the taste of it; he bared his milk teeth at his sisters, but he did not eat it. They rolled and snarled and played until their mother's return, when they ran to her. She had brought an eel, which she bit into pieces, beginning near the tail, but leaving the head above the paired fins. Tarka swallowed little pieces of the fish and licked his small sister's head afterwards, because it tasted nice. Then he licked his own paws. He was cleaning himself for the first time.

The new food changed them almost at once. They grew swift and fierce. Their frolics on the bark often ceased at the cry of a night-bird, or the distant bank of a cattle dog in the village. They started whenever their mother started. They began to fear. Sometimes at sunset, when their mother left the holt, they ran on the bank and mewed to her as she hunted upstream. She would leave the water and chase them back again to the holt. Her smooth movements near them on land were often broken; she would stand still and uncertain, or run on, jerky with fear. Many times she stood upright and listened, her nose towards the village. People occasionally walked over Canal Bridge, which now carried a drive to a house near the weir; and whenever she heard voices she ceased to hunt, and swam down the river to be near the cubs. Human voices frightened her; but the thunderous noises of trains in the valley and the long, whisking lights of motor-cars on the road beyond the railway were ignored because she was used to them, and knew them to be harmless.

The buds of the ash, sullen for so long in their coverings shaped like the black hooves of cattle, broke into browny-green sprays. The cuckoo sang all night. Reed-buntings chattered among the rising green, water-holding stems of balsam; soon Antares would burn dull red in the low southern night sky.

One warm evening when the river was low, the mother swam down to the holt and called the cubs into the water, and although they were ravening, she did not climb up, but waited for them with a fish below the tree. They whimpered and peered, moving their heads sideways and telling her that below was fearful. She lay on her back in the water and let the fish go, in order to catch it, and rise with it gleaming again. The two youngest cubs ran back over the damp, trodden couch to get through the tunnel, but they were too fat to squeeze through. Perhaps Tarka would have gone with them, if he had not wanted the fish so much. His eyes were on it, he smelled it, his mouth filled with eat-water. He mewed, he yikkered, he tissed, but there was no fish. The otter swam on her back and called him into the water.

Tarka watched her. He wanted the fish, but he dared not let go with his feet. The fish came no nearer, so he dropped down into the black, star-shivery water. He was clutched in a cold and terrible embrace, so that he could neither see nor breathe, and although he tried to walk, it smothered him, choked him, roared in his ears, and stifled every mew for help, until his mother swam under him. Pressing pads and tail against her back, Tarka was carried to the stony margin of an islet, where the closed flowers of the water-crowsfoot were floating among their leaves. He spluttered and sneezed and shook water out of his eyes, and saw the stars above him, and felt his mother's tongue on his head.

When he had eaten the fish, Tarka began to enjoy the

36

strangeness. He was playing with the fish-tail when he heard the whistle so often listened to from the holt. When he saw the animal with the wide flat head and great bristling whiskers that had loomed over his head once before, Tarka tissed and snarled at it and ran for his mother. He snapped at the nose sniffing at him. The dog turned on his back and tried to touch Tarka with his paws, in play. Tarka watched him and wanted to roll as well, but he was awed by the stranger's size.

An hour later, the three cubs had eaten their fish happily on the stones. The bitch had grown tired of coaxing the other cubs to enter the water and had dragged them by their scruffs out of the holt and dropped them into the river.

The first otter to go into deep water had felt the same fear that Tarka felt that night; for his ancestors, thousands of years ago, had been hunters in woods and along the banks of rivers, running the scent of blooded creatures on the earth, like all the members of the weasel race to which they belonged. This race had several tribes in the country of the Two Rivers. Biggest were the brocks, a tribe of badgers who lived in holts scratched among roots of trees and bushes, and rarely went to water except to drink. They were related to the fitches or stoats, who chased rabbits and jumped upon birds on the earth; and to the vairs or weasels, who sucked the blood of mice and dragged fledglings from the nest; and to the grey fitches or polecats, so rare in the forests; and to the pinemartens, a tribe so harried by men that one only remained, and he had found sanctuary in a wood where a gin was never tilled and a gun was never fired, where the red deer was never roused and the fox never chased. He was old; his canine teeth worn down. Otters knew the ponds in Arlington woods, and played there by day, while herons stalked in the shallows and nothing feared the châtelaine who sometimes sat on the bank, watching the wild creatures which she thought of as the small and persecuted kinsfolk of man.

Long ago, when moose roared in the forest at the mouth of the Two Rivers, otters had followed eels migrating in autumn from ponds and swamps to the sea. They had followed them into shallow water; and one fierce old dog had run through the water so often that he swam, and later, in his great hunger, had put under his head to seize them so often that he dived. Other otters had imitated him. There was a web of skin between the toes, as in the feet of wolves and dogs, and generations of swimming otters had caused the spread of the toes to increase and the web of skin to widen between them. Claws grew shorter. Tails used as rudders became longer, thicker, and powerful with muscles. Otters became hunters under water.

The moose are gone, and their bones lie under the sand in the soft coal which was the forest by the estuary, thousands of years ago. Yet otters have not been hunters in water long enough for the habit to become an instinct. And so the original water-fear was born with Tarka, whose mind had to overlay a weak instinct with habit, just as his ancestor had done when he was hungry.

When he went into the water the next night and tried to walk towards his mother, he floated. He was so pleased that he set out across the river by himself, finding that he could turn easily towards his mother by swinging his hindquarters and rudder. He turned and turned many times in his happiness; east towards Willow Island and the water-song, west towards the kingfishers' nest, and Peal Rock below Canal Bridge, and the otter-path crossing the big bend. North again and then south-west, where the gales came from, up and down, backwards and forwards, sometimes swallowing water, at other times sniffling it up his nose, sneezing, spitting, coughing, but always swimming. He learned to hold his nose above the ream, or ripple, pushed in front of it.

While swimming in this happy way, he noticed the moon. It danced on the water just before his nose. Often he had seen the moon, just outside the hollow tree, and had tried to touch it with a paw. Now he tried to bite it, but it swam away from him. He chased it. It wriggled like a silver fish and he followed to the sedges on the far bank of the river, but it no longer wriggled. It was waiting to play with him. Across the river Tarka could hear the mewing of his sisters, but he set off after the moon over the meadow. He ran among buttercups and cuckoo-flowers and grasses bending with bright points. Farther and farther from the river he ran, the moonlight gleaming on his coat. Really it was brown like the dust in an October puff-ball, but the water sleeked the hair.

As he stopped to listen to the bleat of lambs, a moth whurred by his head and tickled him. While he was scratching, a bird flying with irregular wingbeats and sudden hawk-like glidings took the moth in its wide gape and flew out of his sight. Tarka forgot the moon-play. He crouched in the grasses, which rose above his head like the trees of a forest, some with tops like his rudder, others like his whiskers, and all whispering as they swayed. The nightjar returned, clapping its wings over its head with the noise of a dry stick cracking. Tarka was glad to hear his mother calling him. He mewed. He listened and her whistle was nearer, so he ran away in the wet grasses. The cub did not know how alarmed his mother was nor did he know that less than fifty flaps away a bird with great eyes and wings spanning a yard was flying upon him. The nightjar had seen the bird, too, and had clapped its wings as a danger signal to its mate whose two eggs were laid among ferns in the wood.

The nightjar twirled and planed away; Tarka scampered on. The great bird, who had raised two tufts of feathers on its head, dropped with taloned feet spread for a clutch. The otter saw it drop and ran forwards so swiftly that the sound of her going through the grasses was like the first wind which uncoils as it runs before the south-westerly gale. The bird, which was a short-eared owl, thought that Tarka was a small rabbit, and fanned above him while it considered whether or not he was small enough to be attacked. It did not hesitate longer than the time of six flaps, but dropped, while screaking to terrify and subdue its prey. But Tarka came of a family fiercer and quicker in movement than the owl. Tissing with rage, he jumped and bit his assailant as a foot grasped his back and four talons pierced his skin. The other foot of the bird grasped grasses and it had turned with clacking beak to peck the base of the cub's skull when the paw-stroke of the bitch tore half the feathers from its breast. She stood on it, bit once, twice, thrice, in a second of time, and so the owl died.

Tarka was nipped in the neck, shaken, picked up, bumped all the way back to the bank, scraped over the stones, and dropped into the water. Obediently he followed his mother across the river, to where the dog was lying on his back and gravely watching two cubs playing with the tip of his rudder.

Fish were brought alive to the cubs when they had been swimming about a fortnight, and dropped in the shallowest water. And when they were nearly three months old their mother took them downstream, past Leaning Willow Island, and across the bend, to where the banks were glidden into mud smoothed by the sea. The tide had lapsed from the mud, leaving fresh water to tear the rocky bed below.

Tarka galloped through the tall green reeds to the river, stopping by a gut to sniff at the tracks of a curlew, which had been feeding there during the ebb-tide. Near the water he found another track, of five toes well spread, and the prick of five claws. The dog had walked there. Just above Halfpenny Bridge they saw him, half out of the water, and chewing a fish which he did not trouble to hold in his paws. He craunched it from the head downwards, gulping his bites quickly, and as soon as the tail was swallowed, he turned and went underwater for more.

The bitch took her cubs to a pool below the bridge and walked with them across a shallow tail of water. She stared at the stones, brown and slippery with sea-weed, and the cubs stared also. They watched the glimmers in the claws of water, sometimes trying to bite them. While they were watching, the mother ran along the bank to the top of the pool and slid into the water. More often than usual her head looked up as she swam from bank to bank, for she was not hunting, but driving the fish down to the cubs. Tarka became excited and, seeing a fish, he swam after it and went underwater to get it. In order to travel faster, he struck out with all four webs together, and lo! Tarka was swimming like an otter near a fish. It was the biggest fish he had seen, and although he kicked after it at the rate of nearly two hundred kicks a minute, he lost it after a yard. He yikkered in his anger, and oh! Tarka was no longer swimming like an otter, but gasping and coughing on the surface, a poor little sick-feeling cub mewing for his mother.

He felt better when he had eaten a mullet caught by his mother. The fish had come up with the tide and remained in the still pool. Late in the night Tarka caught a pollywiggle, or tadpole, in a watery hoof-hole and thought himself a real hunter as he played with it, passing it from paw to paw and rolling on his back in the mud. He was quite selfish over his prey when his mother went to see what he was doing, and cried, *Iss-iss-ic-yang!* an old weasel threat, which, being interpreted, means, Go away, or I will drink your blood!

Old Nog the heron, beating loose grey wings over Leaning Willow Island as the sun was making yellow the top of the tall tree, saw five brown heads in the salmon pool. Three small heads and a larger head turned to the left by the fallen tree, and the largest head went on up-river alone. The cubs were tired and did not like being washed when they were in the holt. Afterwards Tarka pushed his sister from his mother's neck, the most comfortable place in the holt, and immediately fell asleep. Sometimes his hindlegs kicked, gently. He was trying to catch a shining fish that wriggled just before his nose, when he was abruptly flung awake. He yawned, but his mother, tissing through her teeth, frightened him into silence. The day was bright outside the hole.

A kingfisher sped down the river, crying a short, shrill *peet!* as it passed the holt. The otter got on her forelegs and stared towards the opening. Soon after the kingfisher had gone, a turtle dove alighted on the ash tree above the holt and looked about her; she had just flown off her two eggs, nearly dropping through a loose raft-like nest in a hawthorn by the weir. The bird held out a wing and began to straighten the filaments of a flight-quill which had struck a twig during her sudden flight out of the bush-top. She drew the feather through her beak thrice, shook her wings, listened, and went on preening.

Tarka closed his eyes again, breathed deeply and settled to sleep on the youngest cub's neck. He looked up when his mother ran to the opening. The otter was listening to a sound like the high, thin twang of a mosquito. Hair bristled on her neck. From far away there came a deep rolling sound, and a screaming cheer. The otter instantly returned to her cubs and stood over them in a protective attitude, for she knew that hounds were hunting the water.

41

Tarka crouched down, listening to the cries. They became more distinct. Always a deeper, gruffer note was heard among them. The noises, almost continuous, became louder and louder. Nearer came another sound—the wings of the dove striking against twigs as it flew away.

A minute later the pair of cole-tits that had a nest in a hole of the ash tree began to make their small, wheezy notes of alarm. The white owl had flown from the bridge and was perched against the ivy of the trunk, turning its head from side to side and blinking. One cole-tit, about as long as a man's finger, flittered with anger on the twigs a few inches from the gold-grey head. The owl blinked slowly; the baying swelled under the bridge; it swung its head round without moving its body and stared straight behind it. *Chizzy-chizzy-chizzy-te!* wheezed the cole-tit as the owl floated away. Tarka was used to this sound, for usually it greeted him whenever he looked out of the holt in daylight.

Chizzy-chizzy-chizzy-te! the bird wheezed again, and then Tarka saw the big head of the dog-otter by the opening, and his wet paws on the bark. The bitch tissed at him, her teeth snapped at his head, and the dog was gone.

The cries were now very loud. Tarka heard thuds in the wood all around him. The cubs crouched in the darkest corner. Nearer came the shouts of men, until the thuds of running feet ceased on the bank. The water began to wash against and lap the half-drowned trunk, claws scraped the wood, the opening grew dark and the tongue he had heard above the others boomed in the hollow. The otter crouched back, larger than usual, for her body was rigid and all the hair of her back stood straight. Swish, swish swept her rudder. She recognized another sound and tissed every time it cried the names of hounds, in a voice thin and high as though it were trying to become as the horn which so often took its rightful breath. The voice ceased. The horn sang its plain note. Whips cracked.

By their big feet hounds pulled themselves out of the water, except the one who threw his deep tongue at the holt opening. He was all black and white, with great flews, and the biggest stallion-hound in the pack. He was black from nose to neck, except for the pallid nicks of old quarrel scars on his muzzle and head. No hound quarrelled with him now, for Deadlock was master of all. In his veins ran the blood of the Talbots, and one of his bloodhound ancestors had eaten man. He had mastiff in him. His dam and sire had pulled down many a deer at bay in the waters of the moor, and died fireside deaths after faithful service to red coats. A pink weal ran down his belly, for in his second stag-hunting season the great pied hound had been ripped open by the brow-point of a stag; and his pace had gone from him afterwards. The otter-hunters bought him for a guinea, liking his long legs, and now Deadlock was the truest marking hound in the country of the Two Rivers.

He held by his paws, and his teeth tore at the sodden tinder-wood. He could thrust in only his head. While he was kicking the water for a foothold, the otter ran forward and bit him through the ear, piercing the earmark where the blue initial letters of his original pack were tattooed. Deadlock yarred through his bared teeth. Three small mouths at the other end of the holt opened and tissed in immense fright.

Then Tarka heard a cry which he was to hear often in his wanderings; a cry which to many otters of the Two Rivers had meant that the longest swimming, the fastest land-looping, the quietest slipping from drain or holt were unavailing.

Tally Ho!

The cry came from down the river, just above Leaning Willow Island, from the throat of an old man in a blue coat and white breeches, who had been leaning his bearded chin on hands clasping a ground-ash pole nearly as long and as old as himself. From his look-out place he had seen something moving down like brown thongweed just under the clear and shallow water. Off came the hat, grey as lichen, to be held aloft while he cried again.

Tally Ho!

The horn of the huntsman sang short and urgent notes; the air by the holt was scored by the names of hounds as he ran with them to where, amidst purple-streaked stems of hemlock, the old man was standing on the shillets.

Soon afterwards the horn sounded again near the holt and

43

the baying of hounds grew louder. Footfalls banged the wood above Tarka's head, as a man climbed along the trunk. The water began to lap: hound-taint from a high-yelping throat came into the holt: the bitch grew larger along her back when, above her head, a man's voice cried snarlingly, *Go'rn leave it, Captain! Go'rn leave it!* A thong swished, a lash cracked. *Go'rn leave it, Captain!*

The high yelping lessened with the taint of breath. The cries went up the river. The rudder of the bitch twitched. The hair on her back fell slanting; but it rose when something scratched above. Her nose pointed, she breathed through her mouth. She moved away uneasily. Tarka sneezed. Tobacco smoke. A man was sitting in the branches over them.

After half an hour the cries came down to the holt again. They passed, and then Tarka heard a new and terrible noise— the noise as of mammoth iron-toed centipedes crossing on the stones, or shillets, at the tail of the pool.

Tally Ho! Look out, he's coming down!

Iron toes scraped the shillets faster. Here, across the shallow, a dozen men and women stood almost leg-to-leg in the water, stirring the stream with their iron-shod poles to stop the dog-otter passing down to the next pool.

Tarka and the cubs breathed fast again. Deadlock's great bellow swam nearer, with the high yelping of Captain. Many wavelets slapped against the tree. A dozen hounds were giving tongue between Canal Bridge and the stickle above Leaning Willow Island. A shaggy face looked into the holt and a voice cried just over Tarka's head, *Go'rn leave it, Dewdrop! Gor'n leave it!* Boots knocked on the trunk. *Is-isss-iss! Go'rn leave it!* And Dewdrop left it, bitten in the nose.

Unable to break the stickle, the dog-otter went back under the bridge. Baying became fainter. The notes of the cole-tits in the ash tree were heard again.

In the quiet hollow the otter unstiffened and scratched for ticks as though the hunt had never come there. Hounds and men were above the bridge, where another stickle was standing. The water flowed with small murmurs. She heard the rustling clicks of dragon-flies' wings over the sun-plashy ripples. Silence,

44

the tranquil *chee-chee* of a cole-tit seeking a grub in an oak-apple, and the sunbeam through the woodpecker hole moving over the damp wood dust on the floor. The otter lay down, she dozed, she jumped up when sudden cries of *Tally Ho!* and a confused clamour arose beyond the bridge. Now all the sounds of the past hours were increasing together, of tongues, and horns, and cheers; and very soon they were overborne by a deep new noise like the rumbling of the mill when the water-wheel was turning. Then with the deep rumbling came the prolonged thin rattle of the horn, and the triumphant whooping of whips and huntsman. The sounds slowed and ceased, except for the lone baying of a hound; they broke out again, and slowed away into silence, but long afterwards the strange blowing noises made by their mother frightened the huddled cubs.

Sometimes the slits of the owl's lids opened, and dark eyes would watch a drop of water falling from one of the thin horns of lime hanging from crevices between stones of the arch. Yellow ripple-light no longer passed across the stonework of Canal Bridge. The sun made shadows on the meadow slightly longer than the trees were tall. For more than an hour the water had been peaceful. A blackbird sang in the sycamore growing by the bridge. The otter looked out of the holt and listened. She feared sunlight on the field less than the taint of hounds still coming down on the water, and, calling her cubs, she slid into the river and ran out under the bank, and to the grass. *Iss-iss-ss!* The ground in patches was damp with the water run off hounds' flews, flanks, and sterns. Only a carrion crow saw them hastening across the meadow to the leat, and its croaks followed them into the wood where bees were burring round purple spires of foxgloves, and chiffchaffs flitted through honeysuckle bines. Otter and cubs passed low and swift among the green seed-heads of the bluebells; and uphill over blackening leaves, until they saw the river again below them, where the sun-points glittered, and a young kingfisher, one of the sons of Halcyon, drew a blue line in the shade of oak trees.

3

The shock-headed flowers of the yellow goat's beard, or John-go-to-bed-at-noon, had been closed six hours when a grey wagtail skipped airily over the sky-gleams of the brook, flitting from stone to stone whereon it perched with dancing tail and feet. In the light of the sun more gold than at noon the drakeflies were straying low over the clear water, and the bird fluttered above its perch on a mossy stone, and took one. The water reflected the colour of its breast, paler than kingcups. It did not fly, it skipped through the air, calling blithely *chissik chiss-ik*, until it came to the verge of a pool by a riven sycamore. On a sandy scour it ran, leaving tracks of fragile feet and dipping as it took in its beak the flies which were crawling there. It skipped to the ripple line and sipped a drop, holding up its head to drink. Two sips had been taken when it flew up in alarm, and from a branch of the sycamore peered below.

The brook swirled fast by the farther bank; under the sycamore it moved dark and deep. From the water a nose had appeared and the sight of it had alarmed the wagtail. Two dark eyes and a small brown head fierce with whiskers rose up and looked around. Seeing no enemy, the otter swam to the shore and walked out on the sand, her rudder dripping wet behind her. She stopped, sniffing and listening, before running forward and examining all entrances under the bared roots of the sycamore tree in the steep bank. The otter knew the holt, for she had slept there during her own cubhood, when her mother had left the river and followed the brook to get to the White Clay Pits.

The wagtail was still watching when the otter came out of the holt again. It flew away as she whistled. Two heads moved across the pool and a third behind, slightly larger, for Tarka followed his sisters. The cubs crawled into the holt, leaving seals, or marks of five toes and running pad, in the sand with the prints of the wagtail.

The sycamore was riven and burnt by lightning, yet sap

46

still gave it a few leaves for summer. Its old trunk was beloved by two mouse-like birds which crept up the whitest tinder and held themselves by their spread tails as they looked in the cracks for woodlice and spiders. Every spring this pair of treecreepers made a nest between the trunk and the loose bark, of twigs, tinderwood, dry grasses, and feathers. Here burred the bumble-bees to their homes in the crannies, and when the first frosts stiffened the grasses they tucked their heads under their fore-legs and slept, if they did not die, until the primroses came again. Here, when the trees were nearly bare, waddled Iggi-wick, the grunting vuz-peg, or hedgehog, with a coat of the tree's dry leaves, black-patched with autumn's falling-mark, and on the earth he curled and closed meek eyes and dozed into a long rest. The tree was the friend of all, and it had one human friend, who as a child had seen it first when trailing in summer after her father hunting the otters of the brook. She had imagined that the old charred sycamore was a giant with many legs, who had been burnt in a fire and had rushed to the bank to cool himself, and that its roots, bared by floods, were thin legs bent at wooden knees and fixed in the water. The brook was determined to drown the giant, who was burrowing his toes for a hold. The maid grew tall and beautiful, but still the old giant sat cooling his thirteen legs, and every June, when she passed by with her father, following the otter hounds, he wore a fresh green wig.

Many otters had slept in the cave behind the roots; some had died there, and the floods of the brook had taken their bones away.

Mother and cubs curled up together against the dry earth of the holt's end, five feet away from the water. The cubs fell into a deep sleep, torn with dreams wherein an immense black face showed its long fangs. Tarka slept with his small paws on the neck of his mother, and her paw held him there. They snuggled warm in the holt, but the bitch did not sleep.

At dimpsy, when day and night hunters see each other between the two lights, she heard the blackbirds scolding the wood owls; and when the blackbirds were silent, roosting in thorn or ivy with puffed feathers, she heard a badger drinking

47

and grunting as it swallowed. The owls' bubbling quaver settled into the regular hunting calls; then the otter yawned and slept.

She awoke when the wood owl had made a score of journeys with mice to its nestlings in the old eyrie of a trapped buzzard, when the badger had walked many miles from its earth in the oakwood. She was hungry. Leaving her cubs asleep, she crept out of the holt. At the water edge she listened nearly a minute. Then she turned and climbed the bank, running into the meadow where cows snuffled at her as she stood on her hindlegs. Hearing no danger sound, she went down to the river, entered quietly and swam across to the shallows. She walked through a matted and floating growth of water-crowsfoot, and came to summer plants growing out of stones—figwort, angelica, water-hemlock. Returning through the jungle with a crackling of sappy hollow stems and the breaking of rank florets and umbels, she walked among nettles which stung her nose and made her sneeze. Thence she passed under branches of blackthorn, which combed her back as she ran into the marshy field. As in the meadow, she explored as far as the centre, rising to her full height to listen. She heard the munching of cattle, and the harsh *crake crake* of a landrail throwing its voice about the uncropped bunches of marsh grasses and the bitten clumps of flowering rush. Then swiftly back to the brook by another way, through tall balsam stalks to the water, where she climbed on a boulder and lay across it, her head near the stream. She clung by her rudder to the reverse side of the stone, and whistled for the cubs.

Tarka had been peering from the holt, and at the first whistle he moved forward into the water, making hardly a ripple. He swam across the pool with his forelegs tucked under him, kicking with the hindlegs only. The toes were spread at the thrust, so that two webs drove him forward with one kick. Behind him swam the cubs, the arrowy ripples pushed from their noses breaking against each other. They followed Tarka across the floating crowsfoot flowers and reached their mother who lay so still. They spoke to her, nuzzling her with their heads and mewing their hunger. When she would not speak to them they bit her rudder, they cajoled and wheedled, they made angry tissing noises, but she did not move. They left her; and suddenly she sprang up with an otter-laugh, which was not so much a sound as the expression of lips curled back from teeth, and the rolling of the head. She was boisterous with joy after the day's fright, and had been shamming death in fun. Calling the cubs to follow her, she sank into the water and swam upstream.

The cubs knew that she was looking for fish, and they followed her by scent in the line of bubbles that was breaking along on the surface. She looked up with a fish in her mouth and they raced for it, yikkering threats to each other. The otter led them out of the pool and to a shallow; she dropped the fish, a trout of three ounces, and went to the gravelly bank where the water was deeper. Tarka picked up the live trout and took it on a mossy boulder, where he ate it in less than a minute.

The otter caught small fish so quickly in the narrow water that Tarka was soon gorged; and the other cubs in their quick hunger were able to snatch a fish from him while he was rolling on his back in order to have the pleasure of clawing it over his head. The bitch cubs were smaller than Tarka, but quicker in movement. Sometimes they swam along the bank under water, looking left and right; but their mother had scared the fish into their holes, and they rarely saw the gleam which was a fish curving back over her head. Often they snapped at stones or roots, mistaking them for trout.

At the end of the night, Burnt Sycamore Holt lay a mile and a half behind them. It was time to hide when buzzards were seen soaring above the oak and larch woods. The bitch led them out of the water, through willows and ash trees and brambles, and across a narrow-gauge railway track to a fir plantation. Two years before, her mother had taken her to a large rabbit bury near the edge of the wood, and now she led her own cubs there. A scent strange to Tarka was on the dry soil before the tunnel, but his mother did not heed it. She ran down the tunnel and immediately a fox crept out of it by another way, not wanting to meet a bitch otter with cubs underground, or indeed anywhere.

While the otters were cleaning themselves, the fox was sitting down outside the hole, sometimes yawning; he had within him a fill of mice, beetles, and young rabbits. He was drowsy. He remembered his scratching post, the stump of a sapling larch, and walked there, to rub his flanks against it. Reddish hairs lay around it on the ground; one side was polished. When he had scratched enough he walked to a grey stone wall behind a cattle shippen and climbed upon it, waiting for the sun.

The disused rabbit bury was dry and echoed the greater noises of day—the screeching of whistles as light engines, drawing trucks of white clay from the pits on the moor whence the brook took its source, slowly approached the crossing of the lane below; the voice, up the valley, of a man chaunting *coo-coo-coo-coo-coo*, and the barks of a dog running round a field while cows swung in file along a narrow, trodden way, to the milking shed; the buzz, like a blowfly in a spider's web, of a motor-car passing slowly over the little bridge and the rails beyond; the whee-ooing of buzzards and the croaking of crows above the larch wood. These noises did not disturb the otters.

At dimmit light they went down to the brook again, meeting the fox, who was quietly lapping to quench his thirst made by swallowing the fur of so many mice. He looked at the otter; the otter looked at him. The fox went on lapping until the water was spoiled by their musky scent, when he went up the hill to sniff in his earth. For ten minutes he sniffed and pondered, until his curiosity was satisfied, and then he started his nightly prowl—after a little scratching against his post.

The otter took her cubs up the brook and over a field. Away from water her movements were uneasy. Often she stopped in her low running to stare with raised head and working nostrils. A galvanized iron chicken coop in a field caused her to make a wide loop—the scent of man was there. A pair of boots left by a tramp in a hedge made Tarka tiss with fear, turn about, and run away. The cubs were now as active and alert as their mother.

At last they reached the ditch remembered by the otter. She leaned down to the brown-scummed water, clinging to the bank by her rudder. Bull frogs had been croaking a moment before she arrived there, but now they were silent and burrowing in the mud. With paw and nose she sought under the weed, nipping them and dropping them on the grass. The cubs seized them and turned away, yikkering; and when she had caught all she could find, the otter ran back to the cubs and began to flay the frogs, for the skins were tough.

They left some of the frogs uneaten, for there were eels in the ditch. Iggiwick, the vuz-peg—his coat was like furze and his face like a pig's—found the remains, and was gleefully chewing when a badger grunted near. With a squeak of terror the vuz-peg rolled himself in a ball, but the badger bit through the spines as though they were marram grasses. Iggiwick squealed like marram grass in flame. Later in the night nothing was left except the trotters, teeth, and spiny coat of poor Iggiwick.

They were too far off to hear the dying squeals of the vuz-peg, for during the half-hour before the badger caught him they had travelled a mile up the brook. The otter swam in front, the cubs scrambling behind her. Often a fish would dodge back by her whiskers, missing the snap of her teeth by the space of a fin, and the cubs would bump into one another in their eagerness to get it. When this happened, the otter would turn again to her prowling from bank to bank, and leave the fish to be caught by them.

The brook became smaller and narrower, and at the end of the night it was less than a yard across. The next evening they left the rushes in the wet ground where they had been sleeping, and crossing a road, came to a boggy tract where curlew and snipe lived. Tarka ran over the line of a hare, and followed it in curiosity until his mother called him back. Mosses made the way soft and held many scents—of marsh orchid, stinking iris, bog pimpernel; of wild duck, stoat, short-eared owl, magpie, and, once, the rank-smelling flight-quill of a raven.

They reached a thread of water and followed it downward until it was joined by another thread. The two made a stream, which hastened under whitish banks of clay. The otter sought for fish, but finding none, climbed out of the channel by a slanting otter-path and crossed the railway track near a tall, dark chimney that rose out of buildings. It was a brick factory. An otter had travelled before them, and in a hollow behind birch trees about a quarter of a mile on they heard a whistle; and running towards the call, they came to a deep reed-fringed pond, on the clay side of which a grown dog-otter was playing with the wings of a drake. Tarka kept behind his mother, being frightened of the stranger. He had a split ear, done in a fight two years before. Mother and cubs went into the pond, leaving him rolling on the bank and tossing the wings with his paws.

The pond was an old pit from which white clay had been dug. The water was deeper than any the cubs had swum in. Round the edge grew reed-maces; it was early June and the wind-shaken anthers were dropping the yellow pollen on the juicy heads which would pass, with autumn, into the drab hues of decay. Ten ducklings were hiding in the reeds, while their mother circled in the starry sky, telling them, with soft cries of *quaz-qua-a-a-az-quaz*, not to move. She had flown up when the dog-otter had caught and eaten the drake, swimming up underneath it. At the time of capture the drake had been trying to swallow a frog, by quapping with its bill, which held one of the legs. When the otter's teeth had gripped the drake, the frog had escaped; but it commenced to swell on the water and so it could not swim down to the pit's floor. Tarka saw it above him as he pushed about eagerly under water: the frog showed darkly in the dim surface mirror which reflected the grey sludge of the pond's bed. Tarka caught it, and ate it under a thorn bush grown from a haw dropped by a thrush beside the pond.

Mother and cubs roved about in the water for a while, and the dog joined them. The frogs and eels, having seen them, were hiding, and so the bitch climbed out through grey-lichened whitethorn bushes and ran among rush-clumps to the next pit. They hunted through four ponds before they had caught enough to be ready for romping. The fourth pond was larger than the others, and so deep that Tarka had not breath enough to follow the grown otters down in the gloomy

52

water, although he tried many times. He knew they were playing, and mewed to them to come up. Sometimes a string of luminous bubbles shook up and past him, but that was all he saw of the fun; he could see above him, but all was obscure beneath, although he could sometimes hear them.

The old dog-otter was happy, because he had another otter to play with him. His wander years were past; he had killed salmon in the Severn, eaten pollock on the rocks of Portland Bill, and lampreys in the Exe. Now he dwelled among the reeds and rushes of the White Clay Pits, and whenever otters journeyed to the ponds, which formed an irregular chain in a wide flat valley drained by the stream, the old dog, who was rather deaf, would join them; and in the deep pond, he would lure one or another down to a rusted, weed-grown engine that had lain for years half-buried in the clayey ooze. A great joy it was to him to hide in the funnel, and to swim out upon the otter seeking him. Again and again after taking in air he would swim down to his engine, but if any otter except himself tried to hide in the funnel, he would bite it furiously with the few worn teeth that remained in his jaws.

For three years he had lived on the frogs and eels and wild-fowl of the ponds. The clay-diggers often saw him as they went home in the trucks; they called him Marland Jimmy.

The pollen-holding anthers of the reed-maces withered and dropped into the water, but still the bitch and cubs stayed in the land of ponds. Here Tarka tasted his first pheasant, caught by the bitch in the woods where game was preserved. It was a cock-bird, and had only one wing, the other having dropped off in the winter, after a shot-gun wound. The bird was a swift runner, and nearly pecked out the eye of the otter before it died.

By day they slept in the reeds. From his couch of bitten and pressed-down mace stems, Tarka watched the dragonflies which flew glittering over the water. On a reed beside him was fixed the brittle greyish mask of a nymph which had crept out of the pond the day before, having done with the years of preying on pollywiggle, minnow, and water-flea. The sun looked upon it; it dried; it heaved at its mask, which split down the back. Legs and head of a colourless insect crept out with short and flaccid wings. It clung limply to the reed, while its wings uncreased and hardened in the heat. It took the dragonish breath of noon and changed it into gleams of scarlet; its eyes grew lustrous with summer fire. The pond glittered. Its wings, held low near its body, glittered in little, they spread wide and were tremulous for flight. It was gone among the whirring dragonflies, whose bodies were banded with yellow and black, and bright with emerald, and red, and blue.

Cuckoos were calling, and sedge-warblers chattering among the green pennons of the reeds. Sometimes a male bird flew over the pond with a mild and hawlike flight, calling *wuck-oo*, *wuck-wuck-oo*, and the little agitated warblers flew after it. The hen cuckoo did not sing her name, but uttered rapid bell-like notes in one key, a bright necklace of sound to lure a male after she had selected a warbler's rest wherein to lay, and exchange, her small, thick-shelled, greyish-brown egg. Once a cuckoo was flying over with a warbler's egg in her beak (to be swallowed later) when a sparrowhawk dashed at the bird and the egg dropped into the water. *Splap!* Tarka awakened, saw the egg, dived, brought it to the couch, and ate it before the shadow of a grass-stalk had moved its own width on the bank.

4

Tarka was rolling on his back in the beams of the sun one morning, when he heard the distant note of the hunting horn and soon afterwards the tongues of hounds. The bitch listened, and when the baying became louder, she pressed through the reeds with the cubs and took to the bramble undergrowth beyond the north bank of the pond. A south wind was blowing. She ran down the wind, the cubs following just behind her. When she stopped to listen, she also licked her neck; and a human observer might have thought that this act showed her to have no fear of being hunted.

The heart of the otter was beating quickly; and whenever

she stopped to listen, her aroused nervous force was as a burden, only to be eased by movement. Now the hounds were hunting Marland Jimmy, who was swimming about the pond and looking at them from among the reeds. When he was tired of swimming backwards and forwards under water, he crept out through brambles and ran across a few acres of boggy moorland to the stream. He was fat and, for an otter, slow on his broad pads. Hounds were after him when he was half-way across the rushy tract, where lichens and mosses held a distinct scent of him. The old otter reached the stream and went down with the water until he came to a drainpipe, where he had often sheltered. Soon the tongue of Deadlock boomed up the pipe, but he lodged there in safety. Then a terrier named Bite'm crept to within a foot of him and yapped in his face. His hearing having dulled with the years, the otter was not disturbed by these noises; nor was he alarmed by the thuds of an iron bar over his head. Bite'm was called back and another terrier yapped away at him until it, too, was recalled. Voices of men quietened; and after a few minutes the sounds came down the length of pipe behind him, followed by a disgusting smell. Marland Jimmy endured the smell and more thumpings above him; and when, an hour later, he crept out into bright light, the water passed away from him with a coloured smear on its surface. The old otter licked the greyish-yellow fur of his belly, and nibbled the smarting skin between his toes, all the rest of the afternoon, but the smell of paraffin stayed on him.

The bitch and cubs were safe, for although hounds drew down the brook, finding and carrying their line to a wood, the hunt was stopped by a keeper. Young pheasants were in the wood, and gins were tilled for their enemies. Hanging from the branch of a tree in this preserve were the corpses of many vairs and fitches, some green, others hairless and dry, some with brown blood clotting broken paws and noses. All showed their teeth in death, as in life. With them were bundles of claws and beaks and feathers, which once had been dwarf owls, kestrels, magpies, sparrowhawks, and buzzards. The hues and sheens of plumage were gone, and their eyes' light; soon they would drop to the earth, and flowers dream out of their dust.

The brook was a haunt of dippers, whose cries were sudden as the cries of water-and-stones; speedy little brown birds, white-breasted, which in flight were like a drab kingfishers. A tawny owl perching against the trunk of a larch tree also saw the otters coming up the stream, and its eyes, soft with light as the dark blue sloe is soft with bloom, watched them until they crept into a rocky cleft below a fall, where royal ferns cast their great shadows and water-violets were cooled by dripping mosses.

After sunset a swarm of cockchafers whirred and flipped about the top of the larch, and the owl, hungry after huddling still for fifteen hours, flapped up through the maze of cone-knotted twigs and caught two in its feet. It ate them in the air, bending to take them in its beak; and when it had caught and swallowed a dozen, it let out a quavering hoot to its mate—for the tawny owls liked to be near each other in their hunting—and, perched on a low branch of another tree, listened and watched for a young rabbit. After a few moments, its head was tilted sharply downward: the otter and cubs were going through the wood.

At midnight the western sky was pale blue and hollow like a mussel-shell on the seashore. The light lingered on the hill-line, where trees were dark. Under the summer stars a hundred swifts were screaming as they played away the night, two miles above the earth; in fine weather they kept on the wing for many days and nights together, never roosting. Their puny screams were heard by Tarka as he rubbed his neck against the grassy mound of an ants' nest.

While he was enjoying the feeling a loud chakkering noise came down from the wood. The otters swung round. Four heads pointed towards the trees. The bitch ceased to nibble her fur; the other cubs forgot their play with the head of a corncrake. The noise, distinct in the dewfall, was met by other cries as harsh and angry.

When the curious otters reached the wood, other noises were mingled with the chakkering. Green points of light glinted in the undergrowth about them, like moonlight in dewdrops, for many vairs were watching a fight of the two dog-fitches on the woodland path. Running along the bank

56

of a ditch beside the path, the fitches had met at the mouth
of a drainpipe, out of which strayed a hunger-making smell.
The pipe, covered with grass sods, lay beside an oak-log felled
for a path across the ditch. Both ways had been made by the
keeper; one for himself, and the other for fitches and vairs,
whose liking for pipes and covered ways he knew. There were
many such ways in the wood, and to make them more attractive
the keeper had placed the flesh and entrails of dead rabbits
inside the pipes.

Each dog-fitch was trying to break the other's vein by a
bite behind the ear. They rolled and snapped and scratched
with their long claws, their black-tipped tails twitching with
rage.

Every stoat and weasel which heard them ran to watch the
fight on the pathway made by the hobnailed boots of the keeper.
Tawny and dwarf owls peered down from branches of oak
trees, while from afar a fox listened, and prowled on again. A
crow awoke in an ivy-thick holly, muttered *aa-aa!* and laid
its beak among its neck-feathers once more. Tarka circled
round the stoats with the other cubs, mewing and yikkering
with excitement; and then he smelled the rabbit flesh inside
the drainpipe. The youngest cub also smelled it. She was
quicker than Tarka, and her head and shoulders were inside
one end when he ran in at the other. He had bared his teeth
to snatch the flesh when there was a hard snap, a knock of
iron on the pipe, a blow on the side of his head, and a loud
whimpering and tissing from the cub.

Immediately the bitch was by her, running round outside
the pipe in her anguish. She panted and blew as she had in the
hollow tree when her mate was being worried by hounds, she
ran up the ditch and mewed to the cub to follow, she returned
and licked its rudder. The green points of light flicked out
together.

Disturbed by the clatter in the drainpipe, a pheasant crew
in the covert, and a cock defied the pheasant from its roost
among hens in an apple tree by the keeper's cottage below the
wood. The bitch scraped at the sods covering the pipe, blowing
and gasping anew when a retriever started to bark. She ran

57

away, whistling the cubs to follow her, but returned to the cry of the cub, who had fallen out of the pipe and was dangling by its rudder.

The barking changed to an eager whine when a door of the cottage opened and a man's voice spoke. Sounds came up distinctly from the combe below. While the otter tore with her teeth at the chain, the spring, and the closed jaws of the gin, Tarka and the other cub ran among the oak-saplings, rustling the buff leaves of an old year and breaking the stalks of seeded bluebells whose caps dropped round black seeds on the earth. There were faggots of hazel wands just inside the wood, cut and drying for a thatcher, who would split them and make spears for binding the reed of cottage roofs. They burrowed under the faggot, driving out a vair that had been sucking the blood of an aerymouse or pipistrelle bat. The small weasel made a loud *kak-kak-kak* of rage at them and vanished with the limp aerymouse in its mouth. A loud barking was coming from the field, with the yikkering of the otter. Tarka heard the yelp of the retriever, but the sound that followed made him tiss, for it was the shout of a man.

When the keeper, hurrying up the field, was within twenty yards of the wood's edge, the otter left the chain she had been breaking her teeth on and ran away. The retriever rushed at the cub to worry it, but the ferocity of the unfamiliar beast made it hesitate. The otter remained standing by her cub even when the keeper was pushing through the undergrowth. Thinking that a fox or badger was in the gin, he went forward to kill it with a blow of the holly staff he carried. He was peering forward when the retriever, a young animal, ran to him snarling; something flung itself violently against his legs—the otter weighed fifteen pounds—and nearly bit through the leather of his boot at the ankle. He struck at it, but hit only earth. He hurried back to the cottage for his gun, calling the retriever to heel, lest it be injured.

The struggles of the cub pulled the iron peg out of the ground, and it was able to drag itself out of the ditch and slowly away among the saplings. The bitch whistled to Tarka and the other cub, who ran out from under the faggot and followed her.

The mother ran on with them a little way, then returned to the cub that followed so slowly with the gin ripping brambles and clanking against stones and roots. Pheasants in the covert crew from their roosting branches; blackbirds flew from the hollies with wild alarms; wrens and robins complained in the brambles, vuzz-pegs rolled themselves into spiny balls, voles crouched by the withered mosses under the oaks.

Behind the otters came the noise of the keeper crashing through undergrowth, and the retriever's feet pattering near them, *Wough-wough-wough!* to its master. Blood ran down the face of the otter where the wounded cub had bitten her as she was trying to free the gin which gripped its rudder. The cub threw itself up and down, writhing and blowing, and not knowing what had happened, it snapped at its mother's paws, at her ears, at her nose, at her neck. The otter left it to fight the pestering retriever, her eyes yellow and gem-like.

When the keeper came up the cub was gasping with the weight of the iron it had dragged over a hundred yards. He fired at the noise in front of him and the noise ceased. Into the darkness of the wood he fired the second barrel; and listened. He heard stray pellets rattling in the distance and the dragging of the gin as the retriever tried to lift it.

At dawn the crow that slept in the ivy-grown holly saw a new corpse hanging among the fitches and vairs which had run into one end of a drain-pipe, but never run out again. The crow said *aa-aa!* and flying to the gallows tree, picked out its eyes.

When daylight came the otter and her cubs were far from the wood, having arrived at new water, deep and dark and slow moving. They swam to an islet where grew sallows and ashpoles, and swaying at the trees' tops were rafts of twigs roughly pleached, being the nests of wild pigeons. The male birds were awake, and cooing to their mates, when the otter walked out of the water. Green sedges grew by the upper end of the islet, where sticks and roots of winter floods were lodged, and through them the otters crept. The mother trod down a place in the middle and bit off sedges for a couch, and afterwards, hearing a watery croak near her, she sank silently into the pool. Her head emerged by the nest of a moorhen which flew clumsily off six large eggs, brown like the curling tips of sedge and speckled with dark blotches. These were carried back, one by one, to the cubs, who cracked them and sucked the yolks, afterwards playing with the shells. Sometimes Tarka whimpered and stopped play, for the bruise on his head was aching. Then the mother licked it, and washed him all over, and he fell asleep; and the sun had risen when she had cleaned herself and nibbled the lead pellets out of her coat.

Time flowed with the sunlight of the still green place. The summer drake-flies, whose wings were as the most delicate transparent leaves, hatched from their cases on the water and danced over the shadowed surface. Scarlet and blue and emerald dragonflies caught them with rustle and click of bright whirring wings. It was peaceful for the otters in the backwater, ring-rippled with the rises of fish, a waving mirror of trees and the sky, of grey doves among green ash-sprays, of voles nibbling sweet roots on the banks. The moorhen paddling with her first brood croaked from under an arch of stream-side hawthorn, where the sun-shafts slanting into the pool lit the old year's leaf-dust drifting like smoke under water. The otter heard every wild sound as she lay unsleeping, thinking of her lost one. The cubs breathed softly, but sometimes their nostrils worked and their legs moved, as though they were running.

5

When Tarka awoke he saw a small eye quizzing him from among the ash-sprays. He stretched up his head and sniffed, and at the movement the eye disappeared. Ticking cries sounded from the middle of the tangle.

Hearing them, an ackymal that had been searching the stream-side hawthorn boughs for green caterpillars flittered to the islet and chittered beside the crackey. The ackymal had a mate in a stump hole, brooding over a family of thirteen in a nest of moss and feathers, and the crackey had a mate and a family of eight in a ball of grasses hidden in the side of a hay-stack. Both nests were hundreds of wing-flutters away, yet when the hens, both shorter than a man's finger is long, heard the cries of their songfolk, they left their young and hastened to join them. Their scolding was a summons to all small birds. Blackbirds flew in from the fields and let out shrill ringing cries which jerked their tails as they perched above the otters. Soon many small birds were gathered in the trees of the islet, and their mingled cries brought six larger birds, who sloped up one behind the other. They were among birds what the Irish are among men, always ready in a merry and audacious life to go where there is trouble and not infrequently to be the cause of it. Raising their crests and contracting their light blue eyes, the six jays screamed with the noises of tearing linen.

The cubs lay still, but the otter lifted up her head. She had met jays before, and knew that men sometimes go where the pretty crows are nagging. For half an hour she was anxious, ready to take her cubs into the friendly water immediately the jay cries became shorter; which would mean the coming of the greatest enemy, man.

The birds became hungry. The crackeys and ackymals and ruddocks—Devon names for wrens and tomtits and robins—flew away when the otters neither heeded nor harmed them. The jays remained; but when a sparrowhawk dashed into the trees in search of a pigeon, they departed and mobbed the hawk, helped by a pair of carrion crows.

Again the spirit of the green place was tranquil, with peaceful doves cooing in the noonday's rest. All the long day the sun swung over the islet until the hilltops were fiery. Shadows lifted from the waters and moved up the trunks of trees. They faded in evelight. The pool darkened. Over the fields flew a white owl, one of hundreds which like great blunt-headed moths were quartering the pastures and tilth of all the lands served by the Two Rivers. It fanned above the vole-runs, where the craneflies rose in flight from flower and bent. The reeling song of a nightjar on a gatepost ran through the ground mist not high enough to hide the flowers of ragged robin and the harden-ing seeds of the flowering rush. The pigeons settled at the tops of the ashpoles, and ceased their clapping and flapping of wings.

A drop of water splashed, another and another. The otter had withdrawn her head from the river, wherein she had been harkening for stir of fin or wave of tail. Filling her lungs with new air, she slipped into the water and swam to the other end of the islet, where a scour had been formed by the flood-rains of the last south-westerly wind. Here the grown family of the moorhen was paddling. When almost under them, the otter saw the legs and the images of legs joined to them, black in silhouette against the less dark surface. She seized one of the moorhens and drew it under, releasing it to bite it in her jaws, and carried it back to her cubs, swimming with her nose, whiskers, eyes, and part of the dead fowl out of the water. The cubs were waiting, and seeing that she had food, they ran to her and pulled it out of her mouth, tearing away feathers and mewing with their pads on the dead bird. When the otter returned to the scour the moorhens were gone, so she dived and sought fish.

Late at night she returned with the cubs to the wood, and whistled for the lost one. She did not know it was dead; she knew only her longing for it. Her whistles went far in the still night, as she ran with nose to the ground, stopping to whine when her grief became acute. The cock on the apple bough heard her and crew to the dog in the kennel, who barked to its master. Hearing the bark, the otter took her cubs away; and at the end of the night, when they reached the big river, the lost cub was forgotten.

They hunted and ragrowstered for many days under the high wooded hills, below which the river wound and coiled like a serpent. When the moon hung thin and bright in the dusk—the fourth he had seen—Tarka could swim thirty yards under water before he needed to put out his nose to breathe. In one of their haunts, the smaller cub caught a big trout driven upwater by the bitch, and as she dragged the flapping fish on the stones, Tarka seized it above the tail. She snapped at his head, dropping her bite to do so, and he dragged it away. She bit it through the red-spotted skin, and they tugged, while

62

wrenching the fish into pieces which they ate held in pads and munching with their heads on one side, whereas before they had usually swallowed without chewing. At any threat of piracy one whipped round to eat facing another direction; very soon all the trout was gone except a scriddick, or fragment, of the tail.

There was no more yinny-yikkering when they had fed, for then was the time for play. When Tarka had drunk some water, he snapped playfully at the cub's head, and inviting her by his manner to catch him, romped through the shallow into the pool. Sometimes he swam with only his hindlegs, as his mother did when she was not close upon a fish, but when his sister was so near to his rudder that she could touch the tip of it, he used all four webs and swerved by a swish of his rudder which swung him round in his own length. In one of his turns she caught him and they rolled in the water, pretending to bite each other, and kicking as kittens do. And so it was that Old Nog, the wisest heron of the Two Rivers, heard the noise of bubbles breaking on the water as he alighted by the pool side. He watched, prepared to jump-and-flap if there were danger. He saw a swirl on the water, and the roll of two dark sleek bodies. He waited. They rolled nearer. With neck and beak held low—a two-pointed horn spear on a shaft hidden by long narrow feathers—he waded into water over his knee joints. While he paused for a plunge of the spear, which had pierced and held many a rat and eel, the bitch's head arose a yard from him, and at her sharp cry the cubs fell apart and swam under. The heron, with a harsh squawk of anger and alarm, jumped into the air and beat away slowly, with legs stretched out behind him and neck tucked between his lean shoulders. *Kaack!* cried Old Nog, as he flew to his next fishing place.

For several nights after feeding, the cubs went down to a mill-pool to ragrowster, always with the mother, who delighted in playing tricks upon them. Once she whistled the food-cry, and they ran in excitement to her, only to find a large leaf laid on a stone. It was fun, and they chased her. The pool, placid after a dry month, was made turbid by the fragments of leaf, stick, and stone stirred from the silted bottom. She let them catch her, and enjoyed the rage of her little cubs who snarled so fierce and bit so hard, but could not hurt her.

Early one morning the south-westerly wind arose from off the Atlantic, and brought fast low clouds over the land. A blown grey rain hid the trees on the slopes of the valley. At night the young moon was like a luminous grub spinning a cocoon around itself in the sky. The river pushed to the sea with the fresh, or brown flood-water, and at nightfall their holt, rising three feet under a waterside alder, was filled. The otters rode down on the fresh, over the spillway of the Dark weir, where branches were fixed amid long claws of water. They spread their legs and floated. The noise of the great waters filled Tarka with joy. A log rolled in front of him, and he scrambled on it, to jump off again with happy cries. He pretended that froth was fish, and turned over on his back, trying to clutch it. The river swilled him along, while he whistled in happiness. A memory of big fish was moved in the otter's mind by the smell of the fresh, she was taking her cubs down to the river-bend above Canal Bridge, where she and her mate had killed salmon and peal before the cubs were born.

During the journey the clouds were blown to the north-east, over the high and cold moorland, and when the otters had drifted under Rothern Bridge the moon was shining bright in a dark blue sky. Bubbles glinted around Tarka's head, where the water, hurrying too fast over shoals, tumbled back upon itself. Round a bend the river began to slow and deepen —it was dammed half a mile below by a concrete weir built diagonally from bank to bank. This was the head of the weir-pool. The otters drifted on, round another bend until they came to where the smooth and thundering fall-over of the bubble-whitened water slanted across the river, broken near the left bank by the plunge of breakers down the fish-pass. A mist hung over the river. An icicle stood in the moonlight below the fish-pass, a silver spark for an eye.

Below the fish-pass the water rushed in a foamy spate. Above it slid black and polished. Presently out of the lower whiteness a silvery flicker shook and vanished. The silver spark moved and glinted lower. Old Nog, peering below the pass, was so excited that he nearly fell over the three long green toes of each foot, in his haste to overlook more of the water. A second fish tried to leap the weir; with sideways flaps of tail it struggled up the spillway, but the claws of the water pulled it back. The moon in its first bright quarter was smitten into a myriad shimmerings by the lower turmoil. Suddenly, it seemed, the shimmerings were drawn together into a larger quartered moon, which rose out of the water in a silvery curve, and fell into the pool above, soundlessly in the immense roar of the fall.

The otters were lying in an eddy near the right bank, away from the tug of the cascade plunging down the fish-pass. The water in the eddy turned quietly. On its surface revolved a wheel of sticks, riveted by bubbles. The otters turned with it, hanging rudders down in the current. When the salmon leapt the weir, the bitch became rigid and her nostrils widened; but before the burst of the splash had dropped back, she had become supple again. The back of her sleek head gleamed and was gone. The cubs followed her, naturally so swift that a human observer might have wondered what cry or signal had been made by the otter.

They swam by the bank until the pull of the water grew less, when the mother turned into midstream and sought the salmon by working upwater from bank to bank through the gloomy and tumultuous spate. The current forced them to swim with the webs of four feet. Tarka swam on her left flank and the other cub on her right. Sometimes he was flung sideways, or spun in another whirling wheel. He was swimming out of one when the bitch either scented the fish or saw the swift ream of its dorsal fin, for she turned and swam with the current, leaving them behind. Tarka turned after her, and was pursuing with all his strength when a narrow fish, larger than any he had ever seen, swished past him. A few moments afterwards the otter followed, but Tarka had to rise to breathe, and when he swam down again he was alone. He knew that hunted fish usually went upwater, so he swam against the current, swinging from side to side as he had learned by imitating his mother.

When, after several minutes, he could find neither mother nor sister, he climbed on the bank, where wet vegetation and sticks loading the lower branches of nut trees showed how quickly the fresh had risen, and was falling. Plashes of water covered the grassy depressions of the meadow, where moorhens were feeding; and Tarka was returning from an unsuccessful pattering after the birds when he heard his mother's whistle. She had been swept down the fish-pass and hurled against the concrete rim of the middle trough, where the water had pounded her until she had been flung out of the straight rush and left gasping and coughing on rocky shillets heaped against the lower bank by old floods. She was savage in failure, and took her cubs over the plashy meadow to a wood to find rabbits. In this wood she had never heard the *iclack* of a sprung gin, so she had no fear. But the rabbits told their fear by thumping their hindlegs, and those which did not bolt into the open ran to their buries and sat there quivering, with ears laid back over shoulders. The otters followed them to where they crouched, inert in terror, their faces pressed into the earth where the tunnels stopped. Twelve were dragged out squealing, and killed; three being skinned by the bitch. While they were feeding a harsh chattering came from one of the holes, with two pricks of greenish light. Here stood Stikkersee the weasel, who was in a rage because the water-fitches were in his wood. Stikkersee was about half as long as the otter's rudder, but he was not afraid of her. He came within a yard of her nose and raved so persistently at the smell of so much blood that she turned away from the little beast's racket and went back to the river.

When the moon had come to its round shine, Tarka was hunting his own food in the pools and necks of the clear water running round the bend above Canal Bridge, which rod-and-line men declare to be the best beat of the Two Rivers. One August night, after play under the oaken fender that took the leat away from the pool, he had left his mother but a short while and was running along the bank, when a raucous cry in the darkness made him halt. His paw was raised. His nostrils twitched. The cry had come from the meadow, where tufts of rush-grass and sedge were left uncropped by cattle. It was followed by others—slurred and throaty notes which rose

66

slowly into the air and ended in a sweet and liquid cry, something like that of an otter at play. The curlews, which were
feeding with their young flown from the moors where they were
born, were disturbed by something, and had cried the alarm.
Tarka had heard curlews crying during many nights, but never
before in such a way. He heard thuds in the ground; and from
the river the warning whistle of his mother.

Remembering what had come with the ground thuds before,
when the air of the hollow tree had shaken to the baying of
hounds, Tarka ran swiftly to water. The otter had left the
river and was standing on the bank, sniffing the night wind.
The alarm cries of the curlews had ceased, and call notes fell
from the sky. In the riverside sedges two warblers began to
speak to one another. They mixed hastily the notes of song and
alarm, with the gentle under-song voice used only to their
mates when brooding in the cradles woven to the green flags.

The ominous sound of a human voice came to Tarka, and a
hound-like taint which raised the hair of his neck. Immediately
the bitch yikkered a threat, and with her cubs ran down the
bank and hid among the sedges. Clouds hid the shine of the
moon.

On the bank, dark against the sky, appeared the figures of
men, and a long-legged lurcher dog. The men scrambled down
to the river's verge. There was a moment of quiet, when the
trilling cries of the flying curlews rose above the water-murmurs
and the wind in the trees.

A scratching noise and the flickering of a small light. It
went out. Another match was struck and shielded by a hand,
until it spread into a lurid flame, over-casting with ruddy glow
the dim shades of trees across the water. The flare lit the faces
of two men. One held a pitchfork with gleaming prongs. They
stood still and watchful. Then a youthful voice ten yards
higher up the river said: "Fine li'l brown dog going through
the daggers, Shiner! Wish I'd took hold of 'n."

Neither of the men answered. They were staring intently
at the water. Slowly the torch-bearer raised an arm and pointed.
The spear was poised, to quiver over the man's head, while a
ream, or little wave, skated over the pool.

A hoarse voice whispered "Now!" and the fork was plunged into the water. A curved flash of fire scattered its ripple. The torch-bearer threw down his torch and waded into the water followed by the young man, who had run down the bank when he had seen the jumping salmon. They were groping for the fish, guided by the agitated spear-shaft, when the man yelled that one of the prongs had gone through his hand. He held it up, dripping blood, and cursing that the top of one of his fingers was knacked off.

The man on the bank picked up the torch—oily rags tied to a stick—and held it as far out as he could over the water without filling his boots. The youth cried out that he had got a grip on the sow's gills and that he couldn't hold it much longer. Before the man could get to him, he had dropped the fish, yelling that he had been bitten in the leg by the little brown dog.

On the moonlit bank, beside the black-and-red smoking rags, they tried to bind their wounds; and the uninjured man was bending down to pick up his empty sack when the lurcher dog began to growl. Its snarls increased; it ran forward; it yelped with pain and ran back past them, followed by two yellow, glowing eyes.

"Fine li'l brown dog you zee'd in the daggers," growled the poacher called Shiner, who had lost a finger-joint. "Us may as well keep whoam when they sort o' dogs be about!"

6

Yellow from ash and elm and willow, buff from oak, rusty brown from the chestnut, scarlet from bramble—the waters bore away the first coloured leaves of the year. Beeches preserved their tawny form in rain and hail, but yielded more and more to the winds. Sandmartins and warblers deserted their old haunts; kingfishers and herons remained. The reeds sighed in the songless days, the flags curled as they withered, and their brittle tops were broken by the rains.

Eels began to pass down to the sea. They were the females,

travelling from ponds and lakes, from dykes and ditches and drains, from the hill streams of Dartmoor where the Two Rivers had their ancient source. The eyes of the eels grew larger as they were swept down in the turbid waters, as they writhed over wet grass, along cart ruts and drains. These eels were urged seawards by a common desire—to journey onwards from where the shallow bed of ocean broke off and dropped deep below Ireland. To reach their spawning beds across the Atlantic these fish would swim against the Gulf Stream, coming at last to a great eddy, or stagnancy, where, below ancient oak timbers rotting in seaweed, strange fish carrying lights moved in the heaviest darkness. Here the eels of the world laid their eggs, and here they died, far under the floating weed of the Sargasso Sea whence as transparent, flat, ribbon-shaped creatures, they had set out for the inland waters of Europe. After their immense journey the elvers had reached the mouths of rivers and passed up to ponds and ditches, where those that were not killed by man, otter, heron, gull, waterfowl, cormorant, kingfisher, dwarf owl, and pike, lived and grew until desire and instinct moved them to seek their ancestral birthplace in the Gulf of Mexico.

The eels of the Two Rivers were devourers of the spawn and fry of salmon and trout, and the otters were devourers of eels. Tarka stood on the shillets of the shallow stream while they twisted and moved past his legs. At first he ate a small portion of each capture near the tail, but when his hunger was gone he picked them up, bit them, and dropped them again. The more he killed the more he wanted to kill, and he chopped them until his jaws were tired. It was a slimy sport, and afterwards he washed for nearly half an hour, quatting on a mossy rock.

While the eels were migrating the otters found their food easily, as there was no hunting to be done. They followed the eels down the river, eating them tail-first as far as the vent, and leaving the head and paired fins. They played away most of the night. The mother took her cubs to a steep sloping bank of clay which had been worn in past winters by many otters sliding down it. Nine feet below was a pot-hole with seven bubbles turning in the centre with a stick, and as Tarka slid down headfirst he meant to seize the stick and play with it. When he looked up through the water it was gone, and many other bubbles rode there, a silver cluster about the blurred image of another otter. Hearing the strokes of an otter's rudder he looked in the direction of the sound, and saw a strange cub, with the stick in its mouth, travelling under the foamy current. Tarka followed the dim form until he reached a barrier made by an uprooted pollard willow and broken branches lodged in the stream. He climbed on the trunk, shaking water from his ears and eyes, and ran back with jubilant whistles to the slide. There he saw the cub, the stick still in its mouth, standing with a grown otter. Tarka yikkered, and ran back to the water. The grown otter mewed to him, ran after him, licked his face, and purred in his ear. He tissed at her, and whistled to his mother, who came to him, but did not drive the stranger or the cub away.

The stranger had been the mother of many litters long before Tarka's mother had been born. Her fur was grizzled on pate and shoulders, and her muzzle was grey. Her canine teeth were long and yellow, and she had lost three of her incisors. She knew every river and stream that flowed north into the Severn Sea. She had roamed the high cold moors of three counties, and had been hunted by four packs of otter hounds. Her name was Greymuzzle.

She played with the otters at the slide, and remained with them when the low clouds became rosy in the east. That day all five hovered on Leaning Willow Island, and she curled beside Tarka, and washed his fur, treating him as though he were her own cub. Then she washed the other cub, who had a white-tipped rudder. Greymuzzle had met White-tip wandering alone three weeks before, and had remained with her ever since. There was friendship and sympathy between the two grown otters, for they never yikkered or tissed at each other. Indeed, although Tarka's mother did not remember Greymuzzle, the old otter had played with her and her cub brothers all one night in one of the duckponds near the estuary.

The rain was blown in grey drifts down the valley, and the river flooded the martin holes that riddled the sandy banks.

Trees and branches and dead animals bumped towards the sea. So heavy the autumnal fresh that the otters could not see to hunt in the river. They travelled up the valley on land, feeding on little voles turned out of their drowned homes, and on rabbits which they caught in a warren in a wood where the corpses of herons, kingfishers, red-throated divers, cormorants, and shags were nailed to an oak tree. Some had been shot, others trapped. The cormorants and shags were beheaded, for the Two Rivers' Board of Conservancy paid one shilling for every head. The wings of the kingfishers were cut off their tiny bodies, for some women in towns were willing to pay money for the bright feathers, which they wore as ornaments on their hats.

After another gale the bird-nests of old summer began to show in the woods above the winding river. Very beautiful were the wild cherry trees at the fall of their vermilion leaves. The gales of the October equinox stripped them off the branches and whirled them away. The otters went down again on another fresh, sometimes leaving the water to cross bends of marshy ground and fields, following trackless paths which otters had run along before fields were ploughed; before wild men hunted them for their skins with spears of fire-hardened wood. These paths were older than the fields, for the fields were once the river's wider bed, in the mud of which the heavy rudders had whilom dragged. They floated under Halfpenny Bridge, and lay by day in the reeds of the old canal bed. A dog disturbed them, and the next night they travelled inland, and sought a resting place in the hillside earth of badgers. The white-arrowed faces of the Brocks only peered and sniffed at them. A few dawns previously a fox had crept into the same earth among the hillside pines, but the badgers had turned him out, as he stank, and his habits were displeasing to their tidy ways. Had the fox crept there during the day, and his wheezing told them that he was being hunted by hounds, he would not have been bitten and driven out, but given shelter, for man was their common enemy.

The Brocks allowed the otters to sleep in one of their ovens —as countrymen call the chambers connecting the tunnels, for they were the size and shape of the cloam ovens wherein some Devon farmwives still baked bread. The otters were clean, and washed themselves before sleeping, and so to the badgers were agreeable. At fall of night they left the earth together, Tarka keeping close to his mother, for the size and appearance of the old boar who had been snoring during the day on his bed of bitten grass and moss in the next oven made him uneasy. The badgers waddled down their paths trodden through the spindleberry shrubs and blackthorns, but the otters made their own way among the brambles to the sloping top of the hill. They ran along a row of sheep-nibbled rape to the skyline, crossed a road, and pushed through the hedge-banks of many small fields. Travelling down a pasture, and through a wood of oak and holly, they came to a pill, or creek, whose banks were fissured by guts and broken by tidal waters. White-tip suddenly galloped away over the mud, for she re-cognized the Lancarse pill which carried the stream coming down the valley from the Twin-Ash Holt, where she had been born. It was low tide, and the water ran below glidders, or steep muddy slopes. They spread their legs and the water took them under a road-bridge to the river, which ran through a wide and shallow pool crossed by black round iron pillars of the Railway Bridge—the Pool of the Six Herons. Whenever Tarka crawled out to catch one of the little birds feeding by the water-line, his feet sank into mud and his belly dragged. Alarmed by the otters, the birds arose with cries which seemed to awake echoes far down the river. These were the cries of ring plover and golden plover, of curlew, whimbrel, snipe, and redshank, and all the way down into a dim starlit distance the cries were borne and repeated.

The brown water rocked them down, and as they were drifting in a wide curve Tarka saw something which filled him with fear. The constellation of the Plough, which had been before them, was now on their left, with its starry shape touching the tops of the trees far away. The stars were friendly, being of the night and the water, but these strange lights were many times the size of the morning star. They stretched in a twinkling line across the river, throwing a haze above them, like the dawn which the otters of the Two Rivers know as a warning.

Neither of the older otters was afraid, so Tarka swam without diving. The lights made the three cubs uneasy. As they drifted nearer, rumbling sounds came on the night breeze which had arisen two hours since with the flowing of the tide over the estuary bar.

Soon the sweep of the fresh lessened, for the tide was pressing against the river. A wavelet lifted Tarka and passed behind him, another curled like a long razor-fish shell and broke over him. He shook the water from his whiskers, and licked his lips, liking the strange taste. He lapped and drank. The forerunning press of the young tide lifted him up and down, and chopped with playful foam at his pate. On every ribbed shoal and mudbank the wavelets were lapping the stones and rocks, lapsing with faint trickling sounds, and leaving domes of froth which trembled and broke in the wind. As the otters swam down with stronger strokes the mudbanks changed to sandy shoals, and air bubbles out of ragworms' holes shook up in the shallow water through which they paddled. Long dark shapes rode on the water, swinging round slowly in the tide, and the wavelets went flip flup against them. Tarka was afraid of the salmon boats, but the old otters ignored them. The lamplights on the bridge were now very large and bright, and had ceased to twinkle. They passed more boats at their moorings. The rumbling noises of traffic on the bridge were loud, and figures were seen. In front, twenty-four arches, of different shapes and sizes, bore the long bridge. Greymuzzle dived, and the four followed her.

She had caught the scent of men and dogs blowing from the bridge, two hundred yards in front. Under water Tarka swam until he could swim no more, and rising quietly to vent, he turned his head to see if any danger were near, and swam on. He rose to breathe seven times before reaching the bridge, and the eighth rising brought him under one of the arches. He swam hard against the tide pouring between two piers.

This was the first time Tarka passed under the antient Long Bridge, which the monks built across their ford two centuries

before the galleons were laid down in the shipyards below to
fight the Spanish Armada. When the otters had passed under
the bridge they had to swim hard, keeping near the right bank
of the river to avoid the main flow of the tide. Flukes were
caught in the estuary that night by the otters diving to deep
water; they were not easy to find, for the dabs and plaice lay
flat on the sand when they saw the dark shapes above them,
and their sandy-speckled back hid them. The otters raked the
bottom with their paws, driving up the fish which they seized
and took on the bank to eat.

In the nights that followed Tarka learned to eat crabs,
cracking them with his teeth. With the other otters he sought
the shellfish among the rocks below the stone quay of a fishing
village at the meeting place of the Two Rivers, where often at
night they were disturbed by the pailfuls of rubbish flung over
by the natives. Once a pailful of hot ashes came down,
burning both Tarka and White-tip.

By day the otters slept in the reeds of a duckpond which they
reached by drifting with the tide up the other horn of the
estuary, and turning into the Branton pill, where ketches and
gravel barges were moored. At dawn they left the salt water
and ran over the eastern sea-wall to the duckpond shaped like
a ram's horns. In the brackish waters of the duckpond the
otters took mullet which had been washed in when the sea-
wall had broken years before, and rainbow trout put there by
the owner. Old Nog fished these waters, and at night many
kinds of wildfowl flapped and quacked beside the reeds;
mallard, widgeon, teal, coot, dabchick, and strays of the duck
family—shoveller, pochard, and golden eye.

On the fourth night of the otter's arrival at the Ram's-horn
duckpond, the swallows which settled among the reed-maces
at sunset did not sleep. They twittered among themselves when
the first stars gleamed in the water, for they had received a
sign to leave the green meadows they loved so well. They
talked in their undersong voices—which men seldom hear, they
are so soft and sweet—while clinging to the unburst heads of
the reed-maces. They talked of white-and-grey seas, of
winds that fling away the stroke of wings, of great thunder-

shocks in the sun-whitened clouds under, of wild rains and hunger and fatigue to come before they saw again the sparkles in the foam of the African strand. But none talked of the friends who would fall in the sea, or be slain in France and Spain and Italy, or break their necks against the glass of light-houses, for the forktailed birds of summer had no thought of these things, or of death. They were joyous and pure in spirit, and alien to the ways of man.

During the day Tarka had been watching them, being curious. He had watched them sweeping above him with a windy rush of wings that darkened the sky, and had listened to their sharp cries as they dipped and splashed in the wind-ruffled water. As he was stretching himself before leaving his couch at sunset, they flew like a great sigh up to the stars. *Krark! Krark! Krark!* cried Old Nog, standing grave and still in the shallow water at the pond's edge. It was the last English voice many of them would hear, the blue winged ones of summer, who had begun the weary migration from the land of thatched homesteads and old cob linhays.

Some days after the swallows had gone, Tarka heard a short, soft, mellow whistle while playing in the Ram's-horn duckpond. The five otters ceased their play and listened. The whistle came again, and Tarka's mother answered. The answering whistle was keen and loud. The bitch swam towards it, followed by Greymuzzle and White-tip. The whistle made Tarka cry in rage, *Ic-yang*, and when a dog-cub has cried thus he is no more a cub, but a dog-otter.

The night before, the otters had fished in the estuary by the sea-weedy hurdles and posts of a silted-up salmon weir, where in former times salmon were left penned by the tide. They had returned to the duckpond across fields and dykes, along an otter route, and on their trail an old dog-otter had followed.

Now he had trailed them to the duckpond, a big, flat-headed, full-thighed dog with great whiskers, more than double the weight of Tarka. He frightened the crier of *Ic-yang*, who crouched tissing with his sister when the stranger sniffed at her nose and then licked it. This action caused Tarka's mother to behave in a curious manner. Turning fiercely on the cub,

75

she rolled her over, bit her, and chased her under water. Many bubbles were blown up. Tarka dived to see why this strange thing had happened, but the dog turned in a swirl of water to snap at his head. Tarka was so scared that he swam to the bank and crawled out among the dry thistles. Here, while the water ran from his fur, he whistled to his mother. He saw her swimming with her head out of water, with the strange dog behind pretending to bite her. She was heedless of her cub's cries, and dived with the dog in play. For hours Tarka ran on the grassy bank of the duckpond, following his mother as she played in the water. Once the dog rose to the surface with a mullet in his mouth, which he did not trouble to kill before leaving it to float on its side. Tarka whistled again and again, and at last the big dog left the water and chased the small dog for whistling to his mate.

Tarka ran away. He crossed over the sea-wall, and worked up the stony bed of the pill, catching the flukes and green crabs which were feeding at the mouth of an open sewer. He met White-tip and Greymuzzle, and together they returned to the duckpond when the wildfowl flighted over. He was swimming round one bend of the ram's horn when the big dog heard the strokes of his hindlegs and swam after him again. Tarka dived and twisted, and although he was bitten twice in the neck and once through the paw, he was not caught. His mother's training had made him swift and strong. He quitted the water and was pursued through grassy tufts and thistles and bunches of frayed flags to the sea-wall, where the big dog turned and whistled to his mate. Hearing another whistle—it was really an echo of his own—he galloped in rage back to the duckpond. Then Tarka whistled, and the dog returned to kill him. Tarka went up and over the sea-wall at his greatest speed, across the mud and stones of the pill and to the western sea-wall, where he stopped. He cried *Ic-yang!* several times, but if the dog had returned in answer to the challenge, it is doubtful whether Tarka would have waited to drink the blood of his enemy.

Already his mother had ceased to care, although she would never entirely forget, that she had loved a cub called Tarka.

7

He was alone, a young male of a ferocious and persecuted tribe whose only friends, except the Spirit that made it, were its enemies—the otter hunters. His cubhood was ended, and now indeed did his name fit his life, for he was a wanderer, and homeless, with nearly every man and dog against him.

Tarka fished the pools and guts of the Branton pill, eating what he caught among the feathery and aromatic leaves of the sea-wormwood plants which grew in the mudded cracks of the sloping stone wall with the sea-beet, the scentless sea-lavender, and the glasswort. One night a restlessness came over him, and he rode on the flood-tide to the head of the pill, which was not much wider than the gravel barges made fast to rusty anchors half-hidden in the grass, and to bollards of rotting wood. The only living thing that saw him arrive at the pill-head was a rat which was swarming down one of the mooring ropes, and when it smelled otter it let out a squeak and rapidly climbed over the sprig of furze tied to the rope to stop rats, and ran back into the ship. Tarka padded out of the mud, and along the footpath on the top of the sea-wall, often pausing with raised head and twitching nostrils, until he came to where the stream, passing through a culvert under the road, fell into a concrete basin and rushed thence down a stony slope into the pill. Entering the water above the fish-pass, he swam under the culvert, following the stream round bends and past a farmyard, through another culvert under a cart-road, and on till he came to a stone bridge near a railway station. A horse and butt, or narrow farm cart, was crossing the bridge, and he spread himself out beside a stone, so that three inches of water covered his head and back and rudder. When the butt had gone, he saw a hole, and crept up it. It was the mouth of an earthenware drain, broken at the joint. He found a dry place within. When it was quiet again, he went under the bridge and fished up the stream, returning at dawn to the drain.

He was awakened by the noise of pounding hooves; but the noises grew remote and he curled up again, using his thick rudder as a pillow on which to rest his throat. Throughout the day the noises of hooves recurred, for below the bridge was a ford where farm horses were taken to water. Twice he crept down the drain, but each time there was a bright light at the break in the pipe, and so he went back. At dusk he slipped out and went upstream again. Just above the bridge was a chestnut tree, and under it a shed, where ducks were softly quacking. He climbed on the bank, standing with his feet in sprays of ivy, his nose upheld, his head peering. The scents of the ducks were thick and luring as vivid colour is to a child. Juices flowed into his mouth, his heart beat fast. He moved forward, he thought of warm flesh, and his eyes glowed amber with the rays of a lamp in the farmhouse kitchen across the yard. The chestnut tree rustled its last few rusty leaves above him. Then across the vivid smear of duck scent strayed the taint of man; an ivy leaf trembled, a spider's web was broken, the river murmured, and the twin amber dots were gone.

Beside the stream was a public footpath and an illuminated building wherein wheels spun and polished connecting-rods moved to regular pulses which thudded in the air like the feet of men running on a bank. Tarka dived. He could not swim far, for by the electric power station the river slid over a fall. He swam to the right bank, but it was a steep wall of concrete. Again he dived, swimming upstream and crawling out on the bank. For many minutes he was afraid to cross the railway line, but at last he ran swiftly over the double track, and onwards until he reached the stream flowing deep under a footbridge.

He had been travelling for an hour, searching the uvvers of the banks for fish as he had learned in cubhood, when on a sandy scour he found the pleasing scent of otter. He whistled and hurried upstream, following the scent lying wherever the seals had been pressed. Soon he heard a whistle, and a feeling of joy warmed his being.

A small otter was waiting for him, sitting on a boulder, licking her coat with her tongue, the white tip of her rudder in the water. As Tarka approached, she looked at him, but she did not move from the boulder, nor did she cease to lick her neck when he placed his forepads on the stone and looked up into her face. He mewed to her and crawled out of the water to stand on hindlegs beside her and touch her nose. He licked her face, while his joy grew to a powerful feeling, so that when she continued to disregard him, he whimpered and struck her with one of his pads. White-tip yikkered and bit him in the neck. Then she slid into the water, and with a playful sweep of her rudder swam away from him.

He followed and caught her, and they rolled in play; and to Tarka returned a feeling he had not felt since the early days in the hollow tree, when he was hungry and cold and needing his mother. He mewed like a cub to White-tip, but she ran away. He followed her into a meadow. It was strange play, it was miserable play, it was not play at all, for Tarka was an animal dispirited. He pressed her, but she yikkered at him, and snapped at his neck whenever he tried to lick her face, until his mewing ceased altogether and he rolled her over, standing on her as though she were a salmon just lugged to land. With a yinny of anger she threw him off, and faced him with swishing rudder, tissing through her teeth.

Afterwards she ignored him, and returned to the river as though she were alone, to search under stones for mullyheads, and eels. He searched near her. He caught a black and yellow eel-like fish, whose round sucker-mouth was fastened to the side of a trout, but she would not take it. It was a lamprey. He dropped it before her again and again, pretending to have caught it anew each time. She swung away from his offering as though she had caught the lamprey and Tarka would seize it from her. The sickly trout, which had been dying for days with the lamprey fastened to it, floated down the stream; it had been a cannibal trout and had eaten more than fifty times its own weight of smaller trout. Tar from the road, after rain, had poisoned it. A rat ate the body the next day, and Old Nog speared and swallowed the rat three nights later. The rat had lived a jolly and murderous life, and died before it could fear.

The lamprey escaped alive, for Tarka dropped it and left White-tip in dejection. He had gone a few yards when he turned to see if she were following him. Her head was turned, she was watching. He was so thrilled that his whistle—a throat sound, like the curlew's—was low and flute-like. She answered. He was in love with White-tip, and as in all wild birds and animals, his emotions were as intense as they were quick. He felt neither hunger nor fatigue, and he would have fought for her until he was weak now that she had whistled to him. They galloped into the water-meadow, where in his growing desire he rushed at her, rolling her over and recoiling from her snapping of teeth. She sprang after him and they romped among the clumps of flowering rush, startling the rabbits at feed and sending up the woodcock which had just flown from the long low island seventeen miles off the estuary bar.

White-tip was younger than Tarka, and had been alone for three weeks before the old, grey-muzzled otter had met and taken care of her. Her mother had been killed by the otter-hounds, during the last meet of the otter-hunting season, at the end of September.

Tarka and White-tip returned to the stream, where among the dry stalks of angelica and hemlock they played hide-and-seek. But whenever his playfulness would change into a caress, she yinny-yikkered at him. She softened after a while, and allowed him to lick her head, once even licking his nose before running away. She was frightened of him, and yet was glad to be with him, for she had been lonely since she had lost Greymuzzle, when a marshman's dog had chased them out of a clump of rushes where they had been lying rough. Tarka caught her, and was prancing round her on a bank of gravel when down the stream came a dog-otter with three white ticks on his brow, a heavy, slow-moving, coarse-haired otter who had travelled down from the moor to find just such a mate as the one before him. Tarka cried *Ic-yang!* and ran at him, but the dog-otter, who weighed thirty pounds, bit him in the neck and shoulder. Tarka ran back, tissing, swinging and swaying his head before he ran forward and attacked. The older dog rolled him over, and bit him several times.

Tarka was so mauled that he ran away. The dog followed him, but Tarka did not turn to fight. He was torn about the head and neck, and bitten thrice through the tongue and narrow lower jaw.

He stopped at the boulder where White-tip had been sitting when first she had seen him, and listened to the whistles of his enemy. The water sang its stone-song in the dark as it flowed its course to the sea. He waited, but White-tip never came, so he sank into the water and allowed himself to be carried down past bends and under stone arches of the little bridges which carried the lanes. He floated with hardly a paddle, listening to the song of the water and sometimes lapping to cool his tongue. The wheels and rods of the power station turned and gleamed behind glass windows like the wings of dragonflies; over the fall he slid, smooth as oil. Slowly and unseen he drifted, under the chestnut tree, under the bridge, past the quiet railway station, the orchards, the meadows, and so to the pill-head. The current dropped him into the basin of the fish-pass, and carried him down the slide to salt water. With the ebb he floated by ketches and gravel barges, while ring-plover and little stints running at the line of lapse cried their sweet cries of comradeship. The mooring keg bobbed and turned in the ebb, the perches, tattered with seaweed, leaned out of the trickling mud of the fairway, where curlew walked, sucking up worms in their long curved bills. Tarka rode on with the tide. It took him into the estuary, where the real sea was fretting the sandbanks. He heard a whistle, and answered it gladly. Greymuzzle was fishing in the estuary, and calling to White-tip.

The old otter, patient in life after many sorrows and fears, caressed his bitten face and neck and licked his hurts. They hunted together, and slept during the day in a drain in one of the dykes of the marsh, which was watered by a fresh stream from the hills lying northwards. Night after night they hunted in the sea, and often when the tide was low they played in the Pool opposite the fishing village that was built around the base of a hill. The north-east wind blew cold over the pans and sandy hillocks near the sea, but Greymuzzle knew a warm sleeping place in a clump of round-headed club-rush, near the day-hide of a bittern. She became dear to Tarka, and gave him fish as though he were her cub, and in the course of time she took him for her mate.

8

The trees of the riverside wept their last dry tears, and the mud in the tidehead pool made them heavy and black; and after a freshet, when salmon came over the bar, beginning their long journey to spawn in the gravel where the river ran young and bright, broken black fragments were strewn on the banks and ridges of the wide estuary. In November the poplars were like bedraggled gull-feathers stuck in the ground, except for one or two or three leaves which fluttered on their tops throughout the gales of November.

One evening, when the ebb-tide was leaning the channel buoys to the west, and the gulls were flying silent and low over the sea to the darkening cliffs of the headland, the otters set out on a journey. The bright eye of the lighthouse, a bleached bone at the edge of the sandhills, blinked in the clear air. They were carried down amidst swirls and topplings of waves in the wake of a ketch, while the mumble of the bar grew in their ears. Beyond the ragged horizon of grey breakers the day had gone, clouded and dull, leaving a purplish pallor on the cold sea.

The waves slid and rose under the masted ship, pushing the white surge of the bar from her bows. A crest rolled under her keel and she pitched into a trough. On the left a mist arose off a bank of grey boulders, on which a destroyer lay broken and sea-scattered. It had lain there for years, in bits like beetle fragments in a gorse-spider's grey web-tunnel. One of the great seas that drive the flying spume over the pot-wallopers' grazing marsh had thrown it up on the Pebble Ridge. During the day Tarka and Greymuzzle had slept under the rusty plates, curled warm on the wave-worn boulders rolled there by the seas along Hercules Promontory.

Two hours after midnight the otters had swum five miles along the shallow coast and had reached the cave of the headland, which Greymuzzle had remembered when she had felt her young kick inside her. The tide left deep pools among the rocks, which the otters searched for blennies and gobies, and other little fish which lurked under the seaweed. They caught prawns, which were eaten tail first, but the heads were never swallowed. With their teeth they tore mussels off the rocks, and holding them in their paws, they cracked them and licked out the fish. While Greymuzzle was digging out a sand-eel, Tarka explored a deep pool where dwelt a one-clawed lobster. It was hiding two yards under a rock, at the end of a cleft too narrow to swim up. Four times he tried to hook it out with his forepad, the claws of which were worn down with sand-scratching, and in his eagerness to get at it he tore seaweed with his teeth. The lobster had been disturbed many times in its life, for nearly every man of the villages of Cryde and Ham had tried to dislodge it with long sticks to which they had lashed hooks. The lobster had lost so many claws that after nine had been wrenched off, its brain refused to grow any more. Its chief enemy was an old man named Muggy, who went to the pool every Sunday morning at low spring-tide with a rabbit skin and entrails, which he threw into the water to lure it forth from the cleft. The lobster was too cunning, and so it lived.

The otters rested by day on a ledge in the cave under the headland. Here dwelt Jarrk the seal, who climbed a slab below them by shuffles and flapping jumps. Sometimes Tarka swam in the pools of the cave, rolling on his back to bite the drops of ironwater which dripped from the rocky roof, but only when Jarrk was away in the sea, hunting the conger where the rocks of Bag Leap ripped foam out of the tide.

The greatest conger of Bag Leap, who was Garbargee, had never been caught, for whenever it saw Jarrk the seal, its enemy, it hid far down in the crab-green water, in a hole in the rocks of the deepest pool, where lay shell-crusted cannon and gear of H.M. sloop *Weazel* wrecked there a century before. When no seal was about, Garbargee hung out of the hole and stared, unblinkingly, for fish, which it pursued and swallowed. One morning as Tarka, hungry after a stormy night, was searching in the thong-weed five fathoms under the glimmering surface, something flashed above him, and looking up, he saw a narrow head with a long hooked preying beak and two large webs ready to thrust in chase of fish. This was Oylegrin the shag, whose oily greenish-black feathers reflected light. The smooth narrow head flickered as Oylegrin shifted his gaze, and a pollack below mistook the flicker for a smaller surface-swimming fish. The pollack turned to rise and take it, and the shag saw the gleam of its side at the same time as Tarka saw it. Oylegrin tipped up and kicked rapidly downwards, faster than an otter could swim. Its tight feathers glinted and gleamed as it pursued the pollack. Garbargee also saw the pollack and un-curled a muscular tail from its hold on a jut of rock. The conger was longer than a man is tall, and thicker through the body than Tarka. It weighed ninety pounds. It waved above the weedy timbers, and as it passed over, crabs hid in the mouths of cannon.

Bird, animal, and fish made a chasing arrowhead whose tip was the glinting pollack; conger the flexible shaft, otter and shag the barbs. Oylegrin swam with long neck stretched out, hooked beak ready to grip, while it thrust with webbed feet farther from the bubbles which ran out of its gullet. The pollack turned near Tarka, who swung up and followed it. Oylegrin braked and swerved with fourteen short stiff tail-feathers and one upturned web. The pollack turned down a sheer rock hung with thong-weed, but, meeting Tarka, turned up again and was caught by Oylegrin.

The chasing arrowhead buckled against the rock, in a tangle of thongs and ribbons and bubbles shaking upwards. The giant conger had bitten the shag through the neck. Wings flapped, a grating, muffled cry broke out of a bottle of air. Tarka's mouth opened wide, but his teeth could not pierce the conger's skin. The gloom darkened, for an opaqueness was spreading where there had been movement.

Now Jarrk the seal, who had been searching round the base of the rock, saw an otter rising to the surface, and was swinging up towards him when he saw a conger eel wave out the opaqueness, which was Oylegrin's blood staining the green gloom. Garbargee held the shag in its jaws. The undersea cloud was scattered by the swirls of flippers as the seal chased the conger. Garbargee dropped the shag, and the cleft of rock received its grey tenant. Jarrk swung up with a bend of his smooth body, and lay under the surface with only his head out, drinking fresh air, and looking at Tarka six yards away. *Wuff, wuff,* said Jarrk, playfully. *Iss, iss,* cried Tarka, in alarm. The pollack escaped, and later on was feeding with other fish on the crab-nibbled corpse of the shag.

It was not often that the otters went fishing in daylight; usually they lay in the warm noonday sun on the sand of a cove behind the Long Rock—a spur of which was the plucking perch of Chakchek the One-eyed, the peregrine falcon. One morning Chakchek half-closed his wings and cut down at Tarka, crying *aik-aik-aik!* and swishing past his head. It was the cream-breasted tiercel's cry of anger. He was a swift flyer and soon mounted to where his mate waited at her pitch in the sky above the precipice, scanning the lower airs for rock-dove, oyster-catcher, finch, or guillemot. When they had swept away down the north side of the headland, Kronk the raven croaked thrice, deeply, and took the air to twirl with his mate in the windy up-trends.

Near Sandy Cove was the Cormorants' Rock, where five cormorants squatted during most of the daylit hours, digesting their cropfuls of fishes. Each cormorant, as it arrived with steady black flight, would pass the rock about fifty yards, swing round and fly back into the wind, to alight uneasily among its brethren, some of whom had the tails of fishes sticking out of their gullets. They held out their wings and worked their shoulders to ease the fish down into their crops. The top of Cormorant's Rock, where they sat, was above the highest wave.

Bag Leap was a sunken reef stretching about half a mile from the point, over which the tides raced. Here the currents brought many seals, which had followed salmon up the Severn Sea, on their return home to Lundy Island. With them was a grey seal, a stranger, who had come down from the north. For several days the seals fished off the Leap, while Jarrk roared among them and joined in their favourite game of chasing the smallest seal, who was not black and yellowish-brown like themselves, but a rare silvery-white. They would swim round the rocks looking for her, sometimes remaining under water for nearly a quarter of an hour. Once when Tarka was searching for a bass in four fathoms he met Jarrk face to face, and the shock made him blow a big bubble. He turned and kicked up to the light, while Jarrk swam round him in a spiral. Jarrk was always gentle, for he had never an enemy to shock him into fear, and when Tarka tissed and yikkered at him the scymitar-shaped lip-bristles of his broad muzzle twitched, his upper lip lifted off his lower jaw, he showed his yellow teeth, and barked. *Wuff, wuff,* said Jarrk, jovially. *Ic-yang,* yikkered Tarka. The seal snorted; then his back, stretched and gleaming, rolled under like a barrel.

When the seals left Bag Leap for the seventeen-mile swim to their island home, one remained with Jarrk. She was the stranger grey seal, and often while the other seals had been romping, she had been exploring the far dark end of the cave behind the Long Rock, where was a beach of boulders. Grey-muzzle explored the beach for the same purpose, and sometimes otter and seal passed by each other in the pools. On one high-tide the seal swam into the cave, and did not return with the ebb. For three days she hid herself, and then she flapped down the sand and splashed into the sea, very hungry.

Many times during the rise and fall of tides the bitch-otter ran into the cave, and on the morning of the grey seal's return to the sea, she swam round the Long Rock, and crawled out of the surge among the limpet-studded rocks of Bag Hole. Three hundred and ten feet above her, perched on the swarded lip of a sand-coloured cliff, Kronk the raven watched her running round and over boulders. She reached the base of the precipice, and scrambled up a slide of scree, which had clattered down during the rains of autumn. Gulls wove and interwove in flight below the raven, floating past their roosts in the face of the cliff. The scree had fallen from under the Wrecker's Path,

86

made during centuries by the cautious feet of men and women descending after storms to gather what the sea had thrown on the boulders of the Hole. It was not much wider than one of the sheep-paths on the headland. Greymuzzle ran along it, and turning a corner by a lichened boulder, disappeared from the sight of Kronk. She had climbed here alone several times during the previous night.

Less than a minute afterwards the raven jumped leisurely over the edge, and opening his wings, rose on the wind, and turning, swept back over his perching place, over snares pegged by rabbit-runs in the grass, and to a shillet wall a hundred yards from the precipice. One of the brass snares Kronk was watching. It had been drawn tight about the neck of a rabbit since early morning; the rabbit had died after two hours of jumping and wheezing. It was cold; its fleas were swarming in agitation over its longer hairs. Kronk was waiting for a meal off the rabbit, but he did not like to go near it until he knew for certain that the trapper, whom he had watched setting the snare the afternoon before, had not tilled a gin beside it specially for Kronk. The raven knew all about the methods of trappers, and the steel traps and brass snares they tilled. Several times Kronk had sailed with the wind over the snared rabbit; he sailed without checking by tail or wing lest the trapper be spying upon him. In every other act of his life he was as cautious, having learned many things about man in more than a hundred years of flying.

The raven was waiting for Mewliboy, the soaring buzzard hawk, to espy the rabbit; and when Mewliboy had ripped it open with one stroke of his hooked beak, the raven intended to call *krok-krok* and so summon his mate to help him deal with the buzzard, if he were not trapped. And if he had sprung a hidden gin, then both buzzard and rabbit would be safe meat for Kronk. So the raven reasoned.

Greymuzzle came to the end of Wreckers' Path, and climbed up springy clumps of sea-thrift, among gull-feathers and mussel-shells and fish-bones, and ran along another path to the top of the precipice. She looked left and right, often pausing to sniff the air. She picked up a feather, ran with it a few yards, and dropped it again. She cast round over the sward, peering into rabbit-holes, and pulling out dry stalks of thrift that the wind had blown there. Kronk watched her running, swift and low, along the narrow wandering lines pressed in the sward by the feet of rabbits; he saw her stop by the snared rabbit, bite on to its neck, and watched her tugging at it. *Crr-crr!* said Kronk to himself.

He jumped off the wall, which was covered with dry lichens dissolving the stones with acids, and circling above Greymuzzle, croaked a long, harsh note, meant to call the gulls. He dived at Greymuzzle, repeating the harsh cry, and very soon nearly fifty herring gulls were screaming about her. Alarmed by the noise, she ran back the way she had come; the gulls followed, and Kronk had the rabbit to himself. Seeing him, the gulls returned, screaming and flying as near to him as they dared. Kronk pecked and pulled at his ease, knowing that the gulls would give the alarm should a man come round either the south or the north side of the wall, both of which hid approach.

Greymuzzle was slipping down the scree at the end of Wreckers' Path, carrying a brown dry tussock of sea-thrift in her mouth, when the remote crying of gulls became loud above the cliff. *Quoc-quoc-quoc!* many were muttering in anger. Several hundred wheeled and floated above the otter. She heard a soughing of wings, and looking up, saw the beak and eyes of the raven growing larger as he plunged towards her. He had taken nine long hops away from the rabbit, and the tenth had taken him over the precipice edge as a man, walking fast, had taken his ninth stride round the northern wall, three hundred yards off. Kronk opened his wings when half-way down the cliff and sailed without a wing-beat round the Point.

Mewing and scolding, the gulls floated higher in the wind, and hearing them, the grey seal, who had been lolling beyond the break of rollers, swam out twenty yards and turned to watch the top of the cliff. She knew that the tossing flight and the cries of *quoc-quoc-quoc!* meant the presence of man. And although the seal could not see much at a distance, once she had been fired at by a man with a rifle.

Greymuzzle swam round the Long Rock with the mat of roots in her mouth, and crawled out of the sandy surge. Tarka was lying on his back, playing with a smooth green flat pebble of glass that he had carried from the bed of a pool. When he saw her, he turned on his pads—neither bone nor muscle showed in action—and ran to see what she carried. Greymuzzle lifted her burden out of his playful way, but he jostled her, wanting to take it, and knowing nothing of her purpose. He bit off three rootlets, and at the mouth of the cave ran back to his glass pebble.

The seal watched with bleary eyes the man climbing down, and his spaniel dog sitting three-quarters of the way down the path, frightened to follow its master farther. Tarka played with his pebble, below the orange-lichened and towering wall of the Long Rock. In a scattered and unled flock the gulls drifted above the cliff. Over them Kronk the raven, most-powerful and black, cleaved the air on outspread wings; sometimes he twirled on his back, recovering immediately. He was practising the upward or impaling lunge of beak that he had learned from his sire many years before. High above the raven a small dark star twinkled and swept in its orbit, twinkled and poised on its pitch. Chakchek the One-eyed, slate-blue pinioned and cream-breasted, was aloft. *Crr-crr*, said Kronk, as sea and greensward turned up and over and upright again. *Crr-crr-crr*, as the man disappeared round the Long Rock, and Kronk sailed downwind to be over him.

A thousand feet below the raven, Tarka tapped his pebble of glass, green and dim as the light seen through the hollow waves rearing for their fall on the sand. The noise of waves, continuous and roaring on the rocks at low tide, was swelled by the echo beaten back by the cliff, and Tarka saw the man climbing round the Long Rock before he heard him. The man, jumping from boulder to boulder, did not see Tarka; but when he reached the sand he saw the trails of two otters. One trail led into the cave straitly, with regular five-toed prints, except where the track swerved from the impetuous and uneven trail of a galloping otter. Three rootlets of sea-thrift were dropped on the spurred sand. The trail led on; the other

89

turned back to the wetted grey pebbles, where lay crab-shells, corks, fish-tails, and a piece of glass.

The man followed the tracks into the dim cave, clambering over ice-cold rocks, and shining a light in the pools wherein drops glistened and struck loud in the stillness. He moved slowly, with glances over his shoulder at the diminishing circle of daylight. The roof of the cave was red and brown with the iron in the rock. Sometimes his foothold wobbled on a stone that in the motion of tides had worn a cup for itself. Some distance from its mouth the cave turned to the left, shutting darkness and sea-whispers together. The man went on, bending down to find his way by the light he carried. The pools became shallower, without life or weed; the roof lower and dry. A wailing cry ran along the walls. Holding the electric torch before him, he saw four pricks of light that moved, vanished, and appeared again, one pair above the other. The wail went past him again, like the cry of a hungry infant. On the grey boulder at his feet the wan light showed a black mark, as of tar on bitten fish-bones—the spraints of an otter.

Cold struck into him, pale yellow eyes shifted noiselessly in front. The toe of his boot kicked something that clattered on the stones, and looking down, he saw a bone; and near it, other bones, skulls, and shrunken hides. He picked up a jawbone, with grinder teeth, cuspless and oblique, set along it. Many seals had died in the cavern.

Again the wailing, not far away. The boulders sloped upwards, and pressed one against another by his feet, made a noise of *pob-pobble* that rang solidly and echoed down the cave and up again. Before him something white was stirring. Picking it up, he stroked the soft, warm hair of a baby seal, putting his finger in its mouth to stop the wailing. While he was nursing it, he heard the hollow echo of a plunging splash, a grumbling noise like *uch, uch!* and a slapping as of the palms of great hands on flat rocks. Turning his torch down into the gloom, he saw two dull red orbs, and heard the angry bleat of a mother seal.

He carried the white calf to the inner wall of the cave and

laid it down; then hurried to the other wall, where ledges formed natural steps. On the top ledge an otter was crouching. By the shape of the head he knew it was a bitch-otter; an old otter, with grey and grizzled hairs on its muzzle. He climbed as high as he dared, and saw that it had made a couch of dry seaweed and grasses and thrift. He peered into the couch. The otter moved to and fro on the narrow ledge, tissing. He could see no cubs; nor did she appear to be in whelp.

Uch, uch! gasped the seal, exhausted and aching after her anguished journey over the boulders of the cavern. She had hurried by pressing the palms of her flippers on the ground and lifting her body forward by short jumps, moving fast as a walking man. She reached her cub and caressed it with her tongue, making sounds over it between sobbing and bleating. Then she turned her back to the man, and flung sand and pebbles at him with quick scooping strokes of her flippers. The man took from his pocket a wooden whistle, made from an elderberry stick, and played several soft notes upon it. The seal looked at him as though calmed by the simple music. She lay still with her calf, whose head was turned on one side as it sucked through the side of its mouth. The man played on, moving nearer to the seal. Slowly he passed the animals, and went more easily towards the light.

9

The otters were alarmed by the coming of the man, and that night they left the headland, returning to the Burrows, and hunting rabbits in the great warren of the sandhills. A cold mist lay on the plains and in the hollows, riming the marram grasses and the withered stems of thistle and mullein, so that in the morning mildew and fungi in strange plant forms seemed to have grown out of the sand. On the coarser hairs of the otter's coats the hoar remained white, but on the shorter and softer hairs it melted into little balls of water. Everything except the otters and birds and bullocks was white. The sedges and reeds of the duckponds were white, so was the rigging of the ketches in the pill. The hoofholes of cattle were filmed with brittle ice. In the cold windless air came distinct the quacking of ducks and the whistling of drakes as the wildfowl flighted from the ponds and saltings to the sea, where they slept by day.

The otters lay up near a cattle shippen, among reeds with white feathery tops. A dull red sun, without heat or rays, moved over them, sinking slowly down the sky. For two days and two nights the frosty vapour lay over the Burrows, and then came a north wind which poured like liquid glass from Exmoor and made all things distinct. The wind made whips of the dwarf willows, and hissed through clumps of the great sea-rushes. The spines of the marram grasses scratched wildly at the rushing air, which passed over the hollows where larks and linnets crouched with puffed feathers. Like a spirit freed by the sun's ruin and levelling all things before a new creation the wind drove grains of sand against the legs and ruffled feathers of the little birds, as though it would breathe annihilation upon them, strip their frail bones of skin and flesh, and grind them until they became again that which was before the earth's old travail. Vainly the sharp and hard points of the marram grasses drew their circles on the sand: the Icicle Spirit was coming, and no terrestrial power could exorcise it.

The north wind carried a strange thickset bird which drifted without feather sound over the dry bracken of Ferny Hill, where Tarka and Greymuzzle had gone for warmth. Its plumage was white barred and spotted with dark brown. Its fierce eyes were ringed with yellow, the colour of the lichens on the stone shippens. Mile after mile its soft and silent wings had carried it, from a frozen land where the Northern Lights stared in stark perpetuity upon the ice-fields. The thickset bird was an Arctic Owl, and its name was Bubu, which means Terrible. It quartered the mires and the burrows, and the gripe of its feathered feet was death to many ducks and rabbits.

Clouds moved over land and sea with the heavy grey drifting silence of the ice-owl's flight; night came starless, loud with the wind's rue in the telegraph wires on the sea-wall. As Tarka and his mate were running down to meet the flood-tide in the pill, a baying broke out in the sky; whiskered heads lifted

92

fixed to harken. For a minute the otters did not move, while the hound-like baying passed over. The long skein of south-wending geese swung round into the wind, flying with slow flaps and forming a chevron that glided on down-held, hollow wings beyond the pill-mouth. Cries of golden plover, twined in the liquid bubble-link of the curlews' chain-songs, rose up from the saltings.

The white-fronted geese, eaters of grass and clover, had come before the blizzard howling its way from the North Star. A fine powdery snow whirled out of the sky at night, that lay nowhere, but raced over the mossy plains and hillocks, and in the burrows, faster than the grains of sand. Tree, dune, shippen, and dyke—all were hid in whirling white chaos at daylight. The next day thicker snowflakes fell, and out of the storm dropped a bird with white wings, immensely swift in flight, whose talon-stroke knocked off the head of a goose. It stood on the slain, holding by the black sickle-claws of its yellow feet; its hooked beak tore breast-bone and flesh together. Its plumage was brown-spotted like the plumage of Bubu—the hue of snow and fog. Every feather was taut and cut for the swiftest stoop in the thin airs of its polar ranging. Its full brown eyes glanced proudly as any Chackchek, for it was a Greenland falcon.

Beyond the shaped and ever-shifting heaps of sand, beyond the ragged horizon of the purple-grey sea, the sun sunk as though it were spent in space, a dwarfed star quenching in its own steam of decay. The snow fled in the wind, over the empty shells of snails and rabbit skeletons lying bare and scattered, past the white, sand-stripped branches of dead elderberry trees, and the dust of them aided an older dust to wear away the living tissue of the Burrows. Night was like day, for neither moon nor sun nor star was seen. Then the blizzard passed, and the snow lay in its still pallor under the sky.

*   *   *

And the sky was to the stars again—by day six black stars and one greater whitish star, hanging aloft the Burrows, flickering at their pitches; six peregrines and one Greenland falcon. A dark speck falling, the *whish* of the grand stoop from two thousand feet heard half a mile away; red drops on a drift of snow. By night the great stars flickered as with falcon wings, the watchful and glittering hosts of creation. The moon arose in its orbit, white and cold, awaiting through the ages the swoop of a new sun, the shock of starry talons to shatter the Icicle Spirit in a rain of fire. In the south strode Orion the Hunter, with Sirius the Dogstar baying green fire at his heels. At midnight Hunter and Hound were rushing bright in a glacial wind, hunting the false star-dwarfs of burnt-out suns, who had turned back into Darkness again.

*　　　*　　　*

Old Nog the heron, flying over the Ram's-horn Pond, saw Greymuzzle among the reeds, for she was the only dark thing in the white wilderness below. She was hiding a solitary cub by curling herself round it, so that her chin rested on her flank. During the storm she had not left the couch of bitten reed and floss; the heat of her body melted the snowflakes. For two days and a night she kept the snow from the blind cub; and when the air was clear, a black frost gripped the waters of the ponds, bound the drifts, and hung icicles from drain and culvert. Then Greymuzzle arose, and called to Tarka over the ice. He answered from the northern horn of the pond.

He had kept a fishing hole in the ice, which he bit free as it froze. Fish were hard to see, for the top of the water under the ice was a bad reflector of light to the lower water. As it grew colder, the fish buried themselves in the mud, and when Greymuzzle roved in the brown dim water, she saw only her own vague image following her above. More wildfowl flighted to the estuary and the cries of birds when the tide was flowing and covering the sandbanks were myriad as the gold flickerings in the night sky. The otters crossed the swift waters to the sandbanks where they were feeding, swimming under the waves and rising to breathe with only their wide nostrils above. Greymuzzle swam up under a duck and seized it, and the change of note in the quacking was heard by the birds, who threw the alarm over the estuary. Thousands of wings whipped jets on the water. The wildfowler creeping up in his narrow boat pulled the trigger of his gun too late—a long red flame sent a blast of shot swishing over the head of Greymuzzle as she dived. She swam to the mouth of the pill with the duck in her jaws, and ate it on an icy litter of twigs and seaweed left by the last high tide.

The next night the fishing hole was sealed, and no longer marked by a ring of scales and bones, for the rats and crows had eaten them. Greymuzzle was scraping at a fish frozen in the ice when the sheet whanged and whined and creaked, then *boom!*, a crack ran across it, and water spirted in the fissure. When it was still, Orion was reflected there, with the red and green flashes of Sirius; but as Greymuzzle peered the starshine glazed, and mock-trees of the Icicle Spirit grew on the water.

The cold sharpened. To the estuary came sanderlings in white winter dress, running at the tide-line like blown sea-foam. Snow buntings followed, and went south with them. The flat-fish swam to warmer water beyond the bar, and often when the otters dived in the estuary they rose empty-mouthed to the surface, except perhaps for a green crab. Old Nog the heron grew so thin that he looked like a bundle of grey flags stripped by wind and clinging to two reeds. His inland fishing ponds were frozen, most of the streams ran under plates of ice, and the only food he could spare was to be found at low tide in the pools of the Sharshook Ridge, where gravel had been dug.

The pans and plains of the Burrows were crossed by a thousand tracks, the prints of larks, finches, wagtails, crows, and gulls; the presses of weasels, rabbits, and stoats; the pads of badgers and foxes; the triple toes of herons and bitterns, like the veining of leaves. Many of the smaller birds were so weak they could not fly, and their bodies were eaten by rats and weasels, which were eaten by the larger owls and hawks.

Other otters from the Two Rivers came down to the estuary, some of them cubs of ten or twelve pounds in weight, who had kept together with their mothers. Families of three and four and one of five—a bitch and four cubs from the boggy moorland hill where the Two Rivers began in the peat—came to the duckpond along the otter path from the saltings, and finding it frozen, went down the pill and out to the coast. Tarka met White-tip with her mate by an overturned hulk one night; she was scratching at the webmark of a widgeon, frozen in the mud with its scent. One look, and they had passed in the darkness.

Many of the dog-otters wandered solitary. Last of all, slow and fatigued, after weeks of hunger, came Marland Jimmy, the old dog with the split ear who had played the funnel-game with Tarka's mother in the deep clay pit. He limped along the otter-path, which many pads had pressed into ice; the cysts between his toes, inflamed by paraffin, were raw and frostbitten. The tide was ebbing when he crawled over the white sea-wall, and down the dark and hard mud to the water, crackling the brittle ice-forms of the glasswort. Hearing a whistle across the pill, Marland Jimmy walked into the water and swam. He kicked slowly, and the current carried him aslant, amid plates of ice broken off by the last tide. The trickles in the mud channers and salting guts had already ceased. So black and bitter the night that not even the whipper-ing cries of golden plover were heard in the pill. The water ebbed in a blank silence of fixed star-points. Marland Jimmy swam across the pill and crawled out steaming. His breath froze on his muzzle, and his rudder was pointed with an icicle when he reached Tarka, dragging himself on the bank. Tarka was rubbing his head and the side of his neck against a fish longer than himself, with gaps in its dull-shining length. A week before, Jarrk the seal had chased it over the bar, and as it turned past his head, he had taken a bite out of its belly. The dying salmon drifted with the tides until Greymuzzle and Tarka caught it in the pill. What a feast they had had! As soon as they had carried it steaming out of the sea, ice crystals had glittered on the scales.

Tarka rolled on the crisp snow while the aged otter tore at the fish, breaking off bone and frozen pink flesh. He moved from gills to tail, from tail to gills again gulping icy mouthfuls, wheezing with hard swallowing, and when he had breath, yikkering at Tarka to keep away. Tarka, warmed by his fullness, rolled and rolled, until he rolled into the water. *Hu-ee-ee-ic!* whistled Tarka.

The split-eared dog had gorged himself when Greymuzzle returned for another meal. He quaddled down the hard mud to where Tarka was sliding into the water. With a heavy rippling of his body, he ran to the top of the slide, and holding his legs rigid, slipped down on his ruined feet into the water. Greymuzzle heard the happy whistles of the playing dogs, and slid with them until she heard the squeals of rats fighting by the broken carcass of the salmon. The noise made her remember her cub, for rats had squealed among the scrikkits of bones and scales around Tarka's fishing hole during the snowstorm. Tarka played on until he was hungry, when he went back to the salmon. Marland Jimmy played alone at the slide.

The ebb-tide moved along the sea-weedy perches stuck in the mud to mark the fairway. A mist was rising like steam from the top of the water, which moved slower with its weight of surface slush. The slush became clotted, and hardened, and suddenly ceased to move. The star-points dulled. Orion was stripped of his flashing, the green tongue of Sirius was mute, the Swan lost her lustre, the glare of the Bull faded.

Kack! croaked Old Nog, flapping up from the fish carcass as a fox slunk down to it. The tips of his open beak were red with the frozen blood of a speared rat, which was sticking in his gullet. In swaying flight, reed-like legs hanging with weakness, the heron set off for the gravel pools of the Shrarshook. *Kack!* he called to his mate, who was standing in the ebb to her knees, fifty yards beyond the slide. She did not move; nor did the tide.

Krark! called Old Nog at dawn, flying over the pill, and calling his mate again. *Hu-ee-ee-ic!* whistled Tarka to Marland Jimmy, who had not answered since the star-points had suddenly dimmed and vanished off the water. *Hu-ee-ee-ic!*—a thin, hard cry which Greymuzzle heard among the reeds of the duckpond. *Hu-ee-ee-ic!* travelling through the ice-blank in the pill, and out across the estuary.

Bubu stared down at Tarka walking over to the eastern sea-wall; fanned above him before beating away. The Arctic Owl perched fifty yards below Tarka's slide on something that swayed and creaked to its weight, but bore it upright. Staring around with several complete turns of its head, Bubu fixed orange-rimmed eyes on a mask set stiff before and below it. There was no movement; there was no life. The owl stared round again, and flew away, leaving its narrow perch swaying on reed-like legs, as though nodding to the head of Marland Jimmy gazing film-eyed out of the ice.

10

The little thin cub, on its couch among the reeds frozen and bent like the legs of dead spiders, greeted Greymuzzle with husky mewing whenever it heard her coming, and would not be comforted by tongue caresses. Frost had stricken its eyes. Greymuzzle prowled all day and all night when she was not warming and suckling her cub; and although she was so hungry, she still played with Tarka, sliding headfirst down a snowy hillock. They had to travel to the estuary for food, for every incoming tide piled up its floating floes at the pill-mouth, with grinding shrieks and shuddering booms that sounded far over the Burrows. At low tide the frost welded them in a high and solid barrier.

Both otters had blistered their tongues by licking ice, and to ease their thirst, they rasped them against snow on the sea-wall in the middle of the day. Greymuzzle went into the village one night searching the gardens for food. She found the duckhouse under the chestnut tree in the farmyard above the bridge, and although she sought an entrance for more than an hour, she found none. The smell of the ducks was painful.

A fox slunk near her, passing with drooping brush and ears laid back, pad, pad, pad, in the snow.

Unable to get the ducks, she walked down the frozen pill to the estuary, meeting Tarka at the pill-mouth, near the salmon-fishers' hut built on the shillet slope of the sea-wall.

The fox followed her, hoping to get another meal of salmon. He followed her until the dawn, and was near her at sunrise, when she returned to the couch in the reeds of the duckpond. She winded him and ran him, and although he was chased by the marshman's dog when she had left off pursuit, the fox returned, knowing that she had young somewhere in the reeds. His name was Fang-over-lip, and he had wandered far in his hunger.

While the pallor of day was fading off the snow a skein of great white birds, flying with arched wings and long stretched necks, appeared with a measured beat of pinions from the north and west. *Hompa, hompa, hompa,* high in the cold air. Greymuzzle and Tarka were eating seaweed and shellfish on the Shrarshook, but when the swans splashed into the estuary, they slipped into the tideway and drifted with the flow to where the wild swans were floating. Fang-over-lip licked out some of the mussel shells they had dived for, and cracked up a crab's claws, before following along the beach.

The beams of the lighthouse spread like the wings of a star-fly above the level and sombre sands. Across the dark ridge of the Shrarshook a crooked line of lamps winked below the hill. In one of the taverns a sailor was singing a shanty, the tune of which came distinctly over the Pool. The swans moved up with the tide, the otters after them. They were thin and weak; for mussels, winkles, and sometimes a sour green crab were poor nourishment for an otter who, in careless times, had eaten a three-pound sea-trout at a sitting and been hungry two hours afterwards.

The tide beyond the tail of the Shrarshook was divided by a string of froth made by the leap and chop of waters beginning to move north and south, along the arms of the sea stretching to the Two Rivers. The swans turned north, borne by the tide racing past Crow Island. They paddled out of the main flow, and turning head to tide, began to feed in the shallow over a sandbank. The otters drifted nearer, only their wide nostrils above water. When they were ten yards away from the nearest swan the nostrils sank, and chains of bubbles rose unseen above them. A swan saw a dark form under the water, but before it could lift out its head, Tarka had bitten on to its neck. Heavily its wings beat the water. Every curlew on the sandbank cried in a long uprising whistle, *cu-u-ur-leek, cur-r-r-leek!*, and the alarm flew up and down the estuary as fast as sound travelled. The treble whistle of the redshank was piped from shore to shore, the ring-plover sped over the water, turning and wheeling as one bird. Old Nog cried *Kra-r-rk!* Wind from the swan's wings scalloped the water and scattered the spray, and one struck Tarka a blow that made him float slowly away. But Greymuzzle hung to the swan's foot, even when her rudder was nearly out of the water as she was dragged along. The swan trumpeted afar its anger and fear. Bubu the Terrible flew towards the sound.

Before the Arctic Owl arrived Tarka was un-dazed and swimming to help his mate. Seeing and hearing the struggle, Bubu stretched his toes, opened his beak, and gave a loud and terrifying hoot; but when he reached the conflict, fanning above like a shade of chaos, there was nothing to see save only feathers and bubbles. Silent as snow and fog, staring like the Northern Lights, taloned like black frost, the Arctic Owl flew over the Shrarshook and dropped upon Fang-over-lip, but the snarl and the snap of teeth drove him up again.

Across the pull of the tide, among the grating icefloes, the otters took the swan, whose flappings were getting feeble as the death-fear grew less. Tarka had bitten the artery in the neck. When the otters rested the bird lay quiet on the water. It heard the wings of its brethren beating out the flying song of swans, *Hompa, hompa, hompa,* high and remote in the night. It flapped thrice and died.

Tarka and Greymuzzle swam with the swan to the shore, where they bit into the throat and closed their eyes as they drank its hot blood. Soon mouthfuls of feathers were being torn away but before they could eat its flesh Fang-over-lip crept upon them. He, too, was famished, having eaten only a mouse that night—and that small biter of willow bark was but fur and bone. With the boldness of starvation the fox rushed upon them. The snarling brought a boar badger, who had been digging for the roots of sea-beet in the crevices of the stones of the sea-wall. The boar lumbered down the slope, over the seaweed, and across the shingle to where Fang-over-lip, with fluffed-out brush and humped back, was threatening the otters. The badger, who was called Bloody Bill Brock by certain badger-digging publicans, had never before been so hungry. For two days the walls of his belly had been flat. He had no fear of any animal. The otters bit his hide, but could not hurt him, as under the long grey tapered hairs his skin was exceptionally thick. Pushing them away and grunting he seized the swan in his jaws and dragged it away. He dropped it again to bite Greymuzzle; and then he stood absolutely still, except for his nose. Fang-over-lip did not move, nor did Greymuzzle, nor Tarka. Their heads were turned towards the cottage looming white on the sea-wall. A door had opened and closed.

The marshman had with him two bob-tailed cattle dogs, which rushed on the shingle. They found a circle of feathers. Downwind the wave-worn shells tinkled as though a wind had risen off the sea and was running over the beach towards the tarred wooden hospital ship. This was the sound of the fox's departure. Bloody Bill Brock was slower and clumsier, and his black bear-claws slipped on the boulders of the sea-wall's apron. Tarka and Greymuzzle were lying in three feet of water, with only their ears and nostrils showing. They heard the pursuit of the badger, and some moments later the hoarse voice of a man. One dog yelped, two dogs yelped, and both returned to their master on three legs, while the thick-skinned badger continued his way, with the swan, on four sound legs.

Some hours later all of the swan, except the larger bones, feet, wings, and bill, was inside Bloody Bill Brock, who was snoring inside a sandy rabbit-bury, where he slept for three days and nights.

Greymuzzle returned to the duckpond with only seaweed and shellfish to nourish herself and her cub. Unsteadily it dragged its little body towards her, and opened its mouth to greet her. No sound came from its mouth. Its legs trembled and could not carry its head which hung over the couch of weeds. Its paws were frost-bitten, its eye-sockets empty. Grey-muzzle stared at it, before lying down and giving the shelter of her body. She spoke to it and took it in her paws and licked its face, which was her only way of telling her love. The cub tottered away, and sought the milk which it could not find. Afterwards it slept, until she left again to seek food in the wide daylight, following the slot of deer across the snow. The hind, which had come down from the high ground with a herd of red deer, with her calf that had been with her since its birth the previous May, caught the scent of the otter and ran away, the calf beside her. The otter followed, but turned away when she saw a small bird crouching on the snow, unable to fly further. She ate the fire-crested wren—a thimble-ful of skin, bone, and feather. After a vain prowl round the garden of the marshman, she returned to the duckpond, crossing the pill three hundred yards below the place where men were breaking up, for firewood, the bulk of an old dismasted ketch. In the field she picked up the skull of a sheep and carried it a few yards before dropping it. She had picked it up and dropped it many times already.

The ice-talons set harder in the land. No twitter of finch or linnet was heard on the Burrows, for those which remained were dead. Vainly the linnets had sought the seeds locked in the plants of the glasswort. Even crows died of starvation. The only noises in the frore air were of saws and axes and hammers, men's voices, the glassy sweep of wind in the blackened thistles, the cries of lambs and ewes, raven's croaking, and the dull mumble of breakers on the bar.

Every day on the Burrows was a period of silence under a vapour-ringed sun that slid into night glowing and quivering with the zones and pillars of the Northern Lights. More wild red deer from Exmoor strayed to the Great Field, which even the rats had quitted. The deer walked into the gardens of the village, some to be shot stealthily, others to sleep into death. The shepherd of the marsh-grazing stamped at night round his fire, clad in the skins of sheep, and swinging his arms. Beyond the straw-and-sack-stuffed hurdles, foxes, badgers, and stoats slunk and prowled and fought for each other's bodies. Over the lambs in the fold flew Kronk the raven, black and croaking in the moonlight. *Ck!* cried Old Nog, tottering to the Shrars-hook from the sandhills, where he hid shivering during the time of high-tides. The wind whined in the skeleton of his mate broken at the knees, near the skull of Marland Jimmy gaping at the crown, eyeless and showing its teeth in ice.

When two foxes and a badger had been shot, Greymuzzle went no more where ewes pared hollow the frozen turnips and suckled peacefully their tail-wriggling lambs. One night, raving with hunger, she returned to the wooden duckshed in the farmyard by the railway station. High over the shed rose the chestnut tree, black and bare and suffering, with one of its boughs splitten by frost. Other creatures had been to the duckhouse before her.

Fang-over-lip had started to dig a hole under the rotten floorboards, but returning the night after, he had smelt that during the day the hole had been deepened and a gin tilled there to catch him by the paw. When he had gone Bloody Bill Brock had grunted to the duckshed and, putting head between paws, had rolled on the metal tongue holding the jaws apart. The gin had clacked harmlessly against his grey hairs. The badger had scratched farther down and up again, reaching the floorboards by daylight; and departed, to return in the next darkness and to see a gin lying there with jaws as wide as his back—a gin unhidden and daring him, as it were, to roll across it. The gin's rusty jaws were open in an iron leer, its tongue sweated the scent of man's hand. Bloody Bill Brock, who had sprung many gins in his life, grunted and went away.

There were no stars that night, for clouds loured in the sky. As Greymuzzle walked on the ice upstream, snow began to fall in flakes like the breast-feathers of swans. From the estuary the scrambling cries of thousands of gulls, which had returned with the south-west wind, came indistinctly through the thick and misty air. The South was invading the North, and a gentle wind was its herald. The dreadful hoot of Bubu was heard no more, for the Arctic Owl had already left the Burrows.

Greymuzzle walked under the bridge, and smelling the ducks, climbed up the bank. As she was walking past the beehives, she heard a sound that made her stop and gasp— the *ic-clack!* of a sprung gin. Tarka was rolling and twisting and jerking the heavy gin and chain off the ground. It held him. He lay still, his heart throbbing, blowing and tissing and slavering. The sight closed Greymuzzle's nostrils, so that she breathed through her open mouth. She called to him. The gin clanked, the chain clinked. She ran round him until Tarka's leaps, that wrenched the sinews of his leg, ceased in weakness, and he sank across the long rusty spring, blowing bubbles of blood out of his nostrils. A duck quacked loudly, and when its strident alarm was finished, the air held only the slight sounds of snowflakes sinking on the roof of the shed. They floated to rest on Tarka's fur, gently, and shrunk into drops of water. The chestnut tree suddenly groaned, and the corpse of a sparrow frozen for weeks to one of its twigs fell to the earth. It dropped beside Greymuzzle, and was flicked against the duckshed by a swish of her rudder as she stood over Tarka, gnawing in a fury the iron jaws of the gin.

Far away in the estuary gulls were running on the sandbanks through the yellow froth of wavelet-lap. Their jubilant and sustained cries told the winter's end. Under the tree Greymuzzle rasped the bone of the trapped paw with the sharp stumps of her broken teeth. A rat passed near, brought by the smell of blood; it fled when it saw whose blood was wasting. Greymuzzle's face was torn, but Tarka did not know that he had bitten her.

She bit through the sinews, which were strong and thick, and Tarka was free. He rushed to the river. Greymuzzle remained, remembering her cub.

When the ducks heard the gnawing of wood, they began to run round inside the shed, quacking continuously. In the farmyard a dog in its kennel was barking loudly. There was an answering shout in the house that set the animal jumping against its chain. Both Greymuzzle and Tarka knew the sequence of barking dog and the shout of a man in a house!

Greymuzzle stayed until the farm door opened, and then she ran away, splinters of wood in her bleeding mouth.

When the farmer came to the shed with his gun and lantern, he found his gin sprung and three toes of a paw lying in a red spatter about it. Seeing dots of blood leading away over the snow, he hurried to the cottage of one of his labourers and knocked on the door. He shouted, "I've got'n," as his father had shouted in the church door during a sermon half a century before, calling the men to leave and pursue the tracks of a fox through the snow.

The labourer and his two sons put on their boots warming on the slate hearth, and went out to the farmer. Armed with a dung-fork, the handle of a pickaxe, a ferreting crowbar, and the gun, they set out on the trail of the wounded otter. The lantern showed the red dots leading over the railway crossing, and on the snow by the station yard. "Come on, you!" cried the farmer to three men going home after the closing of the inn. It was ten o'clock. One had a staff, and the others kicked up what stones they could see.

The collie dog found the otters for them, in a shed where Tarka had crawled for a refuge. Tarka stood back in a corner on a heap of artificial manure sacks, while Greymuzzle ran at the dog, tissing, and snapping her broken teeth. The lantern light made of her eyes two tawny orbs of menace. Tarka found a hole in the wall, while Greymuzzle fought the collie. Weakened by starvation she was not able to fight for long, and as the farmer said afterwards, it was not even necessary to waste a cartridge, when a dungfork could pin her down and a ferreting bar break her head.

They carried the body back to the farm, where the farmer drew a pint of ale for each of his helpers from the XXXX barrel in the cellar. While they were drinking "Best respects, Varmer," the collie dog began to bark, and as it would not stop after several cries of "Shut that rattle, you," the farmer went out and gave it a kick in the ribs. The collie yelped and went to kennel, but hardly had the farmer gone into his kitchen again when it set up a furious barking. It was banged on the head with the stag's horn handle of a hunting whip, but even this did not check its desire to tell its master that an enemy was in the yard. It kept up an intermittent barking until the dawn, when it was flogged with its head wedged in the door. The farmer was a poor man and not very strong, and a sleepless night made him irritable. When he felt better he gave the dog the skinned carcass of the otter, and praised its courage and virtue in the Railway Inn, telling how it had warned him and how it had tracked the "girt mousey-coloured fitches" to the shed, where one escaped through a hole behind the sacks. He forbore to say how noisy his dog had been afterwards, deeming this a point not in its favour, for how was he, his natural senses dulled by civilization, to have known that an otter had remained all night in the farmyard, waiting for the mate that never came.

Tarka was gone in the mist and rain of the day, to hide among the reeds of the marsh pond—the sere and icicled reeds, which now could sink to their ancestral ooze and sleep, perchance to dream;—of sun-stored summers raising the green stems, of windshaken anthers dropping gold pollen over June's young maces, of seeds shaped and clasped and taught by the brown autumn mother. The south wind was breaking from the great roots the talons of the Icicle Spirit, and freeing ten thousand flying seeds in each brown head.

Water covered the pond ice, deep enough to sail a feather, and at night every hoof-hole held its star.

After seven sunrisings the mosses were green on the hillocks, lapwings tumbled and dived and cried their sweet mating cries, the first flower bloomed in the Burrows—the lowly vernal whitlow grass, with its tiny white petals on a single leafless stalk. Under the noon sun sheep grazing in the marsh had silver outlines. Linnets sat on the lighthouse telegraph wire, wing to wing, and talking to the sky. Out of the auburn breasts fell ravishing notes, like glowing strokes of colour in the warm south wind.

And when the shining twitter ceased, I walked to the pond, and again I sought among the reeds, in vain; and to the pill I went, over the guts in the salt grey turf, to the trickling mud where the linnets were fluttering at the seeds of the glass-wort. There I spurred an otter, but the tracks were old with tides, and worm castings sat in many. Every fourth seal was marred, with two toes set deeper in the mud.

They led down to the lap of the low water, where the sea washed them away.

THE LAST YEAR

11

Bogs and hummocks of the Great Kneeset were dimmed and occluded; the hill was higher than the clouds. In drifts and hollows of silence the vapour passed, moving with the muffled wind over water plashes colourless in reflection. Sometimes a colder waft brought the sound of slow trickling; here in the fen five rivers began, in peat darker than the otter that had followed the Torridge up to her source.

Broken humps, rounded with grey moss and standing out of a maze of channers, made the southern crest of the hill. In the main channer, below banks of crumbling peat, lay water dark-stained and almost stagnant. The otter walked out and lifted his head, sniffing and looking around him. Drops from his rudder dripped into the water and the stirred fragments of peat drifted slowly as they settled. The river's life began without sound, in darkness of peat that was heather grown in ancient sunlight; but on the slope of the hill, among the green rushes, the river ran bright in spirit, finding the granite that made its first song.

Tarka climbed up one of the humps of grey club moss and trod in its centre a bed soft and warm, yet cool for the paw thrust among the long, tight-growing fronds. The moss grew on and over a bush of heather, whose springy stems yielded to his curled body. He had travelled from the estuary, sleeping by day in riverside holts and marshes and feeding at night; remembering nothing, because the moor was unfamiliar to his nose and ears and eyes. When his paw ached, he licked it. It had been a happy journey up the river swollen with snow water, hunting fish and playing with sticks and stones, while mating owls called through the darkness of valleys.

He slept curled in the moss until the last sun-whitened wisps of clouds trailed away into space above the northern slope of the hill, and the plashes took light and colour. The sun awoke him and he heard the twit of a bird—a little drab pipit alone in the fen with the otter. It watched anxiously as the otter warmed the dingy, yellow-white fur of his belly in the sun and rolled to scratch his ears with a sprig of heather. The pipit had seen no enemy like Tarka before, and when the rolling otter fell off his bed and splashed into the water below, the bird flew out of the heather in straight upward flight, twittering as it dropped, fluttering wings that seemed too feeble to carry it higher than its first weak ascent. Up it mounted, to fall back again, until it turned with the wind and slanted down quickly into the heather. Again the wilderness was to wandering air and water, until webbed feet began to patter in the black soft peat, past wan yellow tussocks of withered grasses, and clumps of rushes dying downwards from their brown tips.

Running in the plashes, treading the spider-like tufts of red-rusty cotton grass, he came to a deeper and wider channer fringed with rushes. Down a crumbling sog of peat and into the still brown-clear water. He swam its winding length, seeking eels under the ooze which arose behind him in a swirl of heath fragments, dark and up-scattered by the kicks of his hindlegs. A minute's swimming and the channer widened into a shallow pit above whose broken banks the heather grew, on sprigs dispread and blasted under the sky. Some still bore the bells of old summer, that made a fine sibilance in the wry wind-music of the moor.

Tarka ran past a heap of turves, set around the base of a post marking Cranmere tarn, now empty, whither his ancestors had wandered for thousands of years. A fox had been walking there during the night, seeking the oval black beetles which, with moths, pipits, wheatears, and sometimes a snipe, were the only food it found in and around the fen. As Tarka ran out of the tarn a bird passed swiftly over his head gliding on down-curving dark wings and crying *go-beck, go-beck, go-beck!* when it saw him—one of the few grouse which lived and bred on the lower slopes under the wind. The bird had flown from a hut circle to the south, where seeds of gromwell were to be found. The gromwell had grown from a single seed carried from the lower tilled slopes of the moor on the fleece of a sheep, to which it had hooked itself. Gromwell seeds were the favourite food of the grouse around the source of the Five Rivers.

Tarka watched the bird until it glided below the hill, when he ran on again, finding nothing in the plashes moving only with images of sky and clouds and birds of solitude. Then the sun took the water, breaking brilliant and hot in every plash; the otter galloped with instant joy and sank in bog to his belly. He dragged himself on to a tussock of grass, rolled, shook himself, and set off again, roaming around the fen until he heard again the cry of running water. The cry came out of a hollow, whose sides were scarred by the sliding of broken hummocks—the faint cry of a river new-born. Through a winding channel in the turf, no wider than the otter and hidden by grasses growing over it, the little thread hastened, seeking its valley to the sea.

It fell over its first cascade and cast its first bubbles; and through a groove between hills it found a marsh where a green moss grew with rushes. Beyond the marsh, it ran strong and bright over its bed of granite gravel, everywhere glinting and singing. Over and under and past boulders of granite, splashing upon mosses whose browny-red seeds on the tall stalks were like bitterns standing with beaks upheld. Lichens grew on other boulders: silver with black undersides, and curled like strange pelts curing: grey-green in the shapes of trees and plants: bones with scarlet knuckles: horns of moose: shells and sea-weeds. The lichens fastened to the granite were as the fantastic and brittle miniatures of strange and forgotten things of the moor.

By pools and waterfalls and rillets the river Taw grew, flowing under steep hills that towered high above. It washed the roots of its first tree, a willow thin and sparse of bloom, a soft tree wildered in that place of rocks and rain and harsh grey harrying winds. A black-faced sheep stood by the tree, cropping the sweet grass; and when a strange, small, flashing, frightening head looked out just below its feet, the sheep stamped and bounded away up the hill to its lamb asleep by a sun-hot boulder. Tarka had caught a trout, the first in a mile of river; he ate it, drank, and slipped away with the water.

He caught sixteen fish in an hour, the biggest being three ounces in weight; and then he climbed upon a slab of granite and dozed in the sunlight. High above him a small bird was flying in sharp, irregular flight, mounting high to swoop towards the marsh. Every time it swooped it opened its tail against the rush of air, so that the feathers made a sound between the bleat of a kid and a dove's cooing. Its mate was flying near it. They were snipes, who had chosen for nesting-place a rush-clump in the marsh, and Tarka had disturbed them. He lay still in sleep, and they forgot that he was there, and flew down to find worms by pushing their long bills into the juggy-mire. When the sun sank behind the high tors, Tarka awoke and went down with the river. A small bullock, with long, black, shaggy hair, was drinking by a gravelly ford, and smelling the otter, it snorted and plunged away, alarming the grazing herd.

At night the stars were shorn of their flashes and burning dully through the cold vapour which drifted down from the hills. Everything was moistened—sprigs and faded bells of heather, young ruddy shoots of whortleberry, mosses, lichens, grasses, rushes, boulders, trees. The day rose grey and silent. When the sun, like an immense dandelion, looked over the light-smitten height of Cosdon Beacon, Tarka was returning along a lynch, or rough trackway, to the river. The grasses, the heather, the lichens, the whortleberry bushes, the mosses, the boulders—everything in front of the otter vanished as though drowned or dissolved in a luminous strange sea. The icy casings of leaves and grasses and blades and sprigs were glowing and hid in a mist of sun-fire. Moorfolk call this morning glory the Ammil.

The brimming light gladdened Tarka, and he rolled for several minutes, playing with a shining ball he found in the grass—the old dropping of a wild pony. Afterwards, running down to the water, he found a holt under a rock. It was cold and wet inside, and Tarka always slept dry when he could. He ran out again, liking the sun, and settled on a flat rock in the warming rays.

The rock was embedded below a fall, its lower part green with mosses hanging in the splashes. The mosses dripped and glistened. Tarka washed himself, the water-sounds unheard; he would have heard silence if the river had dried suddenly. The green weeds waved in the clear water with a calmer motion than the tail-fanning of idle fish. And then a sturdy, dark brown bird, with white throat and breast, lit on a stone down the stream, and pausing a moment, jumped down into the water. The dipper walked on the river bed, seeking beetles and shrimps and caddis-grubs. When its beak was crammed, it walked out of a shallow, flew up in a coloured rain of drops, and following the turns of the river, checked fluttering by the rock whereon Tarka lay. It thrust its beak into the moss, six inches above the tumbling water. Rapid notes, as of water-and-stones sharpened to music in a singing bird's throat-strings, came out of the moss, a greeting by the dipper's mate, who was brooding five white eggs in her wet nest. When she had swallowed the food, the water-ousel flew away upstream, low over the water, following the bends of the river. As he flew he sang, sipping his song from the stones and the water.

The shadows moved, and the bright green weeds of morning waved darkly in the river. Many times the water-ousels flew to and from the nest, but they did not see the otter which slept so still in the rocky cup above them.

Tarka gave chase to a rabbit during the next night, bolting it from a hillside clitter of rocks in a hollow at the head of a cleave. Near the clitter a tall stone reared head, shoulders, and body above the rocks embedded there, in the outline of a sea-lion, smooth and curved. The rabbit ran as far as a hole in the north-western base of the stone sea-lion, but turned back in terror as it smelt the dreaded smell of a fitch, or stoat. The rabbit's wits went from it in a thin squealing; its will to run away was gripped in the base of its spine by a feeling of sickly fascination. Its squeals caused an excited chakkering near it, and almost immediately the fitch had it by the side of the neck, and was dragging it into the hole. The fitch,

whose name was Swagdagger, was about to kill it when
Tarka ran through the opening. Swagdagger loosened his
bite to threaten the strange big invader, flicking his black-
tipped tail and glaring at Tarka. One kick of the rabbit's
hindlegs, so powerful for running, could have broken Swagdagger's neck; but it crouched still, its nervous force oozing
away. Tarka ran at it. Swagdagger faced him with an angry
chakker, and was nipped in the shoulder. The fitch ran out
through the opening, but turned outside and gibbered in fury.
Tarka looked once at the green points that were the fitch's eyes,
and went on with his work. Swagdagger went away, to climb
a granite stone, and chakker into the night. The moon was
rising, dim in the mist, and the harsh notes echoed about the
grey stillness of the granite clitter. *Kak-h' kak-kak*, he rattled,
throwing his call one way, then another. He was summoning
the stoats of Belstone Cleave.

Tarka had eaten half the rabbit when a strong scent made
him look round again. He saw in the low opening several
greenish dots, that stared and swung about and stared again.
He went on eating. Delicate sniffs, sudden rustles and paddings,
scratchings, a quick sneeze—he peered for another way out,
wanting to be alone. He found a crack and explored it with
his nose, before beginning to scrape. He sucked in the scent
of fitch, for Swagdagger's mate had her nest of young beyond
the crack.

She had been hunting a rabbit three hundred yards away
when Swagdagger had climbed the stone, and as soon as she
heard the call, she galloped back. Other fitches had run to the
summons of Swagdagger. Sharp-toothed, blood-thirsty, and
without fear, they ran up and down by the opening, sniffing the
delicious scent of fresh-slain rabbit, weaving quick bodies and
lifting their small heads to sniff, sniff, sniff. The noises of
teeth at work made a furious stir in the assembling tribe. The
older dog-fitch yakkered with rage, as he wove in and out of
the swift and impatient throng.

The little angry fitches in the cranny, beyond the nose of
Tarka, heard the cry of their mother and spat at the enemy—
all moving things unknown were enemies to the little fitches.

She ran through the fitches outside in the moonlight and into the cave, jumping in her twisty way for a bite behind the otter's ear. Tarka shook her and tried to kill her, but she ran at him again, and with her ran Swagdagger and all the fitches who had come at his alarm. Tarka trod on stoats; he was pricked all over by the teeth of stoats; he chopped one through the ribs and back, but its biting did not cease; he chopped it again, trying to hold it by his forepaws, but though broken, it was alive and angry, and bit through the skin of his throat and hung there, as long as his rudder. He pushed through fitches into the moonlight, and the fitches followed him, including the four young ones who were excited and eager for play. The pack chased him, throwing their sharp tongues, all the rugged way down to the river, into which Tarka jumped with a splash. Three of them fell in after him, but they did not like the water and crawled out spitting and sneezing, tough and lithe and sinuous as bines of honeysuckle. Unable to find the otter, the dog-fitches started a fight among themselves.

As Swagdagger's mate went up the hill again with her young running behind her, she met a badger, who was going to drink in the river. The grey waddler, animate granite, whose head was heavier than her whole body, lumbered out of the way. He sought no unnecessary trouble with fitches, and he had eaten up the rabbit under the Seal Stone.

The river hurried round the base of the cleave, on whose slopes stunted trees grew, amid rocks, and scree that in falling had smashed the trunks and torn out the roots of willows, thorns, and hollies. It wandered away from the moor, a proper river, with bridges, brooks, islands, and mills.

Soon the oaks above the river would break into leaf. Magpies had topped their nests with thorns, and buzzards were soaring long after owl-light. Kingfishers and dippers had hatched their eggs—there was a dipper's nest, hanging dishevelled like a beard of moss, under nearly every stone bridge spanning the river. The innocent white flowers of the savage blackthorn had withered brown and shaken into the wind. Lent lilies—the wild daffodils of the woods and meads—clasped with their blooms, shrivelled and loving, the seeds of winter's hope. Already the celandines were old thoughts of the spring, their leaves hid by rising docks and nettles and flowering dog's-foot mercury. Badger cubs had been taught to use the latrines outside the tunnels. It was mid-April, swallow-time in the West Country. Otter cubs romped in a big stick-heap resting on the nose of an island above a bridge, eager to play with the moon on the water. Their mother, who was Tarka's sister, attacked him when he looked on them in the stick-heap, and bit him in the shoulder, for she was most anxious, and did not remember her brother cub.

Though the birds scolded, the foxes snarled, and his own kind drove him away, Tarka had many friends, whom he played with and forgot—sticks, stones, water-weeds, slain fish, and once an empty cocoa-tin, a bright and curious thing that talked strangely as it moved over the shallows, but sank into the pool beyond, sent up bubbles, and would play no more.

12

At sunset, as he was crossing a shoal to deep water under an old ash tree, he stopped at the taint of hounds lying on the scour pitted by their feet. Quietly he turned back to the water to swim sunken in the current, rising only to take in air. Round two bends he drifted, then landed and harkened. Ran up the bank, uncertain. Rose on hind feet, dripping and anxious. A dwarf owl making a peacock-like yowling in the woods beyond the meadow, the squeak of mice, the dry cough of a ewe. He ran back to the river, and after eating fish, he played with a rope of water twisting and untwisting out of a drain, trying to catch it between his paws and bite it as it plattered on his face and chest.

An otter-path lay across the next bend, and he followed it to the middle of the field, where he hesitated. Strange smells lay in the dew. He scraped at a place in the grass where paper had been rammed by a pole, near orange peel covered by a loose tuft. He walked on, nose to ground, and smelt man, where hobnailed boots had pressed the turf and crushed cigarette-ends. He turned back, and would have gone straight to water if he had not heard the cry of a bitch-otter at the far end of the path. *Hu-ee-ee-ic!* he answered, and ran along to find her. Near the middle of the meadow he stopped as though he had trod on a gin. The taint of hounds lay thick with the scent of otter. Grasses were smeared with blood and spittle. His hair rose on his back. He blew through open mouth, swung his head about as though looking for hounds, and was gone, silent as his low moon shadow.

The river flowed darkly to the bend, where it broke shallow over shillets that scattered the moonlight. Tarka saw a movement at the tail of the shoal, where an otter was listening. She ran to him and licked his face, then she mewed, and ran on alone by the riverside. Tarka followed her. She was draggled and miserable. She caught a trout and called him, but when he reached her she yikkered and started to eat it herself. She mewed again, and ran into the water. And following her, Tarka returned to the scour opposite the ash-tree holt where that morning the hounds had plunged and bayed. All the way upstream she had been calling, and searching under banks, and on the beds of pools. At length she crawled on the scour with something in her mouth, and dropped it on the stones. She licked it from head to tail, and mewing again, sank back into the water and returned with another, which she laid with the first-found. Perhaps she could not count beyond two; perhaps White-tip had not known in her terror how many cubs she had dropped in the water, when the terrier had driven her out of her holt. The Master had seen them sinking in the pool, lit by a sun-shaft; and hounds were whipped off. They drew on up the river, and found the dog-otter, her mate, and killed him three hours later as he tried to cross a meadow to the wooded hillside.

The old dog and White-tip had wandered together since Tarka had been driven from her in the autumn. Her first litter had been born in January, when the river had frozen, and one day White-tip, returning to the holt, had found them gone. She had called them, seeking everywhere, and in pain, but she had found none to suckle, for a badger walking on the ice had dug them out with his long black claws and eaten them. White-tip's grief had been so keen that soon it had grown less; and she had lain with her mate in the bracken of Ferny Hill.

And now White-tip was grieving again. For two nights, as she travelled down the river with Tarka, she would cease hunting, and run aimlessly on the banks, whining and searching. During the third night she left him and returned to the ash-tree holt, wherein she had been making ready a couch of reeds and grasses. Into the holt she carried a stone, laying it on the couch, and licking it, until a sudden cry called her outside again. She traced the cry to a stone on the shallow, and brought it in her mouth to the holt; soon the couch was filled with wet stones.

Tarka travelled on alone. As the river grew older, so the meadows and cornfields beyond its banks stretched a wider green over the age-long silt filling the valley's groin. Foxgloves claimed the hillsides wherever the oakwoods were felled, storing in their leaves the green power to raise red-purple spires to the midsummer sky. Seen by day from the hilltops, the river lay in its course like a viper broken by a buzzard's beak and claws, marked with brown on its twisted and bluish-white coils. Twin burnished lines were set by the river, touching its banks, straitly leaving it to its windings, and crossing it on stone bridges topped by tarred iron girders. Under the girders jackdaws were building their nests of sticks and sheep's wool and paper picked up in the early morning from cottage gardens. The rolling thunder over their heads did not disturb them, for, like the otters, they had grown used to the noise of trains in the valley.

Below one bridge the river slowed into a wide pool, where the waters of a smaller south-flowing river meditated before turning north with big brother Taw. Tarka was cruising over the bed of the Junction Pool when the moon, shaking and distorted by eddies above, was cut by dark and narrow slips. A down-stroke of his strong rudder and a push off a rock by his hindlegs swung him up for the chase of shoaling fish. They darted away in a zigzag, turning together, up and down and across the pool. Tarka pursued one until he caught it, but as he was swimming to the bank he saw another, and followed it with the fish in his mouth. He snicked it as it darted back past his shoulders. Strokes of the heavy tapering rudder over two inches wide at its base and thirteen inches long, that could stun a fish by its blow, enabled him to turn his body in water almost as quickly as on land.

He shook the fish out of his mouth as soon as he had killed them, for now he was hunting for sport. The dace glinted about the water, the slayer often leaping after a fish that threw itself into the air and jumped as it hit water again. A stain began to move in the water, and a plaice flapped off the bottom and swam in what it thought was the beginning of a flood, when worms came swirling into the Junction Pool. This sea-fish had lived a strange and lonely life in fresh water ever since it had been swallowed in the estuary by a heron and ejected alive from the crop a quarter of an hour afterwards when the bird, flying up the valley, had been shot by a water-bailiff.

The shape of an otter loomed in the water, and the plaice swam down again in a rapid, waving slant, perceived by a one-eyed eel that was lying with its tail inside a bullock's skull redged in a cleft of rock. Thrust through the eel's blank eye-socket was the rusty barbed point of a hook, the shank of which stuck out of its mouth—a hook almost straightened before the line had broken. Tarka swam up behind the eel on its blind side, and opened his mouth wide to bite across the back.

The eel was longer than Tarka. It lashed its tail round his neck and bit on to his nose, when gripped below the paired fins. Bubbles were blown in two strings, one of them fine as charlock seeds, for the hook-shank was rammed up the otter's left nostril. Then the strings ceased, and stray bubbles arose, for the eel was throttling the otter. Tarka clawed it with his paws, but the small claws were worn by many weeks' scratching for trout in granite hides, and the eel's skin was slippery. Flattened on the pool's bed, the plaice watched the struggle of its two enemies.

Tarka knocked it with his paws, and scraped himself against stones and rocks, so that he could be free to swim up and eat it. For three minutes until his breath was gone, he tried to shake off the eel. Then he kicked heavily and slowly up to the surface and tried to climb out by the nearest land—a sheer bank. Its head in the air, the eel lifted its bite on the otter's bleeding nose and sank away down. Immediately Tarka sprang half out of the water and with a *plop!* like a round stone went after it, catching it below the vent. The eel lashed again, and Tarka unbit. He swam under and bit it at the back of the neck, and again released it. The eel tried to wobble down to the bullock's skull, but Tarka dragged it back; and so he played with it, always avoiding the bite of its big jaws. At length it grew feeble, and he took it to a shallow, where, after walking round it and pretending it was not there, he ate what he wanted of the tail-end.

When he had washed his face he went back into the pool, harrying the dace until many score of the silvery fishes floated away on their sides. He harried them until the moon sank under the hill and he grew tired of his sport. Then spreading his legs, he drifted away out of the pool, past an island that divided the river—a narrow island, shaped like an otter, with a rudder of mud carved at its lower end by the swift waters. Alders and willows grew on the island, many broken by uprooted trees lugged down by floods.

Two hours later Tarka was hungry again, and eating a two-pound trout, fat with easy feeding on mullyheads, taken under the third railway bridge after the Junction Pool. Below the bridge, on the right bank, the river passed part of its old course, now dry save for green-scummed pools, left by March risings, among the shillets. The law of life was also the law of water—everlasting change. It had carved this deserted bed through the centuries, raised it with shillets, and turned away to a newer course. Brambles, thorns, elderberry bushes, nettles, and briars grew entangled along the silent waterway. It was the haunt of grass snakes, frogs, mice, and a wild sandy ram-cat without front paws. For the first three years of its life the cat had been lean, feeding on rats in and around a corn-mill and answering to the name of Shaggery. During its fourth year it had gone wild in the woods and grown fat on rabbits, until caught in a gin. It limped back to the mill and became tame again, but when the pad had rotted away and the stump had healed, it had lain rough in the woods. It was caught a second time, losing its other paw. For two years it had lived in the old river-bed, prowling forth at night and living on frogs, mice, beetles, and carrion fish left by otters on the banks and shoals. It moved by bounding hops from its hindlegs, like a rabbit. Its claws had drawn up above the ends of the short stumps, useful for a hugging hold on its prey, but a hindrance in washing its face. Sometimes otterhounds, tearing their way through the undergrowth, had 'spoken to' the scent of this cat, whose hiding-place was in a deep rabbit bury under a thorn brake.

Tarka ran over its scent, and followed it along the old river-bed. The cat was sitting on a boulder, from which it had been watching a vole-run below. Tarka stopped, surprised as the cat. Shaggery's ears flattened, its body increased into a loop of agitated fur, and it let out such a waul that Tarka's back began to twitch. The cry was loud, and slowly champed through teeth. It sank to a low grinding threat when Tarka stood up to sniff what was wauling at him. He steadied himself by touching the stone on which it stood and the ram-cat made a noise like one Tarka had heard before, when a pailful of hot embers had been shot over the village quay by the estuary. He fled remembering a burn. Alone again, the ram-cat lowered body on stumps, and lifted ears to listen for voles.

When the next night White-tip followed Tarka's trail along the dry bed, Shaggery was sitting above the bury, in an old mossy-damp magpie's nest. Again the waul and the grinding of teeth, again the spitting hiss, and again an otter hurrying back to water.

Tarka had gone under the last bridge above the tide, and the sun was rising when he crept out by a mud glidder and curled himself in a bed of green flags. Water ran clear and shallow on its rocky bed below the mud. Swallows flew to and fro over the river channel, winding deeper and broader through the meadows. All things were warmed in the sun. The grass and dock-leaves under the tide-wall were greenish grey with salt and silt dried on blade and stalk and leaf, after the sluggard tide's lapse. Seaweed, black and brittle, lay below the wall with scriddicks of old rush-tops and sticks among white flowers of scurvy-grass. The sun moved above the oakwood that sloped from the rocky bank across the river; the leaves of lower branches were blenched, and weed-hung. A hot, broken glitter, like a flight of silver birds, played lightly on the green flags where Tarka was lying. One brilliant beak of light slipped round a flag and pecked at his eye until he awoke, and yawned, and turned on his back. His nostrils lazily tested the wind that sometimes trembled the tips of the flags. It was a clean wind, and he lay content.

Three buzzards sailed over the river, one above the other, like the stars in Orion's Belt; the top bird moving with steady wings, the lower bird circling, and the lowest veering on broad vanes, cleaver-shaped, heavily with rolling sweeps into the lingering wind that eddied about the top of oak trees. The tree-trunks were dark; only from the high young branches had the sun struck colour, yellow and pale green.

A lustrous blue line was drawn against the dark forest of trunks as a kingfisher sped downriver. The buzzards drifted away south, their wings narrowing with a gold glister, and shrank into the sun.

Peet! The short, shrill cry came from a silver point drawing a ruddy line over the mud. With a fish in its beak the king-fisher sped upriver to its young in a sandy bank above the Mouse Hole Pool. Martins twittered along the river-bank, and hovered about the heads of bullocks, taking crisp-winged flies from their muzzles and between their horns. Tarka yawned, and dozed again.

A dark cloud arose over the crest of the oakwood, and the greenery of young leaves faded. Rain beat on the flags. A million million drops in the river leapt to meet the drops fresh-risen from the Atlantic. The cloud passed, and again the meadow was hot and bright. The swallows flew up the river, quitting at the coils its glitter and yellow kingcups, and fleeing on across the green meadow to the road by the bridge. Here, in the hollows of the broken road surface, was to be found after rain a greyish mud that set harder than the browny mud of the salty scourings in the river. Only by the bridge was this mud to be found, for the road sloped up and down over the river, and the slopes were not tarred, lest the feet of horses slip. The aerial masons were about to build their nests on the rafters of shippen and barn; they flew in pairs, singing their sun-songs.

Beside the bridge grew an elderberry tree, straight and sturdy as a young oak in a park; one of the few soft-cored elderberry trees in the country of the Two Rivers that had not grown up a cripple of the winds. Its leaves partly hid a motor-car, in whose closed body, shut away from the wind and the sun of the English spring, sat some men and women. They were awaiting hounds before moving to the parapet of the bridge, and perhaps, if a kill seemed certain and early, to the meadow over the low wooden fence. Other motor-cars stopped on the bridge. The swallows swooping over the stonework saw the sunlight browned by the smoke of engines, and dived back again over the grass. The baying of hounds above the bridge became louder, for the otter had swum through the lower stickle, and was travelling downstream.

The hunted otter was White-tip. She had been chased for nearly three hours. Always the cries and tongues and legs had followed her, up the pools and down the pools, from holt to holding, from holding to shallow.

Tally Ho!

She saw faces and waving arms above the bridge, but she did not turn back.

Light-laden drops rolled down the green flags as their points drew down the sky. Tarka lay still, watching. They rustled and broke with soft sappy noises. White-tip was pressing through the bed of flags. Her mouth was open. Tarka, who had been listening for half an hour to the distant cries of men and hounds, stared at the movement. A sudden clamour ran down the river, loud and startling, for Deadlock had found

White-tip's deep seals in the mud, where she had crept out of the water.

The two otters ran through the flags and slid down the mud to the river again. Tarka spread himself in the shallow flow, moving with light touches of claws just over the rocks and stones of the bed. He moved slowly, as an eel moves, as smooth as the water, and with sinuous ease. Sometimes he crept out at the edge of the mud, walked a few yards, and slipped back into the water again. Hounds were crushing the flags around his bed, and throwing their tongues along his line.

He swam through a long pool at his fastest pace, putting up his nostrils every fifty yards to breathe, and down again immediately. He left the oakwood behind him, and came to a narrow gut draining the water of a small marshy valley, where bullocks were grazing. The gut lay under trees above a rocky bank. Its other bank was mud. Seaweed hung on the roots of trees six feet above his head. Tarka walked up the gut, partly hid by the broad strongly keeled leaves of river sedge. He followed it into the marsh, and climbing out, ran along a path trodden by cattle, through a gate and down to a lower marsh, hidden from the opposite bank by a tide-wall. The tongue of Deadlock spoke across the river, and Tarka slipped into another gut. He trod through brown mud to a black ooze, in which he moved slowly, owing to his very short legs. The drain led under the tide-wall to the muddy glidder above the river. It led into darkness, with light coming through the chinks of a circular wooden trap, that kept the tides back from the land. He sniffed at a chink, and waited in the ooze.

For two hours Tarka lay behind the wooden trap, while the noises of hunting moved away into remoteness. Slowly the sound of the low running river was stilled into slack water. Tricklings, the lap and slanting wash of ripple-ends, a turning drift of froth and sticks below the mud—the sea was moving up again. A heron alighted at the bottom of the muddy bank, and stalked gravely into water to his knees. Flukes were rising off the silt, seeking food. The heron bent down and peered. He stepped forward on one foot, and speared with a swift plunge. Then he stared up the river. A thin-drawn thread of sound in the air, looped to another and another and another; loosed as four gossamers floating by in the wind. It was the re-call to hounds. In the after-quiet the heron stalked to his spearing again. The murky water twired by the knee-joints of his thin green legs. Splash, flicker, and shaken drops— he swallowed fluke after fluke; but when twenty yards beyond the trap he straightened up his neck, stood on his toes, jumped hurriedly out of the water, and flapped away, pulling up his shanks after him and tucking his long neck and head between his shoulders. He had seen the heads of men.

Smells of the lower river, riding up with the young tide into the Mouse Hole Pit, had overspread the wishy washy otter-scent, and the pack was being taken back to kennels. The horn-like voice of the huntsman, as he talked to hounds by name, came to the otter through the chinks of the sodden elm-wood trap. They trotted on the opposite bank, happy at the huntsman's heels, led home by aged Harper, who had taught them all to mark an otter. Flews to flews with him was Deadlock, and at his stern, Bluemaid, old before her time, worn-out by swimming. Then came Pitiful who worked hard and alone; whenever it was possible to go wrong, Pitiful went wrong; it was Pitiful who, whenever they passed by the dry river-bed, led them on the trail of Shaggery the ram-cat; if a hound were missing, it was surely Pitiful. Near her was Captain, a black-and-tan rough dog, who looked like a lurcher; the huntsman did not take Captain to important meets, for Captain's voice was like a knife whose edge is turned. He did not throw his tongue, he screamed; and sometimes in his excitement he babbled, flinging water-lies about. Bite'm the terrier hurried among them, sometimes sniffing in tufts, hoping to find a rat to shake; and following Bite'm, like an easy-going, big, heavy boy led by a sharp little quick-eyed tacker, came Rufus, who cared more for a nest of field-mice than for a joint or rib of rank otter. After Rufus on the tidewall ran Dewdrop, whose long fawn-coloured hair was curly with wet. Her ears hung long and loose.

Often while the trophies were being taken by the huntsman those ears would flap between blue-stocking'd legs, and teeth would slyly nip through wool, as though it were brown fur of the worry. By the Wharfdale bitch—for Dewdrop was the only true otterhound in the pack—ran Playboy and Actor, whose dingy-white shapes were so alike that only the huntsman could name them truly. Behind them came Render and Fencer, who always tore at roots of a holt with their teeth; Hemlock, with one eye blind, the dark pupil grey-veined with the scar of a blackthorn prick; Hurricane, the ancient Irish staghound with the filed canines; Barbrook and Bellman, Boisterous and Chorister, Coraline, Sailoress, Waterwitch and Armlet, who always stood apart from the pack during holt-marking and bayed moodily like a lighthouse siren. Then came Sandboy, who fought other hounds at the worry, and Grinder and Darnell —hounds who had chased the fox. They trotted on the tide-wall between the short, quick-stepping huntsman and the long-legged whip and kennelboy, whose long loose striding had been formed in early years by crossing ploughlands on his way to school.

Twenty paces behind the pack walked the Master with two members of the Hunt. He was saying that it had been a great day, only lacking a kill to complete it, when old Harper stopped and lifted his muzzle. The air on the water, colder than the land air, was brimming over the sea-wall, and Harper had smelled an otter. Deadlock moved into the airstream, threw up his head, whimpered, and ran down the grassy bank to the broken turf above the glidder. Sterns were waved like feathers. Deadlock leapt into the river, followed by half the pack. Pitiful started patiently to work the water-line of the mud, and Captain babbled in excitement as he lapped and swam.

The water was three feet deep. Hounds scrambled up the glidder, some slipping down, drawing long claw-lines on the harder clay beneath. They whimpered and scratched before the round wooden trap, and Armlet bayed them on from the bank above. Terrier Bite'm pushed his small eager body between their flanks, under their legs, whining and yelping. Five men waded the river, testing a footway with taps of iron-shod poles before them. Thinking that the otter they had hunted for more than five hours was hiding inside, and that the tired hounds would have no chance to kill even an exhausted ·

otter in the rising water, the pack was not withdrawn when
Bite'm was taken to the open end of the drain, where Tarka's
deep seals in the lower ooze showed like big blackberries
crushed in the mud. Bite'm was given a pat on his ribs and
gently shoved into the dark hole. He crept in, quick and
shivering.

The ooze sucked at Tarka's webs as he turned away from
the light-striped lid of the drain. His heart beat as fast as
water-drops drip without dribbling. The hanging sodden door
went *sug-plog-sug* as paws struck it. He looked up and down,
round and up again, for a way of escape. He crawled in the
ooze, away from the immense din, and saw an enemy coming
towards him an instant before he smelled it. *Is-is-iz!*

They met and joined and twisted into shapes smoothed by
ooze. The terrier got a grip on the otter's rudder and hung
on to it. Tarka bit and bit and bit, quick as a striking viper,
in cheek, shoulder, flank, nose, and ear. Noises of bumping and
squelching and snarling and tissing became louder when the
trap was lifted and light showed the red and black shaking
shapes. The otter's rudder, near the opening, was seized and
pulled by a hand. Another hand gripped the terrier's scruff.
The long black smooth shape was lugged out of the drain, the
terrier fixed to it. Hounds were leaping and clamouring up at
the men. A hand held Bite'm's tail-stump, another hand
squeezed, trying to make him unclench. Tarka writhed and
contorted as he hung by his rudder; his back became a bow,
suddenly bending up, and his teeth made a row of holes in
a hand. The jerk made his rudder slip, and he dropped among
boots, to squirm between legs and away down the glidder. He
pulled Bite'm with him.

Hounds trod on him, snarling and thrusting. Tarka was
hidden under their heads, picked up and thrown sideways,
then dropped and picked up and shaken. Eight jaws held him
at one time in the midst of a deep sullen growling. He was
hid in the plunging of white and brown and black bodies. He
bit Deadlock through the flews, and again in the nose, as he was
lifted on other muzzles, Bite'm still joined to the base of his
rudder. The pack bore him down to the tide, where the worry

broke up. Heads were lifted again, and tongues thrown. Hounds stooped to water; some swam after Captain, who was cutting the air with his knife-edge voice.

But Tarka was gone, and so was Bite'm. The terrier came to the surface a minute later, forty yards away, and swam inshore, spluttering and gasping, the short hairs of the otter's rudder still between his teeth.

13

The tide was flooding fast in midstream. It carried with it sunken branches that sometimes showed a stick, and turned under again. Tarka passed them as he swam into a riband of water returning under the steep and broken rock-face that was the river's left bank. The riband moved down again, feeling the roots of oak trees, and reclaiming the seaweed hung there since the morning ebb. The otter drifted to a root and rested his paws upon it, breathing through his mouth. Two pink nicks above his nose welled red immediately; so did his paws. He bled also from rudder, back, neck, flank, and shoulder. While he was among the hounds he had felt neither fear nor hurt, for the power of all his senses had been in movement to escape. Now his wounds smarted with the salt in the water, and he listened in a still dread for Deadlock's tongue. He lay still for a quarter of an hour.

No hound spoke. The water rose, and lifted him off the root, and carried him away. He drifted through the Mouse Hole Pit and beyond the oakwood to the deeper winding bed in the meadow, where oarweed hung dry on the lower branches of thorns, with sticks, grasses, sometimes the skeleton of a rabbit or bird. Dead brambles tangled in the thorns were swinging in the water, combing the scum of the tide. Cuckoo flowers grew above the top of the flood, their small pale gentle faces rising on tall stems from the dead stumps of trees, some broken and wilting, trodden into the mud and asleep again.

Through the soft pasture ground the river roamed, coiling

and uncertain. The tide-water filling it gleamed dully like a seal's hide, greyish brown and yellow freckled. The mud at its edges streamed with tiny bubbles out of the ragworms' holes. It carried Tarka with its other flotsam to the middle of its last sea-bend, where the tide lay like a dead seal. Already it had started to ebb. Tarka crawled into shallow fresh water singing round stones, and reached two rocks covered with green water-moss. Here he sat and licked his wounds, and lapped the salt from his mouth. Long shadows were on the grass, and the faint-screaming swifts were high over the valley, eager for the sunset and their mystic star-games.

Above the tide's head the banks were of brown soil and up-right under the broken turf. Seedling plants of balsam were four inches high. Willows were green and waving in the evening wind. Tarka walked under the bank on dry shillets and sandy scours washed loose of mud, until he reached the roots of a big tree based at the tail of an eddying pool. He crept into darkness, to a dry shelf within, and slept.

The high stars of mid-May were shining through the branches when he came out of the holt, slow and stiff and hungry. Below the two rocks the water gushed in many clear rills. Tarka walked across a bend, down a bank, over the shallow, and up the other bank. He made a landloop that took him to the bottom of the railway embankment, and pushing through a low thorn hedge, he climbed the grassy bank to the rails. Over the wooden sleepers he walked so that the stenches of oil and tar and cinder would mingle with his own scent, in case the enemies were trailing him.

At the next bridge, under which a dwarf owl nested, he left the track and went to water again. Working down the river, crossing from side to side and searching for fish under stones and in deep holes, he left the grassy sloping tide-walls behind and passed by boats resting on a ridge of gravel above a long road-bridge. Swimming with a fluke to the river-side, he could find no bank. The water lapped a stone wall. He swam under an arch of the bridge and ate the fish on a ledge of sand raised over an old galvanized-iron bath thrown away into the river. Below the bridge was a railway bridge, supported by round iron piers sunk into the gravel. A wave washed against the base of the pier near the right side of the river as he swam round it, hoping to find mussels clinging there. The sea was returning again. It poured over the ridges of sand, making a sound with every stone and shell and shillet tumbling before its eager spread. *Hu-ee-ic!* Tarka chopped at the froth, the new smarting of his wounds unheeded. *Hu-ee-ic!* The salt wave was of the sea, and the sea was the friend of otters.

As he was swimming down in a turbulent pool, Tarka saw a big fish turn before him. He raced after it. His hindlegs pushed forward under his body for the full double-thrust, and the arch of his back opened the big bite of Deadlock that had nearly touched the spine. He bled, but felt no pain in the joy of hunting a big fish. The mullet—one of many that had come up from the estuary, feeding in the muddy collar of the tide's head—nearly dashed into the stone wall of the quay in its terror. It saved itself by a leap that took it a yard into the air, and falling back, it sped swiftly down the river. Tarka followed it to where it had leapt, stood head and shoulders out of the water, while he looked round, before rolling under again. He swam up the base of the wall and turned back by the railway bridge, swimming three double-thrusts to the left, then three to the right, while watching for the glint of scales. He followed the wall until he came to an opening in the quay where the tide was rushing. Another fish turned in the turbid swirling water before him, and darted up the pill. Tarka swam up the narrow way, but seeing nothing, swung back into the wide river. He swam across the tide to the opposite bank by a shipyard, then returned along the piers of the bridge, searching by the stone sterlings.

The tide was pouring fast between the piers when he reached the wall again. Swimming along the wall he turned up the pill, and let the tide take him. With easy strokes he explored the water, swinging in a zigzag course from side to side. At the end of each crossing he threw head and shoulders out of the water, to breathe and survey before pushing off again with a thrust of hindlegs from the stones under the glidders. Many times he swerved off his course to peer round and under things that lay on the bed—broken kettles, cooking-pots, basins, and battered oil-drums thrown away in the mud.

He saw fish-shapes in the water beyond and above him, and headed them again as they would dash back to the estuary. The mullet swam away from him at thrice his speed, but he followed surely. The spring-tide was now flowing at six knots and the mullet went up with the press of water. Tarka drove them under another bridge, past which, by some steps in the quay, water from a mill-leat was splashing under a culvert. Above this the walls of stone ended, and rows of weed-hung stakes leaned over the mud glidders. Following the westward curve of the pill, Tarka passed by a timber-yard, and after a minute's swimming, swung north again and then east. The creek was like a great hollow slug filling with water.

Above the next bridge the leading fish rushed back and skurried by him, missing his snap by a curve that gleamed all its side, and a flack of its tail that filled Tarka's mouth with air. It escaped with six of its grey brethren, but the last two were headed again. Tarka drove them up the straight and narrowing pill, through the collar of the tide and into still water, which was strange to the mullet, it was so clear and shallow.

Tarka was now a mile from the pill-mouth. The image of the bright moon rolled in shaken globules in the hollows of the brook's swift waters, blending as quicksilver. Every ten yards two clusters of small bright beads arose out of the blackness and vanished in a dipping streak. Sometimes a delicate silver arrow pointed up the brook and was tangled in a fish-tail swirl. Every ten yards the whiskered head looked up for direction—only the immediate foreground was visible under water—and smoothly vanished. Tarka swam with all his webs thrusting together against the swift current, just above the bed of the brook, ready to leap up and snap should the fish try to pass him.

He swam under a bridge of the small gauge railway, whose shadow darkened the water. As he thrust up his head to vent, Tarka saw beyond the shadow-bar the white blur of water sliding over the sill of a weir. Under water again, he looked from side to side more quickly, for in this dark place the fish might easily slip by him, although the water was not two feet deep.

When midway through the shadow, his rudder swished up sickle-shaped, slanting his body. His hindlegs touched stones; he sprang. The scales of the two fish coming straight towards him in the darkness reflected only the darkness, but he had seen a hair of faintest light where the ream of a back-fin had cut the surface and glimmered with the moon-frosted slide. His teeth tore the tail of the leading fish, which escaped—his rudder lashed for another turn, his body screwed through the water, and struck upwards with teeth into the mullet's gorge. Tarka swam into moonlight and dragged the five-pound fish (despite its beats and flaps) on to a shillet heap under the the spillway of the slide. He gripped it with his paws and stood over it and started to eat it, while its gills opened and closed, and it tried feebly to flap.

The chewing of its bony jaws soon made him impatient, and he fixed his teeth into the shoulder and tore away his bite. For five minutes he ate, then stretched up his head, with its spiky neck-hair raised, and excitedly assayed the air. *Hu-ee-ic!* His nostrils opened wide. *Hu-ee-ic!* White-tip looked over the weir-sill and slid down with the water. *Yinn-yinn-y-y-ikk-r!* she cried, through her white teeth, and pulled the fish away from Tarka who rolled on his back and tried to play with her tail. Then he rolled on his pads again and stared down through the rectangular space under the bridge, remembering the other fish.

He slid off the rock. White-tip ate most of the mullet, before following Tarka.

The leat, with its swift clear water and brown weed—like clusters of stoats' tails—ran parallel to the brook, a few yards away, and past a lime-washed mill with a ruined water-wheel. A fence made of old iron bedsteads was set in the leat's grassy bank, and here White-tip saw the dark shape of Tarka's head against the nobbled lines of framework. He was eating. Seeing her, he whistled. As she ran over the grass, she smelled the scales where he had dragged the fish. *Yinn-yinn!* she cried again, jumping on the fish and clutching its head in her paws. Tarka watched her. Then he licked the blood from his wounds and ran back to the pill. He was going after more big fish.

In the meadow near the lime-washed mill was a dump of house-rubbish, tipped there by dust-carts, and spread about. A sow and her growing farrow were routing in the mess of rotten flesh and vegetable food, crunching up egg-shells and bones and cinders with eager delight. Here, while the moon was waning and the low mist was growing white, the otters returned to play a strange game. It was begun by White-tip making a splash before Tarka, to make sure that he would see her leave the water and climb the bank. When he followed, she ran round the meadow and back again, passing close by, but not once looking at him. After a while, they went back to the pill and romped like porpoises. Then they ran up the bank together and wandered off alone, up and down, passing and repassing many times through the squares of the wire fencing, without recognition or purpose, as though they were both mazed. To the water once more, a drink and a search for eels, and again the strange play in the meadow.

Each was pretending not to see the other; so happy were they to be together, that they were trying to recover the keen joy of meeting.

On the seventh round White-tip ran near a young pig that on sniffing her scent, jumped and grunted and squealed and then stood still. Every black jowl lifted from the pleasant garbage. Hot ears ceased to flap. White-tip moved, and ten pigs jumped and squealed, and hurriedly bolted. The sow, a ponderous and careful animal with eyes sunken in fat, that had eaten two rats and a cat besides twenty pounds of other food that night, pointed her ring snout at the troublesome smell and moved her big shaking body towards it. White-tip threatened her, crying *Is-iss-iss!* If the sow had caught her, White-tip would have been eaten by sunrise, since she weighed only fourteen pounds and the sow weighed seven hundred pounds. She whistled to Tarka, who ran at the sow.

Seven hundred pounds of flesh returned from the fence with pricked ears and a tail-tip gone; and Tarka ate grass blades, although he was not hungry. He wanted to get the taste of sow out of his mouth.

All night the swifts had been racing over the valley, so high that not even the owls had heard their whistling screams. When these birds saw the golden fume of the sun rising out of the east, they poured down in three funnels to the lower airs of the valley. Their narrow wings made a whishing noise as they fell. Tarka and White-tip in the weir-pool lay on their backs and watched them as they linked into chains and chased away, some up the valley, others to the estuary. Suddenly the otter heads lifted, looked round, and sank together—they had heard the otter-hounds baying in the kennels on Pilton Hill.

In daylight they drifted down the mill-leat that drew out of the pool, passing from grassy banks to concrete, above which were walls and windows of houses and lofts where pigeons sat and croodled. Some of the older pigeons were already cocking red-rimmed eyes at the sky, for it was near the time of year when the peregrine falcons wheeled aloft the town of Barum, coming from the cliff eyries of Bag Hole, Hercules Promontory, and the red cliffs along the Severn Sea.

A stag-bird, or farmyard cock, saw the otters from its perch on a bough over the leat, and cried *Wock-wock-wock-wick*, while its comb became redder. Then it saw nothing but water, and crowed in triumph among the hens. Tarka had not forgotten the time when a cock had crowed before.

The leat flowed under a road, and under a brick cliff that was one wall of the town mills, swirled back from the locked wheel and gushed under a penstock and through a culvert to the pill, from which the sea was ebbing. Tarka and White-tip swam over the drowned white flowers of scurvey-grass to the bend where timber lay, and climbing out, sought a hiding-place among the pile of oaken trunks. As they crept along a rough bole a rat squeaked, another squealed, and soon all the rats of the timber stack were squealing. An old buck saw Tarka and fled away, followed by others, who were either bucks or does without young. Some of the rats dived into the water, others ran to farther wood stacks, where lived families that fought with the invaders. Their squeals came out of the planks all the

morning, while the ringing rasp of circular saws was loud in the
sunlight. These rats were heard by the sawyers, and during
the dinner-hour one went off to fetch his ferrets.

Tarka and White-tip were lying in a hollow trunk, curled side
by side, their heads close together. The hollow was damp; its
crevices still held skulls and leg-bones of mice and sparrows that
had looked at Tarka when he was very young. There were also
fishbones with a faint smell, but even these were beyond memory.
In the autumn, long after the cubs had left its friendly hollow, the
tree had been cut off from its roots and dragged by horses across
the meadow and taken away, with other trees, to the saw mills.

Hidden in the pile of trunks, the otters heard the grumbling
of the grist mill across the creek, with the noises of traffic and
the voices of men. During the morning Tarka shook his ears,
tickled by the irritant buzzing of a bluebottle-fly caught and
fanged in a spider's web outside the hollow. Long after the fly
was dead Tarka heard the buzzing, but without twitching his
ears; for similar sounds now came from the bridge, where the
motor-traffic crossed two roads. The noises were quieter when
the sun was on the top of the sky, and the otters heard distinctly
the chirping of sparrows. Then the chirping grew less, for the
birds had flown to feed in the quieter roadways. Tarka ceased
to listen for footfalls, and slept.

White-tip awakened before Tarka, by the time of an eye-
blink. Light from a crevice above, between the trunks resting
on the old tree, made two eyes to gleam like no eyes the otters
had seen before. They were pink as some blossoms of the
balsam, a flower that rose tall by the sides of the Two Rivers
every summer. The pink eyes blinked and moved nearer,
above a white body. The creature's strong smell, blent with
the smell of man, its bold silence, its likeness to an otter, yet so
curiously small, made them move uneasily. It peered with its
pallid eyes, and sniffed at the tip of Tarka's rudder. Tarka
followed White-tip who was more nervous than he was. As
they were moving along a trunk, a rat jumped upon Tarka's
back and clung to his hair, while screwing up its eyes and
yinnering through its bared teeth. It was crying aloud its fear,

not of the otter, but of the ferret. This tamed animal of the weasel tribe, whose name was Nippy, followed the rat in a quiet fury, and while Tarka was climbing up through a gap between the first and second layer of trunks, it leapt and bit the rat through the neck, dragging it from its clutch on the bark and shaking it as it drank its blood. Hearing another squeal, Nippy left the limp and dying rat and rippled after the squealer.

When White-tip looked from under the pile of trunks, she saw a dog peering bright-eyed, its head on one side, above her. A man stood beyond with a cudgel. The dog stepped back three paces as she ran out and yapped as the man struck at her with his cudgel. White-tip turned back, meeting the sharp-faced ferret under a log. She ran round the stack.

The broad sky, grey with heat beating down on the dusty peninsula, dazed the eyes of Tarka, who was stiff with wounds and bruises. He ran to the grassy bank above the creek, slower than the man, who struck him a glancing blow. The blow quickened Tarka, and the man, eager to kill him, threw the ground-ash stick at his head. It twirled past Tarka and scored a groove in the hot and hardening mud. Tarka ran over the cracks beginning to vein the glidder, and sank into the water. He was seen from the bridge, moving round the larger stones like a brown shadow, slowly stroking with his hindlegs and never once rippling the waterflow, which was just deep enough to cover an old boot.

At night Tarka whistled in the creek, but heard no answer. He returned twice to the bend by the silent timber yard, where the eyes of rats were pricked in vanishing moonlight, but White-tip was not there. The flood tide took him two miles up the river again to the railway bridge where a pair of dwarf owls had their eggs, in a stolen jackdaw's nest. These owls, scarcely bigger than thrushes, flew both by day and night, feeding on flukes and shrimps, frogs, snipe, oak-webs or cockchafers, worms, rats, mice, butterflies, and anything small they could catch and kill. When they saw Tarka under the bridge they wauled like Shaggery the ram-cat, they barked like foxes, they coughed like sheep, they croaked like bull-frogs.

They flew over him as he walked up the gut that emptied a small brook from the east-lying valley beyond, blaking like herring gulls a yard above his head. When he was driven away from their eggs they hooted with soft pleasure, and left him.

Tarka walked under the road and climbed into a millpond, where three eels died. Travelling up the brook, under the mazzard orchards growing on the northern slope of the valley, he reached a great hollow in the hillside, shut in with trees and luminous as the sky. Tarka saw two moons, one above the cherry trees, the other in front of him, for the hollow was a flooded limestone quarry. *Hu-ee-ic!* The sweet whistle, like the cry of the golden plover, only softer, echoed from the face of rock across the water. He swam down and down, and could not touch bottom. The sides of the quarry dropped sheer down into the still depths, except at the far end, where was a little bay under a knuckle of land.

He found no fish in the pit, and ran past the deserted limeburners' cottages and kilns to the brook again. Climbing the right bank he ran over grass-grown hillocks of deads, or rejected shillets of slatey rock, to another drowned quarry. Sombre brakes of blackthorns grew in the slag-heaps near the ivy-covered chimney of the ruinous furnace, and willows bound with mosses leaned in the water, which was dark and stagnant. A tree-creeper had her nest in a crack of the tall chimney, which rocked in every gale, for only the ivy, whose roots had made food and dust of nearly all the mortar between the stones, held it upright against the winds. Every April for five years the tree-creeper's young had been reared within the crack, in a nest that always looked like a chance wind-wedging of dry grasses and little sticks. The crows and magpies never found the nest, so cunningly was it made each year.

Fish, big and slow-swimming, lived in the sombre waters of the pit, and Tarka chased one down to the mud forty feet under the surface, where it escaped. It was a carp, more than fifty years old, and so wise for a fish that it knew the difference between a hook baited with dough-and-aniseed and one baited with dough-and-aniseed and cottonwool. Its habit, when it found a baited hook, was to expel through its mouth a flume of water on the dough until it was washed off and then it would swallow it; but dough stiffened with cottonwool was left alone.

Hu-ee-ic!

The sky was growing grey. Tarka could not catch a carp, and he was hungry. He went back to the brook.

Hu-ee-ic!

Only his echo replied, and he wandered on.

14

When the bees' feet shake the bells of the heather, and the ruddy strings of the sap-stealing dodder are twined about the green spikes of the furze, it is summertime on the commons. Exmoor is the high country of the winds, which are to the falcons and the hawks: clothed by whortleberry bushes and lichens and ferns and mossed trees in the goyals, which are to the foxes, the badgers, and the red deer: served by rain-clouds and drained by rock-clittered streams, which are to the otters.

The moor knew the sun before it was bright, when it rolled red and ragged through the vapours of creation, not blindingly rayed like one of its own dandelions. The soil of the moor is of its own dead, and scanty; the rains return to the lower ground, to the pasture and cornfields of the valleys, which are under the wind, and the haunts of men.

The moor knew the sun before it was bright, when it rolled the falcons, and the hawks, pitiless despoilers of rooted and blooded things which man has collected and set apart for himself; so they are killed. Olden war against greater despoilers began to end with the discoveries of iron and gunpowder; the sabre-toothed tigers, the bears, the wolves, all are gone, and the fragments of their bones lie on the rock of the original creation, under the lichens and grasses and mosses, or in the museums of towns. Once hunted himself, then hunting for necessity, man now hunts in the leisure of his time; but in nearly all those who through necessity of life till fields, herd beasts, and keep fowls, these remaining wildings of the moors have enemies who care nothing for their survival. The farmers would exterminate nearly every wild bird and animal of prey, were it not for the land-owners, among whom are some who care for the wildings because they are sprung from the same land of England, and who would be unhappy if they thought the country would know them no more. For the animal they hunt to kill in its season, or those other animals or birds they cause to be destroyed for the continuance of their pleasure in sport—which they believe to be natural—they have no pity; and since they lack this incipient human instinct, they misunderstand and deride it in others. Pity acts through the imagination, the higher light of the world, and imagination arises from the world of things, as a rainbow from the sun. A rainbow may be beautiful and heavenly, but it will not grow corn for bread.

Within the moor is the Forest, a region high and treeless, where sedge grasses grow on the slopes to the sky. In early summer the wild spirit of the hills is heard in the voices of curlews. The birds fly up from solitary places, above their beloved and little ones, and float the wind in a sweet uprising music. Slowly on spread and hollow wings they sink, and their cries are trilling and cadent, until they touch earth and lift their wings above their heads, and poising, loose the last notes from their throats, like gold bubbles rising into the sky again. Tall and solemn, with long hooped beaks, they stalk to their nestlings standing in wonder beside the tussocks. The mother-bird feeds her singer, and his three children cry to him. There are usually but three, because the carrion crows rob the curlews of the first egg laid in each nest. Only when they find the broken empty shell do the curlews watch the crows, black and slinking, up the hillside.

Soon the curlew lifts his wings and runs from his young, trilling with open beak; his wings flap, and up he flies to fetch song from heaven to the wilderness again.

A tarn lies under two hills, draining water from a tussock-linked tract of bog called The Chains. The tarn is deep and brown and still, reflecting rushes and reeds at its sides, the sedges of the hills, and the sky over them. The northern end of the tarn is morass, trodden by deer and ponies. Water trickles away under its southern bank, and hurries in its narrow course by falls, runnels, pools, and cascades. One afternoon Tarka climbed out of the rillet's bed, scarcely wider than himself, and looked through green hart's-tongue ferns at the combe up which he had travelled. Nothing moved below him except water. He walked up the hill, and saw the tarn below him. He heard the dry croaking of frogs, and ran down the bank that dammed the dark peat-water. A yard down the slope he stopped.

A hen-raven, black from bristled beak to toes, hopped along the edge of the tarn when she saw him. Tarka heard small plopping sounds and saw ripples in the water, where bull-frogs had dived off the bank. The raven took three hops to a pile of dead frogs, then stopped, crouched down, poked out her head with flattened feathers, and gazed at Tarka. Her small eyes flickered with the whitish-grey membranes of the third eyelids. The raven was not afraid of an otter.

She had been fishing for frogs by dapping the water with her beak. Hearing the noises, the bull-frogs swam to the surface and turned with bulging eyes towards the dapping. The raven made a dry and brittle croak. When the frogs heard it, the skin swelled under their necks, and they croaked a challenge, mistaking the noises for the struggle of a choking female. They swam within a few inches of the raven's beak. One, perhaps two, would leap out of the water, and then the raven opened her beak and caught one, perhaps two. She was very quick. She hopped with them to her pile, spiked them through the head, and walked quietly to another fishing place. She could carry eight or nine frogs in her craw at once to her nest of young in a rocky clitter near the head of the river Exe. When loaded, she flew with gaping beak.

Tarka lifted his head and worked his nostrils. The steadfast glance of the small eyes along the black beak pointed at him. He smelled the frogs, took three quaddling steps towards the raven, and stopped again. The raven did not move, and he did not like her eyes. He turned away. She hopped after him, and nipped the tip of his rudder as he slipped into the tarn.

Krok-krok-krok! said the raven, cocking an eye at the sky.

Tarka lay in the water and watched her picking up frog after frog and pouching them, before she jumped off the bank and flew over the eastern hill.

When she returned, her mate was with her. They soared above the tarn. Sometimes the cock-raven shut his wings, rolled sideways, and twirled on open wings again. *Krok-krok!* he said to the hen, seeing below the form of the swimming otter, darker than the dark tarn. The raven opened his beak wide, set his wings for descent, and croaked *kron-n-n-n-nk* during the slow, dipping swoop, in the curve of a scythe, from one green-lined margin to the other. Then he tumbled and twirled, alighting on the slope of the hill, and walked down to the water to catch frogs.

Several times each day the two ravens flew to the tarn. The cockbird talked to Tarka whenever he saw him, and pestered him when he was sunning himself on the bank. He would hop to within a few feet of him with a frog in his beak, and drop it just to windward of Tarka's nose. Once, when Tarka was playing with a frog and had turned his back on it for a moment, the raven picked it up and threw it to one side. Bird and otter played together, but they never touched one another. The raven, who was one of the three hundred sons of Kronk, would drop a stick into the tarn and Tarka would swim after it, bringing it to the bank and rolling with it between his paws. Occasionally the raven slyly pinched his rudder, and Tarka would run at him, tissing through his teeth. With flaps and hops the raven dodged him, flying up out of his way only when driven to water.

Day after day Tarka slept in the rushes in the morass at the north end of the tarn. Unless he was tired after the nightly prowl, the *kron-n-n-n-k* of the zooming raven would always wake him, and he would either run along the bank or swim by the weeds to play with the bird. One morning five ravens flew over the tarn, the hen leading three smaller ravens in line and the father behind them—a black constellation of Orion. They lit on the turf of the dam. The youngsters sat on the bank and watched their mother dapping for frogs. Tarka ran along the bank, amid guttural squawks and cronks, to play with them, but the parents stabbed at him with their beaks, beating wings in his face, and hustling him back to water. They flew over him when he bobbed for breath, and worried him so persistently that he never again went near a raven.

When the wind had blown the seeds of the cotton grass and the sedge drooped tawny under the sun, the curlews flew away to the seashore and the rivers. Little jerky flights of pipits crossed over the hollow in the hills, their twittering passed on, and the tarn lay silent as the sky. One afternoon in early September the silence stirred, and along the tawny hillcrest moved something like a leafless top of an oak branch. It became a stag hastening with tongue a-loll to the wooded valleys of the south. Silence settled on the moor until the hill-line was broken by a long and silent file of staghounds running down from The Chains on the line of a deer. Tarka stood on his bed of rushes and watched them until they loped into the sky. When he had settled again a blackcock hurtled down the western hill and flew over the tarn, followed by a grey hen with her two heath poults. Two horsemen in red coats slanted down the side of the hill; and after them came a young farmer riding bare-back a stallion with blown mane and flying tail. Then came a grey hunter, carrying a man with a face nearly as red as his coat. Others followed, singly, and at long intervals, on weary horses.

That evening Tarka quitted the tarn, and journeyed over The Chains to water that hastened in a bright thread out of the bog. It entered a narrow goyal, and the moon was hid by the hill before him. After a mile the water turned north, under the hill whose worn grey feet it had broken for its bed. The goyal widened by the Hoar Oak, whose splintered stump, black as its shadow with the moon behind, glistered with the tracks of slugs. Near the Hoar Oak stood a sapling, caged from the teeth and horns of deer, a little tree by the grave of its father.

And Tarka went down the Hoar Oak Water which, under ridge and common, shattered the moon into shards and lost them under the trees which grew together in the lower valley. Its voice passed from leaf to leaf, up through the woods where badgers were seeking mice and black slugs, and to the night over the summer hills.

Where two waters met, to seek the sea together, Tarka walked over the trail of otters, and recognizing the scent of White-tip, he followed up the water the otters had travelled. Near the end of the night, while he was swimming in a pool scooped in the rocks below a fall, he saw an otter-shape before him. It moved slowly with the sway of water, its head lolled on a stone. It had been drowned some hours. The whistles of otters playing at the fall, during the previous night, had been heard by the water-owner, who had set a gin under the wash of the fall, on a sunken ledge of rock where otters touched after the joyful pounding of the plunge. The otters had come back again.

Iron in the water sinks, and however long cubs call her, a bitch otter cannot swim with three legs for ever.

Tarka heard the clink of the chain as the swollen body rolled; and his bubbles blown of fear rose behind him.

At sunrise he had crossed two miles of woods and fields— stubble with lines of sheaves, stacked in sixes and tied in fours, fields of mangel and sweet turnip where partridges crouched, and pasture given over to sheep—and found other water below Beggars' Roost hill. Ducks were paddling by a farm as he walked upstream, passing under a bridge, by which grew a monkey-tree with leaves as sharp as magpies' beaks. Cottages by the waterside and a mill were left behind, and he came to quiet meadows where only robins were singing. He crossed from side to side, looking for a place to hide during the sunlight. Half a mile above the mill he found a rock in the left bank of the stream, with a wide opening half under water. Hazels grew on the bank above. Their leaves took on the golden-green of spring in the beams of the low August sun as Tarka crept under the rock.

15

He was awakened by the tremendous baying of hounds. He saw feet splashing in the shallow water, a row of noses, and many flacking tongues. The entrance was too small for any head to enter. He crouched a yard away, against the cold rock. The noise hurt the fine drums of his ears.

Hob-nailed boots scraped on the brown shillets of the water-bed, and iron-tipped hunting poles tapped the rocks.

Go'r'n leave it! Leave it! Go'r'n leave it! Deadlock! Harper! Go'r'n leave it!

Tarka heard the horn and the low opening became lighter.

Go'r'n leave it! Captain! Deadlock! Go'r'n leave it!

The horn twanged fainter as the pack was taken away. Then a pole was thrust into the holt and prodded about blindly. It slid out again. Tarka saw boots and hands and the face of a terrier. A voice whispered, *Leu in there, Sammy, leu in there!* The small ragged brown animal crept out of the hands. Sammy smelled Tarka, saw him and began to sidle towards him. *Waugh-waugh-waugh-wa-waugh.* As the otter did not move, the terrier crept nearer to him, yapping with head stretched forward.

After a minute, Tarka could bear the irritating noises no more. Tissing, with open mouth, he moved past the terrier, whose snarly yapping changed to a high-pitched yelping. The men on the opposite bank stood silent and still. They saw Tarka's head in sunlight, which came through the trees behind them and turned the brown shillets a warm yellow. The water ran clear and cold. Tarka saw three men in blue coats; they did not move and he slipped into the water. It did not cover his back, and he returned to the bankside roots. He moved in the shadows and under the ferns at his ordinary travelling pace. One of three watching men declared that an otter had no sense of fear.

No hound spoke, but the reason of the silence was not considered by Tarka, who could not reason such things. He had been awakened with a shock, he had been tormented by a noise, he had left a dangerous place, and he was escaping from human enemies. As he walked upstream, with raised head, his senses of smell, sight, and hearing were alert for his greatest enemies, the hounds.

The stream being narrow and shallow, the otter was given four minutes' law. Four minutes after Tarka had left he heard behind him the short and long notes of the horn, and the huntsman crying amidst the tongues of hounds *Ol-ol-ol-ol-ol-ol-over! Get on to 'm! Ol-ol-ol-ol-over!* as the pack returned in full cry to the water. Hounds splashed into the water around the rock, wedging themselves at its opening and breaking into couples and half-couples, leaping through the water after the wet and shivering terrier, throwing their tongues and dipping their noses to the wash of scent coming down.

Deadlock plunged at the lead, with Coraline, Sailoress, Captain, and Playboy. They passed the terrier, and Deadlock was so eager that he knocked him down. Sammy picked up his shivery body and followed.

Tarka sank all but his nostrils in a pool and waited. He lay in the sunlit water like a brown log slanting to the stones on which his rudder rested. The huntsman saw him. Tarka lifted his whiskered head out of the water, and stared at the huntsman. Hounds were speaking just below. From the pool the stream flowed for six feet down the smooth slide up which he had crept. When Deadlock jumped into the pool and lapped the scent lying on the water, Tarka put down his head with hardly a ripple, and like a skin of brown oil moved under the hound's belly. Soundlessly he emerged, and the sun glistened on his water-sleeked coat as he walked down on the algae-smeared rock. He seemed to walk under their muzzles slowly, and to be treading on their feet.

Let hounds hunt him! Don't help hounds or they'll chop him!

The pack was confused. Every hound owned the scent, which was like a tangled line, the end of which was sought for unravelling. But soon Deadlock pushed through the pack and told the way the otter had gone.

As Tarka was running over shillets with water scarcely deep enough to cover his rudder, Deadlock saw him and with stiff stern ran straight at him. Tarka quitted the water. The dead twigs and leaves at the hedge-bottom crackled and rustled as he pushed through to the meadow. While he was running over the grass, he could hear the voice of Deadlock raging as the bigger black-and-white hound struggled through the hazel twigs and brambles and honeysuckle bines. He crossed fifty yards of meadow, climbed the bank, and ran down again on to a tarred road. The surface burned his pads, but he ran on, and even when an immense crimson creature bore down upon him he did not go back into the meadow across which hounds were streaming. With a series of shudders the crimson creature slowed to a standstill, while human figures rose out of it, and pointed. He ran under the motor-coach, and came out into brown sunshine, hearing above the shouts of men the clamour of hounds trying to scramble up the high bank and pulling each other down in their eagerness.

He ran in the shade of the ditch, among bits of newspaper, banana and orange skins, cigarette ends and crushed chocolate boxes. A long yellow creature grew bigger and bigger before him, and women rose out of it and peered down at him as he passed it. With smarting eyes he ran two hundred yards of the road, which for him was a place of choking stinks and hurtful noises. Pausing in the ditch, he harkened to the clamour changing its tone as hounds leaped down into the road. He ran on for another two hundred yards, then climbed the bank, pushed through dusty leaves and grasses and briars that would hold him, and down the sloping meadow to the stream. He splashed into the water and swam until rocks and boulders rose before him. He climbed and walked over them. His rudder drawn on mosses and lichens left a strong scent behind him. Deadlock, racing over the green-shadowed grassland, threw his tongue before the pack.

In the water, through shallow and pool, his pace was steady, but not hurried; he moved faster than the stream; he insinuated himself from slide to pool, from pool to boulder, leaving his scent in the wet marks of his pads and rudder.

People were running through the meadow, and in the near distance arose the notes of the horn and hoarse cries. Hounds' tongues broke out united and firm, and Tarka knew that they had reached the stream. The sun-laden water of the pools was spun into eddies by the thrusts of his webbed hindlegs. He passed through shadow and dapple, through runnel and plash. The water sparkled amber in the sunbeams, and his brown sleek pelt glistened whenever his back made ripples. His movements in water were unhurried, like an eel's. The hounds came nearer.

The stream after a bend flowed near the roadway, where more motor-cars were drawn up. Some men and women, holding notched poles, were watching from the cars—sportsmen on wheels.

Beggars' Roost Bridge was below. With hounds so near Tarka was heedless of the men that leaned over the stone parapet, watching for him. They shouted, waved hats, and cheered the hounds. There were ducks above the bridge, quacking loudly as they left the stream and waddled to the yard, and when Tarka came to where they had been, he left the water and ran after them. They beat their wings as they tried to fly from him, but he reached the file and scattered them, running through them and disappearing. Nearer and nearer came Deadlock, with Captain and Waterwitch leading the pack. Huntsman, whippers-in, and field were left behind, struggling through hedges and over banks.

Hounds were bewildered when they reached the yard. They ran with noses to ground in puzzled excitement. Captain's shrill voice told that Tarka had gone under a gate. Waterwitch followed the wet seals in the dust, but turned off along a track of larger webs. The line was tangled again. Deadlock threw his belving tongue. Other hounds followed, but the scent led only to a duck that beat its wings and quacked in terror before them. A man with a rake drove them off, shouting and threatening to strike them. Dewdrop spoke across the yard and the hounds galloped to her, hut the line led to a gate which they tried to leap, hurling themselves up and falling from the top bar. A duck had gone under the gate, but not Tarka.

All scent was gone. Hounds rolled in the dust or trotted up to men and women, sniffing their pockets for food. Rufus found a rabbit skin and ate it; Render fought with Sandboy— but not seriously, as they feared each other; Deadlock went off alone. And hounds were waiting for a lead when the sweating huntsman, 'white' pot-hat pushed back from his red brow, ran up with the two whippers-in and called them into a pack again. The thick scent of Muscovy ducks had checked the hunt.

Tarka had run through a drain back to the stream, and now he rested in the water that carried him every moment nearer to the murmurous glooms of the glen below. He saw the coloured blur of a kingfisher perching on a twig as it eyed the water for beetle or loach. The kingfisher saw him moving under the surface, as his shadow broke the net of ripple shadows that drifted in meshes of pale gold on the stony bed beneath him.

While he was walking past the roots of a willow under the bank, he heard the yapping of the terrier. Sammy had crept through the drain, and was looking out at the end, covered with black filth, and eagerly telling his big friends to follow him downstream. As he yapped, Deadlock threw his tongue. The stallion hound was below the drain, and had re-found the line where Tarka had last touched the shillets. Tarka saw him ten yards away, and slipping back into the water, swam with all webs down the current, pushing from his nose a ream whose shadow beneath was an arrow of gold pointing down to the sea.

Again he quitted the water and ran on land to wear away his scent. He had gone twenty yards when Deadlock scrambled up the bank with Render and Sandboy, breathing the scent which was as high as their muzzles. Tarka reached the water-side trees again a length ahead of Deadlock, and fell into the water like a sodden log. Deadlock leapt after him and snapped at his head; but the water was friendly to the otter, who rolled in smooth and graceful movement away from the jaws, a straight bite of which would have crushed his skull.

Here sunlight was shut out by the oaks, and the roar of the first fall was beating back from the leaves. The current ran faster, narrowing into a race with twirls and hollows marking the sunken rocks. The roar grew louder in a drifting spray. Tarka and Deadlock were carried to where a broad sunbeam came down through a break in the foliage and lit the mist above the fall. Tarka went over in the heavy white folds of the torrent and Deadlock was hurled over after him. They were lost in the churn and pressure of the pool until a small brown head appeared and gazed for its enemy in the broken honey-comb of foam. A black and white body uprolled beside it, and the head of the hound was thrust up as he tried to tread away from the current that would draw him under. Tarka was master of whirlpools; they were his playthings. He rocked in the surge with delight; then high above he heard the note of the horn. He yielded himself to the water and let it take him away down the gorge into a pool where rocks were piled above. He searched under the dripping ferny clitter for a hiding place.

Under water he saw two legs, joined to two wavering and inverted images of legs, and above them the blurred shapes of a man's head and shoulders. He turned away from the fisherman into the current again, and as he breathed he heard the horn again. On the road above the glen the pack was trotting between huntsman and whippers-in, and before them men were running with poles at the trail, hurrying down the hill to the bridge, to make a stickle to stop Tarka reaching the sea.

Tarka left Deadlock far behind. The hound was feeble and bruised and breathing harshly, his head battered and his sight dazed, but still following. Tarka passed another fisherman, and by chance the tiny feathered hook lodged in his ear. The reel spun against the check, *re-re-re* continuously, until all the silken line had run through the snake-rings of the rod, which bent into a circle, and whipped back straight again as the gut trace snapped.

Tarka saw the bridge, the figure of a man below it, and a row of faces above. He heard shouts. The man standing on a rock took off his hat, scooped the air, and holla'd to the hunts-man, who was running and slipping with the pack on the loose stones of the steep red road. Tarka walked out of the last pool above the bridge, ran over a mossy rock merged with the water again, and pushed through the legs of the man.

Tally-ho!

Tarka had gone under the bridge when Harper splashed into the water. The pack poured through the gap between the end of the parapet and the hillside earth, and their tongues rang under the bridge and down the walls of the houses built on the rock above the river.

Among rotting motor tyres, broken bottles, tins, pails, shoes, and other castaway rubbish lying in the bright water, hounds made their plunging leaps. Once Tarka turned back; often he was splashed and trodden on. The stream was seldom deep enough to cover him, and always shallow enough for the hounds to move at double his speed. Sometimes he was under the pack, and then, while hounds were massing for the worry, his small head would look out beside a rock ten yards below them.

Between boulders and rocks crusted with shellfish and shaggy with seaweed, past worm-channered posts that marked the fairway for fishing boats at high water, the pack hunted the otter. Off each post a gull launched itself, cackling angrily as it looked down at the animals. Tarka reached the sea. He walked slowly into the surge of a wavelet, and sank away from the chop of old Harper's jaws, just as Deadlock ran through the pack. Hounds swam beyond the line of waves, while people stood at the sea-lap and watched the huntsman wading to his waist. It was said that the otter was dead-beat, and probably floating stiffly in the shallow water. After a few minutes the huntsman shook his head, and withdrew the horn from his waistcoat. He filled his lungs and stopped his breath and was tightening his lips for the four long notes of the call-off, when a brown head with hard dark eyes, was thrust out of the water a yard from Deadlock. Tarka stared into the hound's face and cried *Ic-yang!*

The head sank. Swimming under Deadlock. Tarka bit on to the loose skin of the flews and pulled the hound's head under water. Deadlock tried to twist round and crush the otter's skull in his jaws, but he struggled vainly. Bubbles blew out of his mouth. Soon he was choking. The hounds did not know what was happening. Deadlock's hindlegs kicked the air weakly. The huntsman waded out and pulled him inshore, but Tarka loosened his bite only when he needed new air in his lungs; and then he swam under and gripped Deadlock again. Only when hounds were upon him did Tarka let go. He vanished in a wave.

Long after the water had been emptied out of Deadlock's lungs, and the pack had trotted off for the long uphill climb to the railway station, the gulls were flying over something in the sea beyond the mouth of the little estuary. Sometimes one dropped its yellow webs to alight on the water; always it flew up again into the restless, wailing throng, startled by the snaps of white teeth. A cargo steamer was passing up the Severn Sea, leaving a long smudge of smoke on the horizon, where a low line of clouds billowed over the coast of Wales. The regular thumps of its screws in the windless blue calm were borne to where Tarka lay, drowsy and content, but watching the pale yellow eyes of the nearest bird. At last the gulls grew tired of seeing only his eyes, and flew back to their posts; and turning on his back, Tarka yawned and stretched himself, and floated at his ease.

16

Swimming towards the sunset Tarka found a cleft in the high-curved red cliff, and on the crest of a wave rode into the cavern beyond. The broken wave slapped against the dark end as he climbed to a ledge far above the lipping of the swell, and curled himself on cold stone. He awoke when the gulls and cormorants were flying over the sea, silent as dusk, to their roosts in the cliff.

The straight wavelets of the rising tide were moving across the rock pools below the cleft, where under green and purple laver-weed crabs and prawns were stirring to feed. The weed, so placid before, was kicked and entangled by the searching otter. The crab he climbed out with was bitter, and leaving it, he swam into deep water.

A herring shoal was coming up with the evening tide, followed by a herd of porpoises, which when breathing showed shiny black hides through the waves. Fishermen called them errin-ogs. Once these warm-blooded mammals had ears and hair and paws, but now their ear-holes were small as thorn-pricks, and their five-toed paws were changed into flippers. Their forefathers, who had come from the same family as the forefathers of otters and seals, had taken early to water, shaping themselves for a sea-life while yet the seals were running on land. Their young, born under water, needed no mother's back to raise them to the air of life, for ancestral habit had become instinct.

An old boar porpoise flung himself out of a trough near Tarka and fell with a clapping splash on its back, to shake off the barnacle-like parasites boring into its blubber. Near the boar was a sow porpoise, suckling her little one, who, towed along on its back, breathed during every rise and roll of its mother. Tarka caught his first herring and ate it on a rock, liking the taste, but when he swam out for more, the under seas were vacant.

For a week he slept in the disused lime-kiln on the greensward above the Heddon water, that lost itself in a ridge of boulders above the tide wash. While he was exploring the fresh water a storm broke over the moor, and the roaring coloured spate returned him to the sea. He went westwards, under the towering cliffs and waterfalls in whose ferny sides he liked to rest by day. Once he was awakened by a dreadful mumbling in the wind far above him. As he lifted his head he heard a whishing noise, as of falcons in swoop. Flakes of scree clattered and hurtled past him; then a stag, and three staghounds. The bodies smashed on the rocks, and were of silence again. Soon the cries of seabirds and daws were echoing out of the cliffs. Ravens flew down, and buzzards, and the air was filled with black and white and brown wings, with deep croaking, wailing, and shrill screaming. They jostled and fought for an hour, when a motor-boat, holding a red-coated figure, came round the eastern sheer and drove them into flight. The gulls mobbed Tarka when they saw him slipping down from his resting ledge, but he found the sea and sank away from them. That night, quatting on a rock and eating a conger, the west wind brought him the scent of White-tip.

At dawn he was swimming under the sea-feet of the Great Hangman; and he followed the trail until sunrise was shimmering down the level sea and filling with aerial gold the clouds over the Welsh hills.

At dusk the shore-rats on Wild Pear Beach, searching the weed-strewn tide-line, paused and squealed together when their sharp noses took the musky scent of water-weasels. They ran off chittering as terrible shapes galloped among them. A rat was picked up and killed in a swift bite. The cub did not want it for food; he killed it in fun. He ran into the sea after White-tip, who had been taking care of the cubs since their mother had been trapped under the waterfall.

Six hours later Tarka ran up Wild Pear Beach and his thin, hard cries pierced the slop and wash of waves on the loose, worn, shaley strand. He followed the trail over the weeds to the otters' sleeping place under a rock, and down again to the sea. In a pool off Briery Cave he scented otter again, for at the bottom of the pool lay a wicker pot, holding something that turned slowly as the ribbons of the thongweed lifted and dropped in the water. The red feelers of a dark blue lobster were thrust through the wickerwork; it was gorged, and trying to get away from the otter cub it had been eating. The cub had found no way out of the cage it had entered at high tide, intending to eat the lobster.

Hu-ee-ic! Tarka did not know the dead. Nothing answered, and he swam away, among green phosphoric specks that glinted at every wave-lop.

Autumn's little summer, when day and night were equal, and only the woodlark sang his wistful falling song over the bracken, was ruined by the gales that tore wave and leaf, and broke the sea into roar and spray, and hung white ropes over the rocks. Fog hid cliff-tops and stars as Tarka travelled westwards. One night, as he was drinking fresh water from a pool below a cascade, he was startled by immense whooping bellows that bounded from the walls of mist and rebounded afar, to return in duller echoes as though phantom hounds were baying the darkness. Tarka slipped into a pool and hid under lifting seaweed; but the sounds were regular and harmless, and afterwards he did not heed them. On a rock below the white-walled tower of Bull Point lighthouse, whose twin sirens were sending a warning to sailors far out beyond the dreadful rocks, Tarka found again the trail of White-tip, and whistled with joy.

Travelling under the screes, where rusted plates of wrecked

ships lay in pools, he came to the end of the land. Day was beginning. The tide, moving northwards across Morte Bay from Bag Leap, was ripped and whitened by rocks which stood out of the hollows of the grey sea. One rock was tall above the reef—the Morte Stone—and on the top pinnacle stood a big black bird, with the tails of fish sticking out of its gullet. Its dripping wings were held out to ease its tight crop. The bird was Phalacrocorax Carbo, called the Isle-of-Wight Parson by fishermen, and it sat uneasily on the Morte Stone during most of the hours of daylight, swaying with a load of fishes.

Tired and buffeted by the long Atlantic rollers, Tarka turned back under the Morte Stone, and swam to land. He climbed a slope strewn with broken thrift roots and grey shards of rock, to a path set on its seaward verge by a fence of iron posts and cables. Salt winds had gnawed the iron to rusty splinters. The heather above the path was tougher than the iron, but its sprigs were barer than its own roots.

Over the crest of the Morte heather grew in low bushes, out of the wind's way. There were green places where, among grass cropped by sheep, grew mushrooms mottled like owl's plumage. The sky above the crest was reddening, and he found a sleeping place under a broken cromlech, the burial place of an ancient man, whose bones were grass and heather and dust in the sun.

Tarka slept warm all day. At sunset he ran down to the sea. He worked south through the currents that scoured shelly coves and swept round lesser rocks into the wide Morte Bay. Long waves, breaking near the shallows, left foam behind them in the shapes of dusky-white seals. Bass were swimming in the breakers, taking sand-eels risen in the sandy surge. A high-flying gull saw a fish flapping in the shallows, with ribbon weed across its head. The gull glided down, and the ribbon weed arose on low legs, tugging at the five-pound fish, which it dragged to firm, wet sand. *Hak-hak!* cried the gull, angrily. *Tu-lip, tulip!* the ring-plover arose and flickered away in a flock. Other gulls flew over, and dropped down. Tarka feasted among the noise of wings and angry cries. When he was full, he lapped fresh water trickling over the sand in a broad and shallow bed

Hu-ee-ic! He galloped up the sand, nose between paws. He ran up into the sandhills, where his passing sowed round orange-red seeds from the split dry pods of the stinking iris. Over a lonely road, among old stalks of ragwort and teasel, and up a steep bank to the incult hill, pushing among bracken, furze, and brambles, following the way of White-tip. He found the head of a rabbit which she had caught, and played with it, whistling as he rolled it with his paws.

Already larks were ceasing to sing. When he reached the top of Pickwell down, eastern clouds were ruddy and Hoar Oak Hill, seventeen miles away as the falcon glides, was as a shadow lying under the sky. He descended to a gulley in the hills, a dry watercourse marked by furze bushes, and thorns, and hollies, growing down to sandhills by the sea. The gulley lay south-west; the trees lay over to the north-east, bitter and dwarfed by salt and wind. Under a holly bush, bearer of ruined blossoms and spineless leaves, whose limbs were tortured by ivy thicker in trunk than its own, the otter crawled into a bury widened by many generations of rabbits, and lay down in the darkness.

The wind rushed up the gulley, moving stiffly the black-thorns which squeaked as they rubbed against each other. Dry branches of elderberries rattled and scraped as though bemoaning their poverty. Gulls veered from hilltop to hilltop, calling the flock standing far below on the sands that gleamed with dull sky. The dark base of the headland lying out in the Atlantic was flecked along its length with the white of breaking waves. The sea's roar came with blown spray up the gulley. Tarka slept.

He awoke before noon, hearing voices of men. Mist was drifting between the hills. He lay still until a man spoke at the day-dim opening of the bury. An animal moved down the tunnel, whose smell immediately disturbed him. He re-membered it. The animal's eyes glowed pink, and a bell tinkled round its neck. Tarka crawled farther into the bury and ran out of another hole, that was watched by a spaniel sitting shivering and wet, behind a man with a gun on the bank above. The spaniel jumped back when it saw Tarka, who ran down the gulley, hastening when he heard a bark, a shout, and two bangs of the gun. Twigs showered upon him, and he ran on, hidden by the thorny brake. Two men clambered down the banks, but only the spaniel followed him, barking with excitement, but not daring to go near him. It returned to its master's whistle. Tarka hid under a blackberry bush lower down, and slept among the brambles until darkness, when he left the shelter and climbed up the hillside.

He ran under a gate to a field beyond, and crossing a rabbit's line, followed it through hawthorns wind-bent over the stone bank, to the waste land again. The rabbit was crouching under the wind in a tussock, and one bite killed it. After the meal Tarka drank rain-water in a sheep's skull, which lay among rusty ploughshares, old iron pots, tins, and skeletons of sheep—some broken up by cattle dogs, and all picked clean by crows and ravens. Tarka played with a shoulder-blade because White-tip had touched it in passing. He ran at it and bit the cold bone as though it were White-tip. He played with many things that night as he ran across field and bank.

Following the trail he came to a pond in a boggy field below a hill. Moorhens hid in terror when he swam among them. He caught and played with an eel, which was found dead next morning on the bank, beside the seals pressed in the mud by his clawed feet, and the hair-marks of his rolling back. *Hu-ee-ic!* Tarka ran under a culvert that carried a trickle to a smaller pond in the garden of a rectory. *Hu-ee-ic!* while clouds broke the light of the moon.

He climbed round the hatch of the pond, sniffing the tarred wood, and crept under a gap in the wall which ended the garden. The stream flowed below a churchyard wall and by a thatched cottage, where a man, a dog, and a cat were sitting before a fire of elm brands on the open hearth. The wind blew the scent of the otter under the door, and the cat fumed and growled standing with fluffed back and twitching tail beside her basket of kittens. The otter was scraping shillets by a flat stone under a fall by the road, where farmers' daughters crouch to wash chitterlings for the making of hogs'-pudding. An eel lived under the kneeling stone, fat with pig-scrap. Its tail was just beyond the otter's teeth. White-tip had tried to catch it the night before.

Hu-ee-ic!

The cottage door was pulled open, my spaniel rushed out barking. A white owl lifted itself off the lopped bough of one of the churchyard elms, crying *skirr-rr*. An otter's tiss of anger came from out of the culvert under the road. Striking a match I saw, on the scour of red mud, the twy-toed seal, identical with the seal that led down to the sea after the Ice Winter.

Tarka was gone down the narrow covered way of the culvert, amid darkness and the babble of water. The stream ran under a farmhouse, and through an orchard, under another culvert and past a cottage garden to the watermeadow below. Wood owls hunting far down in the valley heard the keen cries of Tarka.

Hu-ee-ic!

Often the trail was lost, for the otters, which had gone that way before Tarka, had left their seals on bank and scour before the rain had pitted and blurred them.

Tarka followed the stream. At the beginning of Cryde village the water was penned above the curve of the road, the pond being kept back by a grassy bank where stood a hawthorn clipped like a toadstool. Swimming round the edge among flags and the roots of thorns and sycamores, he saw a head looking at him from the water, and from the head strayed a joyous breath. He swam to it—a snag of elm-branch stuck in the mud. White-tip had rubbed against it when swimming by. Tarka bit it before swimming round the pond again to sniff the wood of the penstock. He climbed out and ran along the bank, by the still mossy wooden wheel of the mill. They heard his shrill cry in the inn below. A cattle dog barked, and Tarka ran up a narrow lane which led to the top of a hill. In hoof-mudded patches he found the trail again, for the otters had run the same way when alarmed by the same dog. The trail took him under a gate and into a field, over a bank where straight stalks of mulleins were black in moonlight, to land that had forgotten the plough, a prickly place for an otter's webs. Sea-wind had broken all the bracken stalks. Suddenly he heard the mumbling roar of surf and saw the lighthouse across the Burrows. He galloped joyfully down a field of arrish, or stubble. He travelled so swiftly that soon he stood on the edge of sandy cliffs, where spray blew as wind. He found a way down to the pools by a ledge where grew plants of great sea stock, whose leaves were crumbling in autumn sleep.

The trail led over the sandhills with their thin stabbing marram grasses, and to the mossy pans behind them, where grew privet bushes and blunt-head club-rushes. The way was strewn with rabbit skulls and empty snail shells. Tarka crossed the marsh of Horsey Island—where grew Russian thistles, sprung from a single seed blown from the estuary off a Baltic timber ship years before—until he came to the sea-wall, and below the wall, to the mouth of the Branton pill. The tide took him slowly in a patch of froth which the meeting waters had beaten up, the gossip of the Two Rivers. He ran over the eastern sea-wall, and along the otter path to the Ram's horn pond.

Hu-ee-ic!

He swam to the wooden bridge by the boat-house, and to the withies on the islet.

Hu-ee-ic!

He hunted the brackish waters until the stars were dimmed by dawn, when he pressed through the reeds by a way he had trodden before, but forgotten, and slept on an old couch where lay bones, and a little skull.

17

All day the wind shook the rusty reed-daggers at the sky, and the mace-heads were never still. Before sunset the couch was empty. The purple-ruddy beams stained the grass and the thistles of the meadow, and the tiles of the cattle-shippen under the sea-wall were the hue of the sky. Westward the marchman's cottage, the linhays, the trees, the hedges, the low ragged line of the Burrows, were vanishing in a mist of fire.

The tide was ebbing, the mud slopes grey, with ruddy tricklings. In the salt turf below the sea-wall great cracks wandered with the fire of the sky. Ring-plover and little stints ran by the guts, and their slender peering images quenched the flame in the water. Bunches of oarweed on each sodden perch dripped their last drops among the froth and spinning holes of the gliding tide. The mooring buoys rolled and returned, each keg gathering froth that the current sucked away under its lowest stave. By an old broken wicker crab-pot, only its rib-tops up, a small head showed without a ripple, moving with the water. Men were walking on the deck of a ketch below; other men were sitting at oars in a boat under the black hull waiting for their mates. A dog began to bark, then it whimpered, until it was pushed over the gunwale. It met the water in a reddish splash.

Men climbed down to the boat, oars were dipped, and the dog swam astern, breathing gruffly and whining. The otter head, drifting nearer, sank when a man pointed with his pipe-stem. Fifty yards below, by the chain sagging and lifting from the bows of the riding ship, the head looked up again beside the broken wicker-work. "Artter," said the man who had pointed, and forgot it. They were going to drink beer in the Plough Inn.

Their voices became faint as they walked on the wall. Flocks of ring-plover and little stint flickered and twisted over the mud and the water. A late crow left the saltings, as a sedge-owl swept on long wings over the drooping yellow grass of the wall, and slunk away across the water.

Where the pill merged into the estuary the mud was scoured, leaving sand and gravel. Below the stone setts and pebbles of the wall's apron, whose cracks held the little ruddy winter leaves of the sea-beet, was an islet of flat stones, apart from the wall by a narrowing channel where water rushed. On the stones stood Old Nog, watching for shapes of fish. The broken crab-pot bumped and lurched along the channel, and the heron straightened his neck when he saw a fish jump out of its crown. He peered in the dusky water, where weeds moved darkly, and saw the fish darting before a tapered shadow. It was green and yellow, with a streamer flying from its back. Old Nog snicked the gemmeous dragonet from before the otter's nose, shook it free of his beak, caught it in a jerk that pushed it into his gullet, and swallowed it while the otter was still searching.

Tarka saw a blur of movement above, and swam on under water to the wide sea.

Colour faded; the waves broke grey. Across the marsh a shining fly had lit on the white bone of the lighthouse. A bird flew in hooped flight up the estuary, wheeled below the islet, and began feeding. It saw Tarka, and out of its beak, hooped as its wings in downward gliding, fell a croak, which slurred upwards to a whistle, and broke in a sweet trill as it flew away. Other curlews on the sandbanks heard the warning, and to the far shore the wan air was beautiful with their cries.

Rows of hurdles, black and weed-hung, stood out of the water farther down the estuary. They were staked on three sides of a pool, while every rising tide flooded over the tops of the fences. It was an old salmon weir. The hurdles had been torn away so many times by the dredging anchors of gravel barges and ketches, whose crews were friendly with poor net fishermen, that the owner had let the weir fall ruinous. Herons fished from the hurdles, and at low tide crows picked shellfish off the stakes, and flying with them to the islet, dropped them on the stones.

At half tide Old Nog flew to the seventh hurdle up from the western row, where, unless gorged or in love or disturbed by man, he perched awhile during every ebb-tide. He stood swaying and sinuating his neck; the grip of his toes was not so strong as it had been in his early tree-top life. While he was trying to stand still, before jumping to the rim of the sand-bank awash below him, a salmon leapt in the lagoon, gleaming and curved, and fell back with a thwack on the water. Old Nog screamed, and fell off the hurdle. Three heads looked up, and dipped again. Old Nog walked along under the hurdles, watching the water. The salmon was many times Old Nog's own weight, but it was a fish, and Old Nog was a fisher.

Tarka was drifting past the weir when he heard the whistle

of White-tip beyond the hurdles. His head and shoulders rose out of the water; he listened.

Hu-ee-ic!

White-tip answered him. Her cry was the hunger cry, an appealing almost whining noise, like wet fingers drawn over a pane of glass. Tarka's cry was deeper, more rounded, and musical. He ran across the strip of wet sand, clambered over the hurdles, and down to the lagoon. He touched water, and a ripple spread out from where he had disappeared. His seals in the sand crumbled as they welled water.

Ka-ak! Old Nog ejected the living dragonet in his excitement, for the salmon had leapt again, a glimmering curve. The teeth of White-tip clicked at its tail. Three otter heads bobbed, flat as corks of a salmon net. They vanished before the double splash fell.

The salmon passed through the cubs, cutting the water. They turned together. Tarka drove between them and slowed to their pace, keeping line. Then White-tip, who was faster than Tarka, overhauled them, and the old otters took the wings. The line swung out and in as each otter swam in zigzag. The eager cubs swam in each other's way. Once more the salmon rushed back against the current, straining through the top hurdles, where the water was deeper and safer. Tarka met it; and the thresh of its turning tail beat up splinters of water. The line of otters forced it into the shallow by the lower hurdles. They swam upon it, resting in two feet of water, but it escaped past one of the cubs.

Soon the tide dropped back from the top row of hurdles and the water was cleared of sand. A race poured steadily through a gap in the sand-bank, spreading wider as it drained the lagoon. In the penned and slack upper water the salmon was lying, its fins and tail so still that shrimps rose out of their hiding-places in the sand beside it. While it rested in the water, its gills opening and closing, a dark squat thing was walking on the sand towards it, using its fins as feet. It was the shape of an immense tadpole, covered with tatters of skin like weed. Its head was as broad as a barrel, gaping with a mouth almost as wide. Its jaws were filled with bands of long pointed teeth,

160

which it depressed in the cavern of its mouth when it came near the salmon. Out of the middle of its head rose three stalks, the first of which bore a lappet, which it waved like a bait as it crept forward. It was a sea-devil, called 'rod-and-line fish' by netsmen. During the spring tide it had left the deep water beyond the bar where usually it lived, and moving up the estuary, had been trapped in the hurdle weir.

It crept forward so slowly that the salmon did not know it for an enemy. The close-set eyes behind the enormous bony lips were fixed on the salmon. Chains of bubbles loomed beyond, with otter-shapes; the salmon swirled off the sand, into the cavern of jaws; the teeth rose in spikes and the jaws shut.

Thrice the old otters worked round and across the dwindling lagoon in search of the fish, and then they forgot it, and went down with the tide. Stars shone over the estuary, the cries of wading birds were wandering as the air. The otters drifted down, passing the cottage glimmering white on the sea-wall, passing the beached hulk of the hospital ship, silent and dark but for a solitary candle in a port hole. The tide took them to the spit of gravel, crowned by sandhills bound with marram grasses, called Crow Island, and here they left the water for a ragrowster. While the cubs were rolling and biting, Tarka and White-tip played the game of searching and pretending not to find. They galloped up the sandhills to slide to the hollows again. They picked up sticks, empty shells of skate's eggs, old bones and feathers of sea-birds, corks from the jetsam of the high tide, and tossed them in their paws. They hid in the spines of the tossocks, and jumped out at each other.

The lighthouse beams shone on the wet sands down by the water, and across the Pool the lights of the village lay like wind-blown embers. *Craa-leek, cur-lee-eek!* The curlews saw them as they swam the shallow water to the top of the Sharshook. White-tip and Tarka ate mussels down by the black-and-white Pulley buoy, and the cubs followed them to the pools of the lower ridge.

Salmon, feverish to spawn in the fresh waters of their birth, were "running" up the fairway, and with the flow came a seal, who tore a single bite from the belly of each fish it caught, and left it to chase others. Tarka brought one of the wounded fish to the rocks, and the otters scratched away scales in their haste to eat its pink flesh. They sliced from the shoulders, dropping pieces to feel the curd squeezed from the corners of their mouths. Tarka and White-tip ate quietly, but the cubs yinnered and snarled. Their faces were silvery with scales when they left the strewn bones. Being clean little beasts they washed chins and whiskers and ears, and afterwards sought water to drink in the pond behind the sea-wall cottage.

Among the reeds the four otters lay, dozing and resting, while rain pitted the grey sheet of water and wind bent down the stalks of the wild celery that grew in the marsh. When the clouds became duller they left the pond, and saw the tide lapping almost over the top of the wall, coloured with the fresh from the rivers.

Mullet had come up with the tide, and a school of nearly a hundred found a way through a drain-lid under the sea-wall of the pill. At the end of the night the otters, who had been gorging on eels in the mires—reed-fringed dykes in the grazing marsh, filled with fresh drinking water from the hills—found them in the pit in the corner of Horsey marsh. For two hours they chased and slew, and when every fish was killed Tarka and White-tip stole away on the ebb to the sea, leaving the young otters to begin their own life.

The next night was quiet and windless, without a murmur of water in the broad Pool, on which the lights of the village drew out like gold and silver eels. Sound travels far and distinct over placid water, and fishermen standing in groups on the quay, after the closing of taverns, heard the whistling cries of the young otters, a mile away on Crow Island, lost on the shingle where the ring-plovers piped. They were heard for three nights, and then the south-west gale smote the place and filled the estuary with great seas.

Black bits of old leaves turned and twirled in the flooded wier-pool, above Canal Bridge, like the rooks turning and twirling high in the grey windy sky. The weir in flood was an immense loom in sunlight; the down-falling water-warp was whitey-yellow with bubbles; to and fro across the weir moved the air-hollows, a weft held by a glistening water-shuttle. Below, the bubble-woven waters were rended on the shillets; they leapt and roared and threw up froth and spray. A branch of a tree was lodged on the sill; the rocks had stripped it of bark. Sometimes a lead-coloured narrow shape, longer than a man's arm, would appear in the falling water-warp, moving slowly against the torrent with sideways flaps of tail until washed back into the lower river again, which roared and heaved like fighting polar bears. The sun lit the travelling air-hollow under the sill of the weir.

The salmon never reached the sill. Some fish tried to swim up the fish-pass, but the pound of the flood was mightier on the steps. Above in the weir-pool a bird was swimming, low in the water, watching with small crimson eyes for trout. Its beak was sharp as a rock-splinter. Above the water it was brownish-black, foam-grey beneath—a great northern diver, or loon, in winter plumage. When Tarka saw it first, it was rolling from side to side and stretching out first one wing then the other. The otter on the bank alarmed the diver, which tipped up and vanished quick as the flash of a turning fish, hardly leaving a ripple. When it appeared again the otter was gone. It lay in the water, nearly a yard long, with head and neck stretched out, and swam rapidly up-river. At the top of the pool it saw another otter, and uttering a wailing cry of alarm, splashed along the water to rise, making a dozen oar-like dips with the tips of its wings. With neck out-stretched it took the air and flew round the curve of the river, with wing-beats quicker than a heron's.

Tarka and White-tip had come from the wood in daylight, lured to play by the sun and the flood. Tarka dropped over the sill, the whitey-yellow turmoil bumped and tossed him below. A minute later a narrow lead-coloured shape pushed slowly up the concrete spill-way, and behind it the darker, sturdier shape of an otter. Fish and animal made slow and laborious head-way; they seemed to be hanging in the warp; and then White-tip dropped over in the smooth and glistering water's bend. They instantly disappeared. The racing churn carried them on its top to the bank thirty yards below, and there left them on stones; and there, an hour later, a thirty-pound fish, clean-run, its gill-covers crusty with ocean shellfish, was found by the water-bailiff, with bites torn from behind its shoulder—the marriage feast.

November, December, January, February were past—but otters know only day and night, the sun and the moon. White-tip and Tarka had followed the salmon up the big river, but at the beginning of the new year they had come down again. Drifting with the ebb under Halfpenny Bridge, they crossed the marsh and came to the Pool of the Six Herons, out of whose deep middle reared the black iron piers of the Railway Bridge. Just below the Railway Bridge the muddy mouth of the Lancarse Yeo was washed and widened by the sea, and in here, on the flood tide, the otters turned. White-tip was way-wise in this water, having known it in cubhood. She was going back to the Twin-Ash Holt above Orleigh Mill, where she had been born.

With the tide the otters drifted under the road bridge to a holt in an old rabbit bury above high water mark. It was fallen in, and the home of rats, so they left it, and travelled on in daylight. A mile from the pill-mouth the water ran fresh and clear. After another mile they came to the meeting of two streams. White-tip walked up the left stream, and soon she reached the slide where she had played during many happy nights with her cub-brothers; and climbing up, she was in the remembered weir-pool. It was narrow, and nearly hidden by trees. Past six pines, and round a bend, where two ash trees leaned over the brook. Ivy grew on one, moss on the other. Floods had washed the earth from their top roots, carving a dark holt under the bank. White-tip had forgotten the baying and yapping and thudding one day long ago, when an iron bar had broken a hole in the roof and scared the five of them into the water. She had remembered the bass at night round the bridge piers in the Pool of the Six Herons, the frogging places in the Archery Marsh, the trout and the mullyheads in the Duntz brook, the eels in the millpool; and she had come back to them.

The soft elderberry tree broke into leaf, with the honey-suckle; the wild cherry blossom showed white among the oaks. The green shovels of the celandine dug pale gold out of the sun, and the flowers were made. Oak and ash remained hard budded; these trees, enduring and ancient, were not moved to easy change like lesser growths.

On the first day of March, Halcyon the kingfisher, speeding up the brook, hit the sandy bank with his beak, and fell away. His mate followed him, knocking out another flake of earth, and thus a perching place was made. They picked out a tunnel with their beaks, as long as a man's arm, with a round cave at the end in which seven oval eggs were laid, shiny and white, among bones of fishes and shucks of water-beetles. Then the river-martins came back to their old drowned homes in the steep sandy banks above the springtime level of the brook. In the third week of March the carrion crow, secure in her nest of sticks atop one of the six pines growing over the pool below the Twin-Ash Holt, watched the first chipping of her five eggs, watched the tip of a tiny beak chip, chip, chipping a lid in a green black-freckled shell. The crow sang a song, low and sweet, in the tree-top. White-tip heard the song as she suckled her cubs in the Twin-Ash Holt. Every night Tarka came up from the Pool of the Six Herons to see her.

March winds brought the grey sea-rains to the land, and the river ran swollen, bearing the floods of its brooks and runners. Salmon, languid from spawning, dropped tail-first over the sills and down the passes of the weirs, and Tarka caught them easily in the eddies and hovers, and dragged them on the bank. He took bites from the infirm and tasteless flesh, and left the fish uneaten. Many of the salmon that reached the sea alive were taken in the nets of fishermen rough-fish-catching, in the estuary Pool, to be knocked on the head and thrown back—for the fishermen hated the water-bailiffs who upheld the Conservancy Bye-laws protecting salmon out of season, and secretly killed the fish because of their hatred. The fishermen did not believe that salmon spawned in fresh water, where the rivers were young, but regarded it as a story told to prevent them fishing for salmon throughout the year.

Oak and ash broke their buds, and grew green; the buzzards repaired their old nests, and laid their eggs. The heron's young, after days of flapping and unhappy crying, flew from their tree-top heronry in the wood below Halfpenny Bridge. And one evening in June, between the lights, Old Nog and his mate sailed down to the pool by the Railway Bridge to give the four fledglings their first lesson in fishing. Curlews saw the dark level wings gliding over the mudbanks, and cried the alarm, being afraid of the sharp beaks. Every year Old Nog and his mate taught four fledglings to spear fish in the pool, which lay placid when the sea had lapsed.

Six herons stood in a row eighty yards above the bridge, in the sandy shallow at the head of the pool. *Kack! Kack! Kack! Kack!*—the young birds squawked with eagerness and delight. Dusk deepened over the wide and empty river, the pool shone faintly with the sky. Down by the round black piers of the bridge something splashed. Old Nog raised his head, for he had been awaiting the splash. It was a sign that the bass in the pool were beginning to feed.

Splash, splatter, splash. Soon many fish were rising to take the shrimp-fry on the surface. They were hungry after the daytime rest, having gone up with the tide to Halfpenny Bridge, and returned to the pool without feeding, while men on the banks fished with lines of rag-worm-baited hooks. Usually the men went home to supper, with empty baskets, before the fishes' feeding time. Then to the quiet pool came that wise fisher, Old Nog, with his family, standing motionless while the bass swam into the shallow water;—splash, splatter, splash, as they turned on their gleaming sides to take the shrimp-fry. Old Nog peered with beak held low, and snicked—*Kack! Kack! Kack! Kack!* cried the four small herons, beating vanes and falling over long toes in their eagerness to gulp the silvery fish.

Gark! said Old Nog, swallowing the bass, and thrusting his beak and long feathered neck at the four. *Gark!* They got out of his way; never before had he spoken so severely to them. One saw the flicker of a fish in the water, and stepped towards it; the bass saw the enemy, and sped into deeper water. *Gark!* said Old Nog, sharply, and they stood still.

166

Sucking noises arose out of the pool as it grew darker. These were the feeding noises of male eels, thin and small and mud-coloured, whom the larger blue females would meet in the autumnal migration. In wriggling rushes the eels sought the shrimp-fry in the shallows, and whenever one passed near a beak—*dap!* it was snicked, lifted from the water as a writhing knot, and swallowed.

The Railway Bridge loomed low and black against the glimmer of sky and water. Splash, splatter, the bass were moving about the pool. Two or three lay trout-wise, in the slight downward current by each round iron pier, watching the surface above them for the dark moving speck of a shrimp. The splashes of their jumps echoed under the girders.

A summer sandpiper flew over the bridge, crying in the darkness, for it had been alarmed while feeding under the mud slopes of the empty pill. It was answered by a curlew on the gravel bank above the herons.

Immediately below the bridge the brook poured its little fresh stream into the pool; raising up little ridges of sand, sweeping them away again with sudden little noises. Splash, splatter, the bass were feeding in the weed on the stone piling below the bridge-end. Patter, patter, five dark shapes moving on the soft wet sand of the pill's mouth—the pattering ceased, and the brook slurred its sand-sounds as they slid into the pool. White-tip had brought her four cubs from the Twin-Ash Holt.

The vigorous splashing of the bass was lessening, for many fish were gorged with fry. A whitish shine by the stone piling, and one had risen to seize a shrimp in its large mouth—splash, flicker, splatter, bubble. A dark shape crawled out of the water with the bass. Three lesser shapes followed, yikkering on the stone piling. White-tip turned back into the pool.

Krark! Kak! Ark! Kak! Kack! Kack! Kack! Kack! Kak! Kak! Gark! Kack!

With heads upheld and watching, the herons talked among themselves. They saw three cubs fighting over the fish on the piling; and two heads in the water between the first and second pier. Tarquol, the eldest cub, was following White-tip, for he liked to do his own hunting; and it was in the Pool of the Six

Herons that the strange big otter, who chased him in and out of the piers, never biting or sulking, was to be found. Tarquol, who had two white toes on one of his paws, was stronger than the other cubs, and often hurt them in play without knowing it.

The bass, staying in the flumes around the piers with fin and tail, watched the dim forewater above them. All was dark beside and below them. Tarquol and White-tip swam one on either side of a pier, deeper than the bass, whose narrow shapes were dark and plain above them. A fish darted around the pier before White-tip, and was taken by Tarquol. He ate it on the quick-sand of the right bank, away from the cubs. The sharp point of the back fin pricked his mouth.

The otters caught eels in the shallow edges of the pool, watched by the hungry herons, whose harsh continuous cries told their anger. When the cubs had eaten enough they played on the sand, running on and on until they were behind the six birds, on the ridge of gravel where snags were part buried. Curlews—the unmated birds which had not gone to the moors —flew off the glidders, and away up the tidal reaches of the river.

Hu-ee-ic!

Tarquol, playing with the rotten crown of an old bowler hat —fishermen always kept their bait in old Sunday chapel-going hats—heard the whistle, and dashed back to the pool. *Krark!* cried Old Nog, flying up before him, his toes on the water. *Kak! Kack! Kack! Kack! Kack!* as his mate and youngsters followed. Old Nog flew over the bridge, but seeing and hearing the tide flowing up, he wheeled and beat up the Yeo valley. The five herons followed him, but he dived at them, screaming *Gark! Gark!* Old Nog was weary after many weeks of hunger, of disgorging nearly all he caught into the greedy maws of four grown fledglings, and often, the greedy maw of his mate. *Krark!* a cry of satisfaction. Old Nog flew alone.

Every night for a week the otters came to the pool at low water, until the tides, ebbing later and later, and so into daylight, stopped the fishing. One evening, when the Peal Rock in the river below Canal Bridge was just awash after a thunderstorm, Tarka and White-tip and the four cubs followed a run of peal as far as the weir-pool, staying out until after sun-rise, when several fish were taken in the water, then low and clear again. The Twin-Ash Holt was far behind them, so they slept in a holt under an oak, which was entered by an opening two feet below the water-level. The next night they went on up the river, catching and eating fish on the scours and shoals, before going back to the water for more.

Tarquol swam near Tarka; the cub was lithe and swift as his parent, and sometimes snatched fish from his mouth. They rolled and romped together, clutching rudders and heads and pretending to bite; their joyful whistles went far down the river, heard by Old Nog as he sailed by in the wasting moon-light.

Paler the moon rose, and at dawn White-tip went down with the cubs and Tarka wandered on alone; but he turned back again, calling her to Canal Bridge to play one last game.

Hu-ee-ic!

They played the old bridge game of the West Country otters, which was played before the Romans came. They played around the upper and lower cut-water of the middle pier, while the lesser stars were drowned in the heavenly tide flowing up the eastern sky, and the trees of the hill-line grew dark, and larks were flying with song.

Hu-ee-ic!

Tarquol followed Tarka out of the river and along the otter-path across the bend, heedless of his mother's call. He followed up the river and across another bend; but, scared of the light, returned to water and sought a holt under a sycamore. Tarka went on alone, up three miles of river, to a holt in a weir-pool shadowed by trees, where peal were leaping. The sun looked over the hills, the moon was as a feather dropped by the owl flying home, and Tarka slept, while the water flowed, and he dreamed of a journey with Tarquol down to a strange sea, where they were never hungry, and never hunted.

18

At half-past ten in the morning a covered motor-van stopped at the bridge below the Dark Pool. From the driver's seat three men got down, and at the sound of their footfalls deep notes came from the van. Hearing the hounds, the two terriers —Biff and Bite'm—held by a girl in jacket and short skirt of rough blue serge, yapped and strained against the chain.

Motor-cars were drawn up on one side of the road. The men, women, and children who had come to the meet of otterhounds stood by them, or talked as they stood by the stone parapets of the bridge. Some men leaned on long ash poles, stained and polished with linseed oil and shod with iron and notched from the top downwards with the number of past kills, two notches crossed denoting a double-kill. The women carried smaller and slenderer poles, either of ash or male bamboo. There were blackthorn thumb-sticks, hazel-wands, staves of ground-ash; one boy held the handle of a carpet-sweeper, slightly warped. He had poked the end in some nettles, lest the wooden screw be seen by other boys. It had no notches.

Faces turned to the hound-van. Huntsman and his whipper-in each lifted a rusty pin from the staples in the back of the van and lowered the flap. Immediately hounds fell out and over each other, and to the road, shaking themselves, whimpering, panting with pink tongues flacking, happy to be free after the crush and heat of the journey from kennels. They were admired and stroked, patted and spoken to by name; they scratched themselves and rolled and licked each others' necks; they sat and looked up at the many faces—old Harper solemnly, with eyes sunk by age, the younger hounds, still remembering their walking days, going to seek their human friends, and sniff and nuzzle pockets where biscuits, cake, and sandwiches were stored. The kennel-boy-cum-whip called them by name and flicked gently near the more restless with his whip: Barbrook and Bellman, Boisterous and Chorister, Dewdrop,

Sailoress, Caroline, and Waterwitch; Armlet, who lay down to sleep, Playboy and Actor, Render and Fencer; Hemlock the one-eyed, with Bluemaid, Hurricane, Harper, and Pitiful, the veterans; Darnel and Grinder, who sat behind Sandboy. Then two young hounds of the same litter, Dabster and Dauntless, sons of Dewdrop and Deadlock.

And there Deadlock, his black head scarred with old fights, sat on his haunches, apart and morose, watching for the yellow waistcoat of the Master. His right ear showed the mark made by the teeth of Tarka's mother two years before, when he had thrust his head into the hollow of the fallen tree. The swung thong of the whip idly flicked near Deadlock; he moved his head slightly and his eyes; from upper and lower teeth the lips were drawn, and looking at the kennel-boy's legs, Deadlock growled. The hound hated him.

People were watching. The whipper-in felt that the hound was making him ridiculous, and flicked Deadlock with the lash, speaking sharply to him. The hound's growls grew more menacing. Between his teeth the hound yarred, the dark pupils of his eyes becoming fixed in their stare. Then seeing Dabster trotting off to the bridge the whipper-in gladly went after him. Deadlock looked away, ignoring all eyes.

Other cars descended the hill above the bridge and stopped on the left of the road. For a week in the early summer of each year, known as the Joint Week, a neighbouring Hunt visited the country of the Two Rivers, bringing their own hounds with them, so that the home pack might rest every other day of the six hunting days. Other otter-hunters came from their rivers which flowed into the seas of Britain west and south and east. Their uniforms were coloured as the dragon-flies over the river. There were "white" pot-hats, dark blue jackets and stockings, and white breeches of the Cheriton; the "white" hats and breeches and stockings and red coats of the Culmstock; the cream-collared bright blue coats and stockings and cream breeches of the Crowhurst from Surrey, Kent, and Sussex; men of the Dartmoor, all in navy-blue, from pad-pinned cap to black brogues, except for white stock round the throat; the green double-peaked caps, green coats, scarlet ties, white breeches, and green stockings of the Courtenay Tracey from Wessex. A man like a great seal, jovial and gruff among laughing friends, wore the gayest uniform, in the judgment of two ragged children. It blazed and winked in the sunlight, the scarlet and blue and brass of the Eastern Counties.

Shortly after half-past ten o'clock eleven and a half couples of hounds and two terriers, nearly throttling themselves in eagerness to press forward, were trotting behind the huntsman through the farmyard to the river. The huntsman repeated a cooing chant at the back of his nose of *C-o-o-o-o-orn-yer! Co-o-o-o-orn-yer! W-wor! W-wor!* with names of hounds. They trotted with waving sterns, orderly and happy, enjoying the sounds, which to them were promise of sport and fun if only they kept together and ignored the scent of duck, cat, offal, mouse, and cottage-infant's jammy crust. They pattered through the farm-yard in best behaviour; they loved the huntsman, who fed them and pulled thorns out of their feet and never whipped them, although he sometimes dropped unpleasant medicine at the back of their tongues, and held their muzzles, and stroked their throats until they could hold it there no longer, but had to swallow. The *W-wor! W-wor!* and other cooing dog-talk was understood perfectly; they caused even Deadlock to forget to growl when young Dabster, avoiding a kitten, bumped into him. For the two strongest feelings in Deadlock, apart from those of his private kennel life, were blood-thirst for otters and his regard for the huntsman.

They jumped down the bank into the river, leaping across the shallows to the left bank, and working upstream to the occasional toot of the horn. Almost at once Deadlock whimpered and bounded ahead. Tarka had touched there, on the shillets, six hours before.

They came to the groove in the right bank between two hazel stoles, where Tarka had climbed out to cross the meadows to the weir, for the river-course was like a horseshoe. The grasses still held enough scent for the hounds to own, and they followed the trail to the wood that grew steeply up from the water. A crow, that had been waiting on the weir-sill for beetles and little fish to pass in the gentle film of water near its feet, heard them as they splashed up the leat and flew to the top of a tall tree to watch hidden in the leaves. The crow had seen Tarka as he swam from the leat into the Dark Pool at five o'clock in the morning. Then he had loudly cawed, calling his mate to annoy the otter; now he kept quiet. Hounds swam up the pool.

A furlong above the weir was a ford, where, in summer, horse-drawn butts go for the gravel heaped up by winter floods. By the ford was a tree, and under the roots of the tree was a holt. Deadlock, Render, and Fencer swam to the tree, whimpering, splashing, scratching, and tearing at roots with their teeth. Soon the pack was trying to break into the entrance. They did not obey voice, horn, and whip at once, but had to be urged away by taps of whip-handles on ribs, and by individual commands. *Go'r'n leave it! Go'r'n leave it!* cried one of the honorary whips in a yarring voice, to Deadlock and Render who remained. A little shivering sharp-nosed terrier, off-collar'd, peered with cock-ears and whined on the bank above. The entrance of the holt was under water, and Biff's collar was slipped round her neck again.

The honorary whip, a retired senior officer of the army, prodded with his pole among the roots, and finding soft earth, tried to force the pole to the back of the holt. The water moved away in a yellow muddy wound. He worked until he was hot. He stopped, pushed his hat back from his forehead, and rubbed it with his goatskin glove. "Where's that chap with the bar?" Below the holt, at intervals of ten to fifteen yards, men were gazing into the sun-dappled water of the Dark Pool. Voices sounded high above, where on the road cut in the rock many of the cars were waiting.

A man came hastening down the cart-track with the iron digging bar. A hole was worked in the ground over the holt, while a sportsman in the Cheriton uniform banged the turf with the length of his pole. The hole was made deeper, the bar worked backwards and forwards, and plunged hard down.

The Master, leaning chin upon hands clasping the top of his pole, saw a chain of bubbles rise a yard from the bank, and steadily lengthen aslant the river. Sweeping off his "white" hat, he scooped the air with it, crying *Tally-ho!* Hounds poured down the track and splashed into the river, giving tongue and stirring up the gravel silt. Through shadows of trees lying on the water the lit dust drifted. Many hounds swam mute, striving hard to take the lead, urged by cries and gestures in front of them.

The chain drew out from one bank to another, in stretches of fifty and sixty yards, until by the sill of the weir a ripple was made by a brown head that sank immediately; but was viewed.

Yoi-yoi-yoi-yoi! Ov-ov-ov-ov-ov-ov-ver! Tally-ho! He's gone down the leat!

The dark green weeds were bended and swayed silently by the slow glide of the water. The leat was deep, with a dark brown bed. It had been dug to carry water to the elm wheels of the two mills by the bridge a mile below. Now the larger wheel had been replaced by a turbine, which used less water. Leaves rotted on the leat's bed, the water brimmed almost into the meadow. Tarka swam through the dark green swaying weed, and over the dark brown bed. When he swung up to breathe his nose showed in the ripple like a dead leaf turned up in the current, and settling down again. He swam under the crinkled top-scum by the heavy oaken fender, which was raised to let the water through. A trout darted by him as he passed under the fender, and he caught it with a sudden turn of his body.

Trees made the leat shadowy; ferns hung over it; the talon'd brambles stretched down to the water. It flowed in the low ground of the valley, bending like the river below it. It left the meadows, the tall grasses, and the reddening sorrel, and flowed through a jungle of rushes and grasses, briars and hazel bushes, where the webs of spiders were loaded with bees, flies and grasshoppers. Only a weasel could run on the banks. The blue flowers of borage and comfrey grew in the jungle, where the buds of the dog-rose were opening.

Sometimes a swift, cutting the air with alternate strokes of its narrow black wings, dashed a ripple as it sipped and sped on. Willow wrens flitted in the ash-sprays lower down, taking insects

174

on the leaves. A chiffchaff sang its two-note song. By a briar raking the water the otter's head was raised; he listened and swam to the bank. Hounds spoke remotely; he knew Deadlock's tongue among them. He climbed out of the leat, the trout still in his mouth, and pushed through the undergrowth, among nettles and marshwort, and over soft damp ground. Robins ticked at him, wrens stittered. Burrs and seeds tried to hook to his hair, finding no hold. Warble flies tried to alight on his back and suck his blood; the rushes brushed them off. He ran in a loop back to the leat, and slipped into the water above the hounds, who had gone down. He swam up for a quarter of a mile, then rested by an alder root and listened to the pack running over his land-trail. He looked round for a stone whereon to eat the fish, but hearing Deadlock's tongue, he lay still.

From the wooded hillside above the distant bank of the river came the knock of axes on the trunk of an oak tree, the shouts of woodmen, a sudden crack, the hissing rush and thud of breaking branches, and then quietness, until began the steady knocks of boughs being lopped. After a while Tarka did not hear these sounds—he was listening in another direction. He scarcely heard the shooting buzz of sun-frisked flies over the leat. He felt no fear; all his energy was in listening.

Chiff-chaff, chiff-chaff, chiff-chaff sang the bird among the ash trees. And soon the voices of men, the tearing of brambles against coats, boots trampling and snapping the hollow green stalks of hog-weed and hemlock. Tarka saw their heads and shoulders against the sky, and swam on up the leat.

His scent was washed down by the water, and the hounds followed him. He crept out on the other bank, on soft ground littered with dead leaves, which lay under crooked oak trees. He ran swiftly up the slope and entered a larch plantation, where the sky was shut out. The narrow lines of thin straight boles stood in a duskiness as of midsummer night. All sound was shut out; nothing grew under the trees. A wood owl peered down at him as he ran among the brittle fallen twigs; it peered over its back and softly hooted to its mate. The plantation was silent again.

175

Tarka sat by a bole in the middle of the Dark Hams Wood, listening through the remote sough of wind in the branches to the faint cries below. The smell of the sap was strong in his nostrils. He dropped the fish. Sometimes he heard the querulous scream of a jay, and the clap of pigeon-wings as the birds settled in the tree-tops.

For nearly twenty minutes he waited by the tree, and then the hunting cries swelled in the narrow groves of the wood. The owl flapped off its branch, and Tarka ran down the leat again, passing the hounds nine lines of trees away from them. Sunlight dazzled him when he ran out of the plantation. Then he saw many men and women before him.

Tally Ho!

Tarka ran round them and dived into the leat. When first he had swum down, the water had brimmed to the meadow, floating the green plants in its slow-gliding current; now the bank glistened with a sinking watermark, and only the tags of the starwort were waving. Trout darted before him as he swam against the water flowing faster. Often his head showed as he walked half out of water beside the starwort. He reached the square oaken fender, where only a rillet trickled. It rested on the bed of the leat, penning the water above.

Tally Ho!

Tarka turned and went down the leat again. He reached water deep enough to cover him before he met the hounds who, hunting by the sense of smell, did not see him moving as a dark brown shadow through the channels in the weeds. Hounds passed him, for the wash—or scent on the water—was still coming down.

Tarka swam down to the mill end of the drained leat, now dark with the brown stains of stagnant life on its muddy bed. Trees kept the sun from it. A runner, or streamlet, from other woods joined it at this end, and waited in the pool to pass through a grating to the mills. Tarka swam under the culvert of the runner, but finding shallow water he returned and looked for a hole or drain in the banks. Shafts of sunlight pierced the leaves and dappled the water. A broad shade lay before the grating, where oak planks, newly sawn, were stacked over the water. The ringing rasp of a circular saw cutting hard wood suddenly rang under the trees, overbearing the shaken rumble of millstones grinding corn. Specks of wood settled on the water beyond the shade, where Tarka rested, staying himself by a paw on a rusty nail just above the water level.

He waited and listened. Sawdust drifted past him, to be sucked away between the iron bars of the grating. The noise of the saw ceased. He heard the hounds again, coming down the leat. A voice just over his head cried, *One o'clock!* Footfalls hurried away from the saw. The hatch was closed, the trundling wheel slowed into stillness. Tarka heard the twittering of swallows; but he was listening for the sound of the horn. Deadlock speaking! Up the leat waterside plants were crackling as feet trod them down. Voices of the whips, one harsh and rating, were coming nearer. Heads and shoulders moved over the culvert. When the leading hound swam into the pool, throwing his tongue, Tarka dived and found a way through the grating, where one iron bar was missing—a space just wide enough for an otter. He drew himself on to the hatch and walked slowly up the wet and slippery wooden troughs to the top of the wheel. He quatted low and watched the grating. Hounds swam along it and Deadlock pushed his black head in the space of the missing bar. His jaws pressed the iron and stopped him. He bayed into the cavern where the ancient water-wheel dripped beside the curved iron conduit of the modern water turbine. The place was gloomy; but in a corner, framed in a triangle of sunlight, three ferns hung out of the mortar—spleenwort, wall-rue, and male fern. Five young wagtails filled a nest built on the roots of the male fern; the nestlings crouched down in fear of the baying.

Drops from the elmwood troughs dripped into the plash hollowed in the rock under the wheel. Tarka sat on the topmost trough, his rudder hanging over the rim of the wheel. He heard the shrill yapping of terriers on leash; the shuffle of feet on the road over the culvert; the murmur of voices. Poles were pushed among the layers of planks; feet of hounds pounded the deep water as they swam under the timber baulks. He listened to their whimpers; smelt their breath. After a time the noises receded, and he heard *chik-ik, chik-ik*—the cries of the parent wagtails, waiting on the roof with beakfuls of river flies. Tarka licked his paws and settled more comfortably in the sodden elmwood trough. Sometimes his eyes closed, but he did not sleep.

At two o'clock he heard voices in the gloomy wheelhouse. The men were returning to work after dinner. The hatch was lifted. Water gushed in and over the trough. The wheel shuddered and moved. Water gushed in and over each trough as it was lowered on the rim, and the wheel began its heavy splashing trundle. Tarka was borne down into darkness and flung on the rock. Under the troughs he crept, to the shallow stream that was beginning to flow through a lower culvert to the river. Sunlight dazed him. The bridge was ten yards below.

The parapet before and above him was a smooth line across the sky, except for a wagtail's pied body, the tops of three polypody ferns, the head and shoulders of an old grey-bearded man in a blue coat, and a black empty beer-bottle.

Tally-ho!

19

Tarka became one with the river, finding his course among the algae'd stones so that his back was always covered. He rose beside the middle pier, the cutwater of which was hidden by a faggot of flood sticks. Under the sticks was dimness, streaked and blurred with sunlight. Tarka hid and listened.

His paws rested on a sunken branch. The water moved down, clouded with the mud-stirrings of the leat. He lay so still that the trout returned to their stances beside the stone sterlings.

B'hoys, boys! Com' on, ol' fellars! Leu in, ol' fellars. Com' on, all 'v yer!

The stain spread into the pool below the bridge. Hounds whimpered and marked at the stick-pile. Their many tongues smote all other sounds from Tarka's ears. He knew they could not reach him in his retreat, and so he stayed there even when a pole, thrust into the heap, rubbed against his flank. Then over his head the sticks began to crack and creak, as a man climbed upon them. The man jumped with both feet together on the heap. Tarka sank and turned downstream. Cries from the lower parapet; thudding of boots above. The chain of bubbles drew out downstream.

Tarka swam to the left bank, where he touched and breathed. He heard, in the half-second his head was out of water, the noise that had terrified him as a cub—the noise as of an iron shod centipede crossing the shallows. Way down the river was stopped by a line of upright figures, standing a yard apart and stirring the water with poles. Tarka heard the noise under water, but he swam down until he saw before him the bright-bubbled barrier. He swung round and swam upstream as fast as three and a half webbed feet could push him.

He swam under the heap of sticks again, enduring the massed tongues of marking hounds until the creaking and thudding over his head drove him to open water again. He swam under an arch, turned by the lower sterling, and swam up another arch, to a backwater secluded from the main stream by the ridge of shillets made by the cross-leaping waters of the runner in flood. An ash tree grew over the backwater, but Tarka could find no holding in its roots. He swam past the legs of swimming hounds and went down-river again.

Tally Ho!

He swam through the plying poles of the stickle, and ran over the shallow, reaching safe water before the pack came down. He was young and fast and strong. Hounds were scattered behind him, some swimming, others plunging through the shallows below the banks, stooping to the scent washed on scour and shillet, and throwing their tongues. He could not see them, when swimming under water, until they were nearly over him. He swam downstream, never turning back, touching first one bank to breathe, and then swimming aslant to the other. Once in the straight mile of river under the Town-on-the-Hill, he emerged by a shallow almost by Deadlock's feet;

instantly he turned back. Farther down, by a jungle of balsam, whose top drought-roots were like the red toes of a bird, he left the river and ran on the bank, under trees. He had gone thirty yards on the hot land when Render and Deadlock crashed through the jungle of hollow sap-filled stalks after him. Although his legs were short—it was difficult to see them when he ran—he moved faster than any of the men hunting him could run. He left the land a hundred yards above Taddiport Bridge, by a bank where shards of ancient pottery were jutting.

Below the bridge was a ridge of shillets, long and wide as the broken hull of a sailing ship. Alders and willows grew here, and tall grasses that hid the old dry twigs and reeds on the lower branches of the trees. Floods had heaped up the island. The wet marks of Tarka's feet and rudder soon dried on the worn flakes of rock; but not before the larger pads of hounds, making the loose shillets clatter, had covered them.

Leu-in! Leu-in, b'hoys. Ov-ov-ov-ov-over!

Tarka's feet were dry when he took again to water, after trying to rid himself of scent on the stones so hot in the sun. He passed plants of water-hemlock and dropwort, tall as a man, growing among the stones, some sprawling with their weight of sap. He swam on down the river, passing Servis Wood, over which a buzzard, pestered by rooks, was wailing in the sky. The rooks left it to see what the hounds were doing, and wheeled silently over the river. Their shadows fled through the water, more visible than the otter.

A thousand yards from Taddiport Bridge, Tarka passed the brook up which he had travelled with his mother on the way to the Clay Pits. He swam under a railway bridge, below which the river hurried in a course narrow and shaded. An island of elm trees divided the river bed; the right fork was dry— hawkweed, ragwort, and St. John's wort, plants of the land, were growing there. Tarka swam to the tail of the island, and climbed up the dry bank. The place was cool and shady, and filled with the stench arising from the broad leaves and white flowers of wild garlic growing under the trees. Tarka trod into a thick patch, and quatted low.

Hounds passed him. He listened to them baying in the narrow channel below the island.

Deadlock clambered up the dry bank, ran a few yards among the grasses, threw up his head, sniffed, and turned away. Tarka held his breath. Other hounds followed, to sniff and run down the bank again. Tarka listened to them working among the roots under the island bank, and across the river. He heard the chaunting voices of huntsman and whippers-in; the noises of motor-cars moving slowly along the hard-rutted track-way of the old canal-bed, above the right bank of the river; the voices of men and women getting out of the motor-cars; and soon afterwards, the scrape of boots on the steep rubble path down to the dry, stony bed.

Tarka had been lying among the cool and stinking garlic plants of Elm Island for nearly five minutes when he heard gasping and wheezing noises at the top of the island. The two terriers, Bite'm and Biff, were pulling at their chains, held by the kennel boy. Their tongues hung long and limp, after the two-mile tug from the mills over sun-baked turf, dusty track-way, and hot stones, to Elm Island. Just before, while tugging down the path, Bite'm had fainted with the heat. A lapping sprawl in the river had refreshed the couple, and now they strove against collars pressing into their wind-pipes.

Tarka started up when they were a yard from where he lay. The kennel-boy dropped the chain when he saw him. Tarka ran towards the river, but at the sheer edge of the island he saw men on the stones six feet below. He ran along the edge, quickening at the shout of the kennel-boy, and had almost reached the island's tail when Bite'm pinned him in the shoulder. Tissing through his open mouth, Tarka rolled and fought with the terriers. Their teeth clashed. Tarka's moves were low and smooth; he bit Bite'm again and again, but the terrier hung on. Biff tried to bite him across the neck, but Tarka writhed away. The three rolled and snarled, scratching and snapping, falling apart and returning with instant swiftness. Ears were torn and hair ripped out. Hounds heard them and ran baying under the island cliff to find a way up. The kennel-boy tried to stamp on and recover the end of the chain, for he knew that in a worry all three might be killed. White terriers and brown otter rolled nearer the edge, and fell over.

The fall shook off Bite'm. Tarka ran under the legs of Dabster, and although Bluemaid snapped at his flank he got into the water and sank away.

Tally Ho! Tally Ho! Yaa-aa-ee on to 'm!

By the bank, fifty yards below Elm Island, stood the Master, looking into water six inches deep. A fern frond, knocked off the bank upstream, came down turning like a little green dragon in the clear water. It passed. Then came an ash-spray, that clung around the pole he leaned on. Its leaves bent to the current, it stayed, it swung away, and drifted on. A dead stick rode after it, and a fly feebly struggling—and then the lovely sight of an otter spreading himself over the stones, moving with the stream, slowly, just touching with his feet, smooth as oil under the water. A twenty-pound dog, thought the Master, remaining quiet by the shallow water listening to the music of his hounds. There was a stickle below Rothern Bridge.

The hounds splashed past him, stooping to the scent. Tarka's head showed, and vanished. He swam under Rothern Bridge, whose three stone arches, bearing heavy motor-transport beyond their old age, showed the cracks of suffering that the ferns were filling green. A sycamore grew out of its lower parapet. Deeper water under the bridge; the frail bubble-chain lay on it. A cry above the bridge; a line of coarser bubbles breaking across the stickle, where six men and two women stood in the river.

Tarka's head looked up and saw them. He lay in the deep water. He turned his head, and watched hounds swimming down through the arch. He dived and swam up; was hunted to shallow water again, and returned, making for the stickle. The water was threshed in a line from shillet-bank to shillet-bank, but he did not turn back. As he tried to pass between a man in red and a man in blue, two pole-ends were pushed under his belly in an attempt to hoick him back. But Tarka slipped off the shillet-burnished iron and broke the stickle. The whips ran on the bank, cheering on the hounds.

Get on to 'm! Hark to Deadlock! Leu-on! Leu-on! Leu-on!

A quarter of a mile below Rothern Bridge the river slows into the lower loop of a great S. It deepens until half-way, where the S is cut by the weir holding back the waters of the long Beam Pool. Canal Bridge crosses the river at the top of the S.

Where the river begins to slow, at the beginning of the pool, its left bank is bound by the open roots of oak, ash, alder, and sycamore. To hunted otters these trees offered holding as secure as any in the country of the Two Rivers. Harper, the aged hound—he was fourteen years old—knew every holt in the riverside trees of Knackershill Copse, and although he had marked at all of them, only once had he cracked the rib of an otter found in the pool. Leeches infested the unclear water.

Tarka reached the top of the pool. Swimming in the shade, his unseen course betrayed by the line of bubbles-a-vent, he came to the roots of the sycamore tree, where he had slept for two days during his wandering after the death of Greymuzzle. He swam under the outer roots, and was climbing in a dim light to a dry upper ledge when a tongue licked his head, and teeth playfully nipped his ear. Two pale yellow eyes moved over him. He had awakened the cub Tarquol.

Tarka turned round and round, settled and curled, and closed his eyes. Tarquol's nostrils moved, pointing at Tarka's back. His small head stretched nearer, the nostrils working. He sniffed Tarka's hair from rudder to neck, and his nose remained at the neck. It was a strange smell, and he sniffed carefully, not wanting to touch the fur with his nostrils. Tarka drew in a deep breath, which he let out in a long sigh. Then he swallowed the water in his mouth, settled his ear more comfortably on his paw, and slept; and awoke again.

Tarquol, the hairs of his neck raised, was listening at the back of the ledge. He was still as a root. The ground was shaking.

Go in on 'm, old fellars! Wind him, my lads! B'hoys! B'hoys! come on, b'hoys, get on to 'm.

The otters heard the whimpers of hounds peering from the top of the bank, afraid of the fall into the river. They watched the dim-root opening level with the water. Footfalls sounded in the roots by their heads; they could feel them through their feet. Then the water-level rose up and shook with a splash, as Deadlock was tipped into the river. They saw his head thrust in at the opening, heard his gruff breathing, and then his belving tongue. Other hounds whimpered and splashed into the river.

Pull him out, old fellars! Leu-in there, leu-in, leu-in!

Tarka squatted on the ledge; he knew that Deadlock would follow him wherever he swam in water. Tarquol, twisting and weaving his head, ran down on roots to the water, dragging his rudder for a dive; but a whitish light alarmed him and he ran up to the ledge again. The whitish light was reflected from the breeches of a wading man. A voice sounded near and hollow. Then a pole pushed through the opening between two roots. Its end was thrown about, nearly striking Tarquol's head. It was pulled out again, and the whitish light moved away. Tarka heard the whining of Bite'm.

Hands held and guided the terrier past the outside root. Tarquol tissed again as the dim light darkened with the shape of the enemy, whose scent was on the hair of Tarka's neck. Bite'm whined and yapped, trying to struggle up to the otters. His hind feet slipped off the roots, and he fell into the water below. *Plomp, plomp, plomp,* as he trod water, trying to scramble up the side.

Again the opening grew dark with arms holding and guiding another terrier, and Biff began to climb. *Wough! wough! wough!* Soon she fell into the water. The terriers were called off. Tarka settled more easily, but Tarquol could not rest. Hounds and terriers were gone, but still the voices of men were heard. The sound was low and regular, and Tarka's eyes closed. Tarquol quatted beside him, and for many minutes neither moved. Then the murmur of voices ceased with footfalls along the bank coming nearer: stopping above.

Heavy thuds shook down bits of earth on the otters' heads and backs. The huntsman was pounding the holt-top with an iron digging bar. Tarquol tissed, moving to and fro in fear of the great noises. Tarka slipped into the water, climbed out again, then submerged himself, only his nose and whiskers being out of the water. On and on went the pounding, until he could bear it no longer. He rolled over, and swam out of the holt. Tarquol followed him. He saw Tarka's chain rising bright before him. He turned upstream and was alone.

Seventy yards from the holt he rose under the bank to rest, and heard the baying of hounds. He dived again and went on upstream at his greatest speed. At his next vent he knew that the terrible beasts were following him. He swam out of the pool, turned back again, saw their heads in the water from bank to bank, became scared, and left the river. Galloping across the meadow faster than he had ever run in his life, with the hunting cries behind him and the thudding hooves of bullocks cantering away from hounds on his left, Tarquol came to sheds where farm machines were stored, and going through a yard, he ran through a gap in a hedge into a garden, where an old man was picking off the tops of his broad beans in a row, muttering about the black-fly on them. Tarquol passed him so near and so swiftly that the granfer's short clay pipe dropped from between his gums. He muttered in the sunshine and pondered nearly a minute. Hardly had he stooped to pick up his pipe when a great black and white hound crashed through the hedge and ran over his tetties and sun-dried shallots, followed by three more hounds, and after them a couple, and then his garden was filled with them.

Git'oom!

The hounds were gone, leaving him staring at his broken beans.

Tarquol had run round the walls of the cottage and into a farmyard, scattering fowls in terror before him. One of the hens, who was broody, ran at him, and leapt at his back, pecking and flapping. Tarquol kicked a little dust behind his straight rudder. At full speed he ran into a pigsty, where a sow was lying on her side with a farrow of eleven tugging at her. Seeing him, they stopped tugging, stared together, squeaked together, and scampered away into corners. The sow, too fat to get up quickly, tried to bite Tarquol as he rippled from corner to corner. The baying of the pack grew terribly loud, and still Tarquol darted about the sty, seeking a way of escape. The sow, after many grunts, flung herself on her trotters and bundled her flabby mass to the door, unlocking her dirty teeth to bite Deadlock, who had just arrived. Squealing with rage, her bristly, mud-caked ears flapping on her chaps, she chased him out of the sty, followed him back into the yard, and scattered the rest of the pack. Tarquol had run out behind the sow. He gained three hundred yards before hounds found his line again. He ran with the sun behind him for two hundred yards over grass, then he turned and went through a thorn hedge, climbed the railway embankment, and ran up over Furzebeam Hill, leaving an irregular trail. He ran for three miles on land, hiding among the dry spikes of gorse, and under branches. Sometimes he mewed in his misery.

Hounds ran far ahead of the men and women. Eventually the pack—with the exception of Pitiful, who was lost—hunted him back to the railway line, to where he was crouching low in the thorn hedge. A bird with a loud rasping voice, and a beak like a bent iron nail, clacked and chattered on a briar rising out of the hedge. It was a bird of property, or red-backed shrike, and Tarquol was quatting by its larder of bumble-bees, grasshoppers, and young harvest mice impaled on thorns. The mice were dead, but the bees still moved their legs.

Tarquol ran out of the thorns just before Render's muzzle pushed into his hiding place; but hounds leapt the low hedge and overtook him, before he had gone very far on his short, tired legs. Deadlock seized him and shook him and threw him into the air. Tarquol sprang up as soon as he fell, snapping and writhing as more jaws bit on his body, crushed his head, cracked his ribs, his paws and his rudder. Among the brilliant hawkbits—little sunflowers of the meadow—he was picked up and dropped again, trodden on and wrenched and broken, while the screaming cheers and whoops of sportsmen mingled with the growling rumble of hounds at worry. Tarquol fought them until he was blinded, and his jaws were smashed.

20

When he had swum out of the sycamore holt, Tarka had turned to deeper water and gone under the railway bridge twenty yards below—the line with its embankment and three bridges cut the S from south to north. He kept close to the left bank, in the margin of shade. The copse ended at the bridge; below was a meadow. He rose to breathe, heard the hounds, and swam on under water. He passed a run of peal, which flashed aside when they saw him, and sped through the water at many times the pace of a travelling otter. Sixty yards below the bridge, by the roots of a thrown alder, Tarka rose to listen. Looking around, he saw neither hound nor man, and knew that he was not being followed. He thought of the holt under the oak tree above the next railway bridge and swam on down.

Where the river's bend began to straighten again, the right bank lay under oak trees growing on the hill-slope to the sky. Tarka dived and swam across the river to the holt he had remembered as he left the roots of the sycamore. This holt had a sunken opening, where no terrier could enter. Here Tarka's sire had been asleep when hounds had found him two years before. Tarka swung up, coming into a dark cavern lit by a small hole above, and stinking of the paraffin poured there the previous afternoon. He sniffed the oil film on the water, and turned back into the weir-pool.

Again he made a hidden crossing, to listen under cover of flag-lilies for more than a minute. The river was quiet. He heard the sound of falling water, and swam slowly down, often touching under the bank. He passed under the middle arch of the railway bridge, and reached the weir slanting across the river. The summer water tumbled down the fish-pass, but glided thin as a snail's shell over the top end of the concrete sill. The lower end, by the fender at the head of the leat, was dry. Tarka walked along the sill, nearly to the end, which was two inches above the level of the pool. He stretched his weary back on the warm concrete and sprawled in the sun.

He lay basking for more than an hour, enjoying the sound of water tumbling in the pass and sliding down the face of the weir. Swallows dipped in the pool, and sometimes a peal leapt in the shadow of the bridge. Tarka's head was always raised before the fish fell back, but he did not leave the sill. Warm and brilliant sun-flickers on the shallows below dazed his eyes, and made him drowsy. But when a hound, working alone down the left bank, climbed on the sill by the pass and shook itself, he was instantly alert. Half lying down, he remained quite still, while the hound lifted its muzzle to sniff. Something moved on the bridge—otter and hound turned their heads together, seeing a man behind the railing. At first the man saw only the hound, but when it walked along the sill and ran down the face of the weir, he saw the otter it was following. The man had come along the railway to see if any fish were in the pool; he was a poacher nicknamed Shiner, and the top of one of his fingers was missing. He had no love for otters. Back along the railway line he hastened, and shouted to the otter-hunters.

Followed in silence by the hound Pitiful, Tarka swam leisurely. He watched, from under a tree, a single enemy working down the shallow, crossing to deeper water to seek his scent along the banks. He let it come within a few feet of his head, then dived and swam away. Pitful never saw him, or the chain of bubbles. Often she followed the wash carried down with the current; and when it grew weak, she would amble along the banks until she found where the otter had touched.

Tarka felt neither fear nor rage against the hound. He wanted to be left alone. After several hidden swims from bank to bank, and finding no holding where he might lie up and sleep until evening, he walked out by a cattle-trodden groove in the right bank, and ran away over land. He followed the otter-path across a quarter of a mile of meadow, and re-entered the river by the third oak above Canal Bridge.

Tarka drifted under the high lime-spiky arches of the bridge, and the white owl, roosting on a ledge below the parapet, beside the briars of a dog-rose growing there with hawkweeds, saw him going downstream.

Bees came to the wild roses, crammed more pollen into their laden thigh-bags, and burred away over the bridge. A petal dropped, a swallow played with it as it fell, clipping it with first one wing and then the other, until it sank upon the water, and was carried away, past the gap in the bank where the Owlery Oak, Tarka's birthplace, had been held by its roots two years before.

Then Pitiful swam under Canal Bridge, and after her the pack came down, and many men, and the owl was driven into wavy flight down the river. It pitched in a tree of Leaning Willow Island, as a dull clamour broke out where hounds had marked the otter under a hover.

The water of the pool was swimming deep from the shallow above Canal Bridge to the shallow above Leaning Willow Island. The surface above Tarka mirrored the bed of the river—the dark rocks, the weed, the sodden branches, the legs and bodies of hounds—until ripples broke the mirror into shards of light. In this underwater realm, where sounds were so distinct—the crush of nailed boots on stones, the tip-tap of poles, the thresh of hounds' legs, and even the flip of cyclops and water-flea—Tarka swam until he was forced to vent, which he did at the river verge, under the banks, or by clumps of yellow flags. Sometimes he crept on the stones, hiding himself under overhanging roots as he sought refuge, until dreading the nearness of hounds he slipped into the river again, covered with a silver skin of air. As he swam, twin streams of bubbles came out of his nostrils, raced over his head and neck, and shook off his back to lie on the surface in a chain, watched by many eyes. Up and down the pool he went, swimming in midstream or near the banks, crossing from side to side and varying his depth of swimming as he tried to get away from his pursuers. Passing under the legs of hounds, he saw them joined to their broken surface-images. From under water he saw men and women, pointing with hand and pole, as palsied and distorted shapes on the bank. However hard he swam with his three and a half webs, always he heard the hounds, as they spoke to his scent lying in burst bubble, in seal on muddy scour, on leaf and twig. Once in mid-river, while

189

on his way to a clump of flags, his breath gave out, and he
bobbed up to breathe a yard from Deadlock. He stared into
the eyes of his old enemy; and dived. During forty seconds
he swam a distance of seventy yards, to a bed of reeds, where
he breathed and rested. No one saw him; but they saw the
chain.

Up the river again, past the Peal Rock, and under the middle
arch of Canal Bridge to the shallow, crossed by a line of men
and women, white and blue and green and red and grey,
standing close together.

Tally Ho!

He turned and reached covering water just before hounds.

Get on to 'm! Leu-on! leu-on! Wind him, old fellars!

The huntsman was wading up to his waist in the water,
scooping the air with his grey hat. Bellman, a small-footed
hairy black-and-tan, cross between a drafted harrier and a
Dumfriesshire rough otter-hound, yelped his impatience,
seeming to snap the water as he swam. Sometimes the huntsman gave an encouraging spit-note on his horn. Tarka went
down river, but a blurred and brilliant colour band stretched
from bank to bank above Leaning Willow Island. He tried
to get through the stickle, but stocking'd leg was pressed to
stocking'd leg, a fixed barrier behind plying poles. The owl
flew out of the willow, miserable in the sunlight with small
birds pursuing it.

Tarka turned and swam upstream again, leaving hounds
behind. For five minutes he rested under a thorn bush. Deadlock found him, and on he went, to Canal Bridge once more,
where he lay in the water, weary after the long chase. At the
beginning of the sixth hour he tried to pass the higher stickle,
but his enemies stood firm on the stones. The baying swelled
under the bridge. He was nearly picked up by Hurricane, the
Irish staghound, but the blunted canine teeth could not hold
him.

The chain became shorter. Tarka was too weary to seek
a holding in the banks. He breathed in view of his enemies.
Seven and a half couples of hounds swam in the pool, their
sterns throwing behind them arc-lines of drops on the surface.

Others splashed in the shallows under the banks. The huntsman let them work by themselves.

During the seventh hour the otter disappeared. The river grew quiet. People not in uniform sat down on the grass. The huntsman was wading slowly upstream, feeling foothold with his pole and keeping an eye on Deadlock. Stickles stood slack, but ready to bar the way with pole-strokes. Look-outs gazed at the water before them. It was known that the otter might leave the river at any moment. The boy with the warped pole, on whose cheeks were two patches of dried otter-blood, was already opening his knife, ready to cut another notch on the handle, in the form of a cross.

For more than an hour the sun-thongs flickered across the placid water; and in softening light the owl returned, flying high over the bridge, to the mouse runs in the quiet meadow beyond.

A fallen bough of willow lay in the pool near one bank, and Tarka lay beside it. His rudder held a sunken branch. Only his wide upper nostrils were above water. He never moved. Every yard of the banks between the stickles was searched again. Poles were thrust into branches, roots, and clumps of flag-lilies. The wading huntsman prodded Peal Rock and the rock above it. Hounds sat on the banks, shivering, and watching Deadlock, Render, and Harper working the banks. The crack of a whip, a harsh voice rating—Rufus had turned a rabbit out of a bramble and was chasing it across the meadow. He returned to the river in a wide circle, eyeing the whip.

At the beginning of the ninth hour a scarlet dragonfly whirred and darted over the willow snag, watched by a girl sitting on the bank. Her father, an old man lank and humped as a heron, was looking out near her. She watched the dragonfly settle on what looked like a piece of bark beside the snag; she heard a sneeze, and saw the otter's whiskers scratch the water. Glancing round, she realized that she alone had seen the otter. She flushed, and hid her grey eyes with her lashes. Since childhood she had walked the Devon rivers with her father looking for flowers and the nests of birds, passing some rocks and trees as old friends, seeing a Spirit everywhere, gentle in thought to all her eyes beheld.

For two minutes the maid sat silent, hardly daring to look at the river. The dragonfly flew over the pool, seizing flies and tearing them apart in its horny jaws. Her father watched it as it settled on the snag, rose up, circled, and lit on the water, it seemed. Tarka sneezed again, and the dragonfly flew away. A grunt of satisfaction from the old man, a brown hand and wrist holding aloft a hat, a slow intaken breath, and,

Tally Ho!

Tarka dived when the hounds came down, and the chain showed where he had swum. Many saw his dark sleek form as he walked by the edge of a grassy islet by the twelve trees. The hounds ran to him, and Tarka turned and faced them, squatting on his short hindlegs, his paws close against his round and sturdy chest. He bit Render in the nose, making his teeth meet. In an instant he drew back, tissing, and bit Deadlock in the flews. The narrow lower jaw snapped again and again, until the press of hounds hid him from sight.

He squirmed away through legs and under bellies, biting and writhing a way to the water; and the chain drew out on the surface of the pool while hounds were still seeking him on the stones where he had sat and faced them.

Leu-on, then! Leu-on! Ov-ov-ov-ov-over!

Tarka's pace was slow and his dives were short. In the water by the Peal Rock he lay, glancing at the faces along the banks, across the river, and in the river. His small dark eyes showed no feeling. He turned away from the human faces, to watch the coming of the hounds. He was calm and fearless and fatigued. When they were his length away, he swung under, showing the middle of his smooth back level with the surface, and swimming past their legs. He saw the huntsman's legs before him joined to the image of legs, and above the inverted image a flattened and uncertain head and shoulders. Up and down he swam, slower and slower.

Towards the end of the ninth hour an immense fatigue came over him, greater than his fatigue when in the long hard winter he had lived for over a month on seaweed and shellfish in the estuary. He was swimming up from the lower stickle when the water seemed to thicken at each thrust of his webs. He ceased to swim and drifted backwards. Barbrook touched his neck as he dived. He reappeared two poles' length away, and lay still, looking at the huntsman wading nearer.

For ten minutes he rested, between dives of a few yards only, and then he rolled from Deadlock's bite and went downstream. He swam with his last strength, for upon him had come the penultimate desire of the hunted otter, the desire that comes when water ceases to be a refuge, the desire to tread again the land-tracks of his ancestors. He crawled half up the bank, but turned back at the thudding of many feet, and swam down to the stickle. The sideway ply of a pole in a turmoil of water struck him on the head. He pushed past the iron point, but it was brought down on his shoulder, to hold him against the shillets. Hounds were fifteen yards away, urged on by hat and horn and the yarring cheers of the whippers-in. Thrice Tarka's teeth clicked on the iron pressing his shoulder as he strove against the weight of the sportsman trying to lift him back. A second pole was brought down from the other flank, crossing with the first. The wooden pincers held him; he twisted like an eel and bit into a leg. With furious strength he writhed from the crossed poles, and through the stickle, as Deadlock bore down upon him and pulled him back by the rudder. Amidst the harsh cries of men and women and the heavy tongues of hounds Tarka was over-borne by the pack. The Master looked at his watch—eight hours and forty-five minutes from the find in the Dark Pool. Then the screeching, yarring yell of one of the honorary whips:

Yaa-aa-ee-io! Leu-in on 'im! Yaa-ee-oo!

for again Tarka had escaped from the worry, and had merged into the narrow stream of water that hurried to Leaning Willow Island.

Below the island the river widened, smooth with the sky. Tarka swam down slowly, bleeding from many wounds. Sometimes he paddled with three legs, sometimes with one, in the water darkening so strangely before his eyes. Not always did

193

he hear the hounds baying around him. At the beginning of the tenth hour he passed the banks faced with stone to keep the sea from the village, and drifted into deeper water, whereon sticks and froth were floating. Hounds were called off by the horn for the tide was at flood; and there is no scent in salt water.

But as they were about to leave, Tarka was seen again, moving up with the tide, his mouth open. The flow took him near the bank; he kicked feebly, and rolled over.

Tally-Ho!

Deadlock saw the small brown head, and bayed in triumph as he jumped down the bank. He bit into the head, lifted the otter high, flung him about and fell into the water with him. They saw the broken head look up beside Deadlock, heard the cry of *Ic-yang!* as Tarka bit into his throat, and then the hound was sinking with the otter into the deep water. Oak-leaves, black and rotting in the mud of the unseen bed, arose and swirled and sank again. And the tide slowed still, and began to move back, and they waited and watched, until the body of Deadlock arose, drowned and heavy, and floated away amidst the froth on the waters.

They pulled the body out of the river and carried it to the bank, laying it on the grass, and looking down at the dead hound in sad wonder. And while they stood there silently, a great bubble rose out of the depths, and broke, and as they watched, another bubble shook to the surface, and broke; and there was a third bubble in the sea-going waters, and nothing more.

APOLOGIA PRO VERBA MEA

APOLOGIA PRO VERBA MEA

A year or two after *Tarka* was first published the author made his first visit to the United States of America. In New England he heard, with a welcome feeling of kinship, some of the local West Country words he had used in his story of an otter's wanderings. It seemed that some descendents of the *Mayflower* pilgrims still used Jacobean phrases and pronunciations which had survived in Britain only among the peasantry and in long-established landed families. (A survival due to generations of children, growing up in one place, imitating the speech of their parents.) For example, dog, lost, cost were pronounced dorg, lorst, corst; while proper names like Raleigh (variously spelt in past ages Rawley, Ralegh, Rorley) had not been popularised, as in the industrial areas of Britain with the coming of the Education Acts, into Rally; or, with later genteelism, Rarley.

Here I would like to reprint a letter sent to *The London Mercury*, and published by the editor, J. C. Squire, in the 100th number of February, 1928.

That splendid literary magazine is, alas, no more; and Sir John Squire has gone, too. One day, perhaps, a book will be written about those times, and the weekly meetings in the Temple Bar chop-house in Fleet Street, adjoining the tiny *Mercury* office, where most of the poets and writers of Georgian literary society met together at one time or another. Meanwhile I must record my gratitude to the leader of "The Squirearchy", for it was mainly due to Jack Squire that the Hawthornden Prize for Literature was awarded to *Tarka*.

Sir,
   Your reviewer of my book *Tarka the Otter* complains of "the literary weakness of the excessive use of provincialisms and sporting jargon in the story", therefore I feel that some explanation of the

196

unusual words may be of interest to your readers. Indeed, it would appear to be almost necessary, in view of another reviewer's statement that most of the words are not to be found in the *Concise Oxford Dictionary*, "and possibly, we suspect, not in the complete one". Mr. Arthur Heinemann, a well-known Exmoor character, goes even farther than this, and accuses one of "fathering fake words on the dear Devon dialect". While yet a fourth critic declares that "in the latest edition of the *English Dialect Dictionary*, on the authority of Professor Joseph Wright, M.A., Ph.D., D.C.L., LL.D., Litt.Doc., F.B.A., Professor of Philogy at Oxford, most of the words I suspected are unverifiable therein".

To this last correspondent I have suggested that he might possibly find some of them in the next edition of the *English Dialect Dictionary*.

Ackymal. This word is in general use in the West Country, and is applied to both the blue and great titmouse. (*Chickadee*, in the U.S.A., an onomatopoeic word from the birds' call, is an excellent "fake": possibly by the Red Indians?) I have heard in my wanderings from inn to inn, the following variations: Ackmaull, Hackmall, Hackymall, Eckmall, Uckimol, Hickmal, and most amusing of all, the expression, "Withering things they ackimules: they ought to be kicked to flames!" This was from an old man whose pea-shucks had been hacked open by blue-tits.

Dimity. Twilight. "Between the lights." More common terms are dimmit-light, dimpsey, and dimpse.

Channered. A marshman spoke of the *channered* guts in the estuary saltings. Wandering tracks in the salt turf which look as though made by great worms.

Belving. Common proverb in the West Country is "A belving cow soon forgets her calf". I used the word to describe the note of a deep-chested hound.

Ream. "Unverifiable anywhere" says one critic. Used by a water-bailiff of the arrowy ripple pushed by a fish's dorsal fin, or nose of swimming otter. A wave.

Shillets. Throughout the lengths of the Taw and Torridge the stones (generally flat) of the river bed piled by freshes, freshets, or spates, are so called.

Yinny-yikker. A man heeling-up potatoes with a mattock near Torrington was surprised to see a "g'rt mousey-coloured fitch" run from the river and threaten him. "'Er was roarin' and bawlin' at me, so 'a took me prang (prong, fork) to'n, to give'n a scatt (blow) on th' ade (head) and er ris (rose) up all yinny yikker" (thin snarly chatter or threat).

Pill. Esturial creek. *Cf.* Pilton, near Barnstaple, Pill Town.

Sterlings (pronounced starlings). The stone piling round the base of Bideford Long Bridge is spelt sterling not starling by the Bridge Trust. This masonry is bound by mussels: the taking of the shell-fish is forbidden in bye-law.

Glidders. My own invention, to convey the smooth sloping mud-banks of an esturial creek. Anyone who has dug for rag-worm upon a glidder will smell again the black rotting oakleaves and twigs brought down by spates, to be covered by slower tides with dark grey silt. R. D. Blackmore mentions scree, or rocky flakes that have "gliddered" down some Exmoor combe sides, for example, above Heddon Mouth west of Lynton. The word *glidders* occurred to me as I slipped and slid on the mud (which in one place had hard clay under its loose surface) while spurring, or following the *spoor*, of an otter down to the water.

Spurring. I heard this word while following the Cheriton Otter hounds. Ignorantly I did not then connect it with "to follow the spoor", an Afro-Dutch word presumably. So spur it remains in the text.

Shippen, or *Shippon.* A roofed shed, with one side open for cattle to shelter in. Those built with a tallat, or hay loft, are called linhays, pronounced linneys. In the days of my youth many tallats were the roosting places of white owls, now, alas, in some districts, a rarity.

Vuz-peg. Furze pig, or hedge-hog. Sometimes called aidge-boar (hedge-boar.)

Pollywiggle. Tadpole.

Ruddock. Robin.

Crackey. Common wren.

Oolypuggers. The great mace reed, commonly called bull-rush. Heard from marshmen on the Braunton marsh. James Joyce would have welcomed this word. Ooze, oozy; the white mores (roots) making a puggy noise in ooze when pulled; the seed-head, bull-coloured, soft, puggy. Was not language originally made in the child-mind of man?

Ammil. The thin ice-casing made upon all static objects in areas of Dartmoor during the chill of some nights, and at sunrise shining like a tapestry of gold. Corruption of *enamel*.

Quapping. Invented by me (in so far as I am aware) to express sound made by a duck quickly opening and shutting its bill when feeding.

Aerymouse. The small vespertilian bat. The pipistrelle.

Appledrane. Wasps in autumn slowly drane (too slack-winged to drone) inside ripe apples. Wasp possibly half drunk: sensible wasp, for the night cometh.

Ragrowster. "'Ow they dogs do love vor ragrowster." Heard at Lancross in Devon *Cf.* the Edwardian equivalent *to rag*, a slight amelioration of the grimmer Victorian *to bully rag*.

Brock. Badger. Records in Hartland Church mention money paid for heads of *greys* (Norman), so brock is possibly a Saxon word? *Brock* generally used in the West Country today.

Vair. Weasel.

Fitchey, or *fitch.* Stoat.

Ram-cat. Tom cat.

Stag-bird. A cock among domestic hens.

Twired. Own invention. Used of water, where twirl or swirl would be too forceful. Tide out in estuary: slow and shallow flow of river-water moving past heron's legs, leaving on surface slight raised lines at usual angle of $22\frac{1}{2}$ degrees. Probably precious, but unrepentant.

Tacker. Small child, usually boy.

Clitter. Pile of rocks.

Bubbles-a-vent! An obsolescent otter-hunting cry, superseded at the time of my story (the 'twenties) by "Tally ho!" The submerged swimming otter is always betrayed by the chain of bubbles rising to the surface behind it as it swims under water.

Other hunting terms, such as a hound *"throwing its tongue"*, *"stooping to the scent"*, *"land-loop"*, *"stickle"*, etc., are surely made intelligible to the ordinary reader, even if one reviewer was "wearied and irritated" by them. Another reason for using local words and phrases was to preserve them before they passed away. The daily newspapers, now beginning to reach remote villages, are making a stereotyped speech in rural England; wireless will further a uniform pronunciation. Today even middle-aged men are inclined to be a little shy of their natural speech, sometimes apologising for it when talking with visitors in street and pub; while only the naughtiest children talk as when Shakespeare was alive and listening. Indeed, if one examines the work of this writer it will be found that for the use of "provincialisms and sporting jargon", for exact description of what is to be apprehended by the five senses, there is a sound precedent.—Yours, etc,

HENRY WILLIAMSON

North Devon
12 December, 1927

SALAR THE SALMON

To
T. E. LAWRENCE
of
Seven Pillars of Wisdom
AND
V. M. YEATES
of
Winged Victory

THE SUN IN TAURUS

During the month of May, in all the pure and fast rivers of Great Britain, the smolt are going down to the sea. That to me is a marvellous thing, like the music of Delius, and green corn growing; like swallows nesting in the porch of our cottage, and the moon—the nightingale moon—rising over the moor and shedding her light upon the woods and valleys, the rivers and estuary of the land that is home.

Smolt are little salmon which, born in the headwaters of rivers and their tributaries, and wearing the moorland red-and-black spotted dress of trout for about two years, suddenly become strangely excited, assume a silver sea-coat, and seek the Atlantic of ancestral memory.

No longer than a man's hand at two years and weighing between two and three ounces, a smolt may return to its native river after two or three months in the sea, weighing four or five pounds, the length of a man's forearm. Or it may remain in the sea two years, and return a forty-pounder! For some reason unknown, many of the Wye fish stay two and sometimes three years feeding on herring and prawns off the deep submarine ledges of Europe's end below Ireland; this has helped to make the Wye the most famous salmon river in England.

I have stared at smolts jumping in a Devon river, their foster-mother, as they went down with the currents, always head to stream in the clear water wimpling over the blue and brown stones at the tail of a pool; or, in the fast runs below, prickling broken water as they dashed at the frail waterflies dropping their eggs at sunset.

I have seen the smolts sliding tail-first over the weirs of mill-ponds which were made by damming the river by mortar'd walls of stone, in order to lead water away to work the great wooden wheels of the grist-mills which, when I was young, were everywhere in use along the river-banks of every county;

fascinating it was to watch the gushings of water on the mossy wheel trundling with the grind of mill-stones within a room white everywhere with barley flour, every spider-web heavy white as the beard and hat and eyebrows of the miller; I have followed the smolts down the valley ever widening under its steep hillsides of oak, spruce, larch, and rock-set grasses to the broader pastures which end in the marshes below the tide's head.

From Wye and Shannon, Tay, Coquet and Usk, Hampshire Avon, Tweed, Otter, Taw, Torridge, Teign and Tavy—from scores of fresh rivers in Britain, Germany, Sweden, and the eastern seaboard of Canada—the smolt "drop back" to find their home in the Atlantic; and from there they return in their season to their native rivers, to find new perils during the months of spring and summer (when they do not feed). They wait in shallow water to spend themselves for the spirit, or future, of their race; and, thus achieving immortality, will die, and so return to the Atlantic in dissolution: salts of the sea which is the great father.

In all the pure rivers of Great Britain, the young salmon are dropping down to the ocean. The symbol of baptism, of rebirth, was anciently a fish; and the noblest of fish is the salmon. Yet pollution has temporarily despoiled many of our rivers. In some, inanimate sludge has taken the life out of the water— the oxygen—without which plants cannot grow, mayflies arise, or fish breathe. Chemical discharges poison with false rainbow hues the surface of the gliding masses of dead water. Valuable phosphates and salts are squandered in the estuaries from the drains of great cities. Will that ever be changed? The sludge and the chemicals extracted on land and used for many purposes, among them the fertility of cornfields and pastures?

I hope, despite all, that one day salmon will be leaping again in the Thames: that Salmo Salar, the Sea Leaper as the Romans named him, will jump once more in the Pool of London, and play around the piers of the bridges, showing his square tail in joy of meeting again the sparkling water of his nativity. Will our grandchildren see him and wonder on the darkness of the industrial age, with its wars and mental miseries arising because the true values of living, in a former age, were polluted and lost?

In my boyhood I saw a trout stream, the Darent in Kent, poisoned before my eyes when acids from the new-tarred valley road, once white flinty dust, ran in during a summer storm. In my early manhood I lived beside a moorland stream many miles from that country of the mind of childhood, and spent more than five thousand hours watching the limpid waters of the Bray wherein Salar lived the last months of his life. His fortitude, as you will I hope read, instinctive as it was, and leading to inevitable death, was to me a triumph and an inspiration.

Like *Tarka*, the salmon book was not an easy one to write; for, among other difficulties, I strove to present in words what in those days the films failed to give to people: a sense of living truth, or beauty, of life wild in nature. The camera can record so much; the solitary writer, with but pen and paper, so little.

TIDEWAYS

1

At full moon the tides swirling over the Island Race carry the feelings of many rivers to the schools of fish which have come in from their feeding ledges of the deep Atlantic. The returning salmon are excited and confused. Under broken waters the moon's glimmer is opalescent; the fish swim up from ocean's bed and leap to meet the sparkling silver which lures and ever eludes them, and which startles them by its strange shape as they curve in air and see, during the moment of rest before falling, a thrilling liquescence of light on the waves beneath.

The Island Race is a meeting place of currents over a sunken reef, or chain of reefs. The sea is never still there. Twice every day and twice every night the tide rips over the ledges and pinnacles of the reef, streaming the seaweed under its white surges and mingling the layers of river waters in its green massive drifts.

Salmon feed in the Atlantic and return to the fresh-water rivers to spawn, and, by this arduous and pleasurable act, give of themselves to the immortality of salmon.

For two years after hatching the samlet lives and feeds in the river, and, having survived many dangers, drops down to the estuary in a new silver sea-coat, a slender little smolt no longer than a man's hand, bewildered and brave, entering with others of its school the thickening salt waters beyond the known river-water of its birth. It feels its way by the link of nerves, sensitive to the least pressure or density, along its sides from gill-covers to tail. The smolt, in its first armour of sea-scales, feed eagerly on the new food moving in and stirring the sandy shore of ocean, shrimps and other small crustaceans and fish. In fresh-water life it was always head to stream, poised in eddy or by

206

stone: thus it breathed through mouth and gill, thus it waited and watched for food moving or floating before and above its eyes, thus was it stream-tapered and made strong: a passing act in the everlasting action of its racial immortality. Always it was driving itself forward, to keep its poise, and its place in the stream.

In the sea it drove itself forward, a sideway sinuating movement, boring into the unknown and deepening densities of ocean. It found its new food more easily and frequently, it grew quickly, its shoulders deepened, its white flesh became pink, its forked tail-fin broadened. Always it was travelling farther from the shallow coast, yet following the weakening stream of fresh water beyond the last ribs of sand.

It came to a dark wall of rock from which ribbon weed was unrolling and swaying. The green water moved as in the river, but with greater press, and there the smolt waited in the race of tides, feeding on small fish which drifted past. Many smolts were taken by fish called bass, which, large mouthed and spined of back-fin, roved together down the corridors of the reef, and through the weedy timbers of wooden ships wedged in clefts of rock. The Island was a breeding place of sea birds, guillemots, auks, razorbills, puffins, red-throated divers, and others which oared themselves with their wings swiftly under water, while thrusting with webbed feet. Conger eels lived in dark water-caves, moving darkly and slowly behind broad-nosed heads, and suddenly accelerating along their own lengths to seize a fish before it could turn away. Loath to leave their remembered river-water, which was parent and friend to them, the smolts remained in a straggling school near the reef, among hundreds of thousands of other smolts, brought thither by their weakening parent streams.

The sun in Taurus rose over the land whose watercourses they had left, and set in the Atlantic; the tides poured over the reef, flowing north and lapsing south in light and darkness; the moon moved over the sea, and as its light grew so the tides pressed faster, mingling the river-streams until memory or feeling in the smolts for their rivers was lost in the greater movements of ocean. And in the night of the moon's fullness many shadows moved into the racing tide, and the smolts fled and gathered in confusion before the apparitions, which one after another swam slowly up to the broken, gleaming top of the sea and, near the surface, gathered all their power within themselves to sinuate first one side then the other, faster and faster, gripping the water with one flank then the other to push their tapered lengths violently away from the water: thus a salmon accelerates for the leap. New schools of fish followed, slowly and leisurely, and ranged themselves behind and under and beside the salmon formations already waiting in the tide-race. Fish after fish left its place, swam up, gathered strength, leapt, smacked down on its side, and swam down slowly to its place again.

The tide took the displaced smolts south of the Island, to where beyond rocks the water deepened and was quiet below the lift and roll of waves. So they began a far sea journey, their rivers disremembered. They wandered above rocky glooms of the deeper Atlantic; they wandered in ancestral memory. Here for many scores of thousands of years salmon had travelled, coming to where the last of the continent's foundations fell away into the blue twilight of immeasurable ocean.

In the sea was rich feeding; and when they were grown big, in surfeiture of physical life the unconscious lust for a fuller or spiritual life led them back along the undersea paths they had travelled as smolts, to where ancestral memory became personal memory—to where the river currents frayed away in the tidal rhythms of the sea. The returning salmon thinks with its whole body.

As the different schools found their food easily or hardly, so they grew quickly or slowly; thus salmon were returning to their rivers flowing into the North Atlantic at all months of the year, in varying tapers or sea-mouldings. Nevertheless, the salmon's cycle of renewal is fixed in the orbits of the sun, served by the moon; its spawning time is the end of the year, when days are short and rivers run high with wild rains. What of those fish which enter the rivers at the beginning of the year?

Should the early-running salmon survive the perils of the estuary, of river life in spring and summer, and endure the ardours of spawning and of prolonged starvation (for salmon feed only occasionally, and with no profit, in fresh water), it returns, sick and dislustred, to the sea, where, as fishermen say, it cleans itself; and again it journeys forth against the warm drag of the Gulf Stream with the eagerness of one reborn, yet who must follow the fixed orbit of its kind, unto that darkness which awaits even the sun in heaven. The scattered eggs of salmon in the gravel redds are as the constellations of night; nothing is lost of air or water. In this faith is the story of Atlantic salmon told.

The Romans, sailing their galleys between the Island and the mainland, knew the meeting place by the reef, and named the fish Salar—the Leaper. So shall be called the big keeper, or cock-fish, who sprang towards the moon from the waves of one of the biggest tides of the year on that coast, the Easter tide.

Salar was one of many thousands returning from the ocean feeding banks. As the moon at night rose fuller, he had travelled on, pausing neither to feed nor sleep. He had come at medium ocean cruising speed, travelling about a hundred miles from one sunrise to another, faster with the currents, slower aslant them. The current guided him; his body remembered. His mouth opened forty times every minute, and each time as his mouth closed his gill-covers opened, and red gill-rakers absorbed oxygen from the water for his blood-stream. In that blood-stream were units of life, even as the fish was a unit in the living sea.

Salar was five years old. During the two years of river life he had grown to a weight of two ounces: three years of ocean feeding had added another twenty pounds to his weight. Growth had not been regular or uniform. In two periods of sea wandering he, with other salmon, had increased rapidly, while following herring shoals on their westward migration after their spawning in the shallow waters of the north. The herring had followed drifting clouds of marine plankton, and salmon had pursued the herring shoals. Every day during those two periods Salar had gorged his own weight of herrings, catching a fish across the back as it turned from his upward rush, holding and crushing it in his jaws until it was dead, and then swallowing it head first. Soon his shoulders were hob-curved with stored power.

Pursuing the salmon were porpoises, led by Meerschwein, the old sea-hog. The porpoises hunted by swimming in formation under the salmon, which were under the herrings. They were invisible below. The only warning of Meerschwein's approach was a swirl and sudden varying water-pressure of the upward dash. He swam up under a salmon, gathered and launched himself at the fish, turned on his back and snapped at the salmon's belly. Meerschwein and the other porpoises fed by tearing away their bites; they seldom pursued a fish further. Like all carnivores, they had a sense of sport equal with the sense of feeding.

Following the porpoises were ferocious gladiators, or killers, led by Orca, the strongest, who could crush a porpoise with a single bite in the recurved teeth of his immense mouth. This tribe of killers, like the porpoises, were warm blooded, breathing only in air. They mated and brought forth their young under water. Their young were born with the instinct, or inherited custom, to inspire only when their mothers, to whom they clung, rolled on to the surface to breathe; but they could suck their dam's milk while submerged.

Salar had avoided death by bite of porpoise, shark, ray, and other predatory fish—nearly all fish prey on other fish—and now, five years and one month since hatching from a round egg about three-sixteenths of an inch in diameter in the head-waters of a stream under Snowdon, he was more than a yard long, and his girth was half his length.

He was lying on the edge of a current where it dragged against an eddy or back-trend of water; using one moving weight of water to buoy him against an opposing weight. He lolled there, at rest. He was nearly asleep. His mouth opened to take in water twenty times a minute.

Two lines of pierced scales along each flank covered cells filled with liquid which was sensitive to every varying pressure of moving water; the cells were joined with nerve-roots which connected with the brain. His body moved in idle flexion. Fins kept the body poised in its hover. On his back was the dorsal fin, behind each gill-cover was a pectoral fin. A little behind the point of the body's balance were the paired or ventral fins, by which he held himself when resting on a rock, or the bed of the sea in shallow water. By the caudal or tail fin he steered himself: a rudder. There was a small fixed fin, like a pennon, on his back, aft of the dorsal fin, which served to prevent turbulence or eddy when he was swimming forward. Blue and silver of flanks, porcelain white of belly, with fins of a delicate opaque greyish-pink, with a few yellow-red and grey-green and light brown spots on his gill-covers, and groups of sea-lice under the dark edge of his tail and on his back, Salar was resting in one of the many streaming currents at the eastern edge of the Island Race when Jarrk swam down, driving himself by powerful flippers, peering round and below with grey-filmy eyes. The seal scattered a school of grilse which flickered and flashed away in the tide. The sudden contorted beat of Salar as he accelerated thrummed in the seal's ears.

2

During the time of one wave-crest breaking white and reforming again in phosphoric streaks, nearly a thousand salmon which were resting in the tail of the Island Race had broken formation and were zigzagging into the northerly sweep of the tide. Many schools had been hovering there in echelon, bound for their various rivers—very large springers, five-and six-year-old fish; smaller spring fish with between two and three years of sea feeding; mended kelts—spawned fish which had "cleaned themselves" after spawning—the few survivors of the autumn run, biggest of the year, the authentic spawning run of salmon. The mended kelts would return along the way they had travelled as smolts.

A few of the schools were grilse, small fish which had been less than a year in salt water, weighing from three to eight pounds, slender, silver-grey, unspotted except faintly on gill-covers, with forked tail-fins and gracile "wrists"—the slender part of the body where it splayed into the tail-fin. One of the grilse, of a school of eleven which had been skittering along the moonlit surface and sporting among the wave-crests, was Gralaks, a young maiden salmon who had been born in one of the streams running down from the moor of the wild red deer, in the gravel redds above the pool called Fireplay.

Salar was a fish of the largest salmon river of that coast; he had hatched in one of its many head-waters breaking out of the slopes of Welsh mountains.

Salar saw Jarrk the seal as a luminous shape above him. An instant before he had shot away, the salmon had become alert because the seal's descent had altered the weight of one of the currents maintaining his lie. Jarrk's smooth hide reflected the broken confusion of light which was the surface of the sea, and when the seal had turned, his neck had flashed. Bubbles from his nostrils shone pearly. Salar was away, the fish behind and beside him were away, and the alarm thudded through the sea, felt by the resting salmon above the pressure-roar of the currents.

Other seals were hunting the fish. Among them was a white seal which was followed by a baby seal four months old. The white seal lived on the rocks of Rat Isle, lying off the south-eastern corner of the Island and the home of the black rat, extinct on the mainland. The black rats had come there centuries before on a pirate's ship.

The baby seal when born was white, but now its soft hairs were shed and its hide was grey. Its mother was an albino; she had pink eyes. She hunted usually with Jarrk the bull-seal, and when not hungry they played together for hours, hunting one another around bases of rocks and chasing each other's tails as they swished in bubbled circles that set long ribbons of weed waving and curling and little green crabs scuttling for shelter.

Now the white seal and her cub followed Jarrk into the tidal drift beyond the reef. It was the first time the cub had swum out to sea, the first time it had seen the flash of a salmon. It kicked its linked-flippers and stroked with its skin-flap arms as fast as it could.

They swam with common seals, blotched yellow-brown smaller creatures among the longer grey seals of the Island. Some had come from the coast of Lyonesse and Hercules Promontory, following runs of salmon which came in from the open sea and turned north, seeking their river estuaries.

A slow flicker, a dull gleam with thin strokes of light active beside it, made Jarrk and his mate and cub swim upwards to see what it was. The bull-seal came to rest on the top of his upward sweep with a backward curve that was most pleasurable; for seals, except when they are grown very old and near to death, take great delight in thrusting themselves through water for the upward quiescent glide. Water is not their true or original element: they are warm-blooded animals which ran about on land, and took to water, and which for hundreds of centuries have been acquiring sea-form. The young seal is frightened of water and perhaps would never swim were it not dragged there, moaning miserably, scruff held in mother's teeth, while father grunts in approval and solicitude as he bounces and flaps along beside his family. The little seal enjoys the water very soon, and the joy remains until the time for its final return to the cave of its birth; and there it grows cold like the boulders and skulls around it.

Jarrk swung up on a happy curve of strength, followed by the white seal and her cub. They were invisible to the great conger eel above them. The conger, whose name was Garbargee, was playing with a spring fish which was turning on its side and then on its back, recovering to swim erratically away, to falter, and sink again. A common seal had chopped the salmon as it darted down a submerged chasm of the reef and turned back from a second seal. The seal had torn away its ventral bite, the salmon had staggered away. The tide swept it from the Race. It tried to face the tide, but the nerves of its left lateral line were paralysed, it was weak from shock, and drowning. Garbargee the conger eel—who lived at the mouth of the Two Rivers estuary, his favourite pitch being the weedy chain of the Bar Bell Buoy—tasted the salmon's blood as he gulped water in breathing. Sinuating up the stream of tasty water, the conger came to the dying salmon and pulled a bite from its wound. Garbargee was not hungry, having gorged a small conger, four feet long and as thick as a strong man's arm, two hours before, when he had come upon it beside the corpse of a sea-cow which had drifted two thousand miles on the Gulf Stream since death.

Garbargee was a cannibal eel; he weighed over a hundred pounds. He had outgrown his fear of seals, although he still swam away when he smelled or saw one. There were two greyish scars across his back where once Jarrk, finding him in one of the rusty boilers of a warship sunken off the Island, had tried to chop him. The seal's jaws could not open wide enough, and the canine teeth had made two parallel lines in the eel's tough and slimy skin. Garbargee had bitten one of the flap-hands of the seal, and broken two of the prolonged finger-bones, which had healed, but set irregularly. Ever afterwards when swimming idly, for pleasure, Jarrk did not swim straight, but slightly in a curve, owing to the deformity.

Jarrk recognized Garbargee, and let out a bark. He often barked under water, usually when playing with the white seal or one of his mates or would-be mates. He roared both on top and under water when fighting and chasing another bull-seal, and the barking roar was visible by a gust of bubbles which he blew from his teeth and whiskers.

Garbargee felt the driving strokes of the seal's flippers coming nearer. He abandoned the salmon, and swam downwards. Jarrk reached the listless fish, caught it across the back, bit through its backbone, knew it was dead already, and swam down to the sea's bed to eat the fish. He chewed and swallowed for several minutes, during which time his heart-beats slowed to ten a minute, for his blood was rich in oxygen; after which he rose to the surface to breathe. As he swam down he saw a series of dull gleams in the darkness below, and recognized the conger eel.

Garbargee swam away with the salmon bite still in his mouth. He reached a cleft of rock, and lay there, holding himself still by his pectoral fins. His body was curved for an instant pro-pulsion, should the seal find him. With one eye he watched the forward area of water, with the other eye he stared upward.

One eye saw the quicksilvery form of Jarrk swimming at a downward slant, his bubble-whisker'd head searching from side to side; while the other eye watched the broken fish turning in an eddy of the current, head down.

Jarrk passed over and behind Garbargee, and out of sight. Garbargee lay still, his gills and mouth scarcely opening. A drove of wrass swam down with the current, glinting as first one fish then another turned on its side to take the smaller fish they were pursuing. A lobster walked over his back, but Garbargee did not move. The water-logged oar of a ship's boat came bumping and turning sideways over the rocks, grey streams of barnacles hanging along its length. It moved into the area of total reflection, opaque darkness beyond an angle of $22\frac{1}{2}°$ from the eel's eye. Then Garbargee saw with his right eye a small shape swim into his window or arc of vision, becoming a little seal which shone in streaks as it turned. Strings of bubbles from its nostrils ran over its head and wobbled upwards into the broken dull shiningness of the sea-surface.

Remembering this shape for a small seal, Garbargee slid forward over the rocks, moving with the tide. Strips of ribbon weed as long as himself, fixed to rock by thongs, were waving aslant the current. He swam through the shell-crusted ribs of a ship which had foundered there two centuries before, a French corsair sunken by the cannon of a British privateer. The wreck was another of the homes of Garbargee. Once, by holding his tail round one of the timbers, he had pulled out straight an eight-inch hook, baited with herring, which he had swallowed. The barb had pierced the maxillary bone of his left jaw. Two fishermen in a boat, pulling on the line, had fallen backwards, to haul in a straightened hook of soft steel a quarter of an inch in diameter, a piece of gristle wedged in its barb.

Garbargee swam slowly through the weedy ribs and, reaching the stem, turned into the tide to follow the little seal above. With open mouth the conger approached the cub, which, seeing him, departed as fast as flippers could drive it. Garbargee gave chase. The little seal plunged and twisted, but Garbargee followed every movement, snapping to grip it across the small of its back as it turned. Garbargee meant to catch the cub and take it down to the wreck, where he would tear out its life. But the white seal, its mother, searching for her cub, crossed the line of chase, and, seeing her, Garbargee swam down and slithered into impregnable holding under the wreck.

The white seal led the cub to the surface, uneasily turning down to swim under it, watchful for attack. Amidst the waves they lay, taking in air: then she leapt upon the cub, rolling over and clasping it between her flippers, nuzzling it and biting its head in joy and anger for the scare given her. The dark head of Jarrk looked up beside them, and they talked together, eyeing the moon and shaking drops from their whiskers, peering about with dim out-of-water sight. The shine of a salmon jumping sharpened three heads towards it. Before the splash was smoothed in the wave the heads had vanished.

Garbargee, lying behind the weed-streaming stem of the wreck, saw the shape of Salar reform in a surge of bubbles, and watched it moving away in sea-paleness to the east, towards the estuary, followed by ten smaller fish, led by Gralaks the grilse.

3

Now sometimes a fish fails to find the way to its parent river because it has lost the guiding currents of familiar fresh water, spreading root-like into the sea. When Salar came in from the Atlantic feeding banks the rivers of that coast were low, for little rain had fallen since the New Year. Owing to raids of seals he had left prematurely the meeting place of currents in the Island Race, and now he was travelling in a bay where the fresh-water layers gave no memory-pressures to his brain. He swam on without direction, followed by the school of young salmon which was making for the coast. The grilse were in familiar water, for here as smolts they had travelled during the year before.

Salar, disturbed by a current of colder water in which he had swum, turned across to avoid it. Gralaks, entering the cold current a few lengths behind the big salmon, half rolled and then thruddled up and leapt for joy. The other grilse did likewise. This was water of the Two Rivers, their mother stream, their home!

Salar cruised on slowly, alone. He rose to the surface and flopped out, falling back on his side, irritated by the sea-lice clinging to his skin behind the ventral fins and on the descending taper of his back. Each grilse falling back made a bubbled or seething hole, entering head first, with little splash: this was the joy leap; whereas Salar made the smacking splash of an aimless fish.

He swam on, having crossed the layer of colder, less dense water, and came to warmer salt again. Seeing a pollock above him, he curved up and while on his side gripped it across the back. But he was not hungry; his flesh was stored full of power; it was oozing in curd between his muscles. He expelled the pollack from his mouth, caught it up again head first, and then, after hesitation, closed his gill-covers and the expulsion of water pushed it out. He swam on slowly, a lost salmon.

After four hours he had swum east nearly twenty miles, and reached the first drifts of broken sea-shells on the sea's bed. The quality of light in the sea was changing, as it had changed in water throughout his life. White opaqueness of moon, with the particular glints and gleams it gave on fish and weed and wave-hollow, was being absorbed in a general greyness of the sea. The fish's window or conning area of visibility was becoming clearer, but part of his life was leaving him with the dimming of the moon. Colour was coming back into the sea with the daylight. He swam on without purpose.

He came into an area of strong coastal currents, and turned with them. They swept over jags of rocks faster than his slow cruising speed. This was the race over Dead Man's Reef. Had Salar chanced to stray here a few hours later or earlier he would have entered the current running north and gone with it along the rocky shore and past the Morte Stone and so to the Severn Sea, where he would have found the fresh-water guides to his parent river. Now a strong race was setting south, and not liking white or broken water, Salar turned into the tide, and swimming with it, he came to sandy shallows ribbed by the periodic sway and roll of waves. His nervous liquid-cells knew the rhythm of these waves; it was the same rhythm of the Severn Sea, the pulse of shallow Atlantic rollers at the full of the moon. He leapt through a wave, a gleaming impulse of joy. Through a shoal of very thin and small greenish fish he sped, amusing himself by sucking in some and expelling them from his mouth: a greeting, for as a smolt he had chased and fed upon the translucent gravel-sprats with their greenish dots of eyes. He drove through a shoal of bass feeding on the sprats, which were trying to escape their spine-backed enemies by darting down at the sand and burying themselves with a rapid wriggle. He scattered the bass, remembering how as a smolt he had been terrified by their large-mouthed hunger in the tideway.

So he came to shallow water where the rollers were rising sheer and top-creaming before assembling themselves for a final assault of the shore. Gulls were flying slowly up and down the white spreads of surf, turning on black wing tips and peering down with yellow-colourless eyes for living or dead food. Seeing the salmon leaping on the far side of a wave, the carrion feeders uttered cries as colourless and envious as their eyes.

Of birds, the herring gulls are the most selfish, all the harmony of their lives is in their flight. They never play; they search the edge of the sea and the land for themselves alone. They find peace at sunset. On spread wings, gliding, or flying slowly through the evening air in formation, calmly and in silence they return to their roosting ledges in cliffs, above the sea whose entire being is fretful. The gulls have risen from the land to find aerial beauty, while the sea grows more bitter-blind with the centuries.

Salar played through the green walls of the waves. Sea-trout sped through sand-stirring water before him, and flatfish lay still, their backs speckled as sand, invisible. The sea-trout had been born in the rivers, hatched out of eggs in gravel beside salmon eggs. Some were brown trout which by chance had descended to the estuary and assumed a silver coat; others had the salt-itch in them from the egg, offspring of a tribe which had sought sea-food for so long that now it was an instinct. The sea-trout roved in schools, living a merry life round the coast until the time came to return home for spawning. One of the biggest sea-trout of the Two Rivers was Trutta, the great spotted pug, who was to become the friend of Salar and Gralaks, in Denzil's Pool, and then in the water above Humpy Bridge, and later, in the pool called Fireplay.

The sun rose over the hills of the mainland and splashed its gold on the walls of the waves. Salar swam on, leaping several times in every mile, curving out of the water and curving back. This was the travel leap; he used the weight of falling back to drive him onwards. He must leap: shocks of energy passed through his body, stimulated by the pulses of creation passing through the water: memory-excitations of sand-stirring water, of light-play on corrugations of gravel. He was a smolt again, a sea-sprite.

The sudden appearance of this sea leaper startled a bird that was paddling aimlessly in the foamy back-drag of creaming wave-tops. It hastened seawards, paddling a score of times and then ceasing through weariness. The bird had thick waterproof plumage and a long sharp beak; a guillemot. Its head, neck, and back were dark brown; its breast, which should have been white, was also dark brown, in clotted streaks of featherlets. When it had been white-breasted the guillemot had enjoyed movement in air and water; now it was cold, weary unto death, the filaments of its feather were stuck together with oil-fuel waste cast overboard by a ship. The guillemot had swum up from its chase of fish into a floating mass of crude petroleum, and thereafter it flew no more; its skin was painful, winds and tides drifted it away from its parent island, it starved. Three years before it had nearly caught the little smolt Salar as he swam with his brethren in the strange currents of the Race; now Salar, leaping near it, shocked some of its remaining life from it. He swam on under the guillemot, seeing its two feet and air-glistening body mingled with the reflections of feet and body. Later the bird was thrown on the beach by the surge and dragged itself about until the shore-rats found it dying and feasted on it; soon it was water, air, sand, salt again.

Round the rocks a current was sweeping, and this Salar followed. He swam an oar's length from the base of cliffs strewn with submerged rocks on which limpets and other shell fish were creeping. Anemones were open, waving arm-rays to seize little fish and wandering shrimps. A fisherman standing on a flat rock above the sea and pulling up a lobster pot saw him jump out of the water and cursed with envy. Gulls were soaring and crying above the cliffs, for the fishermen had disturbed the nesting ledges whereon they were beginning to imagine their young. Seeing the salmon leap below, some of the cockbirds dropped down and flew to and fro over the water; for when bass showed there, they were feeding on surface shoals of smaller fish, and the gulls fed among them. The salmon resembled bass, although bass did not usually leap from the water.

Salar cruised on, jumping not so often, as his excitement at finding shallow water grew less. Stimulated by the vivid pulse of his blood, his parasites secured their holds between his scales and sucked that blood. He leapt and fell back on his side with a splash that set the gulls screaming in envious competition. A couple of hundred yards farther on he jumped and smacked down on the water again, this time on his other side. To the lice Salar was the earth, a benevolent and inanimate cosmos which yielded nourishment when cultivated and stimulated with chemical injections. Their earth supported them; they knew the pleasures of feeding and sleeping, and the greater joy of perilous love-seeking and satisfaction. For the search for love involved a slow crawl from scale to scale, while their earth was liable to flex into swift movement and the water strike them violently; their bodies were armoured. Salar carried seventeen sea-lice on his body. Most of them were females which had been successfully sought by the smaller males, since each of the females carried twin strings of eggs. Some male lice had lost their grip during the struggle for courtship, and had died of starvation near the Azores.

Salar came to another tide-race off the headland along whose length he had been cruising, and swam south with it. A common seal spied him by the reef called Bag Leap, but he sped away downtide, and feeling the lightness of a fresh-water stream which was moving inshore against the press of the tide, swam with it, keeping near the rocks of the south side of the headland. And cruising against the current he overtook a school of smaller fish which he knew by their shape and flexion. They were leaping and playing, led by Gralaks the grilse, for they were now in their mother-stream, water of the Two Rivers.

Wizzle the Chakchek, the peregrine falcon, saw the blue-grey shapes moving in the water as he cut his hard swift circles in the sky over the precipice of his eyrie. He saw the rocks under green water as dark blotches. His sight was stereoscopic, keenest of the sun. He could see pigeons flying above the town up the estuary twelve miles away in clear air.

The gift of sight is the sun's greatest gift to the world; it is only by the sense of sight that man clears himself; Truth is clarity, which is beauty.

The sun shone on falcon and fish, greensward and glint of rock; pride of the sun was in them. Chakchek saw the blue back of his mate shoot out of the cliff below, from the eyrie on Bone Ledge which gravely she had been meditating. It was the time of vernal equinox, light and dark were balanced, the sun's eye was to gaze longer every day: the solar stare was life. Seeing his mate Chakchek tipped up and fell over sideways in a dive upon her. She dived to get speed, then shot up in the wind pouring up the rock face, to meet him. They approached one another at a leisurely speed of a hundred and fifty miles an hour. They met and paused, the tiercel checked, the falcon fell; and together they dived to the water, flattening out and skimming a wave crest, and using the currents, eddies, rebuffets, and pillars of the wind, rose without pinion-throw a thousand feet and in the blast stayed, cutting darkly into the day.

They saw Kronk the raven watching them from the look-out scaur near his nest, where his mate was sitting on five eggs hugged between her thighs, her blood fevered with hope. They saw a cormorant paddling in the waves, watching them as it rested before tipping up and swimming down in pursuit of fish. They saw the blurred shape of the common seal swimming round the base of a rock; and, beyond the buoy marking the

sunken reef of Bag Leap, something which made them, in playful mood, slip off their wind ledge and fall to see what they
were—black lengths rolling up, spray-blowing, and rolling
under again. This was a herd of porpoises, led by Meerschwein
the old herring hog. The peregrines cut circles above the porpoises; the tiercel dived at Meerschwein in scornful play, rose
on the gusts of the south-west as though abruptly ending this
wind foolery, and turned and swept away north-east at a
hundred and ten miles an hour, followed by the falcon. Wizzle
wanted a pigeon from the oak-grown valley inland.

The porpoises were following a large school of salmon making
for the Two Rivers estuary. More than sixty fish were travelling
fast before the black glistening bottle-noses, which drove forward in two tiers, one layer or line diving below the other as it
rose to the surface to vent. When hunting, the porpoises
breathed thrice every sea-mile. The lower tier swam under the
salmon, gathering together again after a massed drive. Appearing suddenly from invisibility below, the porpoises scattered the
salmon in terror surface-wards, where they were pursued and
chopped by the upper tier.

Behind the herd of porpoises, travelling fast, was Orca
Gladiator, the grampus, the killer, blowing a jet of spray into
the air as it rose to breathe every quarter of a mile.

Salar, swimming easily with the grilse, was startled when a
hen-salmon bigger than himself thruddled past him, swung
round, and dived to the gravel below, where she remained with
her tail round a rock. He sped away forward, followed by the
grilse, and then sank to the gravel of a clearing, three fathoms
down, in order to see the enemy afar. One eye looked up and
forward, the other eye watched midwater and flank. Beside
and behind him lay the grilse, resting on gravel touched by
their ventral fins, their tails slightly curved, ready for instant
acceleration.

When other fish swam into sight Salar knew by the way they
dashed about what the enemy was. Meerschwein and the herd
of porpoises had harried Salar's shoal when they had been
herring-hunting. Aimless fear possessed Salar as it had the
grilse. They waited with curved tails. A glistening shape drove

forward bubble-shaking: and where the salmon had been resting gravel and shell-speck swirled thickly.

But as he was swimming under a ledge of rock in deeper water Salar came face to face with Orca Gladiator, who had just crushed a porpoise in its great teeth and swallowed the mid part of the body, leaving the head to float away on one side of its jaws, and the tail-flukes on the other. Orca was eighteen feet long and when it could get salmon to eat, it ignored other creatures, except occasionally to chop them in fun. The grampus had followed porpoises for some weeks, having come from the fogs of the Labrador coast, where the icebergs were drifting down from the Arctic Ocean. In those cold waters it had been one of a pack hunting whales, which they tore bit by bit, launching themselves at the leviathan of warm flesh, biting and tugging and worrying until each jawful was free.

Instantly Salar turned and shot away, but Orca was as quick, lunging forward under the salmon. Salar leapt thrice from the wide peg-toothed gape, each time nearly falling back into the jaws. He flickered and doubled, and scurried under an overhanging rock, and lay there with fast-beating heart, hidden by a fringe of bladder weed swaying gently in the tide. His head and body were in half darkness, and pressed against the rock worn concave by the scour of sand and water at low tide. Orca tried to get him, but the head of the grampus was big, round, and blunt: vainly it wallowed about the rock, shoving and blowing the sand. It rose through the waves and gave a loud snorting grunt and swam out to sea, at a tangent to the direction taken by the porpoises. About a mile from the rocks it turned and swam back slowly, swinging down to the base of the ledge where the body and tail of Salar were still moulded in fear against the rock. It came to the surface, grunting angrily, and swam down once more, to swim up and jump clear of the water, showing its black fluked tail and mackerel-like shape in a wide splash. It swam away fast, throwing itself over lines of waves it crossed diagonally in pursuit of the porpoises.

Half an hour later a fisherman in a small boat off the North Tail of the estuary of the Two Rivers watched seven 'erring 'ogs playing with a large clean-run springer not a hundred

223

yards from where he was fishing. The 'erring 'ogs, he told his companions later in the inn, lay roughly in a ring. First one would take the living fish in its mouth and throw it up: a second would catch it, toss it in the air, the others would roll up and bump it with their snouts. Once the fish got away, but was caught again under water, and the game continued nearer his boat. After a while the 'ogs tore a bite out of the fish. Then a master great 'og, four or five times as big as the others and big round as a tar-barrel, came up and they cleared like as if the devil was after them. When they had gone the fisherman tried to pick up the salmon, which was floating head down, on its back, white belly showing, but there was too much swell and broken water on the Tail. As the tide was beginning to flow strong, he hoisted sail and went home to the fishing village with the news of what he had seen. Other fishermen had seen the porpoises, too, and there was much swearing. The lawful season for nets was not yet begun, and here was the spring run of fish, no water in the rivers for them to go up, being protected by law for the sake of they bliddy 'errin' 'ogs.

Fishermen had been taking salmon in the estuary in nets at that time of year for scores of centuries before the Two Rivers Conservancy Board had made its by-laws.

4

An hour before midnight, in bright moonlight, a dozen crews of four men each, silently in rubber thighboots, went down to their salmon boats moored on the sandbank at the edge of the deep water of the fairway. "Let'n come," said one, truculently, with a glance up the estuary. All the fishermen felt an angry but subdued sense of injustice against water-bailiffs employed by the Board of Conservators. They believed that the laws were imposed only for the benefit of rich sportsmen; while they themselves were poor men with families to feed and clothe from what they got by fishing. The Board, they said, stops us fishing before the big fall run of fish, declaring they must run through to spawn; but the rod-and-line men aren't stopped for six weeks after the nets be off. Yet when the spring run begins, they stops us fishin' for to stock the rivers for the rich gentry's pleasure. So most of the fishermen ignored the limits of the season for net-fishing, and fished for salmon all the year through when the weather was favourable. During the close season they fished only at night, beginning two hours before low ebb, and continuing until the returning flow made the drag on the nets too heavy. The tide ebbed brightly; the water looked white, the shapes of boats going down were indiscernible. There was no wind. The night was in the moon's unreal power. Curlew and other wading birds were crying on sandbank and gravel ridge. In each boat two men pulled at the sweeps, a youth sat in the bows, the owner sat in the stern, where the net was piled.

An old man in the stern of one boat sat upright as light flicked on the starboard bow and was scattered in a loud splash. The oarsmen, dipping enough to keep way on the boat, looked over their left shoulders. Salar had leapt near the Pool buoy, at the tail of The String, where the ebbing waters of the Two Rivers met and bickered.

Salar had gone up with the estuary tide in daylight as far as Sunken Tree bend, where the salt water pressing against river water was so cold that he and the grilse had dropped back with the tide, avoiding fresh water and the plates of ice riding down with the river. The salmon's excitement arising from crammed power was chilled by the sleet water. Now in the Pool, below The String, with its irregular line of froth, many salmon were hovering head to stream, avoiding, sometimes playfully, the currents of cold water by rising or swimming sideways or drifting backwards before them, always nosing into the water-flow.

The Shrarshook Ridge, a gravel bank bound with mussels, grew longer and higher as the tide ebbed at five knots. The Pool buoy rolled with the weight of assaulting water, leaning ocean-wards on its iron chain which the salt never ceased to gnaw in darkness, sunlight, and the moon's opalescent glimmer. Ocean's blind purpose is to make all things sea; it understands nothing of the Spirit that moves in air and water.

On the shillets of the lower ridge known among fishermen as the Fat and the Lean, the keel-shoe of the salmon boat grated, the man in the bows sprang out and held the gunwale. The boat swung round to the shore, noisy with the water streaming against its length. When the other three men had clambered out, he shortened the anchor rope in the ring and carried the anchor a little way up the slope of the ridge, putting it down carefully lest the clank of metal be heard over the water. The tide was too strong for shooting a draught, and they waited there quietly, talking in low voices and sometimes standing silent to listen for sound of the water-bailiff's motor-boat.

Soon the boat was heeling over, and they shoved it down into the lapsing water. Splash! My Gor, that was a master fish, thirty pound by the noise of'n. Shall us shoot, feyther? Bide a bit, 'tes rinning too strong yet.

They waited. The youth struck a match to light a cigarette. Put'n out, I tell 'ee! Aw, I ban't afraid of no bliddy bailies. Nor be us, but us wants fish to-night, don't us? 'Tes no sense hadvertisin' us be yurr, be ut? Okay. American films were shown nightly in the converted shed called The Gaiety Theatre. The youth wished he had a machine-gun in the bows of the boat for the water-bailiffs.

Other boats were going down, gliding fast on the ebb and in silence but for the occasional squeak of sweeps in thole pins. A flight of shelduck went by overhead, wind sibilating in a wing where a quill had dropped. Far away down the estuary the piping and trilling of birds running and feeding by the wavelap line was changing to cries of alarm as the first boats reached their stances on shore and sandbank. Two sets of flashes beyond the hollow roar of the bar came from lighthouses north and south of the Island twenty miles away. There was no horizon to the earth, no shape or form to its objects, the moon's light was dead light.

Fish were dropping back with the tide, new schools were coming in over the bar, on whose pitted and shifting sandbanks the lines of waves plunged and broke with a roar, filling the shimmering hollow midnight.

In lessening tide the boat put out, leaving one man on the

ridge. He took a turn of the rope round back and shoulder, trod a firm stand, and gripped the rope in his hands, watching the boat drifting down and across and shedding net from stern as it glided into luminous obscurity. It was a flake of darkest shadow in the moon-dazzle on the water, and then was lost to sight. He braced himself and affirmed his footholds, to take the weight of water on rope and net which hung aslant in the tide, between head-rope buoyed with corks and heel-rope weighted with lead. The boat turned into the tide, and he leaned against the curved drag of the net with its two-inch mesh stipulated by Conservancy by-law for the escape of smolts.

He heard the noise of the boat touching uptide, the others clambering out, the clank of anchor, and one of his mates hastening to help him. Together they took strain on the rope and waited for their mates, who were trudging down to meet them with the other rope. The arc cast by the two hundred yards of net was now an elongated and narrowing bulge, which must be drawn in as quickly as possible before any fish enclosed by the netting walls found a way out by the space between ropes and the ends of the net.

They hauled slowly, steadily, hand under hand, leaning back against the scarcely yielding ropes, pulling against an area of water restrained by eight hundred thousand meshes. The two coconut fibre ropes came in four yards a minute. Each rope ended at a wooden stretcher, to which were tied the head-rope and the heel-rope. At every concerted tug on these less water was restrained, and the net came in not so dead. Now the skipper became more anxious, and ordered two of the crew to haul at the heel-rope to foreshorten the net under any fish which might be dashing about the enclosed water. The men at the heel-rope hauled rapidly, bending down, their hands near the gravel to keep the bottom of the net as low as possible. The seine, or purse net, came in swiftly, seeming to hiss in the water. There was nothing in the net.

The fishermen showed no disappointment. They had been wet in sea-labour since boyhood. The youth fetched the boat and they shook small crabs and seaweed from the net and re-piled it in the stern of the boat. After a few minutes' rest they shot another draught, and hauled in again, bending low as before when the seine came fast and easy near the top of the water, which was asplash and glinting: they lifted the seine and ran back a few paces, while the youth dropped on hands and knees, and gripping a fish by the wrist, his thumb by the tail-fin, lugged it out and struck vigorously the base of its head with a wooden thole pin. It ceased to slap the gravel, and lay still. He killed four other fish, three of them being grilse. A good draught! One twenty-pounder, another fifteen, and the others between five and six pound apiece.

The fish were flung in the well of the boat, and covered with sacks.

Two more draughts were shot, taking three more fish, one of them a lean brown kelt with fungus growing on tail-fin and jaw. They knocked the kelt on the head, and threw it into the water. The kelt had entered fresh water as a clean-run fish weighing eighteen pounds a year previously; it languished in the lower pools of the river all spring and summer, and travelled at the fall to the spawning redds under the moor. During the twelve months it had lived on its stored power; when taken in the net it weighed under ten pounds. A few of the older fisher-men killed kelts because it was a Conservancy law that kelts, or unclean fish, must be returned to the sea. One or two very old fishermen remained in the village who refused to believe that a kelt could mend itself in salt water, and return again the following season as a clean fish. They said it was another lie of the Board to take away the living of poor men. The hard times in which these old fellows had been schooled were passed away, but their effect would remain throughout the rest of their lives.

After a pause of slackwater, the tide began to flow, and with the flow came Salar and the school of grilse led by Gralaks, forerunners of larger schools to arrive from the feeding banks in later spring.

Salar and the eight grilse swam a little ahead of the flow, to breathe and control the current. Suddenly alarmed by a fearful apparition, Salar shot up and across, breaking the water with a bulging splash and a glittering ream or travelling wavelet. Gralaks also leapt, and the watchers saw the arrowy glints of their reaming. They saw too a broader, slower flash, and thought this to be the roll of an immense fish. The boat was already afloat, the rowers waiting at the sweeps, the fourth man holding the post-staff. Immediately the boat put out, the rowers bending the sweeps with full strength across the tide, then with it, and back across: they shipped sweeps and ran ashore: the skipper threw out the anchor and hastened to help the fourth man. They heard and saw splashing, and imagined a great haul, bigger than the record of seventeen fish a few years before. As they hauled he exhorted the heel-rope men in a voice hoarsely earnest to pull faster, and together. Although only half the net was in, they could feel the jags on the walls as fish struck them trying to escape.

Then a shout from the direction of the Pool told them of danger: the water-bailiffs had landed on the ridge. The fishermen did not fear being fined if caught and convicted: they dreaded confiscation and destruction of their net, and their licence for the season, soon to open, not being renewed.

Glancing over his left shoulder, the skipper saw several moving spots of light from electric torches, and realized the bailies were there in force. He knew they could not search without a warrant, and he could plead he was rough-fish-catching; but if the bailies arrived while they were giving salmon a dapp on the head, they would have all the proof needed. Gladly he heard the sound of raised voices upalong, and hoarsely exhorted the others to get the seine in, and away. He began to speak rapidly to himself, wife and children needing food and covering, one law for the rich another for the poor but if they bailies comed near they'd find what they wasn't looking for. An extraordinary plunging and beating of the water inside the distorted horseshoe of corks made him pause in his mental tirade, and haul the stronger on his rope. He realized something other than fish was in the seine; the tugging plunges against the net made him anxious lest it be broken.

The shouts from the upper end of the ridge had ceased; the water-bailiffs, having come upon a boat with net piled for a draught, were moving down, hoping to find one in the act of taking salmon.

'Errin' 'ogs, cried the skipper, with a roar of disgust. Fetch the boat, he ordered his son. Seven porpoises were clashing and threshing about in the seine. Gralaks was there, too, her sides and shoulders scored criss-cross where she had driven against the net and broken her scales. Quick, into the boat, cried the skipper, shouting as a spot of approaching light wavered and dazzled his eyes an instant. Holding the head-rope, he shoved off and scrambled aboard. Pull like something, he cried, taking a turn with the head-rope round a thwart, and hauling over the stern. The skipper did not swear—he was Chapel through and through, as he occasionally informed those who did. Several torchlights were flashing as the water-bailiffs hastened over the gravel bank, wary of falling into pits left by the barges digging gravel. Make'n spark, cried the skipper, and the rowers grunted with their efforts. Then, seeing that the net was safe, the skipper bellowed indignantly, Why don't you chaps stop they witherin' 'errin' 'ogs, can you answer me that, tho'?

The youth wanted to leave the net trailing in the water, to taunt the bailies into giving chase, and then clog the screw of their motor-boat with the mesh. Tidden no sense, grunted his father, who was in shape not dissimilar from the shape of a herring hog. Besides the tide be flowin', if 'twere ebbin', might be some use, 'twould serve the bailies right to be drov' out to sea and wrecked.

The net was taken aboard, with one small porpoise, which was soon battered to death, and the boat made for the sand-bank below the sea-wall of the village.

There they were met by the skipper's wife, who whispered in a voice deep and hoarse that two bailies with a policeman were waiting by the slip, up which they must walk to get home. They witherin' bailies, they deserve to get their boat rammed and zunk below 'em, declared the skipper, in great disgust.

The salmon were taken from under the sack. While the two hands and the youth lit cigarettes at a discreet distance, the skipper's wife removed a wide black skirt much speckled with dried fish-scales. Rapidly the skipper threaded a stout cord through gill and mouth of each salmon. The cord was then tied round the wife's waist, after which the skirt, by a feat of balancing made more difficult on the wet and infirm sand, was put on and fastened. Having anchor'd the boat, and carrying the oars, the crew went slowly towards the slip leading to the quay.

"What have you got in that bag?" one of the waiting water-bailiffs demanded, pointing to the bulging sack on the skipper's shoulder.

"My own property," replied the skipper.

"Of what nature?"

"'Og."

"I don't want no sauce," threatened the bailiff. "I have a constable here. What's in that sack?"

"'Og, I tell 'ee."

"Turn it out."

"You can't make me. Where's your search warrant?"

"I know what you've got. You're caught this time. Do you want me to go to a magistrate and get a warrant, when you'll lose your renewal of licence. I'll ask you once more, what have you got in that sack?"

"'Og, I tells 'ee. For a bailie's breakfast, if you likes."

"Turn it out."

"If you promises to fry it for to-morrow's breakfast."

"I promise nothing."

"Why don't you try and search me?" screeched the old woman, amidst laughter.

"For the last time I ask you, will you turn out that bag?" shouted the water-bailiff. "Or shall I give you in charge?"

"Aw, don't 'ee vex yourself so," said the skipper, in a gentle voice. "Here's an Easter egg for 'ee," and he dropped the heavy weight, and tugged the sack from the blubbery mass.

"It's yours, Nosey Parker," yelled the fishwife, as she staggered away, holding the arm of her husband and laughing stridently.

The curlews made their spring-trilling cries over the water flowing fast up the estuary. Soon the birds would be flying to the high moor for nesting.

Salar swam up with the tide, alone. Within and around and

making the muscle-cluster of his body were fats and albuminous matter sufficient for five hundred and seventy ascents of the river, without restoration by feeding, from its mouth in the sea to its source on the moor. The moon declined to the west, and the estuary was silent.

5

Again Salar went up to the tide-head, again he shifted back with the ebb to avoid cold streams of fresh water. Ice held earth and water while the moon wore away to a dark shell of itself. Salmon waited for warmer water, birds for warmer air, flowers for warmer earth. Spring was held down by frost.

Salar knew now the meaning of a net, and he avoided those places in the estuary where a strange enemy dropped slowly down the water, behind a more fearsome enemy, in shape between bird and seal, which moved with dip of wings or flippers along the surface. Whenever he saw a boat he sped away down the current, seeking a depth of pit or hole from which he watched while resting on the bottom.

As the moon's light grew less, so the tides moved more slowly up the estuary, and with a diminishing press of water. More salmon came over the bar on every flowing tide, with big spotted sea-trout which fed on smaller sea-trout and other fish as they roved the channels between sandbanks and the worm-cast mud of ruined saltings.

Salar became way-wise in the estuary. He returned no more with the ebb to the sandy shallows by the bar, but remained with other fish in the agitation and noise of the two tides meeting above the Pool—for the estuary of one river lay north, the other lay south, and their returning ebbs were in opposition, causing that irregular movement of froth where the tides clashed and jittered, called The String.

At half-tide Salar idled under The String, swung about in eddies and swirls, rising and dipping on trends of the shifting and myriad-varying tide-force. There also schools of bass waited, watching for gravel-sprats, and small fish tumbled down in the twisting and uncertain currents. Other salmon, some marked by nets, waited on the bed of the Pool, cached in neutral water-pockets before juts of rock or boulders. They were uneasy, unspirited, watchful for danger.

A boat sailed slowly up The String, in it a fisherman holding tiller tucked between elbow and side. He held a line in his hand. In his other hand he held a rope, attached to a sail shaking in the wind abeam. On the submerged line was a lead weight, below it a length of catgut, and at the end of the gut was a hook half concealed by an artificial worm of red rubber. A nickel spinner just above the shank of the hook made a bright blur in the water, behind which the worm wriggled. The line slanted in the tide.

Salar did not see the boat until it was nearly over him, then he sped up against the current, turned and went down to the bed of the Pool, to lie behind other salmon whose heads, fins, and flanks had been hurt in escape from nets.

He saw the boat, which was tarred below the water-line, changing in shape and colour as it moved slowly forward. From a scattered blur it assembled into a sharp nose which drew after it splashes and flashes of light amidst its broken surface image. When it was directly overhead it was dark and defined in a skin of slipping light, dreaded porpoise shape. Salar saw the line slanting in the water, light running thinly up and down its length. When the boat had passed out of his inverted cone of vision, he watched the line and saw the artificial bait as something which made him alert and wary.

The fisherman was spinning for bass, which with every flow came over the bar in schools, feeding eagerly on rag-worms, gravel-sprats, shrimps, and small fish. Returning on the ebb, the spiny fish ranged themselves in The String and waited there energetically for food to wriggle into their big mouths.

While Salar was watching the lure, something was watching Salar. This was an enemy he had never seen in his life before —Petromyzon the Stone-sucker. The Greeks were kind when they gave its family that name. Petromyzon was a relative of the Hag-fishes, creatures with a low organization of skeleton.

Petromyzon was like an eel, or a worm, a huge torpid worm. Its body resembled the artificial rubber thing escaped from the fisherman's hook, magnified, discoloured, sunk in living sloven-liness, animated waste-product of the spirit of life. Petromyzon had a scaleless body and a sucker mouth thorny with teeth for rasping off scales and flesh and drawing the blood of fishes. It had no jaws or ribs. It had no real bone in its body. It drew breathing-life through seven-a-side branchial openings instead of gills. It had a single nostril at the top of its head. Now, stuck to a stone on which grew bladder weed hiding its head, Petro-myzon was waiting to sneak up on Salar and clamp itself to the richness of his body.

It clung to the stone, moving its tongue backwards and for-wards for suction. Salar lay behind another stone half an oar's length in front of Petromyzon. The bed of the Pool under the meeting tides was quiet at three-quarter ebb. Above Salar loose weed and small fish, after being swung and swirled in the tidal bicker, were moving fast in the confluent westerly cur-rents; but in the hollow of the Pool's bed there was an area of quiet. On stones and sodden carbonizing trunks and roots of trees, washed out of river-banks in old floods, and now half-buried in gravel, the seaweed lifted in lightly rising water; the salmon resting there were on the point of lifting, their air-bladders repressed to resist the upward trend. On the eastern edge of the Pool, however, the water of the backwash was moving in an opposite direction to the tide; and here fish were facing down the estuary. In one place, by the rusty stock of an old iron-and-wood anchor, Gralaks the grilse was hovering be-tween two layers of water moving at different rates, and facing north; while a large spotted sea-trout less than a fathom below the grilse was facing south. These fish were using the vagaries of the currents to maintain them with the least effort.

Salar lay where the moving fronds of weed stroked the azure-white skin of his belly. Within his body, and under the fore-part of his backbone, was a cavity or air-bladder which auto-matically adjusted itself to the lift of the water: thus he was able to continue floating a few inches above the stone, for the pleasing sensation of being touched by the seaweed.

Every moment the pockets and eddies of the tide were changing with the altering set of currents. Automatically the salmon shifted with them. The two fish by the old anchor moved away as a gravel ridgelet which had been piling up beside the anchor was suddenly scoured by a flume of water that straightened out the eddy; small stones, sand, and broken shells whirled away. A ruinous wickerwork crab-pot was uncovered, the ridgelet's foundation. As the water cut away the gravel, so the wickerwork leaned and loosened, to lurch away over the stones and come slowly to rest on the bed of the Pool between Salar and Petromyzon.

Petromyzon loosened its ringed mouth on the stone, and slithered towards the broken crab-pot, while Salar continued to buoy himself over the waving fronds of seaweed.

A flexible submarine, marbled mud, moved through a hole in the crab-pot, fourteen streams of water moving in and out of its gill-clefts. The thick soft lips of the sucker mouth began to work over the thorn-like teeth. The expressionless eyes were fixed on the salmon's flank. Slowly it moved through the crab-pot. Having no swimming bladder, it could only rise in water by muscular exertion; it quivered, seeming to shorten and thicken, and launched itself at Salar, rearing its head to strike at the scaled side; and instantly clamped itself there.

Salar's acceleration up the Pool, his turn and zigzagging dash down the tide made other salmon leave their resting places and sink together to the bottom, whence they could observe the widest area of water above them. In fear Salar leapt out of the water, causing the boatman holding the line with the red rubber bait to sit upright and puff rapidly at his cold pipe. 'Twas the largest Zeven-Ole I ivver zeed tackle a zalmon, he told them later in the *Royal George*.

Salar could not shake off Petromyzon. The lamprey's mouth was stuck firmly to his left side below the medial line of nerves, forward of the ventral fins. Indifferent to the salmon's slipping and turning rushes, to his rolling staggers as he changed from one tide-pressure to another, Petromyzon sucked the scales closer to his teeth, and began to rasp away and swallow skin and curd and flesh. He drew blood, and fed contentedly.

Salar rested on the bed of the Pool, gulping water irregularly, for his fast-beating heart. In front of him the iron links of the Pool buoy chain turned and returned slowly as the buoy above wallowed twisting in the combined weights of two tides. He could see the movements of the hind part of his enemy's body as Petromyzon allowed itself to be borne on moving water, holding securely with its mouth. Starting forward with pain, Salar rolled and tried to scrape off the lamprey against a stone. Although the salmon weighed twenty pounds, his weight in water varied with his speed of movement: he weighed nothing when motionless: so Petromyzon continued to feed with only slight disturbance. Suddenly frenzied by the feeling of lost freedom, Salar swam up to the surface and leapt with all his strength, deliberately to fall back on his side and knock away his enemy. Petromyzon, accustomed since earliest life to irregular motion when attached to its hosts, most of which were quitted only when they died, endured the buffeting and sucked the harder.

After slackwater, and the returning flow, Salar became accustomed to the lamprey. The pain had gone, and he had no more fear of it. Petromyzon was a hindrance, something to be gotten rid of by leaping and by scraping against stones. He was used to the extra drag, to the queerness of moving aslant when he meant to swim straight. In the tide's swilling murkiness he drifted, past lessening sandbanks and muddy glidders, a large quiet fish, as though unseeing among smaller coarse fish feeding eagerly. He moved slowly through the water, scarcely overtaking clusters of seaweed loose in the tide. Under the harmless looming length flatfish flapped along the bottom, feeding squint-eyed amidst racing gravel and sand and the twirling of black oak-leaves.

Off the shingle tongue of Crow, the channel deepened and the tide raced narrow. Salar swam on slowly through the tide, hardly moving. The dark hull of an anchor'd barge loomed noisily before him. He was accustomed now to the shape of large boats. The barge had been taking gravel aboard during low tide, and the crew were awaiting deeper water before sailing up the fairway to the quays of the port. The exhaust of the ship's kerosene engine thudded hollowly, issuing black smoke. Salar felt the thuds in the water as the hull appeared to race over him.

Other salmon were moving up in the tide. Among them was Gralaks the grilse. The large sea-trout which had been hovering behind the wood-and-iron anchor was swimming below her. This was Trutta. He had spawned seven times in his native stream; during seven springs and summers he had escaped death by net, gaff, hook, wire, poison, bomb, otter, seal, porpoise, heron, lamprey, and disease. On each of Trutta's scales was his life-history engraved. His scales, like those of salmon and most other fish, were irregularly circular, resembling the cut section of a tree's trunk. Just as a tree's life or growth can be read by the rings, so does the scale of a fish tell its age. A scale of an old sea-trout, or pug as fishermen of the Two Rivers called it, seen under a microscope showed the growth of its first two years of river-life in the small inner rings, with two slight corrosions for the two winters, when food was scarce and its growth was delayed. Thereafter its spawning revisits were indicated by wider corroded rings.

The young sea-trout smolt went down to the sea as the Pleiades were rising in the night sky, and when it returned at full summer, three months later, it had doubled its size. It was then called a peal. The widening rings on its scales showed this sudden increase. During its stay in fresh water the little peal fed on flies and other food, except when it was spawning, but it did not grow any bigger, and when it dropped down to the estuary again in February, the outer edge of its scales were corroded. Sea-feeding soon made it plump, the scales grew to cover that plumpness, and in the following summer it returned once more to its parent stream, there to disport itself with other peal, and amuse itself by taking flies and small fish while waiting for the joys of spawning.

After seven returns to his river Trutta the sea-trout was old and cunning, a thick-headed pug, spotted heavily on gill-cover and flank. His tail-fin was convex, the outer edges worn away. He weighed fourteen pounds. On each scale were seven corrosions, spawning marks, among the wavy rings of easy seagrowth. He was a cannibal, like all his family.

The gleaming grace of Gralaks had first attracted Trutta by the anchor, since when he had followed her. Trutta was scarred thrice by the teeth of lampreys. When in the mudbanks of the middle estuary he saw the tails of small river lampreys waving in the current as they bored in search of rag-worms, he tore them out and champed them and swallowed them. He had a jaw like a pike's jaw and three staggered rows of teeth in the vomer ridge or palate of his mouth. Between these teeth and the curved teeth on his tongue he could grind the flesh from the bones of a peal weighing two pounds without working his jaws.

Higher up the estuary swam Salar, quiet among a drove of bass turning on their sides amidst seaweed, crabs, flatfish, and bubbles streaming from mud-holes of cockles and rag-worms. The tide took him past the wreckage of an abandoned salmon-trap, broken weed-grown hurdles silted in sand around a lagoon, where salmon sometimes rested awhile when returning on the ebb. Old Nog was perched on a black oak post, peering low for fish. Three swans were paddling in the back-wash by the shore, moving down the estuary, while a flock of shelduck bobbed rapidly past on the ribbon-froth of the central current.

The tide poured into a deep pool with a rocky bottom and here the current divided, to flow up a creek which was the mouth of a small river. There was no sand or mud on the bottom because every ebb-tide returning down the Pill swirled against the main fairway ebb, stirring the silt deposited on the river-bed by the previous tide's flow. Mussels grew in clusters on the rock of the pool's bed.

A small boat was riding at anchor in the pool. In it was the fisherman who had seen Meerschwein and the other porpoises play with a salmon off the North Tail a fortnight previously. The fisherman had come to visit his lines put down a few hours before. As Salar approached the boat the fisherman was pulling in one line, with its two score of hooks. Flatfish, pollack, and bass were hooked. One of the bass was but a loose bag of skin and bones attached to a head.

This was the work of Myxine, the glutinous hag of the Two Rivers. The hag was a relation of Petromyzon, but one which lampreys avoided. Myxine's eyes were sunk beneath her skin, deep in the muscles of her head. They were without lenses. Myxine did not need sight, for much of the hag's life was spent within the bodies of fishes. While the bass had been struggling on a hook of the night-line, Myxine had fastened to it and bored a way inside, eating steadily hour after hour until, gorged, she lay at rest in a bag of bones and water. The water poured out as the fisherman lifted it up, and the hag's head, with whisker-like barbels, looked out of the bass's mouth.

The fisherman had never seen such a horrid sight before. With a religious exclamation he dropped it in the boat, and Myxine slithered out of the hollow corpse. He picked the hag up to knock it on the gunwale, but was horrified to find that it was turning itself into a length of slime in his hand.

"Ah, git out, you bissley bigger (beastly beggar), you," muttered the fisherman, shaking the long hair grown to hide his ear-stumps—which had been frozen off during a blizzard aboard a whaler in his youth—as he flung the glutinous hag into the sea.

Myxine swam down to the bed of the pool, and rested there. The act of exuding slime from the thread-cells along her body was additionally exhausting, and the hag lay still, unseen by Salar as he moved slowly in the wedge of tranquil water at the division of currents. Petromyzon waved indolently at his side. Salar had no desire to go up with the tide. His bounding sea-vitality had shrunk within him through fear and the draining wound in his flank. He lay inert on a rock. Half his length away lay Myxine.

The hag saw the waving tail of Petromyzon, and the sight made her teeth work. She got under the lamprey's tail, and fastened her sucker there. Petromyzon lashed, but the hag stuck. In fear Salar started forward. By the time he had reached the sunken lime-kiln by the bend of the sea-wall, half a mile away, Myxine's head was inside Petromyzon's belly.

Salar waited in an eddy beside the rounded broken wall of the kiln, until the rising tide swept through the eddy, and he went on, feeling strangely light.

By the Long Bridge of the port three miles distant he leapt, and a boy on the quay saw what looked like a red poppy on the silver flank. Less than three months later, all of Petromyzon was mud again.

239

6

In the night the wind went round from the north to the west and in the morning ice on the saltings and tide-fringes had lost its clarity. Larks sang over the marsh where sheep and ponies no longer grazed tails to wind. A wild bumblebee went humming happily over the wet salt grass. The curlews, whose bubble-link and trilling cries at night arose and fell with the tides, flew away over the hills to the moor, where their cries became more tender. Fishermen in the estuary village hung their nets out on walls and lines between crazy posts of old ships' timbers, looking over the meshes and talking of the seals which were in the estuary.

For Jarrk had come over the bar, as he did every year when the legal net-fishing season was about to open. As the day approached, so the attitude of those men who had been illegally fishing began to change. Why didn't the Board of Conservators see to it that they seals was shot, an old fisherman grumbled. Weren't they poor men trying to earn a living by catching salmon which were scarce enough already, without allowing they bliddy seals and errinogs to come in and drive the fish out to open sea again? Didn't each net owner have to pay five pound a year licence money, to pay the bailies' wages, and what did the bailies do for to earn those wages? Nought but try to stop poor men from getting a few greenbacks in the winter, so that their kids shouldn't rin about the streets bare-foot and hungry. If the bailies went out after errinogs and seals they'd save more fish than were took out of season by half a dozen nets. But the Board was there to look after the interests of the rich man's pleasure of whipping water upalong with rod and line, being allowed to fish a month before the net season opened, and six weeks after it had closed; one law for the rich and another law for the poor, aiy, that's it. The younger fishermen did not grumble; they knew more than the old chaps; they stood against walls, relaxing happily in the spring sunshine.

One or two very old fishermen, wearers of ancient cracked leather sea-boots, did not believe that salmon spawned in fresh water, saying it was a yarn put about by the Board to get fish up for the rod-and-line men. Over their pints they argued that years agone there were lots of fish, but the numbers began to fall off as soon as the barges began digging away the gravel of the Shrarshook. That proved, they declared, that salmon laid their eggs under the Shrarshook. The grandfathers would not hear any argument about it: the 'poor man's right of fishing in the fall, when the big run began, had been stole away by the rich man.'

The Board had been formed, and given power to make its own by-laws for the preservation of salmon, when these old fishermen had been boys. Then no water-bailiff had dared venture in the village, nor near the Shrarshook at night. Even recently there had been trouble: nine years before, when Trutta the sea-trout was born, the water-bailiffs' boat had been rammed in the Pool one dark night, an attempt to drown them.

Soft spring had come, but still the rivers were low, no water for the fish to ascend. Salar had found the school of grilse again, and with Gralaks and Trutta and other fish went up and down on every tide. The rivers were low and clear, cold with ice and sleet water, the sea was warmer. But every day the river water was growing less cold. Then the seal came in again.

Up the estuary blew the west wind, soft and gracious after the weeks of those winds veering from the north star and twilit polar regions: the hard dryness of north-east, the aerial ice of the north, the brutal shaking gales out of the north-west with its slate-quarry clouds quelling all spirit save in falcons cutting with sharp wings into the blasts. Now the west wind rolled waves in the fairway without tearing their tops; the west wind was a light wind, lifting from air and earth and water the heaviness of winter. The life of the elements was relieved.

Salar leapt through the waves in the bay with hundreds of other salmon playing in release. Few fish were in the estuary. Having scattered the schools, Jarrk returned to the Island Race, where every tide streamed with new silver.

The seal came back behind a school of forty-seven fish which had missed their way home to a Scottish river owing to an irregular set of the Gulf Stream in the Atlantic Ocean. These fish were small-headed, thick-shouldered, their flesh was redder than fish of the Two Rivers; on the way back they had fed on prawns inhabiting a rock shelf off the Scillies. By chance their forebears had discovered prawns in this place before the glacial caps dissolved on the mountain slopes above their native river; and to the island shelf their ancestral spirit led them on every home-coming.

Exploring the fresh currents in the bay, the agile fish of Tay came into the estuary of the Two Rivers. Jarrk chased one into a lagoon by the South Tail, and ate it lying on a sandbank while the first waves of the flowing tide scoured the sand from under him. The seal was seen by the crew of a boat, and shouted at, but he went on eating, head, shoulders, tail of the fish held in flippers. He ate the eleven-pounder and then launched himself with a flapping jump into the tide-race cutting away the sandbank.

It was the first day of April, and in the estuary and higher salt-water reaches of the Two Rivers the licensed nets were about to shoot their first official draughts of the year. From now until the end of August, the passage of salmon and sea-trout to their rivers would be barred in narrow fairway and streaming shallow by thirty-six nets each eighty fathoms long. Two hours before low tide, during slackwater, and two hours of the new tide, by day and by night, with a close-time from noon Saturday until noon Monday, one or another of thirty-six nets was liable to encircle them.

Jarrk the seal had fished in the estuary of the Two Rivers for more than a dozen years. His serious fishing began with the net season. He knew the voices of many of the fishermen. They had shouted at him often. One boat carried a rifle, and Jarrk knew that boat, recognizing the figure which ran to the boat before he heard the crack and water-thud of the bullet sometimes rising away into the air over his head and piping like a strange bird.

The rifle had been presented to the Board by a sympathizing

sportsman and given to the skipper of a crew who claimed
to be a skilled marksman. After three years of proximity with
salt water, the rifling of its barrel, when examined casually, resembled a railway tunnel blasted through igneous rock.
Having fired more than a hundred bullets at the seal, the marksman was wont to remark that the animal dived at the flash.
Actually Jarrk, having been scared by the first few water-
thuds and occasional ricochets, had ceased to dive from something which was harmless to him.

The seal used to wait until a draught was shot and then
swim under the heel-rope weighted with leads and cruise along
the bend of netting until he saw a fish. He would remain on
the bottom until the arc was short, and the fish dashed about
in a small space: then he would swim up and seize it, usually
as it tried to turn back between the net and himself. "He picks
up fish like a Christian," and "He'll take salmon for a pastime," and "He's a masterpiece for taking fish," the fishermen
said. Having caught his fish, the seal lifted up the net and swam
away, rising about a hundred yards from the shore and eating
it as he lay in the water.

Jarrk went from net to net for his sport. He never entered a
net until both post-staffs were drawn ashore. At first he had
entered as soon as the fishermen were ashore, and then the
fish, dashing in terror along the dark brown web, had escaped
inshore where only the rope was striking the surface of the
water. So Jarrk, intelligent and percipient—with subtlety of
mind developed and widened in every generation since his
ancestors, land beasts, had taken to water where were few
natural enemies—quickly learned to wait until a net was closed
before swimming under it.

The seal came into the estuary for other things besides the
sport of hunting salmon. Sometimes at night he lay on the
shingle tongue of Crow, listening to the sounds of singing,
and concertina music, which came, distinct and clear, over
the Pool when the tide was in and no wind blowing. Once he
was observed swimming after a small blue dinghy, on which
a portable gramophone was playing a record of dance music.
He had come within twenty yards, while an argent fire of

phosphorescence played behind the slight wash of the boat at anchor.

The tide was making fast, the first tide of the season. Between Shrarshook and Crow shingle-spit were rocky pools through which the sea pressed, swelling and overpouring onwards with many noises which together made a vast sea whisper. Boats at the estuary mouth seen from the Shrarshook were tiny and far away, the crews waiting by them fragmentary black specks, sand-dissolved, moving with puny imperceptibility against a background of breakers white-crinkled under a pale blue immensity of sky.

On the crest of the Shrarshook a few year-old herring gulls which had not mated were chipping off mussels from the blue clusters there, flying up, and dropping them to crack the shells. Two boat crews waited and rested below at the tide-line, a third was rowing with the current, shedding black net behind it.

Gurgling and wallowing, the Pool buoy lay in the fast water, a great rusty-red sea-top spinning on its chain.

A shout, for the rope-man on shore had seen the ream of a fish within the semi-circle of corks. Sweeps were bent as two backs straightened, rubber-booted feet braced on thwarts. Another back-fin cut the water. Tide took the boat, white above water-line and tarred beneath, licence number painted on bows, aslant its inshore direction. Iron keel-shoe grated, crew leapt out, first man flung out anchor, second man ran to help rope-man. The two couples took slow strain on the almost immovable ropes.

The skipper said, "'Tes the seven year glut." Every seventh year spring fish was plentiful. For thousands of years it had been known in the estuary village. Recently, since a century or so, hydrographers had spoken of a nine-year cycle when ocean-currents tended to set inshore. Nine years, said the scientists; seven, said the fishermen. It is the seventh wave that drowns a man, said the deep-water sailors, mast-and-yards men; and it is the seventh son of a seventh son who has power to charm salmon inshore, and he keeps his power so long as he never kills a fish, said the old women.

244

The fishermen hauled steadily. The tide sag-bellied the net. Water ran up and over the leaning Pool buoy. A boat which a few minutes before had been down on the South Tail moved fast up the fairway, rowed in silence over the line of corks. The skipper in the stern carried a rifle importantly across his knees. The boat was going a mile upriver, to a draught opposite the Pill, where Myxine the glutinous hag had hollowed out Petromyzon.

The boat turned north out of The String, and glided swiftly out of sight below the stones and mussel-clusters of the Shrarshook.

After ten minutes the twin twenty-five fathom lengths of net, called arms, were hauled in. Remained the thirty fathom length, mid-piece, called bunt. The bunt was deeper than the arms and the meshes were smaller. Within the bunt fish were moving—the water was a-ream, uneven with bulging rises. "'Tes the zeven year glut," said the skipper. The net came easier. Wet black folds fell on the boots of the four men. Small green crabs hung on the net, menacing insignificant pincers; they fell, and were covered, struggling against new layers dropping on them. Watching, the men saw a dark brown glistening back arise and roll under. The skipper swore. A bulge of water rose and was swirled away with the tide. Faster and easier came the last of the net. They watched intently, grouped together, heel-rope men kneeling. Thresh of water, flicker, tug, boil. "Back 'er comes, boys! Steady, don't drag the seine." Never had they seen so many fish in a single draught. The netted water bubbled and splashed and shimmered.

One by one the deep-shouldered fish were lugged out by the tail, held down on net pile, and thumped on skull-base with an oaken thole-pin fetched from the boat. The skipper would never kill a fish with his own hands. He was a seventh son. He felt a calm elation. At last he was rewarded. He went for a short stroll by himself. Twenty-three fish in one draught. It was a record for the Two Rivers.

Near the Pool buoy, pulsing paired hind-flippers leisurely against the tide, Jarrk lay and chewed the twenty-fourth fish. Having eaten all he wanted, the seal sank away and drifted over the bed of the Pool, turning into the north-flowing river and rising to breathe as he passed the deep shelving slope of Crow.

Soon he came to the Creek Pool, and, bobbing up, saw a boat being rowed towards him. At the familiar sound of *Zeal!* he tipped up and swam down to the bottom, amusing himself by lying there and letting the tide take him among flatfish and crabs. He was bumping along slowly from stone to stone, the tide swilling by him with its marine litter, when Trutta the sea-trout, followed by Gralaks and six grilse, and Salar behind them, swam peacefully over him.

As Jarrk lunged upwards, the fish flashed away inshore, and so came within the hanging net. Jarrk followed them. They sank to the muddy-sand bottom, to hide. Jarrk cruised round the net, and seeing them within, rose to the surface and waited.

Seeing his blunt whiskered head by the corks, the skipper ran to the boat for the rifle, which was lying with its muzzle in the bilge. Jarrk watched while the rifle was loaded and aimed, expecting what happened: a cracking thud in the water near him, a report that raised gulls and wading birds from tidemarks far up and down the estuary; and nothing else. The seal was used to swimming down when the rifle was fired, and so he rolled under, and the marksman said this time he had hit the limmer. Some 'opes, replied his mates, watching the water as they lay back, boots sinking in wet sand, while the third man flacked the rope on the water in vain hope of scaring the seal away.

They hauled hand under hand, watching. They saw the water cut by a back-fin. Trutta, having seen Jarrk behind the net, skidded, and fled. They saw the ream of another fish, and another; a boil and jabble on the surface. Salar, Gralaks, and the grilse swimming up and down the net, seeking way of escape, had met in confusion.

The fishermen knew the heel-rope was dragging over sandy troughs and holes scoured by the previous ebb, and now being silted and rescooped by the flow. Salmon could escape in the pot-holes. So they hauled slowly, for the leaded heel-rope to conform as much as possible to the irregular bottom. Two piles of net arose slowly on rope coils and post-staffs, by their feet.

Jarrk lifted the heel-rope with head and flippers, and swam inside the net. The farthest corks were a dozen boat-lengths from the shore. The seal, his immense appetite satisfied for the moment, was playing with the fish: chasing first one, then another, rolling and blowing and tumbling. Within the net, dashing up and down to find a way out and finding none, while also fleeing in terror of meeting the seal, were Salar, Trutta, Gralaks, and six grilse. Smaller and smaller grew the arc of the net enclosing them.

The fishermen, pulling methodically, saw, an oar's length inside the corks, the leap of a grilse, and the head of the seal looking up an instant afterwards and disappearing. They swore steadily. They saw, before they had hauled three more fistfuls, a bigger salmon jump out and in and out in a series of plunging leaps along the surface, and heard the seal's teeth click behind the tail-fin. This was Salar. As they pulled less slowly, now that the weight on the ropes was not so heavy, they saw the wave of a fish approaching inshore at its greatest speed, then the boil and break of sand by their feet. "Pug!" cried the skipper, for only a large sea-trout could turn, in a few inches of water, with such invisible swiftness. They saw the ream moving back the way it had come, and the skipper shouted, "Pay off" for it was a big fish, and would strike at an angle now that the tide had carried the bunt upriver. As they dropped the ropes to slack the net, Trutta, travelling at his greatest speed, struck the mesh with his nose, and drave through.

Only dabs, seaweed, and crabs were in the seine when it was lifted ashore, to be picked up and looked at. The mesh twine was new; a single strand could not be broken by a steady pull between a man's hands. The sea-trout had broken nine meshes, and through the rent all the fish had escaped.

SPRING SPATE

7

Rain fell from grey clouds over the estuary at floodtide, and Salar leapt for the change in the water. From the hills, clouds in close pack could be seen apparently following the valley which was the estuary; but this was condensation in the colder, windy air above water. Wind from the south-west pressed skits on the waves, and the rain spread to the hills and the moor, and by nightfall every drain and runner and ditch was noisy with falling water. Through pipe and culvert and chute the water hurried, with its differing loads, matter inanimate and suspended, dead leaves, soil, tar-acids from the broken surface of second-class roads, oil, decaying things, and the gases arisen from the disturbance of mud in eddies of the river and its influent streams. Rain poured from a sky without star or moon but luminously stained by the lights of the town under whose ancient bridge the ebb moved heavily and swiftly to the river's mouth: thickly the tide ebbed, overpressed and overweighted by the volume of the spate.

There was no fishing from gravel ridge or sandbank that night. Old tree trunks and roots rode down in the grey-brown water. Far out in the bay the sea was distained when daylight came. The landscape was dissolved in falling grey rain.

Salar had gone up under the familiar piers of the Long Bridge the night before, but, meeting the freshet's thrust, he had turned aside to avoid the thick-water irritations in his gill-rakers. Under the stone wall of the quay there was an eddy of salt water, where with other salmon he rested; but the rising turbid volume of road and field washings swept the eddy away, and the fish turned and swam towards the sea. They gulped unevenly in water which, saturated with carbonic acid gas released from rotting vegetation and silt in ditches and pool eddies, was additionally acid with peat-water run from bog-plashes of the moor. Soon this brown opaque water, loaded with leaves and sticks, was absorbed in the wider waters of the estuary; and into the half-ebb Salar turned, to move across the currents until he found a good stream. Other fish moved with him.

Forward into this they felt their way, turning instantly as they ran into a layer of water which caused them to gulp with choking. This water had been cutting into the mud banks of rotted turf overlaid with sludge below the town's open sewer in the quay wall. Avoiding its acrid taints, Salar found the clearer and faster streams of the secondary freshet which now was coming down. There were no tar-acids or oil-scums in this wide and pleasant water, although leaf-fragments and black twigs were moving thickly over the bed of the fairway. It was runnable water, and he leapt, and drove quickly against its exhilarations. Finding that the good stream continued and broadened, he sought slower water by the edge of sandbank and salting, and moved up faster, but always at the verge of the main or parent stream.

Salar had moved up through this channel many times during the moon's wax and wane; he had drifted with the water, letting the tide take him, slower and slower, until the tidal pool was reached. Here fresh water had lain over the heavier salt, stagnant, chilling, brackish. Roots of trees and rocky juts were slimy with fine mud suspended and settled in the lifeless lake. Disillusioned, he had drifted back with surface flotsam and wreckage and froth which began to return the instant it reached the tide-head; every time the tide-head water had moved back without pause, waveless, assoiled, Salar with it.

But now the stream was alive, and he took life from it. This water was coloured, but not turbid. It was the spate fining down after the first load of drain water had carried away stagnant deposits of used life awaiting recreation. It was not yet water springing from the rock, but it was water enlivened by percussion and repercussion against the living rock and air of earth. A million million bubbles of air had been beaten into it by the force of gravity, a million million fragments of rock had dragged against and resisted its momentum; every swirl and tear and crashing fall had been attended by watchful air. It

249

was saturated with oxygen, sparkling water, life-giving water, faithful to the spirit of Salmon. It was grand running water, and the fish leapt to it, fleeing fast after shadowy companions in play, and, as the spirit sank in them after its exaltation, boring steadily onwards again.

Salar passed under a railway bridge, its tubular iron pillars ringed by marks of old tides. Above, the river ran under sloping banks of mud, gliddery stuff, frittered by castings of rag-worms which had their vertical tunnels deep in black sand beneath the mud. This sand was black with the carbon of ancient oak-leaves and twigs and turf covered by salt of tides after the sea-wall had been raised to reclaim marshland otherwise drowned by every spring-tide. At low tide draining water from the marsh gushed through wooden traps hinged above the culverts opening under the wall; the pressure of high tide kept the traps closed, and behind them the water accumulated until the tidal level dropped.

Enclosed and dociled within grassy walls, the river wound eel-like through the marsh. Soon Salar was passing under another railway bridge. He slid forward by a pillar against which the stream was divided and flung out, causing underwater recoil. He was lifted up and back, but swam out of the turbulence, which would have drowned a powerful human swimmer, with three easy sinuations.

The smooth sandy bottom of the estuary was left behind. The waterflow was torn by rocks and boulders of angular and linear shape. They lay between the sea's abrasiveness and the river's smaller polishing. Seaweed grew poorly on the lumps of rock, fretted by alien silt during tidal flows and then swilled by enervating saltless water: enduring alien air while awaiting the sea's brief benison twice every day. And because it was broken water, mud-streaming, unrhythmic, Salar ceased his leaping. To avoid bruise and jar, constantly he had to rise, to swing sideways, to pause and waver before feeling a way around sharp rocks and the rough higgledy-piggledies of the formless watercourse. It was hybrid of sea and river; it was artificial, man-altered, unnatural. The water spirit did not dwell there: its laws and verities were changed and obstructed.

Like all hybrids, it was unproductive, outside its cycle established in the great orbit of the sun. The life it created and nourished —except the rag-worms which were there temporarily— mullet, bass, flatfish, eels, and shrimps, was tidal-transient. One day the deposits of carbonized leaves and turf, on which the worms fed, would be tunnelled through, assimilated, refined as silt and raised to the surface as castings; then the worms would perish. It was negative land and negative water, belonging not to composition or life, but to dissolution and death.

Salmon, stream-shapen and wave-wrought, were made un-easy, fatigued, in the pill or creek at low water. Many injured themselves, bruising skin and flesh as they hastened to pass through the area. Salar had journeyed here many times before, but always on the flowing tide, in water a fathom deep and more. But this was fresh water rushing in spate over a bed silted by the slower, lesser streams of more than a hundred days.

A small trout was washed past Salar, belly upwards, poisoned by gas bursting suddenly out of a black wad of old leaves in the eddy where it had been resting. Only a small part of the gas had been absorbed as the bubbles wriggled upwards, but it was enough to poison the fish after three gulps.

Salar pressed on, although discomfited and gill-stung, because the water cleared as he went forward. He swam around the wider bends, where the current was less strong, and where usually an eddy moved against the main direction of the river. By the roots of the first oak, a massive tree growing in knotted strength out of rock bared cliff-like by a streamlet entering the creek, he rested, hovering near the surface to avoid the silt-drag below.

While he was hovering there he saw a form move beside him which made him turn and swim away at his fastest speed. The form was seal-like, and slightly smaller than himself, but he recognized it instantly as an enemy. This was a young otter, which had been equally startled to see so large an object appear beside it. The otter had come down to play in the water after hunting rabbits in the hillside oakwood; for during a spate it could not hunt in water. Realizing, after the thudding shock of Salar's acceleration, that it was fish, the otter began to hunt around the ledges of rock in which the oak's roots were grown, hoping to surprise fish there. And, groping and peering, the otter came face to face with Trutta the sea-trout, who immediately drove past the otter and knocked it sprawling. Trutta had met otters before, and knew them for slow swimmers who could not hurt him unless they got him into shallow water.

Searching the bed of the eddy, where water turned against shillets at the base of the rocky wall, the otter came upon a smaller fish which was resting there, cowed by the presence of a small river-lamprey which was eating into its side. The fish was one of the six grilse which had travelled from the Island Race with Gralaks at the full of the moon. The grilse was cowering there, its body curved and taut. The otter sprang sideways off webbed hind-feet with a sweep of its thick tail and as the grilse started off its snapping teeth bit the lamprey, pulling it away from the fish's flank. Swimming up, the young otter crawled out along a root and began to eat the lamprey tail-first, as it had eaten eels with its mother and fellow-cubs during the eel-migration of the previous fall. The taste of the lamprey was unfamiliar, and the otter left it, departing into the wood again to hunt rabbits. Shore rats found the lamprey later, and ate it up.

Meantime Salar had gone up the river, which ran slower through a long pit with rocky side and bottom under the oak-wood. Now the water was running slower and clearer, and he swam comfortably through a regular surge of water. The opposite bank was walled, but rough marshy ground was giving way to grassy pasture. Here the first alder grew; the true river was not far away, for alders cannot grow near salt-water.

So Salar came at last to the natural river, where it wound widely and was allowed to make its own pools and back-waters, to cut into its ancient bed and form its own islets. Its gravel was clean and its music was sharp after the sombrous rhythms of the sea.

8

Trutta moved over the shillets where water was slow and unbroken. The shillets were flat fragments of rock, not yet ground to gravel, lying below the pools which had been cut

out of the bends above. During a spate every part of the river
bottom, except bedrock, was in movement, however gradual;
and where the stream slowed the shillets and gravel slowed, and
accumulated. At every bend Salar avoided deep and fast water,
but kept to its edge, moving steadily upstream. Trutta followed.

A dark stain was slowly deepening on the sea-trout's head,
on the back of his neck and behind the gill-covers. His dorsal
fin was torn and scales on his back were scraped off. He was a
sick fish, and Salar was piloting him. Salar was unaware of
Trutta's weakness and pain, but he knew he was being followed,
and was content thereby. His tail was guarded. Also he
knew Trutta for something like himself, a familiar form
accompanying his life, making the same journey.

The sea-trout was using Salar's sense of direction for himself;
he was weary, desirous of reaching the Junction Pool, where
he might trust himself to the river and rest. He ached along
his entire body. The shock of breaking through the net had
injured the nervous tissue between brain and the balancing
levels in his head. These water-levels were three in number,
two of them vertical and at right angles one to another, the
third was horizontal. Sometimes Trutta lurched sideways,
losing his balance. This made him fearful, and so he followed
Salar, keeping just behind the salmon's tail.

At mirk midnight Salar moved up the river as easily as he
had moved when the sun was high. He felt his way, as he was
swimming, through the varying pressures of the stream. Currents and wedges and back-lies of water were being formed
and shaped by every ledge of rock and boulder in the river;
each rock and boulder was thereby sensed before it was encountered. Every moment the salmon, through the linked
nerve-cells down his sides, was adjusting himself automatically
to the different flumes and countering swirls which were as
vibrations or little shocks: rock and stone echoes in fluid
motion about him. He did not need the sense of sight; but
Trutta, dismayed and sick, the automatic balance and levels of
his brain upset, was travelling by sight, following Salar's tail.

Salar avoided the deep rushing water of the main stream.
Sometimes he moved in water scarcely deep enough to cover

his back-fin, water streaming fast over gravel banks thrown up on inner bends of the river's course, usually below pools. These gravel beds remained there because the water-force was not sufficient to shift them. The river bed was always moving, even at low summer level, when perhaps only grains of sand were stirring. The sand accumulated behind a small stone, forming a tiny scour which as it increased altered the echo-set of its flumes, which in turn disturbed and swirled other particles of gravel. A piece of stone as big as a man's fist, suddenly shifting, caused disturbance or rearrangement over an area many times its size. But when the river was in spate its cutting powers were increased a millionfold. Every snag lodging temporarily against a rock caused the beginning of movement in a thousand pebbles and shillets; and with every movement they were diminished, chipped, ground, rubbed, and abraded. Every river and stream was helping to cut through the world.

Stray seeds, washed down and lodged on gravel banks below bends, sprouted and grew in summer, many of them enduring winter floods to grow in glory of air and sun during their second and final summer. Salar swam over plants low on the gravel, tansy, soapwort, hemlock, water-celery, and silverweed. Among them were brown stalks of docks, relics of last summer's greenery, and against these stalks, some broken off and others bent, dead leaves and loose water-weed and twigs were fixed by the water-flow. The docks put down a deep tap-root into the gravel and flourished there many seasons.

Salar swam by roots binding themselves into the rock of a mid-stream island, and came to a weir which was built diagonally across the river. Under the weir the water was harsh and white. Followed by Trutta, he felt a way across the spread of little water, seeking the power of the main stream. The other end of the weir was built into a second island, and after putting his nose hesitatingly into the fussy shallow water below the apron of the weir, he rested in the eddy of the island-end.

The weir had been built in another century to dam the river and so to store water for the working of a mill. Beyond the end of the weir a salmon trap had been made. This was a narrow channel, faced and floor'd with stone to prevent cutting-away by fast water when in use. The water passing through could be regulated, and stopped altogether, by sliding fenders or doors.

In the days of the trap's usage, before the Conservancy Board had bought out the rights, salmon were taken this way. During a freshet, when fish were running, the upper fender was lifted a couple of feet, and water gushed through at great pressure from the deep mill-pool above. The lower fender was opened wide, so that fish, reluctant to ascend the white slopes of the weir, would find an easy and secure way under it. But when they got to the upper fender, and attempted to explore the strength and direction of the constricted water before launching themselves into it, invariably they were forced back. So they waited under the wall, in eddies and secondary streams, for the pressure of water to lessen. Soon many fish were resting there.

Then the weir-keeper and his assistant dropped the fenders, the salmon were netted out, knocked on the head with a small lead-weighted bludgeon called a priest, and sent to market. In a good season the riparian owner made several hundred pounds out of his salmon trap.

Before the Board of Conservators was formed for the protection and maintenance of the stock of salmon and trout of the Two Rivers, there were many weirs and traps obstructing the free running of these fish. Very few salmon reached the spawning redds of the head-waters of the river. Every weir was an obstacle; and there were frequent weirs, damming the river for the water to turn the wheels of mill-houses. The invention of the steam-engine was indirectly the cause of much pollution of rivers, and the consequent destruction of river-life; and it was also the indirect cause of the general dereliction of water-mills. When Salar and Gralaks and Trutta were born, most of the weirs which had stopped their ancestors from journeying up the river, except in the big floods, were washed out. The fish-traps were ruinous, too.

Salar, followed by Trutta, found an easy way up fast and deep water pouring past the mossy posts of the fenders which long since had decayed. They entered a slow, heavy pool, with a muddy bottom, and swam up under the right bank, against the flow swinging and wimpling about the roots of oaks and alders. They passed submerged rocks on which grass was flattened, and willow withies swayed bending, stemming the flood with loads of dead leaves and twigs. Salar rested in front of a willowy lodge, maintaining himself in the cushion of water in rebound from the rock.

Something behind him glimmered strangely, as with moonlight. He tried to approach it by rising in the water, when it vanished, since it was then beyond his cone of vision. Other fish had seen the glimmer, and waited beside the rock, in the riffle it caused in the stream, attracted to the light. It was the corpse of a kelt which had died of exhaustion and fungus disease a month before. It was held in the withies. Broken, its skin torn and most of the scales stripped, it was glowing with the phosphoric fires of ocean, the last of its life-flame burning out.

The fish watching and rising to the light were curious; it was a fixed object, their curiosity was for movement, and so they passed on.

Salar came to another ruined weir, over the foundations of which the river pushed, determined to wash the last traces of man's work from its course. Rows of wooden posts driven into the gravel slanted across the river, battered and gnawn by the water and the life it nourished and held. The weir had been made of oaken posts and planks filled with shillets; but one day the river had worked its way through one small place, and everlastingly had pushed through the crevice, shifting first one small gravel speck, then another little stone, and at last had cleared a way between the lowest plank and the bedrock. Wider the way was cleared, and the smaller the river in summer drought the greater the pressure of water gushing through, sweeping the pit under the weir and cutting out gravel packed around the posts, until one day a freshet swilling down the river had burst a way through, and the millpool, with its thousands of tons of silt and snags and eels, went rushing down the river.

Now alders and willows, which had been brought down in old floods, were rooted behind the posts, causing the high water to pour over and beside the clumps of their roots and accumulations of leaves and twigs lodged there, and to swirl about the posts, thus slowly washing away the gravel in which they were bedded.

Salar rested in the deep pit still remaining on one side of the weir, and then swam up between two posts, and past a much-polled willow, followed by Trutta. As they moved into the slower and deeper flow under the farther bank, they felt weighted shakings in the water, and sped up fast, fearing an enemy, and came to watchful rest upstream under a shelf of rock. The cause of their alarm was a train passing, for the railway here lay beside the river.

Since they had swum through the long Carrion Pit below the oakwood, the water had been dropping back under the river banks, but now it was rising again, and thickening with colour of the fields. Very few of these fields were under the plough, although they were rich for corn; first the mills declined with the general use of the steam-engine; then the price of corn, due to the steam-engine in ships which brought grain cheaply from the great plains of America, fell below the cost of its cultivation. The riverside cornlands were now pasture for sheep and cattle, and thus the ditches between them drained water less turbid than in the storms of a previous century. Also the draining of swamps and marshes and roads caused the surface water to run away more rapidly, and so the spates rose and fell quickly.

As the river was rising Salar moved on, to find a seat where he might rest safe from surprise and near deep water if so he needed to escape from an enemy. He came to a rock, swung about behind it, and swam on exploring; then he drifted backwards and settled in the riffle of water below the rock. The edge of the fast water gripped him comfortably, and maintained him with the least effort; so that the sea-lice on his body, which had been growing more and more agitated since their host had entered fresh water, hung inert in sleep.

Salar lay contentedly, for the wound in his side had ceased to ache, while the fast stream passed an inch off his nose—at the least startle of danger he could get to safe water.

Innumerable salmon, during many centuries, had been

caught on flies of feather and steel and silk while idling behind
hat small mid-river rock, taking stray nymphs swimming by.
From father to son that salmon lodge had been known, and in
later ages, tenants of the fishing beat learned of it; poachers
knew it; herons, flying slowly over in summer weather when
the river was low and clear, were used to seeing a salmon
dawdling there. At low summer level the top of the rock was
streaked white, and small-splotched with greenish-black scriddicks of fish-bones, the spraints of otters. The rock, owing to
the position of ledges in the river-bed above it, was at the tail
of a pool and at all heights of water in the fairway was a
rest for salmon, a touching place for otters, a stance for herons.

Salar rested behind the rock, and soon another salmon was
resting there also, and then a third salmon; since lodges were
occupied by a varying number of fish when they were running.
The salmon lay behind and beside Salar, knowing of one
another without sight in the roaring water-darkness. More fish
moved into the rock's riffled after-quiet, sheltering from fine
sand now moving generally in the river—for the second fresh
was disturbing the fine gravel-scours deposited by the spate in
decline—which hurt their gills. Soon salmon were lying side
by side and touching, and in four layers, one above the other.
Behind the rear fish lay Trutta, and beside him was a kelt, a
slender fish with new sharp teeth, which had been going tail-
first down-river when it met the first clean-run fish, and there-
upon became much excited, and began to travel upstream with
them. It had eaten five trout since meeting the new salmon.
This fish was what rod-and-line fishermen called a well-
mended kelt, because it had the silvery appearance of a fish
new from the sea although it was thin. They said a kelt mended
itself, that it changed from river-brown, the tarnish and dis-
lustre of stagnation, to an argentine anticipation of ocean: and
how it mended itself, they declared, whether or not it fed
during or after its perlustration, was a mystery, like the primal
sea-change of smolts while yet in the river. The bright deposit
was an armour against corrosion, a temper for brine-weighted
water, and it was made from an excretion of the body, a waste-
product, a kind of solder sweated on each scale. Thus the kelt,

exhausted salmon, was reborn; its sharp teeth and bright scales were a death-desperate hope of resurrection.

Salmon new from the Atlantic had few teeth in their mouths, for their teeth had worn and dropped out, and they needed none when their bodies were full-stored for the ascension of their rivers.

The kelt's silveriness had come rapidly, made by guanin, excretion from its flaccid stomach. When it had begun to feed again, the chemicals of indigestion were generated, and thereby were its scales sweated bright. Those scales were much broken at the edges: serrated.

The kelt lay beside Trutta, and Trutta lay beside Gralaks the grilse, and the water rose higher until there was a phalanx of salmon behind the rock. Heavier fell the rain and soon the river was over its banks and bending the lower branches of alders which in summer would bear masses of sticks and leaves like old bird-nests many feet above the river.

A tree came lurching and bumping down-river, and struck the rock and scattered the fish sideways into the current and then downstream. They turned again to bore into and get the weight and feel of the water against their flanks. Unsure of himself, Salar swam across the stream until he was under the left bank, where the rush of water was slowed down against alder branches.

He did not remain there long, because he was unsure of a way of retreat, having come across the main stream; so he worked forward until he was clear of the branches and in deep water that moved slowly. It moved over reeds which bended palely to its flow. Various wildfowl were feeding here, and Salar saw them above him, for some of their feathers and feather-reflections were fluorescent in the darkness. This was in ordinary times a back-water, lying in an old bed which the river, ever cutting stone from stone under its banks, had deserted—for a while: since all the level valley was old river-bed, gradually being discovered and recovered by water falling between hills to the sea.

Salar, liking the quiet steadiness of the water flowing there, nosed forward into the stream. Very soon it ran fast and shallow, over its olden bed which was now an irregular part of a field. He swam up, over flattened grasses and nettle clumps whose yellow roots were stringing from the stones. He was swept back, and rested behind the nettle clump, in surging water, holding to a stone with his pectoral fins. A pink flat-headed lob-worm, dug out by the water, was swept past him, and he opened his mouth, sucked it in, and crushed it between tongue and vomer, swallowing it.

Then, feeling that the force of the water was lessening, and being more confident of the way, he swam up strongly and reached calmer water which was revolving in a pit below the roots of an oak-stump pushed there during a greater spate two winters ago. He rested awhile, his left flank swept by the twisting roll of water, which kept him almost immobile, except for an occasional flexion of the body, against the gravelly upsurge in the pit. Soon he was joined by Trutta, followed by Gralaks, and the slim kelt.

9

Salar had been resting in the pit for a short while when he realized that the water was falling less. He pressed forward into the wide and shallow rush above the tree stump. There he lay awhile, exhilarated by the water, which was ringing with bubbles of oxygen. He knew the way back, and lay there enjoying the keen and tingling feel of the water as it prepared to sweep up and over and around the trunk. His tail played gently with the playful water.

The stump was massive. For years it had been travelling down the river, after being washed out of the river bank above the Fireplay Pool. Five centuries the oak had grown there, in its maturity leaning mossy, fern-clad, and massive over the water. Its summer leaves were shady; in them mingled the songs of air and water. Wild duck had laid their eggs in the forks of its lower branches, water-ousels hung their water-moss nests in holes of its trunk overhanging the stream. Yellow wagtails nested there too, and little brown wrens, and dimmit-flitting water-bats. Otters sometimes lay sunning themselves along its boughs, watching the shadow-play of leaves on the gravel below; herons perched among its topmost branches and surveyed the surrounding land for human enemies before gliding down to fish at the tail of the Fireplay; voles and moor-hens walked under its water-side roots, through which the winter spates pressed, carving the brown bank under. The tree stood, or leaned, year after year, unmoved by the power of water, for its main roots were far into the parkland through which the river ran. But one day an old man died; and many of his trees died with him, felled to pay death-duties to the state. For scores of years after its trunk had been made into gate-posts, furniture, and coffin boards, the irregularly circular base of the tree remained in the river bank while dry-rot ate the hidden roots away, and at last it fell into the water and was shifted down the river by freshets, lodging against rocks and in eddies until a heavy spate became a flood over water-meadows and fields and it was taken down the valley as though it were one of its old leaves.

Now it was lodged in the old river bed, near the place where its parent tree had stood nearly a thousand years before. A wood dove, having swallowed some of the parent tree's acorns, had flown up the valley, to be seen by Chakchek the Smiter, whose talon-stroke ripped open its crop. The acorn had fallen to the bank above the pool, and in the following spring had put down its tap-root among the grasses.

There is a graveyard of ancient oaks by the South Tail of the estuary of the Two Rivers, trees drowned by sea and buried in sand before the Danes' galleys sailed in from the west; when the wolf howled under the moon, and the sabre-toothed tiger strode low and tense upon moose and elk and red deer of the forest. The stumps and roots are now brown coal in the sand under the beat of Atlantic rollers, with flint arrowheads, and bones and skulls of men and animals. Here on coloured ebb-tides the uprooted trees of the river are borne, carried out to sea and returned on calmer waters, to lie sodden in the sand, with their ancestors beyond leaf-memory of sun or star.

Above the tree stump Salar lay, enjoying rich breathing in a muse of himself, until the tree root shifted, and he became aware of shoaling water. He swam strongly forward into a fast racing stream, feeling his dorsal and tail fins in air. This

261

scared him, and he swam with all his strength, tearing the water; Trutta followed him, not so alarmed, for the sea-trout was used to travelling in shallow water by night. The two fish came to a shallow pit smoothed with grass, at the bottom of which the water was moving in a direction opposite to the tangled surface flow. Salar followed up the main flow barrelling along at the sides of the inverted eddy, and entered an area of shifting shillets and sand-streaming rapid water, from which he turned, and, going back to the grassy pit, he rested his pectoral fins on the drowned grass and idled there at rest. Trutta lay beside Salar, but not on his pectoral fins, which were narrower and not so strong.

The level of the water was sinking rapidly. It was a freshet from the valley of one of the tributary streams, a temporary head of rainwater from a cloudburst above hillsides of scrub-oak. Trutta began to rove round the pit. The old sea-trout knew the river, having returned to it from the sea seven times before; but he did not recognize this place, and he was uneasy.

His uneasiness was given to Salar, who prepared to swim up the rough slide from which he had already turned back. He cruised round the pit against the roll of water and made a half-leap, showing head and back and tail above water, and then swimming down again he sought the main rush and bored upwards into it. Trutta followed him after a short interval. The sea-trout was used to swimming through stickles—rough stony shallows—working a way from stone to stone; but Salar lost his nerve. He struck himself against large stones in his efforts to get quickly to safety. Four of his sea-lice were crushed, and fell away with some of his scales. These parasites were already sick, and for some hours previously had ceased in feebleness to suck Salar's blood.

He reached a stretch of rippling shallow through which he could move only by the most violent threshing of the water. He lost himself in fear, and drove into a stone, striking his head, and lay on his side, washed by the water. Then with a sweep of his tail he turned downstream to the pit and continued through it past the oak stump and so to the deeper water whither Trutta had already returned. Another salmon which had been moving doubtfully up the side-stream turned when it met him, and then swung round again, to drop back slowly, tail-first, with the current.

The fish remained in the pool whereon the wild-fowl were splashing and feeding until the flow from the old river bed ceased, when they turned away and sought the main stream. This was swift and deep and narrow under brown cliffs of meadow land which it was fast undercutting. Salar worked across the main stream to the edge of its swiftness, swimming in water less than two feet deep, and over many small green plants of balsam which had sprouted from seeds lying since last summer in the gravel.

The balsam plant in summer was as tall as a man, a hollow red stem filled with liquid, and bearing amidst its narrow leaves clusters of pink and white flowers becoming, after pollination by bees, pods which on a hot sunny day catapulted their seeds several yards with distinct snapping noises. This ingenious method of assuring its immortality had planted many millions of offspring along scores of miles of river bank since a single plant had started to spread itself from a cottage garden half a century previously.

Rain fell no more, the air lightened with the last of the clouds dragging away into the north-east and the high hills of the moor. Stars shone, the wind was warm. There was release in air and water; owls hooted softly with pleasure in the spruce-fir plantations of the valley sides; foxes shook their coats and flaired the wind; rabbits lolloped and paused, ears lifted, lolloped on and paused before settling to nibble new grass around their forepaws; salmon half-leapt as they left eddy and lie and moved into the broad flow of the river.

Salar swam with quiet ease, watchful yet trusting himself to the greatness of the river. Mud and soil were gone from the water, which now was almost clear for fish; although to human eyes, were it daylight, the river would have appeared fawn-brown in colour, opaque. Rapidly the spate was fining down, depositing sand and leaf-fragments, borne in its myriad mingled streams, by its myriad eddies and pockets. On wet branches of bankside alders and oaks dripping platforms of stalks of bramble and rush and tree sticks were lodged with torn water-weed and other cast flotsam—rusty cans and medicine bottles and hens' feathers from valley farmhouses—and an occasional green ivy spray torn away by the south-west gale.

The river moved with immense power, irresistible yet confined. Its tortuous volume held many deep sounds of rock resistance, lesser noises of gravel movement—defeated rock— and the protests of water against tree trunks and branches. By the air most of these sounds were unheard. The air was free of its conflict with water, it flowed with its own life unconfined, a free element; and to the air the salmon, embodied spirit of water, leapt in joy of freedom.

Over the moor the young moon arose with the morning star, and water everywhere rejoiced in their light. Raindrops on thorns and lichens of the moor glinted, hill trickles and rillets ran gleaming threads, odd slates on farmhouse roofs were ashine, each branch carried a thin line of light, the broad river was silver-splayed. *Krark* cried Old Nog the heron flying darkly over, his eye glinting.

When the sun rose Salar was resting behind one of the columnar piers of a railway bridge crossing the river. After a while he drifted backwards and rested at the tail of the pool because rain-water dripping from the bridge was acrid. Twenty-four jackdaws perching in a row on the iron parapet were croaking unhappily one to another, for their nesting hopes had been checked by the recent tarring of the steel framework. The railway workmen had thrown into the river nearly a hundredweight of old sticks.

A drowned black-faced lamb with legs and head hanging below its body floated under the bridge, revolving with the swirls of the stream. It had fallen off a boulder on the granite moor where it had played with other lambs in the cold sunny weather of its eight weeks of life. Often it had jumped, all four legs at once, and with flourish of long tail, across the river; for the river there was only a short way from its source in the morass where five rivers began. But when the rain had been falling an hour the rivulet was roaring big, and the lamb, running to its playing boulder after a fill of its dam's milk,

264

either did not heed or did not hear the low *baa-aa* of warning, and slipping, was carried away, bumped and hurled over other boulders and rocks until its cries were lost in water. Yet the ewe heard them still as she ran and leapt in distress down the valley, the sight of her causing other black-faced ewes to stand and stare and knock their front hoofs with alarm. The ewe ran down the valley calling her lamb.

Salar saw head and legs before him, and imagining otter, sped away across the river, sinking under the opposite bank where other fish, with Trutta and the kelt, were resting. His coming alarmed them and they turned and swam downstream. The lamb was borne away in the surging water, and soon they forgot their alarm and returned to their places; scarcely heeding the shape of the ewe floating over them; for it was on its back, legs in air.

10

By noon Salar had travelled under two more railway bridges and one road bridge and come to a deep and wide pool above an elongated islet on which trees were growing. This was the Junction Pool. Its width and depth were carved by another river flowing into the main river at right angles.

The islet, a haunt of otters, had been formed when the railway was made in the valley nearly a century before. A bridge on steel columns filled with concrete was built across the main river fifty yards above the Junction Pool, where it was gravelly and shallow. Soon winter spates, pressing against and around the obstructing columns, had scooped all gravel off the rock and carried the gravel down into the Junction Pool. This new gravel-bed altered the set of the streams in the pool; and these streams began to cut it away at once, spates swirled the loose stones and shillets and dropped them in the first slack water. So a ridge was raised, narrow and streamlined. Water-celery plants, docks, nettles, balsam helped to bind the gravel. Seeds of alder and willow sprouted in its compost of dead leaves. It became an islet. Every flood raised it, silting its vegetation,

leaving piles of sticks and leaves against its trees. The sticks
and leaves rotted, a more luxuriant vegetation arose.

In that time before the railway was built, before the new pool
was carved below the piers of the bridge, most fish ascending
from the sea passed through the stronger and more direct
stream of the large river and so came eventually to the head-
waters in the green and granite moor. Now the larger river
flowed deep, sluggish, uninviting. The lesser stream from the
side valley rushed in fast, with its song of clean gravel. Thus
the majority of salmon and sea-trout, after resting in the
Junction Pool, turned north and entered the smaller but keener
stream, coming at last to the spawning redds under the moor
of the red deer.

Between the two moors were small valleys and hills divided
by banks and hedges into scores of thousands of small fields.
Some of these fields, called splatts, were so small that the
potatoes they grew would hardly feed one man in a season.
Most of them were rough grazing, and very few were larger
than ten acres. They lay between boggy tracts with scanty
sheep-bite on them, where curlews, plover, snipe, and wild
duck nested, and wildered thorns were grey with lichens and
shaggy with green moss. It was a high country of winds and
rains, glowing before twilight with stupendous Atlantic sunsets.
From this land, watered by the distillations of ocean, the river
drew its being.

A litter of sticks and leaves lay on the broken edge of the
meadow north of the islet, marking the nocturnal height of the
spate. The banks of the meadow were sheer, cliff-like, for the
water between islet and mainland ran swift and gliding there,
undercutting the field.

From the smaller river the stream swept in, to be pushed and
deflected by the slower, heavier water flowing from under the
railway bridge. After certain confusions, the combined waters
began to move off together, but almost immediately they
divided into two fast runs past the islet.

The inflowing stream was elephant-grey, waving and swinging ponderously, slowing deliberately as it swung across the
pool, there to curl upon itself with innumerable whirls and

irregular sudden expansions and reversions of water. That was the tail of the run, the eddy; and there the salmon lay, a contented and loose formation of fish, some on the bed of the river or in mid-water, while others were poised on the edge of back-trends apparently broadside on to the flow of the river.

The varying movements and weights of flowing water maintained various movements and weights of fish. Slower, heavier salmon, which had been in the estuary for weeks, a coppery tinge on their scales of dull silver, lay in slower, deeper water. Salar was among them. With other large spring salmon he was lying over weed-waving stones on the edge of rapid water, just clear of the eddy-tail, above the islet.

Gralaks and six grilse, forerunners of the main shoals of grilse which would enter the river at midsummer, swam near the surface. Sometimes one rose easily and half-lobbed itself out of the water and sank down to its place in the formation.

A school of small spring fish lay beside the heavier salmon, but in the quick water gliding past the islet. These fish weighed about nine pounds each; but one was a pound lighter, and one was almost twelve pounds. They had left the river two years before as smolts, weighing about two and a half ounces each, but one had been slightly smaller than the others, and the other weighed three ounces. They had roamed the sea together and come into the estuary on the flowing tide following the ebb into which Salar had run. They had travelled fast and in great zest of the oxygen in the river, and leaping continually, all the way from the Island Race to the Junction Pool in less than forty-eight hours. They were keen in pride and strength of the sea, their backs bluish like new-cut lead, while their flanks were a soft whitish silver, or rather the hue of tin, which of olden time was mined and streamed in all the rivers of the granite moor. It is a purer and more lustrous metal than silver.

The small spring fish, which had just entered the Junction Pool, were assured and confident. They had come direct from the ocean, finding the water of their parent river immediately in the Island Race. Indeed the sea was stained for several miles beyond the Bell Buoy with brown flood-water. In the estuary they had encountered neither seal nor net; they had run straight through on the tide. These salmon lay in swift water because its swiftness was their own.

Trutta the sea-trout had pushed himself under some alder roots growing matted along the left bank, one of his homes, and there he lay, asleep, oblivious of all river life, even his own, yet automatically ready to move alive should the retina of his eye, or the nerve-cells of his lateral line, be affected by alien movement.

Small brown trout, each having its hiding hole under bank or root or stone, were lying everywhere on the gravel except in the fastest runs. They were watching for food, displaced nymphs and stone-fly creepers, to move near them.

A shoal of resident dace, pink-finned, lay in characterless water near the old sea-trout, idly waiting for drowned worms and insects to drift into the pit.

The kelt, long-headed and lean, ravaged of spirit and consumed of body, its gills hung with maggots and its scales broken-edged, roved round the Junction Pool, unable to rest, gigantic disillusioned smolt in search of a scattered identity. It lay awhile behind Salar, imitating his complacency; then wriggled upwards to Gralaks and her companion grilse, and sinuated quickly with the movement of young fish. Gralaks swam up slowly and leapt in a low curve; the kelt swam up too quickly, rose on its frayed tail-fin, and fell back with a splash that made the seagulls, fleeing crook-winged in the wind over the valley, to wheel and slant down, uttering cadaver-cries of wild inhuman ocean.

The hovering indifference of the grilse set the kelt roving again round the pool. He lay behind a stone by the clean-cut fish in the throat of the glide; they shifted diagonally, keeping their formation. He was longer than Salar and yet less thick than one of the small springers. The water of the glide was too strong for the kelt, and he wriggled up to the trough of the Pool.

Gradually the air was growing less cold in the valley. The wind eddied slower, warmer. Sunshine heated the opening buds of alders and for a while their lichened branches steamed slightly, with iridescence, then invisibly. A spider drew itself from shelter behind loose dead bark, walked into the sun-rays, rested and warmed itself, moved as a branch-shadow moved; and towards noon, with sudden elation, threw a gossamer into the air. It gleamed red and blue as it drifted twisting. Other gossamers were floating. They were signals of the air's buoyancy. Water was absorbing oxygen rapidly.

And of a sudden, as though they had been awaiting a signal, all the salmon in the pool began to move, slowly at first, cruising just under the surface; then accelerating, one after another they leapt at the air. Far up and down the river, in the tails of pools and from the braided edges of the eddies, mile upon mile of grey swilling water broke with splashes.

Not only was the spirit released in fish, but also in smaller forms of water life. Nymphs of the olive dun, which since hatching from eggs the summer before had lived under stones and among the dark green fronds of water-moss, were now leaving the element of water for the element of air. They were swimming to the surface, breaking their confining nymphal skins, and, having unfolded and dried their new wings as they rode down on the water, were rising into the hymenal brightness of the sky. Trout and salmon parr shifted into the eddies, watching forward and upwards, rising to suck them into their mouths. The larger parr, most of them two years old, were already assuming the silvery sheen of smolthood. They fed eagerly, swimming up faster than trout of the same size, in their vehemence sometimes leaping out of the water. Those on the gravel, amidst salmon at pause in their sporting, appeared to vibrate with eagerness while waiting to turn on their sides to take the nymphs leaving their shelters.

Salar, having cruised round the pool, showing back and fin thrice above water, leapt and returned to his place. He saw above and below him gleams of small fish as they half-rolled to take nymphs. He saw larger gleams, the half-rolls of Gralaks and other grilse as they opened their mouths to do the same. Salar began to take them too. He was not hungry: he was stimulated by rich breathing, excited by parr-memory and joyous river-life come again, disporting himself.

The kelt took a smolt that flashed before him, sank down

269

holding it crosswise in his jaws, while its body writhed deeper into the sharp teeth; and when it was still he turned it head-first on his tongue, and gorged it.

Some of the duns hatched, and flew slowly up on pale wings, to cling to branches and twigs of alder in frail wonder of the new world of air and light.

The kelt leapt and fell back formlessly with a furrowed splash. From on high as they straggled over the hill on their way to known ploughlands, a flock of herring gulls saw the splash, and swung round, wheeling with petulant cries.

11

The splash was also seen by a boy as he was walking hurriedly across the meadow, carrying rod in one hand and tailer in the other. At the sight he began to run. When near the bank, he bent down, and approached more slowly, lest his footfalls be felt by the fish.

Kneeling, and giving repeated glances at the tail of the run, he drew a box of Devon minnows from a pocket and selected one. It was a two-inch length of phosphor bronze, a dull yellow. This he threaded on a trace of thin steel wire set with swivels. At the extremity of the trace was a red bead above a triangle of hooks bound together. The minnow slipped down against the red bead. Then he drew line from the reel through the agate rings of his rod and tied it to the wire trace. The minnow dangled gleaming in the sun. One of the treble hook points touched the tweed cloth of his trousers, and instantly, although slight the touch, was fixed there by its barb. The minnow suggested the shape of a tiny fish, with pectoral fins that were a two-bladed screw. These, when the lure was drawn through the water, caused it to spin on the pivot of the red bead.

The rod was four feet long, made of steel, thinner than a rapier. It belonged to the boy's father, who had used it when fishing for black bass in rivers of Florida, which moved deep and dark under cedar trees hung with air-moss.

The reel also was American, small, simple, and level-winding. It ran smooth as oil, silently releasing plaited silk line through the rod rings while the lure dropped to the grass. The boy wound the minnow to the top of the rod, and screwed up the clutch until the minnow, weighing little more than an ounce, just ceased to pull line off the drum. The clutch would prevent back-lash of the line on the drum when casting.

Now everything was ready. He crept to the roots of an alder recently cut, found and tested foothold, stood upright cautiously, secured balance, gripped the rod in his right hand with thumb on bevelled side of reel drum and index finger crooked round the special hold, and then, with a sweep and jerk of the little rod as he had often seen his father do, sent the minnow three-quarter way across the river. As it fell with a slight splash he slowed the reel by pressing on the bevelled drum edge with his thumb, and, changing hands on the rod, began to wind in slowly, feeling the spinning drag of the lure under water. He quivered with excitement as a fish launched itself half out of the water behind the line, showing pointed dark grey head and white throat above its own wave.

It was Gralaks who had jumped; or rather, she had driven her body along the edge of the water to drag off the sea-lice from under her tail. They had ceased to feed, being sick in river water, and their unusual stillness was as an itch. The grilse had seen the lure, but had taken only the least notice of it, since a length of trace also had fallen into her cone of skylight.

The boy wound in the minnow, and tried to cast it in the same place, but it fell farther across the run, in front of Salar, who saw with his right eye a whir of light moving away in the water before him. Although it was moving centrally away from him, Salar did not see it with both eyes because his left eye was sun-dazed. It wobbled in the faster surface water, sometimes scattering behind it small bubbles. Salar had a desire to take it. He swam up and was turning under it with open mouth when something flashed hugely beside him and seized it.

As the kelt's bony jaws clashed on metal with sharp pain he opened his jaws to take in water and so to expel it; but it remained hard in his mouth. He could not close his jaws. He was not frightened, because in his past sea-life he had occasionally taken food which hurt his mouth by its hardness and gave pain by its poison when crushed. He turned down to the bed of the pool to find a stone against which to rub it off.

To the kelt's surprise and alarm, he could not get to the bed of the pool. He could not swim freely as hitherto in his life. He shook his head violently; the thing in his mouth stabbed him, and tugged at him strongly. A shock of fear jagged through his body, stimulating him to violent action. Desperately he shook his head again, and leapt quickly from the water three times without knowing what he was doing until it happened. The aerial scene was a tilted blur of blue and green and white. In his open gills the air was harsh and choking. When in water again he turned with the flow and swam away with all his strength, causing the hovering grilse to scatter and instantly to sink to the bottom. A fresh-run cock-fish of forty pounds' weight who had just moved up through the fast glide by the islet was so scared by an apparition rushing upon him with open jaws that he gave a jump and found himself unexpectedly in air and then falling on water on his back.

The terrified kelt turned in the rough water which had been pressing his gills open, and lay behind a boulder, curling his tail against a stone that was not there.

Eighty yards away on the bank the boy held the rod with both hands, one thumb pressed tightly against the drum, and wondered what he should do. He put a steady strain on the steel until his wrists were aching, and he feared the line would snap. It was of plaited silk, with a breaking strain of fifteen pounds. At last in fatigue he eased the strain on his trembling arms.

Behind the stone the kelt lay in distressed bewilderment. He could not understand this enemy that prevented him from breathing (for one barb of the triple hook was fixed in his tongue and a second barb in his vomer ridge or palate) and which held him although it never pursued him. Indeed the kelt did not yet define an enemy, although he was hiding in fear from the wire trace which extended taut in front of him, which vibrated its menace through his head and body.

He lay there, feeling weak and gulping jerkily, until the trace slackened, and feeling free, he moved sideways to rub his jaw against the edge of the stone. Since the trace did nothing to him his strength returned, and he swam hard against the stone, striking it with his head. The smolt and other food he had eaten were disgorged involuntarily in the struggle. The hooks drove deeper, and levered one against the other as he strove to wrench the thing from its hold in his mouth. The wounds, enlarged by the barbs, began to bleed. In pain and fury the kelt dashed the trace on the stone, with such force that the minnow was impelled up the trace, and the barb pierced the main artery of his body, which lay under the tongue.

As he bled he weakened. He began to swim up into the pool again, away from the slight drag of the water on the trace behind him; but when the pull came from before him he swung round again and in desperation of life swam down the river to the sea, imagined refuge.

He could not breathe, swimming downstream less fast than the stream. He had to turn, and in a frenzy of fear he swam back into the Junction Pool with jaggered strength and leapt to shake off the wounding hardness in his mouth. Falling back, he felt the water too strong for him, it swept him away, he lost sense and power of direction, his body heavy with fatigue. The drift rested him, and he recovered, to swim feebly the way he was being drawn, sometimes trying to swim aside, but in vain. He was exhausted. Drawn near the bank, into slower water, he saw his enemy, and the shock stimulated his wasted muscles. He struggled to reach the run, and in his effort to bore down into deeper water the river became strange and unfamiliar.

Exultingly the boy drew in the salmon to the bank, where it turned on its side, and lay still. Holding rod in one hand, with the other he passed the loop of the tailer over the fish's tail. It was like a short-handled whip with a loop of twisted steel wire for thong, and when lifted up with a jerk, the spring loop slid small, noosing the tail.

The kelt struggled as it was being lifted, it flapped feebly on the grass, but three blows of the priest on its head killed it. Its captor was trembling with pride and joy, and with these feelings was a slightness of regret that it was no longer alive and free in the river. Later when he reached home the stannic lustre of the kelt was gone, its skin had shrunken, and its head looked too big for its body. To the boy's mortification, his father said it was a kelt. But, declared the boy, it was so bright that surely it was a clean-run fish, although there were no sea-lice on it. Then his father showed him the fresh-water maggots on the gill-rakers, a sure sign, he said: and for confirmation, there was the spawning mark on the point of balance by the paired fins —where scales and skin had been worn away by the act of digging gravel, he said. The mark, however, had not been caused by spawning (as such abrasions were generally regarded by anglers of the Two Rivers), but by prolonged resting on gravel or rock during the stagnancies of summer river life.

When cut the flesh was seen to be pale and infirm, and the carcase was buried under an apple tree in the orchard.

12

Clouds were slowly filling the air, paling the sun to a small white disc, gradually absorbing colours of sky and land until the afternoon was dull and cold. No fish showed in the Junction Pool. An angler with a double-handed rod of split cane sixteen feet long fished the water patiently, departing at sunset, which showed as a purple-grey heaviness down the valley.

The wind was from the north-west, piling up massive dark clouds which fell in cold hard rain upon the moors. Since the larger river, descending from the granite moor, lay below a main traffic road with its hundreds of lesser roads passing by hamlets and villages, it was soon turbid, and tainted with artificial fertilizers washed into its water; while the smaller river, passing undrained meadows and few houses on its way from the moor of the wild red deer, changed but slightly in colour and volume. By sunrise it had risen two inches, while the larger river was a foot higher. Fish moved farther up the pool, and to one side, lying in clearer water.

Later in the morning more fish moved into the Pool behind them, fresh-run from the top of the tide, and soon the salmon which had been resting there began to rise short, showing only the tops of heads and tails: slow, lackadaisical movements, as excitement or power began to spread through their bodies. When the water pressure began slightly to lessen, they set off, swimming slowly, as though leisurely, into the fast water of the new river, which swirled with air bubbles around its gravelly bed.

Had Salar and the larger fish been visible to a human eye, they would have appeared to be moving forward against rapid water while remaining immobile. Seldom would the sideway flexion of any fish have been apparent. Under a swift and broken stream a fish would be seen advancing as though the flow of water were without force. For while the surface streams of the river ran confused and fast, irregularly conforming to the rocky irregularities of the river-bed, the lower water was in reaction against the river-bed. Where it rushed fast on top, it might be almost still below, or even in reverse movement. In the river were innumerable weighted streams in competition for the force of gravity, delayed by friction in passage over obstructions of rocks, trees, pools, and banks. The salmon moved forward with casual ease in gaps and lanes of the streams' traffic, usually in delayed water.

At length Salar came to a bend in the river where on the edge of broken rapid water a circular pool was in motion. Many fish were waiting in the pool, which was caused to revolve by a great bubble-churning rush of white water surging down the face of a sloping weir. The sill of the weir had been built with a cut or nick in its centre for the passage of fish. Here, therefore, the water was most violent in its descent, flinging itself in white surges against the edge of the deeper water below, making it to turn.

The nearer edge of the water lapped a bank of shillets which had been dug out of the pool and left there by spates after the building of the weir. The bank of loose flat fragments of rock shelved deeply. Sometimes the tail-fin of a waiting fish showed a yard or less from the edge, to sink again casually. Nearer the pool's centre dorsal fins lifted above the ruffled surface. A heron flying overhead saw a blotch of dark blue in the water, where fish were massed.

Other eyes too were watching, from behind a hurdle of sticks and weeds left by the receding spate against the trunk of an alder tree on the bank a score of yards below the pool.

One of the fish resting there shook its tail and swam down slowly, rolling on its side and turning up again in another direction, cruising around the pool against the circular current. It was a fish which had been in the lower reaches of the river since the New Year. It was about to make its fourth attempt to ascend the weir. At three points on the rim of the pool it rolled out of the water, showing dorsal and tail fins as it gathered its will within itself; then, heading resolutely into the secondary rush of bubbled water alongside the white, it moved along the rocky bottom, and straightly swam up, accelerating with all its strength.

The winter salmon, flanks of tarnished silver and rust, leapt just beside, and clear of, the white thrust of water. It fell on the lower edge of the weir's apron, entering the thick cord of water descending from the gap in the sill above. The apron or face of the weir sloped at an angle of about 20°. Slowly the salmon, swimming with all its power, ascended the cord, and when half-way up its strength grew less and it ceased to advance: it stayed during the time of a double wing-beat of the heron wheeling overhead: desperately it turned aside in the hope of finding easier water, and was swept down on its side, tossed from wave to wave of the white surge to which it abandoned itself, and, reaching the end of the water's thrust, with a slow sweep of the tail entered the circular pool and took place among the other fish which had failed to get over the weir.

On the farther side of the weir stood a pine tree. The heron alighted on the topmost branch, and perched there swaying, holding its head up as anxiously it watched for its only enemy —man. The grassy bank below the tree ended in a masoned wall, under which the broken water surged over steps made to help fish over the obstruction of the weir. It was not known to the designer of the weir that a series of ledges, one below the other, would be avoided by salmon, although they had been built specially for them; the plan had seemed perfect. But running water usually does the opposite of what is expected of it by those not water-minded. The spate pouring over the sill down the steps made a white turbulence feared by every fish which ventured into it. There was no direct force of flow: it was water in rebound from stone and again in rebound from rebounding water: white shallow meaningless water which salmon dread. While the heron watched in the pine tree, Salar, after one preparatory roll, swam under the main stream and leapt tentatively, testing its force and direction. He was flung over backwards.

The scoop in the centre of the weir was made for the ease and safety of running fish, a spillway to enable them to ascend in moderate water. In the spates of early spring and late autumn, when salmon were running most numerously, the steps were impassable; and the central spine or flume was too strong. So salmon sought the easiest way, which was up the smooth slope of the weir rising from the inner bend of the pool below. This slope or apron was made of stone smoothed with concrete. The edge lay a few inches below the grassy slope of the meadow. Water ran thin at the edge, gradually deepening towards the central flume. The graduated weight of water falling made a diagonal line of white-bubbled surge across the pool, which thereby was one great revolving eddy. After exploring the major streams and finding them unswimmable, salmon either waited for less water or ventured to ascend at the point of least resistance, which was at the edge of the concrete slope, where it adjoined the sward of the meadow. Thus were they, in leaping, exposed to the danger to avoid which the weir was so designed: the gaffs of poachers.

Perched swaying in the pine top, the heron gazed around for human enemies; while behind the rough hurdle of sticks and leaves against an alder other eyes watched the heron, that unconscious sentinel for the men waiting there.

A bronze-coloured salmon, with black and green gill-covers and frayed tail-fin, jumped from deep water at the edge of the concrete slope and fell with a splash on its side, where it lay inert for a moment before the water washed it against the grass. It was half stunned, but the unfamiliar movement of water breaking over the nerves of its lateral line caused it to curve upright, steady itself with its pectoral fins, and with a wriggle to slip down the slope. As it did so, a string of yellowish pink eggs was washed away from it, into the pool below. This fish was a rawner, a female which had come in from the sea late, in the second week of December, and been unable to find a mate; nearly half its thirteen thousand eggs had been aimlessly shed. Some of those eggs, extruded by the shock of falling on the weir-face, were seized by a trout on the bed of the pool watching the edge of the bubble-turn, before the dark and gleaming shape of the rawner slid into and out of the trout's window of vision.

One of the men squatting behind the stick-heap was binding with string the shank of a gaff to a six-foot length of ash-plant which he had cut lower down by the river. The gaff was forged of iron, a large barbless hook. The shank was eight inches long, convenient size for concealing in the pocket.

The poachers were hiding because they had heard that one of the water-bailiffs was in the neighbourhood, having only that morning come upon two boys worming in the big junction pit below, without a salmon licence. After taking the boys' names and addresses, the bailiff had gone on up the valley, and might be about by the weir. They kept still, knowing that the heron's eye would detect the least movement. About half-past twelve, they reckoned, the bailies would be at their dinners, a good time to snatch a few fish, hide them in a sack until darkness, and away.

Up in the dark green branches, tipped with the brown of new growth, the heron flapped to shift position, and then looked around anxiously, lest the flapping might have attracted attention from its enemies. Like most of the herons fishing the valleys of the Two Rivers and their feeder streams, the bird had often heard a loud crack followed by the whistle and rattle of shot when surprised by man. Quite half the bird's working hours were passed in waiting and watching lest one of its enemies appear suddenly to surprise it.

When one of the men waiting below had whipped the gaff to the ash handle he took a small stone from a torn pocket of his coat and began to stroke the point to needle sharpness.

Down the side slope of the weir a kelt, with broken back-fin creamy with fungus disease, its back and sides also blotched, its head black and its underjaw prolonged in an upturned hook or kype, its body lean and brown, was washed, rolled over by the water it could no longer control. This fish had ascended the weir in its dashing Atlantic pride exactly a year before, a master of water which served its species and was servant to all fish only while they were strong with its running strength. Exhausted by disease below the point when it could mend itself by a spurt of its last stored strength, the fish was passing beyond the life-stream which flowed within the flow of the river. It had been resting above the weir since the night before, apprehensive of the water's roar below. Now the water turned it over and the scooping roll of bubbles took it into the pool, where it swayed into balance and rested, gulping water irregularly through its gills.

Salar lobbed himself half out of water, feeling suddenly playful, and enjoying the nearness of many other fish like himself. Without real determination to ascend the weir, he swam strongly under the white thrust and up through it, appearing to the watching men to stand on his tail a moment before toppling backwards and disappearing.

The January-run fish tried again. It leapt from the deep water at the lower edge of the apron and splashed down on the slope, flapping sideways at the rate of nearly two hundred flaps a minute, appearing to plough its way upwards, a plume of water over its head. Making no progress, it altered direction and travelled aslant the glide, until it was within a foot of the edge of the grass, when it felt itself heavy with fatigue and ceased to swim, lying there, a crescent fish, a moment before turning its nose down and slipping back into the white churn several yards distant from where it had leapt.

Its long green toes gripping scaly boughs with excitement, and cursed in a low throaty monotone by a female carrion crow sitting on five eggs in her nest in a lower fork of the pine, the heron, giving a final hasty twist of its long neck as it glanced around, prepared to jump up and glide down to the side of the weir.

As the lanky grey bird paused, Trutta, big, black-spotted and dark stain of bruise three inches deep on his shoulders, lobbed himself vertically out beside the central white thrust and was swept over on his back immediately. He knew by experience that the fall of water was too great. The old sea-trout had swum over the weir more than a dozen times, and on the last half-dozen occasions he had swum up easily, although strenuously: always at night, and when the water was the right height. Trutta had jumped in lighter noon airs because the feeling of the many salmon in the pool was stimulating; and because the pain behind his head was lessening. His neck itched, and he was trying to knock the itching away against the water.

The sight of the large white belly and red of open gills made the heron launch itself from the tree and glide steeply down over the river, to alight with counter beat of wings on the grass above the sill of the weir. From this vantage point it waited, watching for movement of a hidden enemy. The heron was very old, and it knew that men with guns often hid by trees. Every time it came to this weir it spent several minutes in the top of the pine, and an equal period on the bank above the sill, before stalking slowly down to its fishing stance at the bottom of the water-slide.

Behind the screen of flood branches the man who had been sharpening the point of the gaff restrained his younger companion by a finger lift and part closing one eye.

Gralaks and the other grilse remaining from the shoal which had travelled together from the Island Race to the estuary were swimming under the cliff by which the surge from the weir swirled and swung before flowing as normal river again. Blue-grey heads and fins showed in the rocking surface. The grilse were in high glee with the boisterous water, parr-spirited but free of the selfish concentration of their parr-hood. One of the hiding men stared, because the tail-fin of one fish looked black, sharply forked, more like a mackerel's tail than a salmon's. It had been snapped at by a porpoise, which had bitten away the centre of its tail-fin. These grilse curving out of the surge had a greenish tinge above the medial line: finishing diet of sprats off the south-west coast of Ireland. "Greenbacks," muttered the elder of the two men, "rinned up late". Greenbacks usually arrived in early winter.

The heron stood on the bank above the top of the weir, where the water from the pool was led away in the leat to the grist-mill a quarter of a mile distant. On the tree-top his suspicions of possible enemies had slowly been stared away; now a different aspect upon the landscape recreated them once more. The heron swayed its head in the hope of being able to look round the trunks of trees. It searched the path across the river, above the small cliff under which the river surged, and the top of the vegetable garden wall beyond. It had seen a man work-ing in the garden while flying over, but as he was always there and had never shown notice, the heron looked away after the least glance.

A fish splashed into the white skirts of the weir, and was kicked back immediately. The heron started to walk down the grassy slope, but hesitated in alarm that its field of vision was diminishing with every step; it paused and lifted up its head and looked around. It saw the miller, a familiar figure, come out of the mill-house a quarter of a mile away, and with a bar lever up the fender by the wheel, for the sluice to run away during the dinner hour. The wheel had already stopped turn-ing; it was one o'clock. The heron also saw another man walk-ing down the road. This was the water-bailiff, who had been inquiring of the miller if he had seen any fish under his mill-wheel.

The miller's stag-bird, a gamecock living arrogantly among various hens, shook its wet wings on the bank of the water-course below. The opening of the fender had sent water sluicing down in a wave, and the bird, walking in the thin stickle of water and hunting small fish, had been swept off its feet. This did not bother the gamecock, which often before had been soused like this. Whenever it saw the fender being closed this bird ran to the bank and entered the stream as the flow was sinking and struck with its beak at any trout it saw reaming in shallow water. The bird was a clumsy and miniature heron; but it had a measure of skill, and when in summer and early autumn the small sea-trout, called peal, were running, and the fender was closed, it ran with flapping wings to the stream-side, to take the spotted mother-of-pearl fish and open them on the bank for the orange-pink eggs within, its favourite food. The miller was an honest man, and never took a salmon from the pit below the sluice; and he told the water-bailiff, with equal honesty as he went to dinner, unrolling shirt sleeves over thick forearms, that never yet had he seen any poacher take salmon or peal from his mill-stream. As the water-bailiff walked away, the cock crowed, and then proceeded to inspect its hens while waiting for the fender to close again at two o'clock.

Its hunger at last overcoming anxiety, the heron stalked stiltedly down the grassy slope and stepped on the edge of the concrete at the base of the sill, by a crack where a dock root and a thistle root were about to unfurl their first leaves of the year. It assured itself of a good hold for its long green feet and peered over the water, holding beak down to strike should any sizeable fish appear. Then it gave a jump and uttered a skwark and beat up violently, seeing two men rising out of the gravel bank near it. With long legs trailing, it flapped down the river, swerving as it saw the figure of a man looking over the road bridge.

This was the water-bailiff who wondered what had disturbed the heron, for he knew it had been startled by the quick way it had been beating its wings when it had first come into view. The weir was hidden by a bend and trees from the bridge. He decided to go to the weir.

Crouching by the edge where the heron had been standing, the man with the gaff waited for a fish to show. His mate kept a look out on the bank above.

A salmon, which had not seen the men, suddenly leapt in

panic from the far edge of the pool and as it did so the poacher saw something thin fall from its head.

The poacher was waiting, as still as a heron but not so well clad, gaff in hand ready to snatch the first fish to come within reach, staring at the water, when his mate turned casually towards him and shouted out "Bailie!" while pretending to crouch from an imaginary wind in order to light a cigarette. Without turning his head or shifting his position, but with an instant movement of the lower parts of his arms, the poacher lanced the gaff into the white strakes of the surge. It turned up in the water before disappearing. Putting hands in pockets of torn jacket, the man stood there looking at the water until, a couple of minutes later, he turned his head slowly to the voice of the Bailie saying, "Ha, caught you this time, have I, Shiner?"

The poacher, known as Shiner for his work during moonlit nights, replied, "Have 'ee got a fag in your pocket, midear?"

"Aiy," said the bailiff. "And have 'ee got a gaff in yours, by any chance, Shiner?"

"Aw, I ban't no water-whipping rod-and-line gentry, you should know that, midear. What be the like o' me wanting a gaff for? You'll be asking me for a gennulman's licence next, or the loan of a maskell's guts and kid's coloured fishing fly. Search me if it will plaize 'ee, midear."

A maskell was the local name for caterpillar, and the old fellow's reference, which the slower-witted bailiff did not understand, was to silkworm gut.

"You know I ban't allowed by law to search you," retorted the water-bailiff, disconcerted by the poacher's good humour. "Got a gaff hidden under they bushes, have 'ee?"

"I ban't stopping you from searching, midear."

"Well, then, will 'ee answer why you'm waiting yurr?"

"Elvers be running, midear. They'm poaching your fish, too, I fancy. Why don't 'ee summon they elvers, midear?"

He pointed to the water turning back under the bank, where a diseased and dying kelt had turned up slowly on its side, a dark mass of midget eels wriggling round it. Its gills were clustered with wriggles. The fish swam away slowly, doomed to be eaten alive.

"There ban't no law against a poor man taking a dish of elvers for his tea, be there?" inquired Shiner, as he took off a weather-stained felt hat. He knelt down and dipped it in the water. A dozen elvers swam around inside. He threw them back, and banged the hat on the grass to knock off the water. "Well, midear, us mustn't keep th' old crane from his dinner, must us? Else they Cruelty to Hanimals people will be after us, won't 'n?"

Shiner pointed to the heron passing over high, flying slowly, legs straight out behind and neck tucked in. He walked away, laughing loudly.

13

The elvers were running. They darkened the green shallows of the river. The eddies were thick tangles of them. They had come into the estuary on the flood-tide, and in a gelatinous mass had moved into the still water of the tide-head. All fish in the river sped from them, for elvers were gill-twisting torture and death.

For nearly three years as thin glassy threads the young eels had been crossing the Atlantic, drifting in warm currents of the Gulf Stream from the Sargasso Sea. Here in deep water far under floating beds of clotted marine wreckage, all the mature eels of the northern hemisphere, patient travellers from inland ponds and ditches, brooks and rivers, came together to shed themselves of life for immortal reasons. From blue dusk of ocean's depth they passed into death: and from darkness the elvers arose again, to girdle the waters of half the earth.

Salar lay in fast water between Sloping Weir and the road bridge. He lay in front of a large stone, in the swift flume rising to pass over it. The flume streamed by his head and gills and shoulders without local eddy. No elver could reach his gill without violent wriggling, which he would feel. He was swift with the swiftness of the water. There was the least friction between fish and river, for his skin exuded a mucus or lubricant by which the water slipped. The sweep of strong water guarded his life. Other salmon were lying in like lodges in the stony surges. Salar lodged there until dusk, when he moved forward again. Gralaks moved beside him. They recognized and knew each other without greeting.

Many fish were at Sloping Weir now, waiting beside the lessening weight of white water, in the swarming bubbles of the eddy. They lay close to one another. As soon as one fish waggled tail and dipped and rose to get a grip of the water, to test its own pulse of power, another fish took its place, ready for the take-off. Salar idled, alert, apprehensive, seventeenth in line. Sometimes two or three fish left the phalanx at the same time and after nervous ranging set themselves to swim up through the heavy water looking like snow under the rising moon.

At the edge of the turning pool, where the poachers had waited and watched during the day, stood Shiner's 'ould crane'. The bird was picking up elvers as fast as he could snick them. His throat and neck ached. A continuous loose rope of elvers wove itself on the very edge of the water, where frillets sliding down the concrete apron-edge washed elvers into the grass.

After a return to the tree-top heronry where three hernlets had craked and fought to thrust their beaks down his throat to take what he had, Old Nog flew back to the weir and picked and swallowed slowly, his excitement gone, for the elvers were not for him. He flew home again, and by the light of the full moon returned with his mate to the weir. They crammed their crops and necks and flew back to their filthy nest, where by midnight the three hernlets were crouching, huddled and dour with overmuch feeding. Old Nog then flew back to the weir, to feed himself. Most of the elvers were by then gone, but he managed, for the moment, to satisfy his hunger.

On the way home, however, an elver wriggled down his windpipe, causing him to choke and sputter and disgorge; the mass fell beside a badger below rubbing against its scratching-thorn, causing it to start and grunt with alarm. Having cautiously sniffed for some minutes, from various angles, the badger dared to taste; after which it ate all up and searched for more. For the next few nights it returned specially to rub itself against

285

the thorn, in the hope of finding such food there again. As for Old Nog, not an elver that year reached his long pot, as countrymen do call the guts.

During the time of the moon's high tides, more than two hundred salmon passed over the weir. Salar swam up on his second attempt; at first he had been unsure of himself, and dropped back almost as soon as he had got a grip on the central cord or spine of water. Swimming again with all his power, he moved slowly into the glissade of water above the white surge, stayed a third of the way up, as though motionless, vibrating; then had gained over the water and swum stronger in jubilation, and suddenly found the sill moving away under him, release of weight from his sides, and calm deep water before him. He flung himself out for joy, and a young dog-otter, which was rolling on its back on grass at the pool's edge, where a bitch-otter had touched earlier in the night, instantly lifted its head, slipped to the edge, put its head under, and slid tail last into the water.

Salar saw the otter swimming above him, shining in a broken envelope of air on head and fur and legs. The pool took the dull blows of his acceleration and in three seconds, when the otter had swum nine yards against the current, Salar had gone twenty yards upstream into the mill-pool, swerved from a sunken tree trunk lodged in the silt, zigzagged forward to the farther bank, startling other salmon resting there, and hidden himself under a ledge of rock. The otter, which was not hunting salmon, since in deep water it could never catch any, unless a fish were injured, crawled out on the bank again to enjoy through its nose what it imagined visually.

An elver wriggled against Salar, and he swam on. The pool was long and deep and dark. He swam on easily, restfully, slower than the pace of the otter's pretended chase. The wound in his side began to ache dully, and he rested near the surface, near water noisy over a branch of alder. At dawn he was three miles above Sloping Weir, lying under a ledge of rock hollow curving above him, and therefore protecting him from behind, with an immediate way of escape from danger into deep water. The salmon slept, only the white-grey tip of the kype—hooked end of lower jaw—showing as the mouth slightly opened. Fifteen times a minute water passed the gills, which opened imperceptibly.

Salar slept. The water lightened with sunrise. He lay in shadow. His eyes were fixed, passively susceptible to all movement. The sun rose up. Leaves and stalks of loose weed and water-moss passing were seen but unnoticed by the automatic stimulus of each eye's retina. The eyes worked together with the unconscious brain, while the nerves, centres of direct feeling, rested themselves. One eye noticed a trout hovering in the water above, but Salar did not see it.

The sun rose higher, and shone down on the river, and slowly the shadow of the ledge shrank into its base. Light revealed Salar, a grey-green uncertain dimness behind a small pale spot appearing and disappearing regularly.

Down there Salar's right eye was filled with the sun's blazing fog. His left eye saw the wall of rock and the water above. The trout right forward of him swam up, inspected that which had attracted it, and swam down again; but Salar's eye perceived no movement. The shadow of the trout in movement did not fall on the salmon's right eye.

A few moments later there was a slight splash left forward of Salar. Something swung over, casting the thinnest shadow; but it was seen by the eye, which awakened the conscious brain. Salar was immediately alert.

The thing vanished. A few moments later, it appeared nearer to him.

With his left eye Salar watched the thing moving overhead. It swam in small jerks, across the current and just under the surface, opening and shutting, gleaming, glinting, something trying to get away. Salar, curious and alert, watched it until it was disappearing and then he swam up and around to take it ahead of its arc of movement. The surface water, however, was flowing faster than the river at mid-stream, and he misjudged the opening of his mouth, and the thing, which recalled sea feeding, escaped.

On the bank upriver fifteen yards away a fisherman with fourteen-foot split-cane rod said to himself, excitedly, "Rising short"; and pulling loops of line between reel and lowest ring of rod, he took a small pair of scissors from a pocket and snipped off the thing which had attracted Salar.

No wonder Salar had felt curious about it, for human thought had ranged the entire world to imagine that lure. It was called a fly; but no fly like it ever swam in air or flew through water. Its tag, which had glinted, was of silver from Nevada and silk of a moth from Formosa; its tail, from the feather of an Indian crow; its butt, black herl of African ostrich; its body, yellow floss-silk veiled with orange breast-feathers of the South American toucan, and black Macclesfield silk ribbed with silver tinsel. This fly was given the additional attraction of wings for water-flight, made of strips of feathers from many birds: turkey from Canada, peahen and peacock from Japan, swan from Ireland, bustard from Arabia, golden-pheasant from China, teal and wild duck and mallard from the Hebrides. Its throat was made of the feather of an English speckled hen, its side of Bengal jungle-cock's neck feathers, its cheeks came from a French kingfisher, its horns from the tail of an Amazonian macaw. Wax, varnish, and enamel secured the "marriage" of the feathers. It was one of hundreds of charms, or materialized river-side incantations, made by men to persuade sleepy or depressed salmon to rise and take. Invented after a bout of seasickness by a Celt as he sailed the German Ocean between England and Norway, for nearly a hundred years this fly had borne his name, Jock Scott.

While the fisherman was tying a smaller pattern of the same fly to the end of the gut cast, dark stained by nitrate of silver against under-water glint, Salar rose to mid-water and hovered there. Behind him lay the trout, which, scared by the sudden flash of the big fish turning, had dropped back a yard. So Salar had hovered three years before in his native river, when, as parr spotted like a trout, and later as silvery smolt descending to the sea, he had fed eagerly on nymphs of the olive dun and other ephemeridae coming down with the current.

He opened his mouth and sucked in a nymph as it was swimming to the surface. The fisherman saw a swirl on the water, and threw his fly, with swish of double-handed rod, above and to the right of the swirl. Then, lowering the rod point until it was almost parallel to the water, he let the current take the fly slowly across the stream, lifting the rod tip and lowering it slightly and regularly to make it appear to be swimming.

Salar saw the fly and slowly swam up to look at it. He saw it clear in the bright water and sank away again, uninterested in the lifelessness of its bright colours. Again it reappeared, well within his skylight window. He ignored it, and it moved out of sight. Then it fell directly over him, jigging about in the water, and with it a dark thin thing which he regarded cautiously. This was the gut cast. Once more it passed over, and then again, but he saw only the dark thinness moving there. It was harmless. He ignored it. Two other salmon below Salar, one in a cleft of rock and the other beside a sodden oak log wedged under the bank, also saw the too-bright thing, and found no vital interest in it.

The fisherman pulled in the line through the rod-rings. It was of plaited silk, tapered and enamelled for ease of casting. The line fell over his boot. Standing still, he cut off the fly, and began a search for another in a metal box, wherein scores of mixed feathers were ranged on rows of metal clasps. First he moved one with his forefinger, then another, staring at this one and frowning at that one, recalling in its connection past occasions of comparative temperatures of air and river, of height and clearness of water, of sun and shade, while the angler's familiar feeling, of obscurity mingled with hope and frustration, came over him. While from the air he tried to conjure certainty for a choice of fly, Salar, who had taken several nymphs of the olive dun during the time the angler had been cogitating, leapt and fell back with a splash that made the old fellow take a small Black Doctor and tie the gut to the loop of the steel hook with a single Cairnton jam-knot.

Salar saw this lure and fixed one eye on it as it approached and then ignored it, a thing without life. As it was being withdrawn from the water a smolt which had seen it only then leapt open-mouthed at a sudden glint and fell back, having missed it.

289

Many times a similar sort of thing moved over Salar, who no longer heeded their passing. He enjoyed crushing the tiny nymphs on his tongue, and tasting their flavour. Salar was not feeding, he was not hungry; but he was enjoying remembrance of his river-life with awareness of an unknown great excitement before him. He was living by the spirit of running water. Indeed Salar's life was now the river: as he explored it higher, so would he discover his life.

On the bank the fisherman sat down and perplexedly re-examined his rows and rows of flies. He had tried all recommended for the water, and several others as well; and after one short rise, no fish had come to the fly. Mar Lodge and Silver Grey, Dankeld and Black Fairy, Beauly Snow Fly, Fiery Brown, Silver Wilkinson, Thunder and Lightning, Butcher, Green Highlander, Blue Charm, Candlestick Maker, Bumbee, Little Inky Boy, all were no good. Then in one corner of the case he saw an old fly of which most of the mixed plumage was gone: a Black Dog which had belonged to his grandfather. Grubs of moths had fretted away hackle, wing, and topping. It was thin and bedraggled. Feeling that it did not matter much what fly was used, he sharpened the point with a slip of stone, tied it on, and carelessly flipped it into the water. He was no longer fishing; he was no longer intent, he was about to go home; the cast did not fall straight, but crooked; the line also was crooked. Without splash the fly moved down a little less fast than the current, coming thus into Salar's skylight. It was like the nymphs he had been taking, only larger; and with a leisurely sweep he rose and turned across the current, and took it, holding it between tongue and vomer as he went down to his lie again, where he would crush and taste it. The sudden resistance of the line to his movement caused the point of the hook to prick the corner of his mouth. He shook his head to rid himself of it, and this action drove the point into the gristle, as far as the barb.

A moment later, the fisherman, feeling a weight on the line, lifted the rod-point, and tightened the line, and had hardly thought to himself, *salmon*, when the blue-grey tail of a fish broke half out of water and its descending weight bended the rod.

Salar knew of neither fisherman nor rod nor line. He swam down to the ledge of rock and tried to rub the painful thing in the corner of his mouth against it. But his head was pulled away from the rock. He saw the line, and was fearful of it. He bored down to his lodge at the base of the rock, to get away from the line, while the small brown trout swam behind his tail, curious to know what was happening.

Salar could not reach his lodge. He shook his head violently, and, failing to get free, turned downstream and swam away strongly, pursued by the line and a curious buzzing vibration just outside his jaw.

Below the pool the shallow water jabbled before surging in broken white crests over a succession of rocky ledges. Salar had gone about sixty yards from his lodge, swimming hard against the backward pull of line, when the pull slackened, and he turned head to current, and lay close to a stone, to hide from his enemy.

When the salmon had almost reached the jabble, the fisherman, fearing it would break away in the rough water, had started to run down the bank, pulling line from the reel as he did so. By thus releasing direct pull on the fish, he had turned it. Then, by letting the current drag line in a loop below it, he made Salar believe that the enemy was behind him. Feeling the small pull of the line from behind, Salar swam up into deeper water, to get away from it. The fisherman was now behind the salmon, in a position to make it tire itself by swimming upstream against the current.

Salar, returning to his lodge, saw it occupied by another fish, which his rush, and the humming line cutting the water, had disturbed from the lie by the sodden log. This was Gralaks the grilse. Again Salar tried to rub the thing against the rock, again the pull, sideways and upwards, was too strong for him. He swam downwards, but could make no progress towards the rock. This terrified him and he turned upwards and swam with all his strength, to shake it from his mouth. He leapt clear of the water and fell back on his side, still shaking his head.

On the top of the leap the fisherman had lowered his rod, lest the fly be torn away as the salmon struck the water.

Unable to get free by leaping, Salar sank down again and settled himself to swim away from the enemy. Drawing the line after him, and beset again by the buzzing vibration, he travelled a hundred yards to the throat of the pool, where water quickened over gravel. He lay in the riffle spreading away from a large stone, making himself heavy, his swim-bladder shrunken, trying to press himself into the gravel which was his first hiding place in life. The backward pull on his head nearly lifted him into the fast water, but he held himself down, for nearly five minutes, until his body ached and he weakened and he found himself being taken down sideways by the force of shallow water. He recalled the sunken tree and it became a refuge, and he swam down fast, and the pull ceased with the buzz against his jaw. Feeling relief, he swam less fast over his lodge, from which Gralaks sped away, alarmed by the line following Salar.

But before he could reach the tree the weight was pulling him back, and he turned and bored down to bottom, scattering a drove of little grey shadows which were startled trout. Again the pull was too much for him, and he felt the ache of his body spreading back to his tail. He tried to turn on his side to rub the corner of his mouth on something lying on the bed of the pool—an old cartwheel—again and again, but he could not reach it.

A jackdaw flying silent over the river, paper in beak for nest-lining, saw the dull yellow flashes and flew faster in alarm of them and the man with the long curving danger.

Fatigued and aching, Salar turned downstream once more, to swim away with the river, to escape the enemy which seemed so much bigger because he could not close his mouth. As he grew heavier, slower, uncertain, he desired above all to be in the deeps of the sea, to lie on ribbed sand and rest and rest and rest. He came to rough water, and let it take him down, too tired to swim. He bumped into a rock, and was carried by the current around it, on his side, while the gut cast, tautened by the dragging weight, twanged and jerked his head upstream, and he breathed again, gulping water quickly and irregularly. Still the pull was trying to take him forward,

so with a renewal by fear he turned and re-entered fast water
and went down and down, until he was in another deep pool
at a bend of the river. Here he remembered a hole under the
roots of a tree, and tried to hide there, but had not strength
enough to reach the refuge of darkness.

Again he felt release, and swam forward slowly, seeking the
deepest part of the pool, to lie on the bottom with his mouth
open. Then he was on his side, dazed and weary, and the
broken-quicksilvery surface of the pool was becoming whiter.
He tried to swim away, but the water was too thick-heavy;
and after a dozen sinuations it became solid. His head was out
of water. A shock passed through him as he tried to breathe.
He lay there, held by line taut over fisherman's shoulder. He
felt himself being drawn along just under the surface, and only
then did he see his enemy—flattened, tremulant-spreading
image of the fisherman. A new power of fear broke in the
darkness of his lost self. When it saw the tailer coming down
to it, the surface of the water was lashed by the desperately
scattered self. The weight of the body falling over backwards
struck the taut line; the tail-fin was split. The gut broke just
above the hook, where it had been frayed on the rock. Salar
saw himself sinking down into the pool, and he lay there,
scattered about himself and unable to move away, his tail
curved round a stone, feeling only a distorted head joined to
the immovable river-bed.

14

All day Salar lay dull in the pool, under the roots of an alder,
never moving. After the sun had set and other salmon
were leaving their lies and lodges, he swam forward slowly,
painfully. The wind had veered to the north-west, bringing
hard-edged clouds towering in blackness above the moor.
Down in the estuary at midnight fishermen hauled on nets
which held, draught after draught, only seaweed and crabs; they
said nothing at all, they had been wet in empty sea-labour most
of their lives. Salmon from the sea jumped in the wide spate-

water of the fairway and passed up one or other of the Two Rivers. Some of them, fast travellers, moved beside Salar when next evening's sun was spreading rubicund on the hill tops.

Salar followed these new keen fish, his weariness eased, and by sunrise was lying with them in a pool called Denzil's, wide and deep, above another grist-mill weir and the joining place of a third river. In this pool, which was deep because a ledge of rock crossed the river-bed, the clay below having been scooped out by the centuries' spates, lay thirty salmon.

Many of these fish moved on at nightfall, and new fish came in, with Trutta the sea-trout, but Salar remained there. He was apprehensive, and deep water gave serenity. Many times he turned on his side and tried to rub off the iron lacerating the corner of his mouth. Soon most of the skin was rubbed off his jawbone. Body movement was no longer painful, but all his muscles ached.

After a week had passed, the alder leaves growing on the banks above Denzil's Pool were large as the ears of mice which at night moved among the drying litter of twigs, marking the height of the spate on the bank above. One evening a field-mouse fell into the water, and was swimming to the bank when there was a plop, a black scarred neb showing, a jaw opening to reveal many teeth, a swirl on the empty surface. Garroo the cannibal trout had his home under the alder roots.

Atlantic rains falling on the moors had filled the springs in the rock, and the river kept its level for another week. Then it ran slower, and salmon in the middle and lower reaches of the Two Rivers settled down in their lies and lodges.

Every day Salar, resting at the edge of the deepening water, saw lines and lures, which he now recognized as enemies, moving, flickering, spinning at varying speeds over him. For a week the wind continued from the north-west, and nymphs delayed their hatching; and no salmon were taken from the pool, except one foul-hooked by a spinner which caught it in the gill, causing it to bleed to exhaustion in the water.

Salar had been waiting there nearly a fortnight when to-wards the end of a night, as the hollow ruin of the moon was rising through trees, two fish sped past him, turned in shelving

water, and sank beside him. All the fish shared an alertness of
fear. A light darted in the water, moved about, and went out.
Another light shone behind them. Salar swam into the deepest water, where he could see most—forward, above, and
behind. Fish swung and thudded about in alarm. A strange
smell came to him in the water, and he accelerated to the
farther side of the pool.

Two men were wading above the pool, on the edge of the
transverse reef. They carried armfuls of net, which they let
down into deep water. A third man held the end of the rope
under the bank. Sixty yards away two other men were taking
a trammel across the river, in shallowing water below the
pool. A sixth man stood on the bank, waiting silent and listening in the last darkness of night. A heap of old potato sacks
lay near him, the temporary bed of a lean hairy dog with
long thin legs, head, and tail. This was a lurcher, shivering,
curled as though to sleep, but flair-nosed, wide-eyed, cock-eared.
It never barked or growled. It knew the smell of every water-
bailiff in the catchment area of the Two Rivers. The dog
and its master shared a soundless language, of attitude, glance,
and movement.

Across the stickle, where lay the gravel scooped out of the
pool, other men were fixing the trammel, consisting of two
lengths of net, the outer of small mesh for holding, the inner
of large loose squares for entangling, fish.

The six men belonged to a gang which worked pools of
the Two Rivers only at night. The leader, who owned dog
and nets, was a mild-mannered, bespectacled cabinet-maker
by day. The lenses of his spectacles were of plain glass: he wore
them to protect his eyes from wood-dust, and also, by their
absence at night, as a disguise. Four of the men had been fined
by the magistrates of the local town, for poaching. The fining
had occurred before they had formed themselves into a gang,
under the leadership of the cabinet-maker, since when none
had been caught. Its members blackened their faces before
leaving the old and unlicensed saloon car in which they travelled
on their planned raids. One man, however, knew why the
car was used only at night; and that man was Shiner.

Shiner had made and owned and used the trammel net, until he had been surprised one night by the bailiffs, who had confiscated it. Shiner had been summoned, convicted, sentenced to imprisonment; and the Court made an order for the destruction of the trammel net which had been produced as evidence against him. The trammel, however, had been stolen from the court room, during the second prosecution by the clerk to the Board of Conservators—a retired rear-admiral taking salmon with a trout licence only, the excuse being loss of memory due to the war.

The trammel net was never missed, because the local police authorities thought the water-bailiffs had carried it away, and the bailiffs thought the police had removed it. When he had served ten days in prison, Shiner, who had watched the net being taken, said nothing, although he knew who had it. He disliked the gang, because they sometimes worked with methods he considered dirty—they poisoned whole stretches of river by the use of chloride of lime, and blew the pits with gelignite, which destroyed all life in them. Shiner was awaiting an opportunity to get his own back in his own way; for he was not the sort of man to write anonymous letters to police or river-owner.

The gang did not know, when they left their car behind a haystack in a field by the road a quarter of a mile away, that Shiner was watching in the next field. His tool-cart—he was an odd-day gardener to various houses—was hidden behind another haystack. When the gang had left for the river, Shiner climbed through the hedge and, opening the bonnet of their car, unscrewed all the leads to the sparking plugs, fixing them again in wrong order; and then, to make sure the engine would not start, he emptied a small bag of sugar into the petrol tank. After this, struck by a sudden thought, he climbed through the hedge again and removed his tool-cart to the other end of the field, concealing it in a dip of the ground.

Some minutes later he crossed the lane and listened. Then he wetted a forefinger to reassure himself that the breeze was moving from Denzil's Pool in his direction. Afterwards he hid behind an oak tree on the bank above, and waited.

While he was standing there the drift net was spread across the river. Its lead-weighted heel-rope sank into deep water, its line of corks was bellied out by the surface current. Two men, one under each bank and holding an end of rope, began to work their way down the sides of the pool, wading sometimes to their armpits, and gripping branches which overhung the water.

As the drift net slowly moved upon them the salmon became agitated, and moved at great speed up and down the pool. One shot through the wide netting of the trammel, turned immediately from the closer netting beyond, and was caught by the gills. The poachers heard the threshing of broken water, and began to work faster with the drift net. "Go easy," said the leader, standing on the bank above, a dim silhouette against the resolving twilight of dawn. Another fish began to splash.

In the centre of the pool lay Trutta, and near him were Salar and Gralaks. Trutta had known netting in Denzil's Pool two years before. Now, as the drift net came down, he swam aside to the alder, the roots of which in water were like many crayfish huddled together, and pushed under them. Because they recognized Trutta in the stimulation of fear which started old actions in memory, when they had followed him before and so escaped from a like danger, both Salar and Gralaks followed him now and thrust themselves under the matt of alder roots. They stayed there even when the noise and movement of legs was very near. As the disturbance went away another fish pushed in between Salar and Trutta, a terrified brown trout with a black and irregular under-jaw, immense head, sharp teeth, and lean body. This was Garroo the cannibal trout, who was fifteen years old, and weighed seven pounds, and who had long forgotten the fevers of spawning, but not the taste of trout and salmon eggs. In a fury of fear at finding his retreat occupied Garroo bit the tail of Gralaks, and received a slap on the side of his black horny head that caused him to lie limply, for several minutes, diagonally across the parallel bodies of Trutta and Salar.

While the four fish were hidden under the root-clump, the

drift net was approaching the trammel. "Go easy," said the leader. The area between the two nets was slashed with gleams as fish turned and returned. Up to their middle in water, the men who had dragged the drift net were now hauling in the twin ropes of heel and head, only a few yards away from the trammel. The net-ends met on shelving gravel. Gradually the other end of the trammel was brought over, outside the drift net. Within the rocking corks more than a dozen salmon were struggling, torn of gill and tail, scales scraped off skin. The mass of fish was dragged to where the bank was broken by drinking cattle, and one by one they were hauled out on a gaff, and beaten on the nose by the cabinet-maker with a short club of yew-wood weighted with an inlaid spiral of brass.

Nine fish were laid out on the grass, the largest twenty-eight pounds, the smallest seven pounds—one of the grilse of the school led by Gralaks. Quickly nets were stowed into sacks, and the gang, jubilant and now smoking fags, set off across the fields to the lane. It was half an hour to dawn, the shine was already gone from the moon in the great azure glow spreading up the eastern sky. Clouds, hedges, haystacks to the west were black. Their feet rustled frosty grasses. Bullocks which had been crowding and snuffling, black-massed, into the corner by the gate, cantered away, ignored by the lurcher dog, which lifted one ear and glanced at its master, as a cock in the farmyard half a mile away crowed to the morning star.

For nearly an hour they tried to get the car started. First one, then another swung the handle, falling away and cursing in exhaustion.

The cabinet-maker took down the carburettor, and saw a dark sticky liquid, like crude petroleum, in the float chamber. Peering in the tank with the aid of an electric torch, he saw more of it lying at the bottom. He was bitter and blasphemous. It was run off; carburettor reassembled; handle swung again, many times, desperately. The eastern hill-line was a haze of shining, soon the sun would rise and labourers be about. They began to quarrel. Some wanted to divide the fish, and make off homewards across the fields: others, supporting the leader, argued that bestways they should be hid in the stack, and fetched at night. At last the others agreed; but one said, wouldn't the car give away the hiding place? So the salmon, wrapped in sacks, were carried to the adjoining haystack, which had been cut down one side, and concealed on the loose top of it. The nets were hidden in the hedge some distance away, and then, having washed the black from their faces in the ditch, the gang separated and went home across the fields.

A couple of hours later Shiner was wheeling his tool-cart, apparently laden with horse dung, across the market square of the small town. "Do you reckon it be time to till early tetties, midear?" he asked the police sergeant, who every year won prizes for potatoes in the local flower show. "Wait until the ground's in temper; 'tis no use mucketting," replied the sergeant, with amiable importance.

"You'm right," said Shiner, promptly. With a grin he added, "You'd like what I've got in this cart, I dare say? 'Tes proper stuff for growing big tetties."

The sergeant, who had had a kind thought for Shiner since he had been in prison for merely taking salmon, replied, "You keep it for yourself, Shiner; you worked hard enough for it, I reckon."

"You'm right, midear," agreed Shiner, as he went on his way.

That night many of the leading citizens of the town, including several magistrates, dined on salmon which had been bought, surreptitiously, at their kitchen doors.

The old car was abandoned, and the gang broke up.

SUMMER RIVER

15

By the edge of the shallow water two sand-pipers were walking, little brown-mottled birds with long beaks and gentle eyes; meditative waterside birds, who had just flown from Abyssinia to their summer home by the stream. They were still in a dream of migration, their eyes saw the river and green meadows and great oaks and chestnuts on the hillside; but those eyes were sea-dazed, they were tired, they were content to be together by the edge of the grass and gravel, to hear the low song of water, to take a stone-fly just hatched from its larval skin on a dry stone, to see the white clouds in the blue above.

The sand-pipers had crossed the sea, arriving at the Island at dusk, resting there all night, and in the morning had flown to the estuary, and up the valley, following the river as it grew smaller and ran quicker, as it tumbled white between rocks and ran clear over stretches of yellow gravel.

A few miles away, on high ground under the northern sky, the river began its life in the rushes and cotton-grass bogs of the moor. Thither the minds of the sand-pipers were set, as they walked by the waterside, feeding lightly; sometimes rising scarcely higher than the level of the stream to fly a few yards, tremulously, as though flight for them now were a short trilling song of the gentle English spring.

Here the stream ran through a park, where fallow-deer roamed of olden time; now it was pasture for bullocks, black sheep, and horses. The horses were tall and powerful, muscles rippling under glossy skin, long tails swishing as they drank at the ford above the bridge. They were out to grass after the fox-hunting season. They drank slowly, sucking long and delicately, pawing the gravel, content in one another and the windy warmth of the April sun.

Half a dozen striding plunges took the leading horse, a black gelding called Midnight, across the river. The other horses followed, the water of the ford torn by their knees. They climbed out on the opposite bank, whinnying, as though teasing or challenging one another, red-nostrilled, bright-eyed, and suddenly they were galloping away, tails streaming from brown and grey and black. The sand-pipers arose at the thud of hooves and flew on a few yards with tremulous slowness, before sinking again and walking gravely at the water verge.

Salar felt the thuds of hooves as the herd was crossing the ford. He was lying in deeper water twenty yards below, where the run slowed and glided uneven above the uneven stony bottom. Alders hung over the water, giving shade now the sun was across the meridian. He lay with his chin on dark green water-moss, which grew on and covered a smooth shelf of rock. Cold clear water flowed by him. He rested, lightly, on sand graded to the length of his white belly, motionless while the sand stirred in grains by his grey fins with their pinkish tinge. He rested, away from himself in an unconscious dream of water flowing from everlasting to everlasting. The wounds on jaw and flank, and the bruises gotten in attempts to ascend the two weirs above Denzil's Pool, were healing.

A few lengths behind him Gralaks was swimming, in the slow current wimpling by water-growing alder roots. She hovered a few inches under the surface. Sometimes the tip of her dorsal fin drew a fine riffle through the undulating reflection of leaves and trunks and sky. And farther down, in shadow by the stone base of the middle pier of the bridge, lay Trutta.

The bridge was hump-backed, built towards the end of the eighteenth century, in an age of the picturesque and landscape ornament among the landed proprietors of England. Water flowed under its three arches and slid whitely into a deep pit beneath. Salar had reached this pit four nights after leaving Denzil's Pool. Immediately above the bridge he had found a lodge, both pleasant and safe, in deep water beside the middle pier. The deep water continued under alder roots and hollows of the bank. Salar explored these, and then swam up the throat of the pool into swifter water, where he rolled in delight. For an hour or more he lay in the run, then he let the current take him, tail-first, over ledges of rock, to the water rebulging from the central pier. There Gralaks was lying, and the two lay side by side, enjoying the clarity and taste of the water, the feel of loose gravel under them, the gleaming movement of trout before them, and the nymphs swimming down one after another. Secure and happy, they enjoyed the river life as little fish again.

Shiner, who worked two days a week in the garden of a house just outside the Deer Park, saw sudden-broad gleams in the dim green water as he peered over the northern parapet of Humpy Bridge during his dinner hour. It was as though first one fish, then the other, turned on its side to scoop something off the gravel in its mouth. In front of the salmon, and to the right in shoaling water, he saw an occasional tiny gleam, not whitey-green and slow like the salmon, but yellowish swift flashes, trout half-rolling to seize hatching nymphs. All the fish were feeding on them.

As Shiner lounged on the bridge, peering down, he wondered how long it would take him to get those fish out: less than a couple of minutes when the water was low.

A week later when the old man went there, the water-level had dropped. The stream no longer bulged back from the piers, but slid in shadow darkly past them. The noon sun shone on the gravel above, revealing every stone and waving green tuft of water-crowfoot growing out of the gravel. Yellow stones were now brown; purple and grey shillets were dulled. Everywhere the algae was growing, making the riverbed dark. Larger stones were speckled with the shelters of crawling larvae of flies: little cabins of stone-chip and sand cemented together by the larvae, which browsed on the river-pastures of the algae.

Shiner knelt on the grass-edge under the stone upper parapet of the bridge and stared at the trout and parr lying on the gravel, their black and red spots vivid in the sun. They might have been lying under glass, so still and bright were fish and water. The midday sun was hot on the old man's back, the beams pierced his coat which was ragged like lichen, and the colour of the stone of the bridge. He wondered if the salmon had been gaffed out; he could not see any long blurred shapes in the water. While he peered a trout sprang for a fly, and the ripple-shadows were golden on the gravel. He watched another sidle to a floating leaf-fragment, eye it, hesitate, and then return to its hover.

A few minutes later, as he was washing his hands beside the stream, a thought came suddenly to Shiner that astonished him: the fish in the river must enjoy swimming in such clear, cold water, and they were alive just as he was alive.

Swallows returned from Africa, and flew over the river, gliding down to dip their breasts in the water, and arise dark-forked of wing and tail, twittering their joy of azure air and gliding stream. When next Shiner looked over the parapet, while munching bread and bacon between his gums, the gravel was a darker brown, long strings were tangling out from the crowfoot plants, and dark green flannel-weed was beginning to cover the stones of the shallows. An edge of gravel showed dry and bleached under the rushes of the bank opposite the alders. Many more gravel-speck cabins were on the under-water stones. No trout were visible. He wondered if someone had limed the water at night; that would account for no fish.

All the trout were in the fast run rippling in the throat of the pool. Beside the run horses stood and swished their tails, pawing the loose stones and dipping their noses in water which cooled their feet and swirled by their fetlocks. Behind and beside one another the trout lay, watching for stone-fly creepers which were leaving water for air. From the shelter of the undersides of flat stones the insects were creeping, making for the shallows. Some were washed down, struggling and clutching with their six legs, each multi-hooked, at the gravel. They were miniature flattened alligators, with wide bullfrog heads. Each had a tail of two long, slender prongs. The trout watched for them, each fish before or behind a stone which gave shelter from the bubble-rushing water: the biggest trout in the best position, the next biggest in the next best position. The best position was where four flumes, each a food-stream sweeping over a different part of the gravel ridge, met by a mossy stone which stayed the quadruple flow momentarily and intertwined them. Thus a fourfold supply of food was to be sucked in there.

A trout of a pound and a quarter, unusually big for that moorland stream, lay with its tail-fin pressed against the stone. Its eyes were fixed on the four-fold twist, which often enswirled a brown, yellow-bellied creeper. *Snap*, and a complex mechanism, in course of changing its motive apparatus from swimming to flying, was sucked into wide jaws, crushed and reduced to fragments, dissolved by acids into a liquid which would be used in building up tissues in the trout's muscles for the maintenance of itself before the stone.

Many times a red-spotted pennant fin showed and vanished in breaking water; the stone-fly creepers, drawn by the lightness of the water, were moving thickly from their retreats.

Once the big trout turned and rushed at Graula the smolt, which had dashed into its feeding place and taken a creeper before the trout had fully opened its jaws for the force of water to sweep the insect into its mouth. Opening its mouth wider, the trout slashed at Graula, who skipped along the water and escaped while the trout, falling sideways after its turning rush, was borne away from its stone. Two other smolts flashed away from the sight of big yellow belly and blue neb. When the trout got back to its place, it found another trout there, one nearly as big as itself, which had moved up from behind the stone. This other trout was driven off, and returning to its place behind the stone, it found Graula there. The smolt slivvered away to another feeding position.

Graula and the other smolts were more slender than trout of their own size. Most of them were two years old, as long as a man's hand. Graula was three years old, and bigger. They were changing their moorland coats for the coming sea-venture. The black and red spots were overlaid by a blue sheen; the back also was blue, and on each gill cover was a purplish mark. The smolts were stronger and swifter than the trout; smaller mouthed, tail-fins forked, bodies more slender for the whip of speed.

Graula remained feeding on creepers until the shadows of the alders lay short in the water; it was afternoon: the hatch was over. Then the smolt dropped back with the current, passing the root-mass below which lay Gralaks.

Attracted by the lithe gleam of the little fish, the grilse rose and swirled the surface with her tail-fin; an action of pleasure, for the sight of the smolt stirred within her a feeling, beyond memory, of a journey to unknown great waters. The smolt saw the salmon, and a strange excitement played in it, adding to the feeling which had been growing more strongly day after day, as the river carried it from stickle to pool, from pool to glide and surge and run, always downwards to an unknown excitement. So they passed—Graula and Gralaks, two units of the water-spirit, sisters as it chanced: for they had hatched together from a redd above the Fireplay Pool, dug by the same parent, nearly three and a half years before.

The earth and her seas turned from the sun, and the first twilight brought the water-bat from its hanging perch under the middle arch of the bridge, the white owl floating over the grass, and rabbits looking forth from their burrows scrabbled among the roots of the ancient oaks and chestnuts of the Deer Park. Graula was then in the deep pool above Sawmills Weir, hovering on the edge of the fast glide before the lip of the fall, fearful of dropping tail-first into white water, where enemies would be lurking.

In the night Graula went down the leat, with other smolts, and was swept under the fender with the overflow; for the mill-wheel was not working.

When the earth revolved into sunlight again the smolts were lying under a hillside of tall fir trees. On the crest of a Douglas pine stood a heron, gilded by sunrise on a field of azure.

By next dimmit light the smolts were come to Steep Weir, most dreaded by all kelts returning that way, for the river fell sheer from an overhanging irregular lip, to rock beneath, on which the water broke heavily. Only in high spate were clean-run fish able to surmount Steep Weir, by swimming up the solid brown curve of water.

On May Day, when black swifts from Ethiopia were hurtling through the upper air screaming with almost reptilian excitement at their return to the valley, Graula was below Otter Islet and the Junction Pool. The dark bars on her sides, as though inky fingers had clutched her, were silver-blue, and she had grown longer, slimmer, more forked of tail. During the midday hatch of duns the water was everywhere dippled by the migrating schools. Sea-trout smolts moved with them, all their dorsal fins straked with white; the pennant fins of some were single-spotted, others blotched with vermilion. Their cousins the salmon smolts had no red on their pennants. Down the river they went, Graula among them, under railway bridges and round wide bends, through pool and stickle and jabble and run, and so to the deep Carrion Pit, where the final soft stannic lustre was put upon their scales. They drew the sea into them, they leaped among the first tidal waves, they knew the fear of nets although escape was always sudden swift through the large meshes. Among the strangeness of seaweed Graula swam, rejoicing in the new food which was so plentiful by the sides of deep rocks.

For awhile the smolts travelled with the tides, until one day the river was forgotten, and they went down over streaming gravel banks under The String, meeting place of the Two Rivers; past the weedy chain of the Pool buoy, leaping as the ebb took them under the Shrarshook Ridge, watched by fishermen whose unformed thoughts were for the welfare of the little fish. Beyond the lighthouse, white at the edge of sandhills, past the beach where pied oyster-catchers stood thick in flock, under the keels of small yachts heeling to the western breeze, through the tide-rip over the rocks called Hurley-burlies, and so to the tolling bell-buoy, and the open sea over the sandy shoals. There big grey bass, spined of gill-cover and dorsal fin, were waiting for them; and of the sea Graula knew no more.

16

Under most of the bridges and by the waterfalls of the Two Rivers, small and sturdy black birds, with white breasts, were calling their young from domed nests made thickly of water-moss and lined with dry beech leaves. These nests were hung on ledges or in crevices of rock near the water. Some were fixed in the face of falls, dripping wet with drops;

but dry inside. The birds, called dippers or water-ousels, delighted to perch on points of rock in the stream, or bankside snags, and sing to the water. They turned about as they sang, restless as water, bobbing and curtsying; they quitted their singing places abruptly, flying with strong flight, usually following the river course, but sometimes cutting across bends.

When Salar had swum over Steep Weir, a mile above Denzil's Pool, a bird had been flying agitatedly in the spray and thunder of the fall: its nest was in the face of the stone weir, behind the barrage of white water. The dipper had built it during the drought of February and March, when it had flown fearlessly through thin water. For two days the bird had flipped about the weir, crying its sharp watery cries, and on the third day a tree branch had lodged on the sill and split the solid overfall; the bird had dived through to its eggs, cold and white on the beech leaves. Since she had not begun to brood them when the spate had risen, they were unharmed. They hatched out two weeks afterwards, when Salar was settled in his lodge above Humpy Bridge.

There was a dipper's nest under the middle arch of Humpy Bridge. The bird had sat there serenely while the spate was lapping its foundations. Trutta lying at the base of the middle pier was used to black and white flickering at the nest above him. He heeded no longer white splashes in the water, as the bird cleaned its nest before flying away. Trutta had often seen a dipper flying down the river: a blur ploughing the quicksilvery surface, forming into white-black over him an instant before blurring out again.

Every day the water moved slower and warmer, and Trutta left his lie by the cutwater for a trough in the pool upstream. The last sight he had of the dippers before he moved away was four heads thrust out of the side of the nest as the parent flew and clung there, with caddis grubs, and sometimes the fry of trout and salmon, in its beak.

Two days after the sea-trout had moved upstream, Midnight, the black hunter, wading in water under the shade of the bridge, swishing its tail, sniffed at the nest. Immediately there was a brook-chatter of noise, and four young dippers fell out and dived into the water. Midnight drew back in astonishment. The nestlings, who had never before left the dark interior of the nest, swam away from the horse's legs, underwater. First one, then another, bobbed up after a dozen wing-oarings. Their plumage was a greasy blue-black. They lay in the water like miniature cormorants, heads low and necks outstretched. The current took them over the fall, down amidst a swarm of bubbles to a sandy bed wherein sodden branches were embedded. They oared themselves to the surface, and scrambled out on the rocky walling beside the pool, to crouch shivering in a row, blinking at the unfamiliar bright sky and loud noise of the river. Soon the parent birds found them, and fed them; the noon sun looked in upon the shelf where they were perched, and they ceased to shiver.

When the rays of the sun touched Trutta, as he lay still in the deepest part of the pool above Humpy Bridge, he pushed in under the alder roots, to the brown-green dimness of a hiding place. The movement dislodged many fragments of algae which had been growing on the roots, covering them with a brown slime. The fragments were borne slowly to the surface, lifted by small bubbles glinting on them. This algae was in decay, and the bubbles were of carbonic acid gas. It grew fast in sunlight and heat, absorbing oxygen for growth, and giving off the gases of death.

Everywhere except in the fast runs this algae was growing, rising in fragments with the lightness of bubbles, and floating to the surface. No fish were in the stagnant backwaters where it grew most thickly. Only water-snails crawled there. Between the runs and the edges of still areas of water scores of fry, of salmon and trout, were quivering to maintain position, watching for cyclops and daphnia and minute larvae of water-flies. If one of the fry came too near the hover of another, it was driven away, and within the space of a quarter-second the rightful owner of four cubic inches of water was back in its place, watching for approaching food. These fry were no longer than the top joint of a man's finger. They had tiny red and black spots on their scales. Some of them were already double and triple fratricides.

By mid-May the mossy stone in front of which the largest trout had lain during the hatch of stoneflies was above the water, its top was white where dippers had perched, the moss was brown and dry. Mingled grey lines showed old levels. Amidst the dry moss clung the shucks of creepers, brittle and vacant, each burst at the thorax whence a damp fly had writhed a way into air and sunshine. Male stoneflies had short stub wings, but the wings of females had grown and uncrinkled as they hid on the undersides of stones, waiting for twilight mating.

Sometimes a stonefly, as yet unaware of flight, would attempt to cross to the farther bank, its six legs moving fast as it was spun about in the glittering rapids—a narrow, dark fly, long as one of the salmon fry which darted themselves at it with scarce-perceptible splashes. The fly skated on, suddenly disappearing into a suck-snapping noise amidst the running babble-glitter.

While Salar and Trutta and Gralaks were hiding in lethargy from the glare of the day, other things rejoiced in the water. Bullocks stood in the shade of alders, chewing the cud, meditating coolth and the inanity of themselves. Drawing a line of startling blue down the middle of the river, Halcyon the king-fisher shot through the centre arch of the bridge, seven fry held in throat and beak for his seven young perched on a willow in the pool of Sawmills Weir. Soon he was back again, drawing a line less straight because his flight was rising. He left a cry, hard and keen as an edge of glass, in the shadow of the bridge.

Then daintily flitting, sipping through air as it sipped from water, a slender grey bird with yellow breast and long tail lit on the mossy stone and undulated there, never still but never restless, lilting with colour and movement of water, and calling with rillet voice to its mate seeking stoneflies by the river verge. Men called this dancing bright slim bird a dishwasher! It skipped off the stone, twirled to take an olive dun in air, returned to the stone, danced and rose again, took two other flies and skipped away to its nest under a rock by a waterfall.

When the sun was central in his burning arc many nymphs were hatching. Dusky alder flies crawled laboriously up the trunks of trees and the stonework of Humpy Bridge; yellow sallies ran there hastily, as though in astonishment of their own quickness; olive duns flew up almost vertically from the surface after hatching, to seek the shade of leaves and there to dry the dew from their wings, and await the final brightness of life.

Down to the ford came the glossy hunters, led by Midnight and a little ancient pony. This small horse, thin of leg and neck but otherwise rotund, had wandered about the deer park disconsolately, for many weeks, until the hunters had been turned out to graze; then the pony had found a friend. Before their coming it had moved about alone, scarcely able to enjoy a pensioned life of freedom: a mere observer of sheep, hens, pigs, and bullocks. But now these high-stepping tail-fleeing lordly ones were come, the pony enjoyed every moment of life, following them at an energetic canter when they paced away at a long trot; and neighing shrilly when they thundered away at the gallop. No longer did it suffer an extended rotundity, caused by indigestion and a dull landscape. It always grazed beside Midnight, by this act most proud of itself.

The horses stood on the stickle, while drinking and pawing the gravel, causing innumerable small stones and specks of sand to move away, disturbing the lives of nymphs, snails, limpets, shrimps, larvae of gnats and other two-winged flies, leeches, fry of salmon and trout, elvers, lampreys, caddis, water-spiders, and myriad differing forms of small life.

One of the pawing strokes of the pony nearly killed a little squat fish called Gobio, and her ninety-seven young, which Gobio was guarding under a stone about as thick as a man's finger and half as large as his hand. Gobio lay still; there was little else to do in life but lie still and pretend to be part of the gravel. She clung with fins like two fans to the edge of the stone, her yellow body spotted and blotched as gravel. When the waterflow became regular again, she wriggled under the stone, to be beside her ninety-seven offspring, which she had stuck to the stone for safety.

Once Gobio had been to Gralaks an apparition with huge open mouth trying to prise away great rocks whither the alevin had hidden for safety. That was three years ago. To the new-hatched Gralaks, her egg sac yet unshrunken to be a belly, stones smaller than walnuts had been great rocks: and Gobio, little more than an inch long, had been the most fearful thing in the river.

Actually Gobio the mullhead was almost the most frightened thing of the Two Rivers. She was food for nearly everything that swam or dived or peered into the water. Although two years older than Gralaks, Gobio was only a little longer than her pennant fin. Eels were her worst enemies; they thrust their snouts under stones, and writhed to lever them up with their necks—rippling strength turning and screwing and waving while the mullhead resembled more and more the fixity of gravel. The night before Salar and Gralaks had moved into the pool above Humpy Bridge, Gobio had been in dire peril. A big blue-black eel which lived there for the pigs' and rabbits' guts and other things which sometimes were tipped into the river from the near-by farm, was digging for Gobio, when, just in time, an otter had come along. The eel lashed in vain; it writhed itself into a knot of slime about the head of the otter on the bank; all but its heart, near the tail, was eaten. A fox ate the head, later.

Now Gobio was waiting under her favourite stone, to which her ninety-seven eggs were stuck. Within each egg two dark eyes were rolling about, as though signalling to escape. Gobio was on guard, valiant defender against the raids of any caddis or dragonfly larva; and also, a meal ready for any trout, salmon, eel, otter, duck, kingfisher, heron, moorhen, or dab-chick. The stone, and her gravel-coloured skin, were her only protection.

Having cooled their feet and drunken their fill, the horses walked away to renewed interest in grass. The gravel settled again. The last of the hoof-frog scent was carried past the hiding place of Salar. Under the big fish was a silt of decayed leaves and dead weed and residue of old spates. Snails drew their wandering lines through the algae which gave the mud a covering as of velvet. Sometimes from this soft dissolution a bubble shook upwards, the vapour of death. The temperature of the slow eddy rose slowly, and there came a moment when Salar's breathing made him aware of the heaviness of his head; he moved out, into dazzling sunlight, to meet the shock of cold water which made him leap for the pleasure of falling back into an illusion of sea waves. For a while he remained in the run, his back fin just under the surface, and his paired fins hardly clearing the ledge of rock which crossed the river there. Feeling his leap, Gralaks edged out of her hide, and lobbed herself out of the water a few lengths ahead of Salar. Trutta was more cautious; he hovered, with slow sinuations of pinkish-grey tail in shadow, close to the mass of roots which hid him from enemies.

Soon Salar became used to the golden dazzle behind him, the sharp clearness of rock and stone and weed before his eyes, the distinctness of leaves and branches and flying birds over him. He felt uneasy in thin water under the bright sky, and returned to his hide, pushing under the roots until his tail-fin was hidden, and only his head was showing. There he fell into a torpor, breathing slowly, sometimes twice in rapid succession.

For nearly half an hour Shiner had been kneeling by the upper parapet of the bridge. He watched the grey-white mark appearing and disappearing in the water by the alder roots, as Salar opened and closed his mouth. He went back to the garden and told his boss what he had seen, and how the big salmon was "slunging his chine down there in the moots of th' harlder". The old man added that he would be sorry if anything happened to the fish. Then looking at the small globules of green-gages forming on the tree spread against the south wall of the cottage, he said, "They birds wull be after they plums in a few weeks; I've got some old netting put back in the shed to my place, I'll bring it along, 'tes a nice tree, and I reckon they old blackbirds can find all the food they wants among the snails and slugs."

17

Motionless, save for movement of mouth and gills, Salar lay under the mass of dead and living roots. Above the water-roots, and from those exploring the earth of the river bank, arose three trunks of alder. They were lichened; their branches died easily; the alder was a tree that spread itself by earth and water, easily abandoning its injured limbs and off-shoots, and creating others.

One of the trunks of the alder under which Salar was sheltering had been dead some years. Its branches were all fallen away from it. Fungus, lichen, and moss grew on it. Many holes of woodpeckers were picked in its soft wood, where grubs had tunnelled. One of the holes was neater and rounder than the others: entrance to a nest gouged by Hackma and his mate, woodpeckers. They were little black birds capped with red, with white-speckled wings. In the nest six young woodpeckers were chissiwissing incessantly. Before they had come into the woody hollow as eggs, while the nest was being gouged, the dead branch of one of the great Spanish chestnuts on the hillside had often resounded with the excess excitement of Hackma; he used its hard core to amplify his drumming song, which sounded as though he were striking the wood with his beak many times a second. But now Hackma's energy throbbed no more between tongue and palate. He was too weary to sing. For eighteen hours a day he sought for and fetched for and filled six (seven were his mate at home) chissiwissing throats in the hollow of the dead alder.

Salar heard the noises of claws and of wings rustling. They were audible in the roots. He watched something moving slowly up one root, and connected the movement with the noises. The thing he watched was like a small prawn, with a pointed tail, grey, crawling slowly up a root from which fragments of algae fell away. It had a plated mask-like head and jaws which had eaten many fry of salmon, creepers, and elvers. During its wanderings in mud it had torn out small lampreys by the tail from the silt in which they lay buried. This creature's life in the river's backwaters was a preparation for solar life of brittle and flashing splendour.

Salar watched the slow crawl up the root and the reflexion of the larva crawling down to meet it, until the two met, merging into one at the scintillant surface, to proceed upwards in the blurr of air. It crept straight up the bark of the dead trunk and as it rose higher Salar saw it clearer, for it was directly above him.

While watching, he forgot the itch in his gills, where small white maggots were hanging, sucking his blood.

The grey crawler stopped under a dried patch of fungus and became fixed there. It did not move; and yet there was violent movement within the shell. Legs, eyes, thorax, body, tail, were being urged away from the fixture of old life by an irritation of power which caused it to strain and twist, until it broke away.

However, its freedom was not yet gained. It was still shut away from the sun which, for the first time in its life, was to be sought, not avoided. Its head, with the rapacious mandibles, was pivoted on the armour of its thorax; and forcing it round within the grey shell, which was becoming more brittle every moment, it bit with its mandibles and strained to reach the sunlight. When the shell was dry it split, and at once a different being began to tear a way out.

Salar watched the head moving outside and getting larger as it dragged itself out of the shuck. It came out backwards, as though to crawl down to the river. After a rest it began again, and pulled itself clear. It walked away, unsteadily, then clung to the fungus with its six legs, which were set with hooks to the knees. It was colourless, flaccid, unmoving; and lost shape in Salar's sight.

The salmon dozed, lying there aimlessly, he who was formed for piercing leagues of ocean, who had leapt away his power's excess in the foam of waves a thousand miles from land. He too was being changed by a Spirit of which he knew nothing except in a dim recurrent rhythm of excitement.

When next Salar fixed the sight of his left eye on the trunk above, an hour later, the brittle shuck was still clinging to the bark below the clot of dry fungus. Beside it was Libellula the dragonfly, a tremulous movement of body and four wings held to the sun. In the first hour of her freedom the wings had sprouted from the buds and uncurled to crinkle as the sun poured its fierceness into their network of nervules which strengthened the membranes. The dragonfly clung there, wings quivering with waves of feeling flowing to it from the sun.

And while it skimmed there, drawing colour from the golden dragon of the sun, it felt the need for movement, and with a sudden rustle of wings was away on its first flight. Its luminous eyes, with their many facets, quested a crinkling sheen like to itself. Hour by hour it absorbed more colour, until it was an emerald green.

Many times during the days of hotter sunshine Libellula returned to the dry alder trunk, and Salar saw her there, brown against the sky. From above, Libellula was a deep green, with black head and legs. When clouds hid the sun, and at night, she lay quiet, a being neither of air nor water, the metallic sheens gone from her wings, desire gone from her; but when the fiery breath of the solar dragon touched her, she became swift and fierce with the very heat and light of life. Her globular eyes were inpouring with sunlight; they fixed upon other winged flight, her prehensile mask moved forward from her face, she pursued and snapped her prey, clipping off wings and legs and tearing and swallowing.

In flight Libellula met others like herself, and the matings were fierce and selfish as all her life. Wings and mandibles of male dragonflies clashed by her; she drew to herself all who came. Her wings burnt to a darker green; until the fire passed from her, and she clung to the alder below the phantom of her old life, her eyes unfixed from aerial movement, and filled with the vacancy of sky.

Salar watched Libellula clinging there, without interest. The itch in his gills was irking more every day as the river moved slower and warmer. When he had first leapt in the pool the river had been running bank-high; but now it was scarcely trickling over the shallows, where more stones were grey-white with bleached algae.

Soon after the sun had passed the meridian he moved out of the shelter of roots and tried to scrape off the irritation on the top of the water. He was seen below, on his side, pushing his head along the surface, half roll, half leap. His colours revealed his staleness. The back which had been like new-cut lead was now a brownish-blue; pink was tingeing the dulling scales of his flank; and the underpart, which had been white as porcelain during the journey from the sea, was now a yellowish grey, with a worn resting patch at the point of balance. The lower jaw was smudged with black, and greenish with the slime of stagnation. Along the split of the tail-fin were two lines of opaque yellow, and the skin around the lamprey-wound was also ringed with yellow, which was spreading slowly on the dead tissues of the skin. It was fungus, as on the dead wood above him. This fungus disease spread only at night, when the water was cold; warmth of day checked its growth. It grew also along the bony edge of his lower jaw, where the hook had been stuck, and where skin had been scraped against gravel, trying to ease the maggot-itch in his gills.

Salar's shape was slowly changing, too. His head had grown longer, and the kype at the end of the lower jaw was more hooked, so that he could not entirely close his mouth. His skin was thickening, his stomach had shrunk away. He had taken neither nymph nor fly for more than a month. His spirit was depressed and dull as his appearance. Long since the sea-lice had sickened and died and dropped away, and in their place fresh-water shrimps flipped about on his back, sometimes clinging to the fins and nibbling the edges, the salmon unmoving, penned under the roots, in a little shrunken river that Midnight could almost jump across. In the low summer level the deepest water of the pool was hardly up to the hunter's chest.

Brilliant sun: absorption of radiant heat increasing: temperature of water rising above that of air. Not a trout moved, even to flies which fell on the water. Decaying algae absorbed oxygen. All the trout were lying in the fast stickle, where it rippled and dashed and took from circumambient air oxygen which was the life of the river. Salar breathed irregularly; the colder, fresher water did not pass by the roots, but in the middle of the river.

Below Humpy Bridge, below its deeper pool, cattle stood in the shade of alders, knocking tails against branches and hips in torment of gadflies whose low buzz they had heard for the first time that year. The flies settled on their red backs, boring through the skin until they tasted blood; the flies gorged themselves, swelling lazy and content and dozing, to awaken and dig deeper until their heads were liquid. Some fell into the water, to be carried down struggling feebly; trout looked at them, and let them pass. The fish were used to prisms of light, diaphanous wings and delicate touch of waterflies.

316

Wild pigeons and the smaller turtle doves flew down to the shallows by the run, to drink, and cool their feet in the murmurous water. On long green strings the water-crowfoot waved and twisted, its flowers and buds drowning as the current turned them over; slowly they swung back, untwisting, and white cups of blossom looked at the sun a moment before the water swept them under once again. Nearly every dry stone bore its creeper case, frail and empty, clinging there in still life, wind-trembled.

The salmon waited dull, prisoners of the drought. Other things rejoiced in the heat and light. The white of its breast increasing, the dipper sped down under the shadow of the alders, diminishing sturdy blackness. Other dippers, less white of breast, grey-brown of back, young birds, followed. The leading dipper rose over Humpy Bridge and dived down again to follow the river. When the family had gone, the kingfisher— smaller, faster, keener—drew his straight blue line through bends and curves: flashing brilliance of emerald and sapphire changing to tawny of underwing as it passed, narrowing blue again to shoot under the middle arch and pierce with silver lancing cry the stone-reflected water-shadow.

Jackdaws with ashen pates, and azure eyes as of heat's insanity, flew over and floated down like burnt paper to the ford, to lower heads and sip and raise black beaks, and fly away with cries less querulously jangling. Old Nog the heron drifted over, hesitated, wheeled on hollow wings, vol-planed down, and alighted on yellow stilt legs upon a grassy mound by the bank. After staring around with bone-splintered sharpness, while the black plumes of breast and head waved against his smoke-grey plumage, the heron stalked into the shallow water where he stood still, blinking at his own reflection wavering and sun-splashed. Seeing the neb of a trout show for an instant as it took a fly, he walked forward, with head down-held, to the first riband of fast water, from under which little shadows darted. He waited for them to return, settled into stillness, yellow-spindled, emaciated long neck extending from humped shoulders, narrow head with its thin black plumes of mock-mourning for death of many fish he struck, but never ate.

317

After waiting there a couple of minutes, Old Nog saw a change of wavelet shape in the run. He peered lower. A sea-trout, fresh from four months' feeding in rock pools and sandy surf of the coast, after its return from spawning during the winter, had moved into the run. It was the first of the summer run of small sea-trout, and had left the estuary six days before, resting by day and travelling by night. With a precise stroke of slightly open beak the heron stabbed it; with another he held it. Holding it aloft, curving and recurving in struggle to be free, Old Nog walked to the bank, up which he clambered with the help of elbow'd wings, and dropped it on the grass. There it flacked and writhed, while he watched it with a gravity of narrow head and small yellow eyes.

Two crows saw the fish from on high, and flew down. They alighted near, and began to walk around as though they had seen neither heron nor fish. Old Nog ignored them. The crows looked in the grass for beetles, then abandoning the mock-search, stood still, watching the heron; but remaining well beyond the striking range of the beak One flew up and settled on the other side of the heron. Old Nog gave each a glance, then peered down, picked up the sea-trout, which weighed nearly two pounds, as though it were no bigger than a smolt, and dropped it again, turning it over.

After an apparently careful inspection of the fish—he was really watching the male crow which had walked closer behind him—Old Nog picked it up once more, and let it fall, as though it were distasteful. Then he lifted it and tossed it, caught it by the head, and tried to swallow it. With scissor-beak wide open and legs braced, he gulped. Immediately the male crow flew at him, cawing angrily, and pecked at his eyes. Old Nog jerked the fish away and a grey feathered snake struck at the crow, who avoided the thrust and hopped away, to squat on the grass as though it had never seen a fish or a heron, and scratch its poll with the claw of the middle toe of its right foot.

Again the heron, ignoring the crows, peered at the silver-shining fish, as though examining the clove-shaped spots along its length, to which fragments of dry grass and earth were sticking. After turning it over several times, rubbing it along the turf, picking it up by the tail and dropping it again, Old Nog began to break it open, for the amber-pinkish eggs which he knew, from the fish's shape, might be inside it. This was his favourite food, as it was of most living things in the river. The eggs, however, were ungrown, a small mass of orange specks which he swallowed. He was not hungry, having eaten many smaller sea-trout, half a pound and under, at the edge of Sloping Weir only an hour before.

Had the crows not been there, Old Nog would have abandoned the fish on the bank, and returned to the water; but as they were waiting there he stayed too, looking anywhere but at the birds directly. Thus he was alert for instant action. He saw the figure of a man before they did; but the change in his attitude told the crows that a common enemy was near, and they were in the air before the heron was. With circular sweep of wings to push the air behind him, and with scaly knees bent for a jump, Old Nog got off the ground and swept himself away upriver.

The man, who was Shiner, shut the deer park gate behind him and walked under the tall lime trees towards the bridge. Knowing why the crows had been waiting there, he crossed the river and walked fifty paces to the ford, where he saw the mutilated sea-trout. Thus Shiner acquired a good supper for himself and his kitten---as he called a cat which had lived with him for more than thirteen years.

18

When Shiner had gone back to the garden to work, a small bird flew to the river and waited on a branch of alder for something it had seen arising from the water. The bird was a female chaffinch, and its nest was in the fork of an apple tree in the garden, two hundred yards distant. So lichened and mossy was the apple tree, so nobbled and flaked and twisted in its effort to escape its parasites, that the nest had not been seen even by the sharp eye of Shiner. During the second week of April the chaffinch had moulded her nest to the fork, using horsehair, spider-web, moss, feather, and lichen: smoothing the cup in its centre by squatting within and turning round, pressing breast against pleached hair and feathers.

Now eight halves of eggshells lay below, and the young chaffinches were nearly fledged, with nestling down waving on their new and quill-scurfy feathers.

From before sunrise until after sunset every day the hen chaffinch, helped irregularly by her mate, collected insects in her beak, and flew to the nest, where four mouths were nearly always outstretched to take them from her.

The name of the cock chaffinch was Coelebs. He was more gaily coloured than his hen. From various vantage perches he sang a monotonous interrogative song which sounded to the gardener's ears like *Will-you will-you will-you will-you will-you kiss-me-dear?* During the courtship he had repeated this refrain all day; when the eggs were laid he had sung with less excitement; when they were first hatched the quality of his song changed to a flat monotony; and now that the young chaffinches were nearly fledged, Coelebs sang only occasionally, and usually from a distance, and at sight of strange hen chaffinches. The fledgelings knew his voice and song, and listened for it.

During the previous winter he had flown with many other chaffinches as gay as himself: the Romans, who had observed this habit of cockbirds flying in a flock, gave to the bird the name of Coelebs—the bachelor.

The hen had seen something fluttering palely from the river, and had flown to an alder branch to await the arising of another. She remembered this luscious food from the spring before during her first nesting. Wiping her short, blunt, pointed beak —made for seeds rather than insects—on the branch in anticipation, she looked about her, turning her head to one side for a moment as she heard, from far away down the river, the familiar *Will-you will-you will-you will-you will-you kiss-me-dear?*

A shadowy movement in the river below—which the bird saw clearly to its bed of rock and gravel and dark green moss —made her turn her other eye to see what was happening. A greyness was moving in slow diagonal, with slow waves of tail, into clear water with rippling golden shadow-lines on the rock under. It lost outline as it entered fast water, but the chaffinch saw it there, a shadowy blur, lying still.

Again she cocked her head sideways, to assure herself that the big bird swinging over the valley was not dangerous. *Gor-ock!* cried Old Nog, seeing that the sea-trout he had left on the bank was gone. *Gor-ock!* His craw was tumultuous with two eels, black corkscrews which he had lifted from the river by the carcass of a salmon left, the night before, by a family of otters. The broken fish lay on a sand scour behind a tree-root embedded in the gravel, ten minutes' flight up the valley.

Gor-oo! One eel was trying to move up his gorge. Old Nog did not want to lose the eel, nor did he want his crop continually to be coming into his mouth like that. His cries of indecision were heard by the crows, which had been searching for pheasant chicks and young rabbits in the fir plantations of the hillside, and *kaa-kaa-Nog!* they cursed him.

The heron flew away, and immediately the chaffinch forgot it. The bird's eyes were never still. They looked at the river, at the sky, at the branches, at the troop of horses moving towards the ford, at the sky again, at the water, not fixing sight anywhere yet instantly aware of any movement, which was scrutinized for danger or food. In one of the water glances the bird saw what it had been awaiting: a pale green fly arising from the deeper water beside the run, where rock and gravel were covered by silt. Fluttering to meet the green drake, which arose slowly in spite of rapid wing-fanning, the chaffinch hovered before it and took it in her beak; and away to the nest in the apple tree.

About a minute later the bird was back again on the perch, scrutinizing the undersides of leaves for smaller flies while awaiting other duns of the mayfly to hatch from the silt.

Thereafter at intervals of less than two minutes the chaffinch flew to and from apple tree and alder, taking every green drake she saw. Sometimes she returned as though large-whiskered, with six or seven crumpled and moving feebly in her beak. Coelebs also flew to the nest with bunches of green drakes; but the young birds were sated, they could not keep open their eyes, they sank down one on the other, filling the nest solidly to the brim, so that the hen could not clean it out. Coelebs also was sated, and sat on a branch among small cankered apples, not knowing what to do with his beakful. At last, recalling a hedge-sparrow's brood in the bank among hart's tongue ferns of the sunken lane leading up the hillside, he flew off and put the food into yellow gapes that waved to him as soon as he alighted on the edge of the nest. Having got rid of the drakes, he flew to the hedge-top. Dozing in the apple tree, the hen heard, with only the least interest, his *Will-you will-you will-you will-you will-you ki*—suddenly cease. A sparrow-hawk, silently gliding down the lane, saw him and flung itself over backwards, turned on a wing-tip and thrust out a talon'd foot. A pair of swallows pursued the hawk with ringing cries as it flew away with the stricken Coelebs; but over the river they turned back and dived down to the water, to cool their breasts and sip; and flying back, they caught each a floating coppery breast-feather for their nest in the rafters of a cowshed.

While the hen chaffinch was dozing uneasily on the heads of the fledgelings, sheltering them from heat with wings spread over them, and while the swallows were playing with feathers in air, another mayfly was about to appear out of the stream. Danica, pulling herself from the nymphal shuck which had split as she reached the surface, shook the creases out of her new wings, and found herself arising, with the strangest feelings of fear and wonder and joy, to a shining freedom.

Spotted gold gleam and splash was a trout leaping at the pale green cloudiness of light moving upwards, steadily, to the shelter of leaves. There Danica the mayfly clung, twisting her body, with its tail of three whisks, in release of joy which poured through her eyes. On long and slender legs she walked from the leaf to its stem, and thence to the twig, and remained there, her body curved upwards to the sky, and her wings, pale green and diaphanous, drying in the warm air that moved through the trees.

Libellula the dragonfly, in final fury of hunger, with brittle rustle of wings passed by and saw Danica, paused, then swooped to take a blowfly whose coarse buzz made lambent fire of her eyes. Libellula was possessed with a frenzy; she was heavy with eggs; feelings burned wildly within her; the dark green of her wings and body was almost black, sun-charred. She ripped the wings off the blowfly and champed it, but could not swallow. Dropping the hairy blue shell, Libellula fluttered to the waterside, lighting on alder roots by the base of the dead trunk on which she had hatched.

The westering sun threw shadows of trees half-way across the river. Having refreshed himself in the run, Salar went back to his hide in deep water. He did not push under the roots, but lay beside them, concealed by shadow, in water that moved slowly and gave easy breathing. And lying there, he watched Libellula rising and falling over the little bay of still water, at each fall touching the water with the end of her body. Minute after minute the dragonfly stabbed the water, each time dropping an egg; nearly two hundred eggs a minute sank down to the silt.

After a short sleep the hen chaffinch returned to the alder. and seeing no mayflies hatching, began to hop from twig to twig, peering under the leaves. The bird saw Libellula below, but the colour did not attract her. She searched the leaves, taking ephemerals of large and blue-winged olive, and flies of willow, alder, and hawthorn. Since no more green drakes were hatching she sought away from the still water of the outer bend, at each return visit flying nearer to the bridge.

Danica rested on her twig, feeling a dry tightness about the now familiar airiness of herself. This was because the pellicle, or fine skin which enveloped every part of her, was about to split down the back. Then Danica would be to herself all beauty of sky and water. For this final losing of herself in love the unknowing nymph had toiled in the silt of decay and darkness, feeding on diatoms, little vegetables of the river: now she was a spirit in resurrection, without appetite, her mouth sealed, needing neither food nor drink, a being of beauty and light whose doom, or reward, was to die in the sunset of her day of aerial life.

The pellicle broke, and Danica was transformed, her wings clear and iridescent.

Pale blue-grey, empty, the fine sheath from which the mayfly had flown trembled on the twig in a wind too slight to stir an alder leaf. The afternoon sun gave a brazen light to the valley, with lengthening shadows of hilltop oaks extending in advance of a general shadow. Leisurely the horses walked down to the bend to drink; there were fewer gadflies to worry them. Swallows dipped and wheeled and rolled over the grass; higher up swifts raced in a thin black chain, crescent-linked. Above them Danica was flying, in a tiny cloud of her own wings, palest grey. Near her another mayfly, streaked black and white, with large luminous eyes, was flying. When Danica had floated up the sky, the black drake had been flying with seven other males by the parapet of Humpy Bridge, in a rising and falling formation: they were spinning, flying up and pausing, to drop with closed wings, to rise again, one close by the other, spinning their racial dream of imminent and immortal life. When Danica had arisen, the black drakes had followed her, rising into lucent sky until but one was left to pursue.

To the moon's pale phantom flew they, to find in sweet shock the everlasting river. Then they were falling, apart, the black drake empty of hope and illusion; the grey drake to the winding gleam below, bearing thither a strange secret joy.

Over the river many smaller flies were moving; some in shifting dark clouds, tiny dark flies, two-winged, called fisherman's curse, since trout preferred them to other flies, and they were too small to be imitated in silk and steel and feather. From the bridge the black drakes were gone. Other ephemerals were spinning there—pale wateries like little white ghosts, blue-winged olives and iron blues, their delicate legs and whisks trailing, iridescent with the hues of sunset and decline.

Salar now lay in midwater, idle, without movement, his chin resting on a ledge of rock, nearly alseep. He had seen Libellula the dragonfly fall at last into the water, struggle feebly, and be carried slowly away.

Gralaks moved from her shelter, and lay beside Salar. Three leeches hung to her tail-fin. A trout with a dark thin body and large head sidled past them, and hovered under the surface, watching for one or another of the dark cloud of flies—they had hatched from the shelters of sand and gravel-speck which encrusted most of the larger stones of the river-bed—to touch the water. The trout was dark brown and thin because its gut was filled with a thread of worms, a dark brown family joined together in a string, male to female, female to male. So numerous and flourishing was this family that its youngest offspring were hanging, desperate and miserable, outside the trout's vent. The head of the family was secured by hooks to the lining of the fish's stomach; it was this head that absorbed most of the fly-juices before they could be passed to the trout's liver. Thus the trout was starved and lugubrious.

Another trout moved into the run spreading out with bubble and foam patch into the slower water. It had been sleeping in the shadow of one of the arches of the bridge, and during sleep its golden-yellow hue had faded into vertical bars of black and yellow, a pattern of protection. Within a few minutes of being in sunlight again—for the hill-shadows were not yet half-way across the valley—its red spots had changed from scarlet to vermilion, the dark bars had faded, and the fish was again its gravel-bright self.

A salmon's length above Salar, another trout was lying, in its early evening place: a slight saucer-like hollow in the rock. This fish was dark green on its back, resembling the water-moss which grew on the rock. Near it lay a smaller trout, almost lemon colour, hue of the fine grains of sand which sloped down from a lip of rock, its usual feeding place when the spinners came on the water towards evening.

Shadows of alders crossed the river; the water was cooler; floating bines of crowfoot ceased to give off oxygen. The air was yet dry and warm; swallows and swifts played in the upper sky, where a lone herring gull was tumbling and twirling among them as it took spinners in their nuptial flight.

Rings of ripples began to spread on the river. The clouds of fisherman's curse had ceased to drift and sway; black knots moved slowly, as though aimlessly, midges in marriage. Two pairs of wings upheld the union, until one partner faltered, and the little mass of life sank down, to touch the surface, and struggle, and vanish in a lip of water spreading in a ring of ripples.

Side by side the two salmon lay, watching the flies, but inert to move. Some distance below them, in the deep pool cut by the triple falls of the bridge, lay Trutta, under a pink curl of bubbles which stroked his purple head. Not for Trutta the slime and stagnancy of roots; he was way-wise in the river; this was his eighth return from the sea. Behind the pug, in the deepest part of the pool, adding to its floor litter of rotting leaves and sticks and bones, a large eel lay twisting brokenly: an eel thick almost as a man's wrist, blue-black head and slimy back. Until an hour ago this eel had feared nothing in the pool; it had fastened on to salmon kelts and hung there, eating the sick and living fish alive, bite by bite; it had drowned ducklings, dragged down full-grown dabchicks, pursued dippers, and eaten two or three trout every day. But when—the colour of the old sea-trout's skin having suggested a sick fish—it had swum up behind Trutta and bitten between dorsal and pennant fin, it had the enormous surprise of being chased about the pool and, as it swam into its hold under the stone-facing of the bank, of being seized and pulled out, gripped in teeth and spat away, seized again and shaken, and then being gripped across the middle and held there while it twisted and lashed in vain; and only when Trutta had crushed it into two pieces, still joined but writhing independently, was the eel free to move whithersoever it pleased.

Trutta lay under the cascade, waiting for dimmit light, when he would swim up the water slide and join Salar and Gralaks in the run above.

As he lay there, ruddy light lifted from the cascade; the sun was behind the trees on the western hill.

In the coppery glow still brimming the floor of the valley the spinners were burnished points until they dropped into shadow: they were thin streaks of sunset fire rising to fall vanishing.

326

To the dipper speeding in relayed jerks upstream, the water had the colour of the sky, a leaden whiteness; while the king-fisher cutting downstream across a curve flew amidst a vast hue of its own breast.

High overhead the lone gull flew, slowly into the day's end, silently flying to the headland of the west, to the sea murmurs and cliff cries of its brethren.

A bead of gold was shrunk bright on the coppery glow of sunset, Venus the evening star. At the zenith, the sky was pale and clear; its pristine azure was cold with starlight journeying from distant night-suns before salmon leapt in the Island Race, before mayflies rose from water, before the sea grew bitter with earth's dissolution.

When the sun had gone under the hill Danica rose from a leaf whereon she had been resting, and flew down to the water. She was azure-pale as space, a fleck of sky fallen and dancing over the river. Lightly she touched, paused to drop a cluster of eggs, which sank to the bed of the river as she flew up again, to dance over the ripples, to fall again to her own wraith rising to meet and embrace her from the water.

Brighter shone the evening star. Another heron passed in the height of the sky. The roar of the triple falls grew louder under the bridge in dimmit light. Her gauzy wings and body becoming grey as passion ebbed in her, Danica danced away her life's day, while the water-wraith called to her, and she sank to a last embrace, and floated, wings spread and head down, under the arch of the bridge, and fluttering feebly, was borne over the fall to where Trutta watched and waited, resting on a rock within which was a mayfly set in stone a thousand thousand years before.

19

As Nirra the water-bat flittered from her cave under the bridge, a wave arose from the smooth river and travelled rapidly downstream, as Salar leapt and smacked down on his side. The sight of the great pointed head so sudden near

327

made Nirra loop and flitter back to the arch, in fear for her baby clinging to her breast. Nirra rustled into a larva blow-hole in the stone, and licked the black head burrowing hungrily into her warmth. Two grey horns of lime hung from the mortar which bound the stone of Nirra's home, inverted pillars for the doorway. They were not the wrong way round for Nirra, as the water-bat always hung head down when resting, delousing herself, or biting and being bitten by her mate, Nirro. For the past moon, however, Nirra had been at peace, except for her lice. Nirro had vanished shortly before the birth of the batlet, and thereafter no high petulant screaming and grinding of needle-sharp teeth had been heard coming from the larva-hole.

Another splash, as Gralaks flopped half out of water, across the slow-moving current. Nirra was accustomed to the noise and sight of the big splashes in that place at twilight, and flew happily over the water, flitting in sudden stoop and return, snapping midges and moths, and sedge-flies which had hatched from underwater homes built variously:—of minute pebbles, diminutive empty shells of water-snails, fine sand and stones in the shape of turrets and pinnacles; or from cabins made of silk to which were fastened twigs, stems and stalks of butter-cups, and dead leaves. At the end of each turret or cabin was a small grating, which let in water but kept out enemies. Thus the caddis lived until the time when it bound itself completely in silk and slept: to awaken into flyhood, bite a way from the cocoon, swim to the surface, break from its special swimming suit and emerge a sedge-fly ready to instant flight.

The night-flying sedges crossed and recrossed the water, while Nirra snapped, and tumbled as she put the insects in the pouch of her tail.

The bat saw Salar and Gralaks swimming just under the surface of the water, side by side. They were released from the glare and fear of day. Salar's tail-fin idled out of water; it was more brown than grey. Gralaks swam away slowly, turned on her side, and tried to rub the itch in her gills against the stones. The grilse gleamed a yellowish green in several sideway slidings along the river-bed. Salar swam around slowly, and then went

328

down to scrape the sides of his head on the stones, showing broader gleams of worn silvered copper by the grilse's tallow-yellow. The bone of one side of Salar's jaw was worn rough, where he had rid himself of the hook two months before; the place still irked him, where fungus had its hold.

Soon the feeling of elation sank in the two salmon, and they rested on the stones, and mused on the green twilight of the water as they waited for the glowing hues of darkness.

A splash, a shake in the middle fall, brown back-fin and tail-tip zigzagging up the glide; a ream drawn through the shadow of the arch: Trutta had joined them. His flanks were dark-spotted, currants and raisins and cloves; his back marbled rufous and green. He could not quite close his mouth because of the thickening of the kype of his lower jaw.

Trutta moved up into the run of fast water, and Salar followed him, with the ease of confidence; and while the sea-trout lay at the head of the run, the two salmon half-rolled and played in water scarcely deep enough to cover their backs.

Nirra the water-bat was now flittering erratically near the surface of the river, after flies which had come there for warmth: the air was colder than the water. Invisibly in deepening twilight swifts sped, their shrill whistles faint in the height of the sky. The dark heavy shape of a wood owl appeared on a branch of alder, and with a squeak Nirra rustled into the larva-hole, zeedledeedling her alarm to the batlet, who continued to nibble a teat in sleepy play, unaware of what its parent was declaiming. A swelling appeared in the owl's throat, and a hollow cry bubbled from its open beak. It saw the gleams of the salmon below, and the phosphoric glow of fungus on Salar's side and tail-fin; it saw every spot on Salar's gill cover: for the owl's eyes were large, each iris blue like a grape with bloom. It saw the sedges and the moths, some dark red and others cobalt; a duck's feather floating down glimmered; a water-vole gnawing the root of a rush on the farther bank was grey, although by daylight its hair was dark brown. The owl jumped off the branch and vol-planed down with legs hanging and toes spread; the vole also jumped, *plop!* it was in and under the water, and the owl was perching on another tree, peering down for small fish moving there. In the past it had taken trout and salmon parr in its claws; all movement caused its irises to expand, liquid grapes with softer bloom.

As soon as the owl had flown away a wild duck that had been waiting in the still water beside the middle arch of the bridge quacked discreetly for her ducklings to follow, and paddled upstream. Hardly had she gone beyond the angular cutwater when she turned silently and swam back beside the arch, the nine ducklings quiet beside her. The duck had smelled something in the cold air moving down the river.

A fox had slipped across the grass from the edge of the fir plantation on the hillside. It stopped on the bank to assay the air, and then crept down to the ford to drink. First it must smell the hoofmarks of the horses, each one very carefully, as though its life depended on no strange horse having joined the herd since its nasal inspection of the night before. Satisfied with the familiar scents, it drank a little, then withdrew from the bank to sniff about, as on second-thought, possibly to discover a stranger which had not drunken, but stayed away from the river lest it leave scent there for the fox to detect. Finding nothing new, it raised its sharp snout to flair the breeze before slinking over Humpy Bridge, to follow along the other bank to the broken bay, where damp sand and silt held the press of many more hooves. The fox learned that pigs had been wallowing there during the day; and also that a dog of strange scent had visited the ford to drink. This was alarming, for it could not recognize the smell; so after wetting it, thereby removing the smell from the earth and the doubt from its mind, the fox went away, satisfied, towards the hen-house and the rabbit warrens by the avenue of chestnuts.

A soft quacking under the bridge: having smelled the fox away, the wild duck paddled upstream beside the pier, followed by nine ducklings nearly as big as herself. They had come from their day-haunt in the deep tree-hung pool above Sawmills Weir. The duck had made her nest of dry grasses in a higher fork of a mossy oak, twelve feet above the water. The lower or main fork of the oak was bare of moss; an old dog-otter lying there during the many summers had worn the bark

330

smooth. The otter had been killed by hounds a year before, but the moss had not grown again on the rank place. One by one, when they had dried after chipping out of their shells, the ducklings had been carried to the water, held between the duck's thighs. Every night, now that they were nearly grown, the family travelled up the river, eating snails and caddis in the backwaters and eddies, and turning over stones for creepers of stone-fly and march brown, and fry of trout and salmon.

Under the bank by the alders the family paddled and splashed and played. The smallest duckling had a habit of climbing out on the bank and standing there on one leg, its head sunken on its shoulders, in an attitude of sleep. Then, when the rest of the family had gone upstream, the duckling would queep loudly, causing the duck to delay further progress and gather the others about her, while she called the truant to her. Night after night the small duckling did this, and always at the same places.

Salar did not see the ducks going upstream, for they moved in the still water of the bend, by the opposite bank. Nor did he see the white-flipping tails of a family of moorfowl following discreetly after the louder ducks. The cock and the hen led the way, followed by the four remaining and grown birds of the first brood, and then by six smaller birds of the second brood. Three of the first brood were hens. These looked after their six small brethren; but the fourth, a cockbird, had no interest in anything except feeding itself.

When the ducks and the moorfowl had gone upstream, Nirra the bat flittered alone in the darkness, clasped by the batlet, now exploring her body. Nirra talked to it in squeaks sharper and higher than the needle-notes of mice running over the roots of trees, with their litter of old leaves and twigs of bygone spates. Larger moths were now fluttering over the river, their wings sometimes striking against the alder leaves; spiders were on their webs; stars shone in sky and water. Venus was gone, far beyond the Island and the rim of ocean; the moon leaned on the hill: Night was come to the valley.

With the sinking of the moon came full darkness, and many things began to glimmer on earth and in water. A pale green

331

wandering fire in the grass was the love-light of a glow-worm, herself wingless, beacon for some dark-flying rescuer. Trees were a deep velvet blackness. The pole star held its fixed light above the Plough; northwards the sky had the pallor of ice. As the water-bat flittered between starry river and starry sky, it heard and saw what was now a familiar thing: the noise of iron rolling on iron, and the ruddy dilations of fire on steam. Far up the valley a late train rumbled across the viaduct.

Salar felt the distant vibrations in the rock. He lay in the run, behind Trutta. Both he and Gralaks, behind him, were watching for food, but only the sea-trout was feeding. Salar had the illusion of continuing a journey to the unknown and final haven of his being: for which he had travelled from deep ocean to the Island Race, and thence to the estuary and the higher reaches of the river. The river was no longer a stagnancy of warm, betraying water; it flowed fast and keen, glowing with life.

After lying there an hour he became restless, and turned and swam back to the deep water, to swing again into the current and hover just under the surface. Then forward again, slowly, seeking fast water. He saw the rock glowing darkly red under him, the luminous wings of moths, the deep-blue-blackness of the alder roots, the brown and green hues of the gravel. Some floating objects passing on the glimmering surface were seen darkly; others shone with colours. A cast breast-feather of a heron, grey by daylight, was now a rich red; while one of the white breast-feathers of a dipper was a dim black. He saw the alder trunks lambent, crooked as with moon-fire.

At midnight the solar rays reflected from the middle of the Atlantic laid an ocean pallor along the western sky. The Plough, seven points of light, had swung round the pole star. New constellations arose as the western stars of nightfall set beyond the hills and the sea. Sky, rocks, water, glowed with the fluorescence of their own dark lives.

Salar and Gralaks lay in fast water, close to the tail of Trutta. The water was running cold from the springs in the rock of the moor. A stag which had been lying with other red deer in the spruce plantations of the hill came to the ford to drink.

It crossed below the fish, which neither saw nor heard it. The stag walked across the park and up the hillside, making for a hedge where the young leaves of ash and ivy were to its liking.

Just before dawn, when the density and coldness of the water was greatest, a strange salmon moved up beside the others. This was Gleisdyn, who as a smolt had migrated to the sea with Gralaks fourteen months before. He was longer and deeper than the grilse; the extra ten weeks of sea-feeding had made him four pounds heavier. With other grilse who had escaped the nets in the estuary, Gleisdyn had come up the river, running at night in the thinnest water, and resting by day. As the face of Steep Weir was dry, with docks and other plants growing in cracks of the stone of the sill, Gleisdyn had not come to it; he had followed the stream running into the river-bed lower down, overflow from the raised fender by the mill-wheel. Swimming through the mild gush of water under the oaken barrier, he had followed the stream up the leat and into the millpond, past low muddy islets to fast shallows under tall trees, and round a bend into deep water, following the way of the spring salmon in April. Three miles above Steep Weir he had come to another side-stream, which also led under a raised fender, and into another leat. This carried the water from the millpond to the wheel of the sawmill; the fender was open to release the water when it was not working. So with the least effort Gleisdyn had entered the pool above Sawmills Weir, which, like Steep Weir, had been dry.

Gleisdyn swam into Sawmills pool just before midnight; and two and a half hours later he reached the water above Humpy Bridge, and saw Salar and Gralaks. He had left the estuary four nights previously, having come in over the bar during the weekly close-time, when netting was forbidden, from midday Saturday to midday Monday. The sea-lice remaining on him were only just alive.

Stirred by the white and silver of the stranger, Gralaks swam down the run, throwing herself out of water. Gleisdyn followed, and after a while Salar drifted down tail-first, turning as he reached deep water, and accelerating, drove in beside them. They were half-rolling around one another in play when Trutta swam down, and turning, sank to the deepest part of the pool, and lay still.

Alarmed by his attitude, Salar and Gralaks ceased their sporting, and lay behind him, in mid-water, moving their tails nervously, like small trout hovering. Trutta lay still as a stone. Gleisdyn half-rolled beside Gralaks, and then, turning in alarm as he saw something, shot away in an immense ream or wave, towards the piers of the bridge. He slashed round in fear of shallow water of the glide, and returned, piercing his own ream. The wavelets slopped against the bank, while the four fish lay motionless, inert, on the bed of the deepest part of the pool.

Trutta had been startled by the glimmer of surface movement coming upon him rapidly. The wild duck and her ducklings were swimming so fast downstream that they appeared to be running on the water.

Less than a quarter of a mile above the ford was another waterfall, by tall beeches which had been planted when the fall was built for ornament. The family of ducks had been happily bobbing and flapping and talking there, all of them in the water, except the littlest duckling. A flat stone leaned in the pool below the fall; and on this the littlest duckling had been perching, on one leg, feigning sleep, when the duck had started to quack loudly and beat her wings for running flight down-river. The others immediately followed her, but the ninth duckling remained perched on the stone. To turn attention of the otters from him to herself, the duck returned and splashed about in the shallows, dragging a wing as though wounded; but soon the cries of the duckling ceased, and terrified by the musky smell, the duck flew down-river to pitch beside the others and lead them in the race for distance and safety.

They saw the gleam of turning fish, and heard the drumming vibration as the salmon speeded away. Through the western end of Humpy Bridge the family hastened, sliding and bobbing over the white water, moving like a broken string of large oval beads in the shadow of the stonework, slithering round the roots of an alder, and down the noisy stickle of broken shallow water.

A low whistle, softer than the cries of flighting curlew, came from above the ford. The otters were coming.

20

An hour before, while the stag had been drinking at the ford, the dog and bitch had met by chance in the Fire-Play Pool, just below the railway viaduct. They had not met for five months, since just before the cubs had been born in the marshes of the river-head.

The dog had been travelling up the river, after salmon shut in the low pools; but before coming to Humpy Bridge he had gone up a runner or streamlet, remembering the eels there. The bed of the runner, which trickled at the bottom of the garden wherein Shiner worked, was alive with stick-caddises, therefore of mullheads; and eels went after the small squat fish, burrowing under stones for them. The otter's best-liked food was eel. The claws of his forepaws were worn small by scraping under banks and large stones. Sometimes the otter-hounds drew up the runner; but it was boggy and shut in with undergrowth and scrub, and the huntsman in consultation with the master soon decided that hounds were hunting heel— that the otter had come down the runner, not gone up it.

Many times the man living in the cottage, for whom Shiner worked, had heard the soft, water-musical cries of otters travelling up the coombe. The otter lived all of itself, and so spent many hours in playing and whistling.

Usually the otters quitted the thread of water at the head of the coombe, crossed fields and went down another runner which joined the river below the railway viaduct.

The dog-otter, working down the second runner while the stag was leaving the fir plantation for the ford, heard the cries of otters playing, and hastened after them. In the deep slow water of the Fireplay he met his mate, and the cubs he saw for the first time. The bitch had a white patch of hair on her pate, in the form of a star; her dam, who had died toothless during the last winter in the Seals Cave of the headland, had had a white tip to her rudder. The bitch's sire had been a bold otter who, after being hunted many hours, and escaping from worry

335

after worry, had drowned a hound with his last strength. His name was Tarka.

At first the cubs were scared of the big strange otter. He caught a trout wedged in fear under an old pail filled with cement, and left it for them on a shingle bank. Soon they were playing as merrily as before, wrostling in the water and rolling together down the narrows and cascades, and sniffing beside his wide jowl at the scent of ducks on tufts of rush and riverside scours. They went down with the river, and heard the roar of their first falls, echoed from the beech trees. The old otters had often played there, falling over head first and climbing up to slide down again, whistling their joy. As they went over this time the dog sank away in the white rush and when the cubs went over they fought around him, to seize the duckling which was flapping and crying at the base of a leaning stone. They tore its wings off and left it only when it was dead, to frolic after the bitch calling down the fast thin water.

It was nearly night's end. The fox, returning from the bracken of the rabbit warrens, heard noises at the ford which sounded like horses crossing. Webbed feet and thick pointed tails were striking the water as the dog and the bitch clutched one another and struggled in play. Seeing nothing, the fox was puzzled and anxious. It lay down, flairing its nose to smell the reason of noise. Made most curious, it crept slowly towards the alders, ready to run at the first sight of danger.

In the deepest water lay the three salmon, motionless with fear. Trutta lay some way behind them, on the edge of the waterfall. When the short-legged beasts came darkly into the dim cone of fish vision, Gleisdyn turned and shot away, followed by Salar and Gralaks. The otters heard the thumping vibration, and, separating, swam down and peered around with swift movements very different from the heavy clumsiness of their play movements. Before, they had been land beasts sporting in water; now they were of the water. They became longer, slimmer, their heads sharpened. They tucked in their forelegs and swam seal-like, swimming about with sweeping movements of tails which had become rudders. A gleaming form drove suddenly between them, turned with a roaring

336

noise, and after it had vanished they were lifted by water surging solid under them. Gleisdyn, not knowing the river above the bridge, was rushing about in terror, his accumulated sea-strength stripped from him by shock after shock.

Salar and Gralaks were sunken on the gravel at the base of the western pier of the bridge, as though made of lead.

Trutta was hidden under the largest mass of roots, where Salar usually lay by day. The pug was afraid, but he knew what he was doing. He lay still as the roots, one flank protected by the bank. He was ready to move from whichever way the enemy should approach.

Gleisdyn drove downstream from two large and four small dark enemies. His bow-wave smacked against the two piers of the middle arch when he was ten lengths upstream again. In a thruddling zigzag he shot through the pool, swerving from one otter and throwing himself out of water to avoid the bubble-glimmering turn of another. He slid along thin water, driving a furrow in the gravel.

As the bitch, neck-hair raised, leapt with purring growl upon Gleisdyn, he threshed a way past her into deeper water, and sped upriver. The noise of his ploughing up the run made the watching fox trot away from the alders and turn back again, ears upright, nose and whiskers twitching.

The dog-otter bobbed out of the deeper water, and stood on the surface a moment, on his webbed hind-feet. In several quick movements of his head he fixed the glimmer of fish and bubble travelling upstream, and as he fell back with a splash, called the others to follow.

Gleisdyn sped up a gorge between rock and gravel where the river hastened round a bend. He passed a small groove in the rock, and returned to it when he learnt that the river spread thin over shallows above the bend. He fitted his length into the groove, and lay still.

The dog, swimming upstream from side to side and bobbing out of the water to breathe and peer every few yards, passed Gleisdyn and, coming to the shallows, ran out on the bank to listen for the noise of the salmon's passage upstream.

Meanwhile one of the cubs had found the fish, and had

scratched it timidly with its paw to see if it would move. The next moment the cub was swallowing water as it gasped from a blow which caught it across its middle and hurled it against the rock.

Gleisdyn had not struck the small otter deliberately. His strength was going from him in shock after shock of fear as he fled from sight and smell of one or another of the otters. Twice more he went down to the bridge, and upstream again, followed by a wide wave. On the third rush downriver he came face to face with the bitch, whose teeth as he slashed round bit into the wrist of his tail. His momentum tore him free, and in wildest fear he swam up the run again, driven by the feeling that he must get away from the ford. Past the gorge he arrowed, and soon was threshing amidst flat stones and thin water, desperately driving himself forward, breaking his skin on sharper edges of larger stones. The otters ran upon him, curled their hair-spiky necks over him, clasping the cold body with their stumpy forelegs and slicing off scales and skin with their teeth. Curving and slapping as he escaped, Gleisdyn writhed to the water, but the dog caught him by one of the fore-fins and dragged him back, rising up and falling upon him to tear flesh from the thick part of the shoulder. Soon the large bones of the back were exposed, and the fish bled to death. When it ceased to move they left it, for they were not hungry: this was their sport.

The fox had been watching, a coming and going tall-ear'd shadow on the bank, during the hunt. When he was satisfied that they were gone—for once, and once only, he had questioned an otter walking into the badgers' sett which the fox had taken for his own earth—he crept down over the stones, shaking first one delicate pad, then another, as it got wet, and sniffed carefully along the entire length of the salmon. After a long interval, during which the chase was reconstructed by sense of smell to its satisfaction, the fox braced his legs and set himself to drag the carcass to the bank. This was done after some slipping; after which the fox kicked his heels against the grass, and shook his coat. Then he nibbled a piece of red flesh, tasted it thoughtfully, looked round for the otters, walked away as though uninterested in the meal awaiting it, rolled on the grass, wetted a dried patch of cowdung to conceal his own scent, and returned to tear away mouthfuls of flesh and swallow them in lumps which soon made his throat dry and thirsty.

The otters went down the river, passing Trutta lying under the roots, and sliding over the middle fall of the bridge into deep water below. The sky was growing pale over the eastern hills, and they did not linger, but let the stream take them down the valley, under a road bridge, and to secluded water where branches of trees hung over the river, sometimes dragging at the stream. Through the slow stretches they swam, six flat whiskered heads pushing each a watery arrow from its nose. At the beginning of the long pool above Sawmills Weir the dog left them, crawling out by the roots of an oak whose leafy branches stretched over the water to the farther bank. After sniffing round the base of the tree, which was half hollow, and leaving his blackish-green spraints on a root beside other faded marks of bitten fishbones—relics of former visitations of otters —he climbed up the sloping trunk and lay in the fork, where he had not slept for nearly a year. After licking his hair and washing paws and face, he curled to sleep, as a cockerel crowed in the garden of one of the cottages beyond the sawmills.

He left again before sunset, and went down the river, couching at dawn in the thicket of the islet above Steep Weir. There a few hours later the otterhounds found him, and hunted him for four hours, and caught him at last, very tired, in shallow water, even as he had caught Gleisdyn, and slew him.

While the otters had been killing Gleisdyn, Salar and Gralaks had gone down under Humpy Bridge and through the pool, swimming fast, often with backs out of water, down the shallows until they came to deeper water, where they swam easier, but always downstream. Only when they came to Sawmills pool, with its deep pits, and shelter made by willow branches dragging in the water, did they pause and swing into the current again.

Day after day they lay in the dim light of deep water. Day after day the water flowed slower and warmer. Plants of celery and hornwort growing in the shallows toppled with their own weights of green; cattle treading the ford higher up broke off strings of crowfoot, which floated until they caught in snag or stone, to put out small white roots for holding. From their base on Humpy Bridge new blackberry brambles stroked the water; sow-thistles grew there, too, with hemp agrimony, hart's-tongue ferns, water-violets, and yellow flowers of mimulus at the edges of rock and river. All had grown there from seeds left by spates.

The lime trees in the Deer Park were murmurous with bees at the blossoms; heavy thunder clouds—travelling quarries of the sky—trundled over the moor. Village boys swam in Saw-mills pool, white bodies and brown legs and arms moving slowly and irregularly, with much shouting and splashing. At night mists, hiding the stars, moved over the river and the meadow short with aftermath of cutting.

One afternoon of intense air-heat, as Salar lay asleep under the clogged willow boughs, he awakened to a thudding and agitation of the water. He saw much shapeless movement on the bank of the meadow. The other side of the river was dark with trees growing on the steep valley side. When something shook the willow branches, he sped away, up the river, but turned at the sight of many men and horses, some of them in the river-bed, where the water was only a few inches deep. Something ran staggering and plunging down, wading slower as the water deepened, and swimming.

It was the stag which had come down from the fir plantations to drink at the ford every night when Salar had lain above Humpy Bridge. The stag had been roused some hours before, to run many miles across fields to the moor, trying to outrun the staghounds which followed its scent everywhere its slot pressed. Eventually it had come back to the valley and the river, running down two miles of water, sometimes clambering out to make a loop, and then returning to the water which bore no scent. But the huntsman knew the ways of deer; and now hounds had come up to the stag at bay in Sawmills pool.

Salar fled up and down the pool, alarmed by the swimming legs of hounds. Shiner, standing among horsemen on the bank saw Salar drive between the dark green weeds on the gravel at the mouth of the leat, and watched his bow-wave hit the iron doors of the fender.

The stag was turned by hounds from the deep water, and as it walked towards the sill of the weir the huntsman shot it with a pistol. The bullet pierced its shoulder. The stag paused, and walked on. The huntsman fired again. A dark spot opened on its neck. It shuddered, and lurched uncertainly, its head beginning to hang, its tongue lolling, blood thickening in strings from its nostrils. The huntsman fired again. The stag stopped, swaying on its feet. It was dead. Hounds bayed around it, while the whippers-in waded to the stag, to keep off hounds. The stag's head, with its thirteen points, dropped forward and its knees sagged and it fell over in the water.

The mill-wheel was locked, no water passing; the smaller fender of the overflow, by which Gleisdyn had swum up, was open. It sucked Salar down, to a little brook beneath. In the shadow of brambles and hazels he drifted, tail-first, coming back to the river again, to a small pool and then another pool in smoothed grey rock. His life was suspended by reawakened shock; his wound was open again; he let the river take him. In the night he went down the leat of Steep Weir, and by morning he was in the Junction Pool, where listless fish lay in water nearly stagnant.

After noon a thunderstorm broke over the moor, and a freshet came down, flushings from half-dried bogs and marshes, warm and turbid water saturated with gases of decay, from which the salmon turned. By morning the river was at low summer level again, the dark algae on its gravel thickened by a fine silt.

The next day a summer visitor was drowned in the estuary of the Two Rivers. He was bathing, at low water, at the junction of the tides. They ebbed quietly away in a string of foam, taking the body with them. It was a Sunday afternoon, and the weekly close-time for nets; but that night, towards low water, all the fishermen were on the Ridge, sweeping with nets, to take the body, they said. Forty salmon were caught. Salar saw one of the nets, and remembering, swam away fast. When the sun arose over the mainland, he was in the bay, and feeding on prawns and sand-eels. That night he lay, with other salmon, a few river-stained like himself but most of them fresh from the ocean, in the tides of the Island Race.

WINTER STAR-STREAM

21

At the equinox, when summer and fall shared a day of rain that dissolved all colours of land with the moving greyness of sea, the highest tide of the year moved up the estuary. Neither sunrise nor sunset were seen. The grey day grew duller in the afternoon; the waves, piled up by the south-west gale, rolled bigger and slower.

An hour before high water the sea flow ceased, checked by the volume of fresh coming down the river. A brown lagoon lay wide between the sea-walls strewn with froth amidst branches and roots of trees, drowned chickens, cabbage leaves, and the scriddicks of old tide-lines become flotsam again. It rose until the water was level with the top of the walls, brimming above the grazing marshes. At the hour of high water the wall-tops were weirs, marshes were flooded, cattle floundering and belving, sheep drowned, the marshman in the bedroom of his cottage on the sea-wall watching water lapping the lower stairs.

The day was darkened out long before nightfall. As the tide began to move back the wind dropped, and rain fell straight and black. The clouds burst over the hills and the estuary. Trillions of water-thistles arose on the wide lake of the marshes. Mallard and shelduck flighted in from the sea, joyfully to discover the new world. Shops and cottages of the village beyond the Great Field were flooded. Eels ate the dough in a baker's ovens where fires had burned an hour since. Two cormorants sat together on the gilt weathercock of the church spire above a jabble of brown water hiding tombstones. A heron fished from the radiator of an abandoned motor-car on the new concrete highway, perched beside the mascot of a miniature heron in white-metal. Later, the heron was found drowned:

in over-excitement of the world becoming water and the annihilation of Man it had struck a grey mullet between operculum and gill, and unable to free its beak, had been dragged into the water by the fish eight times as heavy as itself.

The lighthouse beam was invisible across the estuary. As the tide pressure ceased, the fairway became a mighty rushing river. Row-boats above the Long Bridge of the town were filled with water thrown over their bows, torn from their moorings, and taken nearly so far as the Island in what was still the river: brown water, unsalt, thick with the soil of many fields.

There was no estuary: only a new great river, muddy and very fast, claiming all its old courses and beds used and disused since its beginning. Everywhere the resurgence of its primitive spirit was hostile to the work of men. At night the town by the Long Bridge was without light, its engines and dynamos bedded in smooth brown mud. The rain fell heavily all night; and all night the engineers worked in the power-house, wherefrom at dawn came the beat of engines; but also at dawn the tide pushed the water over the quays and embankments again, and into the power-house, washing away barriers of sandbags and replacing the mud which had been removed.

Railway lines rusted. Culverts were torn away. Trees which had stood for centuries on the river's banks were uprooted and carried down, to lodge against the arches of the Long Bridge, to collect lesser trees and bushes and form dams which made a vast lake above. For years some of the town councillors had urged the making of a lake there, for both power and pleasure: now they had it: but the river had the power and what the councillors called the unruly elements had the pleasure—seeing, among other things, the Town Bandstand going out to sea.

A herd of porpoises, led by Meerschwein, went miles up the river after the runs of salmon which old men said were the greatest ever known. For days, as the river ran lower and clearer but still with many times its normal autumnal flow, salmon were seen leaping in the wide, water-gleaming valley.

Nearly a hundred hours' continuous heavy rain had filled

343

the underground lakes of the moor so that every spring was gushing. Sunken lanes—tracks worn deep by sleds of olden time—were noisy with cascades, their rugged surfaces washed away to reveal rock grooved and worn by iron and wood and horn.

As the flood withdrew from field and ditch and hollow, many fish were left in closed pits and shallows. There was a saying in the country of the Two Rivers that in a bygone age the agreements whereby boys were apprenticed to moorland farmers had a clause which stipulated the feeding of salmon to the boys on not more than three days a week during a year. This saying was often repeated in books of the familiar kind which are derived from other books; but no such agreement had ever been found to prove the truth of the saying, which was intended to show how in other ages Atlantic salmon were as numerous in the rivers as their Pacific cousins were in later times in the rivers of the Coast.

In the Great Deluge by which Salar returned to the stream of Red Deer Moor nearly all the pigs, dogs, cats, and hens of the valley farms which remained alive turned away, after three days of feeding, from the flesh of salmon. Some said the sudden immense volume of water running into the Atlantic was so charged with the salts of artificial fertilizers washed in the soil from fields that most of the fish coming to the Island Race were unable to find the sea-currents of their native rivers, and so all followed up the one overwhelming waterway to the Two Rivers.

Below Sloping Weir the bed of the turning eddy was covered by salmon, which were covered by a second and a third layer of fish. The water of the eddy was a dark purple. Every moment the circular racing surface showed a brown tail-fin, a dark rolling back, a lead-grey or copper-brown neb. Fish six and seven together were trying to get up the weir. At the side of the concrete apron, where Shiner stood, small trout and sea-trout leapt and slithered on the watery slope so frequently that he could, he told himself, have filled a bucket any moment by simply holding it there.

But Shiner was not there to get fish. Now that he had regular work he was quite happy watching them. Indeed, he felt the secondary feeling of all conquerors towards a subjected race: an attitude of benevolence and protection. Shiner had no gaff in his pocket. He was there because most of his life thought with the way of salmon. All day he had stood there, watching them. He ate no food; his hunger was to see the fish.

Shiner's arrival at the weir had disturbed Old Nog the heron who had been killing every fish it could strike and lift from the edge of the slide.

So many peal—small sea-trout—were leaping and falling within a few inches of the grassy edge that soon the old man's trousers were wet to the knees with the splashing. The female peal were long and fine. Some were seven or eight inches in length—fish which had migrated to the sea as smolts five months before, and found scanty coastal feeding. They were lilac-coloured, unspotted. Others were silvery over their spots; these were the brown trout which had found a way to the estuary, and returned for spawning. The sea-trout were all of one family, although in most the desire for ocean was inherited, not an accident. All had had white flesh before going to salt water, but now their flesh was pink from eating prawns and shell-fish.

A few salmon, the tired ones which had remained in the river since early spring, tried to get up the weir at the side, leaping among the smaller sea-trout whose water it was. Shiner saw fish with long heads and out-thrust kypes, brown as summer algae, the gristle of underjaws worn by rubbing and ringed with fungus. They sprang from the edge of the broken surge which slanted across the pool's circle: some fell on their sides, heavily on the concrete covered by water less deep than their bodies, and lay stunned a moment before being washed down; others jumped too high, falling on the curl-over of white water and being flung back before recovering poise and swimming down with easy stroke of tail-fin. Other stale fish had green on gill covers, their jaws looked smoke-grimy, their scales rusty. They were all shapes and sizes. The pool was more fish than water, fish flushed with the cold fever of spawning, all trying to get to the redds in the higher reaches of the

345

river: danger for themselves but safety for the alevins hatching in the shrunken waters of Spring.

Every minute several fish leapt askew and fell on the grass beside the concrete. Shiner eased them back into the water, wetting his hands lest his touch scald the sensitive skin. When he had arrived at the weir-side that Sunday morning, a thistle had stood beside a dock, both growing out of a crack in the concrete; but during the morning both plants were so beaten by blows of falling fish that at midday their stems were shredded from their roots, and washed away.

Nearer the roaring centre of the weir, stronger fish were jumping. Most of them hit the water and lost impetus before they could grip and bore a way up the slope. Shiner saw roseate hog-backed fish, with heads a canary-yellow: these were males of a late run, full of zest for spawning. They had no appetite for food; excitement had released much uric acid in their systems, which gave their skins the livid colours.

Other salmon were pink-silver, others flushed a deep red. One very big fish, a fifty pounder, which had been returning to the Wye, ploughed up the slope, a plume of water curling over its head. Two-thirds of the way up it was in water falling with its weight and strength: it swam with all its power, seeming to vibrate in green glass: then it was moving back, always swimming hard, until suddenly it gave up and was swept down to where the glide was shattered and tossed in ragged white peaks. The sight made Shiner feel in his pocket for a gaff, and then he sighed, for the confusion of feelings within himself.

The spawning coats of the salmon were varying as their shapes and weights. Shiner saw fish that varied from light brown to the colour of bronze, greenish as though corroded by the sea. These were the females. A few clean-run bluish-dark fish had net marks on them; although the official net-season had ended with August. Fish were jumping at all angles, some to be thrown over backwards immediately, others to strike the water and be swept and tossed away. A few straightly entered the narrow central spine, to find, as they swam with all their strength, the under-layers of water which, dragging against the stone of the apron, delayed the thrust of the over-slidden top water. They moved up, flattened images of fish vibrating within green glass.

They made such slow movement because the weight of the top water, pressed by the gliding and swirling masses above the sill of the weir, was many times the weight of each striving fish. The water was alive with the spirit of salmon-life. It was the master-spirit which had given salmon their shapely beauty, and their speed. The pointed power which in water could burst through netting strong enough to support the weight of a man in air, could not pierce the massive violence of the spate. When the water fell, they would go over, one behind and beside the other.

But while he watched, and as the sun broke through clouds, Shiner saw a fish leap from the midst of the most broken turmoil —a curve of white and tarnished silver which fell and pierced the surge and moved up steadily, vibrating fast and surely, a fish that had learned a way through the varying pressures and water-layers, beside the glassy spine raised from the gap in the sill above. It got nearly to the sill, where it seemed to hang, moment after moment, then it was advancing, inch by inch, to where the spine was flattened just below the break in the hidden sill; and as Shiner watched, it shot forward out of sight, to leap high from the calm deep water of the mill-pool and reveal, in the moment of rest at the top of the curve, a soldered mark on its side, as of a wound healed. Such was the return of Salar—the Leaper.

22

As the fed heron flies, Steep Weir lay about six miles above Sloping Weir; but the journey was longer for fish. The river wound through the grazing meadows of its own past making—now running close to the feet of hills yellow and red and brown with the colours of leaves' failing life, now winding to the other hillside; to recoil upon itself, in wide pools of currents in confusion, rushing swollen and gleaming.

Steep Weir had been built in a past century, diagonally across the river, a barrier of slabs of rocks raised and mortared vertically ten feet on the rock. The top layer of slabs overhung a vertical wall; water falling over fell clear of the wall's base. And it rebounded, because it fell direct on rock. There was no pool underneath, no deep water from which a fish could take off. It was the most harmful weir in the country of the Two Rivers, and, since it was usually unpassable, a favourite place of poachers when fish were running.

Where the sill of the weir stopped, a bank grown with alders continued to a half-rotten sluice. This consisted of a frame of three upright posts, bedded into masonry and morticed on cross-pieces. In the grooves of the upright posts two doors or fenders had not been moved for more than thirty years. They were ruinous, and silted on the higher side.

Early one morning Shiner went to Steep Weir. He knew that some of the chaps from the town would be there, snatching fish. Since he had come to watch salmon for their own sakes, Shiner had appointed himself a sort of honorary elusive water-bailiff. Herons and otters and snatchers he regarded as half-enemies of his own life. Water-bailiffs were enemies of the other half of himself, and when he saw one Shiner became elusive. He muttered to himself, feeling they would not believe that he was by the riverside for the sake of the fish. Not for the sake of the Conservancy Board, which was made up of men there to represent and serve their own interests: nets-men for the increase of nets and extension of time to net, rod-and-line men to increase the number of fish in the rivers, by keeping the number of nets as low as possible, and limiting the season of estuary fishing. Shiner knew all about the Board; and he muttered when he saw a bailie, for old time's sake and also because he was a solitary.

Shiner had a special grudge against the water-bailiffs. Recalling the number of fish he had snatched from below Steep Weir, he now thought of salmon jumping there hour after hour in vain, bruising and breaking themselves. Why hadn't they bailies seen to it that the fender was raised? 'Twasn't proper! Very well, he, Shiner, would do it himself.

Soon after sunrise on the Monday morning he climbed over the fence by the road bridge below the grist mill, and walked along the river bank. He was tall and thin, looking like a humanized alder trunk. His coat was shredded and grey like lichen, his arms and legs long and loose. He had a small face with pointed goatee beard and high pointed ears sticking up beside the upright brim of a very ancient and discoloured billy-cock hat. His eyes appeared to see nothing, he never turned round, or glanced about him; yet he saw all he wanted to see. He was a grey heron of a man, owning only his clothes, a few gardening tools, and himself. In summer he often slept out, beside ricks or in lofts of cattle sheds. He knew white owls which nested in the barns, and they knew him. He liked wandering about alone, in the open air. During winter he lived in a·room over a disused stable, for which he paid rent of ten shillings a year. He insisted on paying rent. The landlord, an innkeeper, allowed him to boil and fry in the rusty grate of the small disused harness room, hung with cobwebs. Shiner's only mate was a cat, an aged beast, which he called Kitten. It was the great-great-grandkitten of the original cat he had owned. He neither begged nor borrowed, nor would he claim an Old Age pension: he hoped thereby he would escape notice. His secret fear was that in extreme old age he would be destitute, and put in the Union, when he would not be able to see the river or the fields.

He walked along by the river, slowly, with an ash-plant nearly as tall as himself in his right hand, continually glancing at the water moving almost bank-high on his left. Forward, and across the river, stood a plantation of thin trees almost hiding the mill-house. He heard the roaring of the weir as he walked on. A raised bank of stone and earth, on which ash and other trees grew, was between him and the weir. Peering through a gap, he saw the figure of a man standing there, and recognized one of the gang which had stolen his trammel net in the police court. Then he saw the hats of two other men moving behind some low-growing furze bushes. The river was over the bank beside the sluice, running down the grass, and pouring over the edge into the race-way below.

349

Moving to another gap, Shiner stared at the weir. Fish were jumping into the white, to fall back again, and be tossed and turned in the churn of water rebounding from the rock below. They were jumping all the time, and most of them were coloured in shades of red and brown. "They'm in full tartan, surenuff," muttered Shiner, using a phrase he had heard years before from a visiting Scots fisherman.

In a bed of rushes fifty yards above the weir Shiner had found a rusty iron bar while poking about there a few months previously. This, he guessed, was the bar by which the fenders had been lifted up years before. But if he went to get the bar now, and started to open the fenders, he might be pitched into the water while he was doing it, and no one any the wiser. They chaps wasn't worth twopenn'oth of cold gin, they would pitch him in if they thought no one would know. And taking red fish, too! Why, the eggs of a ten p'un sow-fish weighed two p'un! 'Twas no sense in it, snatching full ripe fish.

Shiner had taken many hundreds of fish at Steep Weir, and had often stated his opinion that October fish tasted better than clean springers; but that was when he had been younger and "lived for devilment", as he said. But a full ripe fish! 'Twasn't no sense to it.

After wondering for some time what he could do, Shiner clambered over the gap in the bank and walked, looser legged than ever, towards the men. The man standing back from the water saw him casually, and paid no heed to him. His two mates had been informed, however, of the approach, and when they saw who it was, they bent down and withdrew each a long ash-pole which had been hurriedly thrust into the growth of bramble and alder.

The poles had been cut from a near-by copse. To the slighter end a noose of twisted strands of brass wire had been tied. These were for tailing the fish waiting below the sluice.

Shiner went to the edge of the sluice which joined the water-roar at the base of the fall a few paces distant. Fish of all lengths and shapes and colours were jumping vertically under the spread of the weir. None could get up. One great fish— it was the fifty pounder Shiner had seen the day before at Sloping Weir—fell back on a hidden pinnacle of rock and was washed away belly upwards. Shiner cracked his fingers, and muttered to himself.

"You won't do nought with that li'l old rabbit wire," said Shiner. "I was working here with a gaff when Adam was a proper pup. Besides, you'm too late. There ban't enough water here to carry the fish over. Now if you could open the fenders a bit, to let some good water under, you'd attract the sojers upalong the gully." Soldiers was the poaching term for red autumn fish. "Aiy, midears, that's what us did in th' old days. And if I don't misremember, there be a bar lying about yurr."

He began to mooch around, peering under bramble clumps and kicking tufts of grass with his boot. He returned to the others, mumbling half to himself, "You med get a fish by fixing a gaff on t'other end, and cutting the stick in half, maybe you'd get a vish thaccy way, but you med be careful, midears, leaning over all that water, 'tes a turrible master weight of water valling to-day. Aiy, it be, too true it be." And shaking his head, he ambled away, pretending to be looking for the bar. "Th' old fool be wandering i' th' 'ead," said one of the men, lighting a cigarette. Seeing this, Shiner came back, talking in a broader, old-fashioned way. "I minds th' time when us took vower butt-loads of vish from thissy place. But then us had th' bar vor open the sloos, do 'ec zee?" and shaking his head he went away. "Proper mazed fool," said the young man, inhaling deeply of the fag.

Shiner was staring at the fenders of the sluice, his billy-cock pushed over one ear, scratching his head. Jets of water were spirting through holes in the oaken planking, and gushing underneath, hissing white from the pressure of water above the fenders.

As he watched, a small sea-trout slithered up the white hiss of water, and turning by the wood, slithered down again. "You'll soon be upalong, midear," said the old man. "Shiner knoweth."

He found the rusty bar in the nettles, and returned to the sluice. An oak plank stretched across behind the framework,

351

and on this he stood, pushing the end of the bar into an iron notch. Each fender was the shape of a large square shovel: in the handle of which was a vertical row of notches. Levering against the cross-piece, he tried to raise the fender. It was wedged in the lower grooves of the posts, held tight by the weight of silt against its other side. By crashing the bar against the plate Shiner at last shifted the wood and immediately the gush below changed to mud colour.

He shifted the end of the bar to a lower hole, and raised it another notch. Thus slowly one fender was raised; then he began to raise the other. While he was doing this one of the men came to him and asked him how much more he was going to "rise" it. "Hey?" said Shiner, pausing to put a hand to ear, and then bending down to lever again. The man shouted at him, soundlessly in the roar of water now passing under. "Hey?" said Shiner, pausing a moment. The man came on the plank and bawled in his ear. "If you open it to the top, you bliddy old vool, all the fish will rin through, won't 'm?"

"Aiy, you'm right, midear," replied Shiner. "B'utiful water, b'utiful rinning water!"

"I said to you, you old vool, I said, You'm letting all the vish dro, ban't you?"

"No, I ain't got no gaff," replied Shiner, lifting the fender another notch. "If I had, you should have it, midear."

The man seized the end of the bar. "Stop, wull 'ee?" The second fender was almost as high as the first.

"Aiy, you'm right," said Shiner. "Only don't you go telling they old bailies that I was a hacsessry after the fack of this yurr raisement o' the fender," as he inserted the end of the bar into the last hole.

The second man now stepped on the plank and gripped the bar. "What's the flamin' bliddy idea?" he shouted. "Here, you give the bar to me——" and he raised an arm with clenched fist while pulling with the other.

"Yurr, take it," said Shiner, suddenly thrusting the bar at him.

The man who had shouted had been braced for resistance; he lost his balance. He clutched at the other man, who in turn grabbed the third man. The trio leaned back, swaying and clutching. The weight of the bar pulled the first man askew, and all three fell into the water. Instantly they were swept down the race. One got hold of an alder bough in the eddy by the curve of the race, the second held to him; but the third man was carried down into the main rush of the river. He could swim, and so kept his head up. He was washed helplessly down river until he found himself in a backwater. Shiner, who had been following downstream, helped him out.

When the three were together again he said, "You'm a proper double couple o' Adam's pups! Goin' givin' an old 'un like me a proper scare! And where be the bar you was so anxious to get hold to? Like as not in the flamin' sae by now. And I can't reggerlate no fenders just as I was preparin' to do when you wild bathing boys thought you knowed best. I tell 'ee, midear, they be wedged tight by now, and nothin' will shift 'em. Hullo, hullo! Did 'ee zee that li'l b'uty? My Gor, 'twas a b'utiful sight!"

A salmon had leapt out of the white curl-over below the open fenders, had pierced the green glissade descending and had swum through, a dark shadow vanishing. Above in the pool it leapt again—Salar.

23

Shiner walked up the valley, beside the river. He did not hurry. He stared and quizzed and wondered. The cottage garden where he worked was under four miles from Steep Weir, and there was little to do at the fall of the year; and Shiner was not the sort to make work. He was a free man. It took him all the forenoon and two hours after midday to arrive at Sawmills Weir. There a gamekeeper saw him. The gamekeeper was also a local preacher.

"Up to your old games, I see," was his greeting to Shiner.

"Aw, you must have second sight, midear," retorted Shiner, looking at the water. "How be the fezzans this year? Got this yurr grouse disease from Scotland yet?"

"You'm a smart one, Shiner, you be. Got a gaff in your pocket, by any chance?"

"You got any baccy in yours, midear?" countered Shiner.

"I ban't a smoker, you knows that."

"Nor be I."

"Then why do 'ee ask?"

"Aw, just another idle gossip question, midear. Hullo, did 'ee see that g'rt old black poll? Proper old berry-gatherer, I reckon."

Garroo the cannibal trout, who had hidden with Salar and the others under the roots when the gang had worked the trammel in Denzil's Pool, had just jumped and fallen back. He was lean and thin; his head was the shape of a lobster's claw. He looked like his own effigy in a glass case; for his spots were large and very distinct, the red very red and the black very black, while he glistened as though newly painted in hues of blue and brown, and over all a high gleam of varnish. Garroo was too old for spawning, but that did not prevent him from doing what he had done for many years: joining in the general excitement of migration upstream, and gorging on salmon eggs —whence Shiner's description of berry-gatherer. The keeper, who knew almost nothing of fish, thought the old man was merely stupid and garrulous. His Lordship did not fish; and his Lordship's agent always let the fishing to tenants. Shiner knew this; he had no ill-feeling against the keeper.

"Maybe a master g'rt wind after frost will blow away the leaves for 'ee soon," he remarked, changing the subject to suit the keeper. "I see'd many young fezzan chicks as I was in the swamp tilling tetties (potatoes) for my chap this spring. Th' ould birds eat my cabbage plants, but us don't grudge them a bite or two, sir. Live and let live, my chap saith: all complaints at the Judgment Seat. He be proper mazed about salmon, writing a book about'm, he did tell me, so I bin and opened the fender down to Steep, you'll see no more snatchin' there, like I used to do before my guts dried up."

The keeper looked at Shiner with a new interest. Shiner, knowing this, began to speak about the fish which were trying to get up the Sawmills Weir. He pointed out how salmon made

354

many attempts to feel the weights of the water; that they were not jumping every time they showed. They were feeling their way, time after time. Different parts of the weir suited different sized fish. Directly below them salmon were showing, half leaping; but none would try and get up there, said Shiner. That was the small sea-trout place, where the school peal got "up auver".

The weir was built in a series of steps or ledges descending; the water fell from ledge to ledge, toppling in ragged violence. A salmon appeared to push itself out of the lower white and to swim up in foaming water: actually it was slithering on mossy rocks which gave it a good grip. But the water there was too broken for its length, and it fell back, to lie in a trough in the rocky bed below, beside three other salmon which were touching; and over whom the bubbled water raced. The middle fish was Salar.

"'Tes no good for a large fish, just down there, you'll see," said Shiner. "But the li'l tackers go over for a pastime." Almost as he spoke a sea-trout long and nearly as narrow as a man's fore-arm shot out of the white at an angle of forty-five degrees and appeared to fly through the spray at that leaning angle, to alight on a hidden step of rock two feet under the sill, and cling there with its fore-fins. They saw its tail only; its body was beaten by the hard white water. It was pounded there for nearly a minute and then flung itself off the stone and swam vertically up solid falling water, moving gradually up to the bend over the sill and then, with a flick of its tail, it shot forward over the rim. It skipped out a dozen feet away, in exuberance of feeling.

At the other end of the weir the water plunged with more ragged violence off a large flat stone midway between upper and lower river levels. Below the foot of the weir, at this place there was depth for the take-off. New salmon arriving at the weir moved up the main stream which fell from the end where the two men were standing. Only when they had failed many times to reach the lip of the weir did they explore across to the other side, and find, after many trial jumps, the right way up.

"That be the place, my li'l dear," cried Shiner, to something in the water under the far end of the weir. The keeper looked at him with amused tolerance. The old fellow was proper mazed, he thought.

A salmon had shown there, turning on its side. It was Salar, who had arrived at Sawmills at the same time as Shiner. Immediately on arrival Salar had moved into the leaping-off place, and sunk to rest. He let the water seethe over his head and tickle the underpart of his body pleasantly. Salar did not like breathing bubbled water any more than any other salmon; but he lay there easily because, although his body was enswirled and stroked by bubbles, his mouth was thrust into a crevice where water welled in the dark green moss as from a spring.

After enjoying the highly-oxygenated water for a while, Salar moved back with the churning strakes and sank down to the bottom. There he balanced himself under the fog of bubbles. Above him the bubbles hissed; under him the rock rumbled. He lifted himself off the rock, felt the rhythm of power along his muscles passing into the water. He gaped faster at the water, while the flexions of his body rippled faster. He fixed his sight above the fog of bubbles, and sprang; but checked at the last moment. Shiner saw him, a fish of new-cut lead and new-cut copper sliding up moving snow.

Salar had checked on a sudden doubt. The doubt was due to the change of his nature, a change which had been coming slowly all the summer, delayed by return to the sea and renewal of feeding, and now was hastening upon him with the season of coloured leaves and sap sinking in trees and plants. His nature was drawing into itself; he lived more an inward than an outward life. He had no interest in moving things, food, while he was swimming up the river; but when he rested, his old nature returned upon him, and he was irritated and stirred by smaller fish swimming above him and by leaves and twigs and other movement. He took many pieces of black water-moss in his mouth, holding a piece sometimes for a minute or more before expelling it. Then all interest in moving things, which might have been food, was gone; he would sink into himself, his power withdrawn to give colour to his body—

skin and fins—to lengthen his head and give strength to the hook of his lower jaw. His skin was thickening, a pattern as of green and brown and yellow marble scrolled thereon.

A confusion of personality had checked Salar's jump; but after another rest he gathered himself and swam up and leapt, to be shocked by the warmth of air, and to fall beside the stone and swim up against the blank gush of water. He knew the way, and swam more strongly, reaching the straightness of the wall at the back of the weir, two feet from the top. The water gushed off his back, and then he was lying beside the wall, parallel to it, in a narrow trough no wider than himself, and well under the curve of water.

He slithered along, and then found he was lying behind the tail of another salmon. The tail was dark brown. This was one of the grilse which had followed Gralaks into the river.

In front of the small fish lay two other salmon, one a yellow-headed cock-fish with a porpoise bite out of its tail-fin: the other was Gralaks, who had been washed down the falls by the flood, and now was making her way up again.

Soon afterwards a fifth salmon wriggled up and rested its chin behind Salar's tail. An almost continuous line of salmon, hidden by the curve of falling water, was now lying directly under the sill of Sawmills Weir.

When Gralaks, the leading fish, was ready to go over the lip of the weir, she slewed her tail round so that the falling water beat on it. She lay between two mossy slabs of rock. She curled her tail for a jump; she sprang; her flanks gripped the hard descending mixture of air and water with scale and caudal fin; she bored upwards with nose and eye and gill and all the determined strength of life being urged forward. She slapped the water with sideway sweeps of her body, and then she was gone, her passing over the lip of the weir revealed by only a momentary bulge in the smooth bend of water.

24

High over the valley the last swallow was hurled in the wind which streamed the leaves from the oaks and kept the tall spruce firs of the hillsides swaying in slow wariness of grey clouds of sky. By the river the bullock paths were pitted and splashed yellow, under alders dispread black and bare. Over the viaduct a miniature train moved in silhouette, creeping across the sky, antiquated goods trucks on webbed wheels swept about by scattered steam.

From the top of the hill, reddish brown with larch and dark green with spruce plantations, came little reports flattened away by the wind, the first pheasant shoot of the year. Old Nog the heron was trying in vain to outfly the winds over the hill. Higher and higher they took him, turning and slanting and flapping without forward movement, scared by the reports of guns which he thought were all aimed at him. When a thousand feet high he gave up and swung round, and swept across the valley; but a report louder than the others, coming direct to him in a pocket of wind, made him tumble and turn and fly into the wind once more, determined to fish in future only in the wide safety of the estuary. Old Nog had made this resolution a hundred times before; he always forgot it when out of gunshot.

Within the river many salmon and sea-trout were moving. The sluice at Steep Weir was gone; posts, doors, framework weighing more than a ton, had been jostled to the sea, no more to the river in spate than a few twigs and leaves. Already barnacles were laying their eggs on the wood, beside the jelly-sacks of river-snails' eggs killed by the salt.

Every tide brought in more salmon, which reached Saw-mills with their lice still alive, four days from the sea. The gravel of the river-bed was stirred and shifted by a myriad changing weights of water pouring around and eddying from fish on the move. And by mid-November, when the river level was steady with fast water running clear as glass, the gravel was being cut up by the tails of female fish—from the Carrion Pit to the runners on the slopes of the moor: in many streamlets, scarcely wider than the step of a boy, salmon were preparing to spawn.

Gralaks lay above the Fireplay Pool. The roe which had been growing within her all the summer were now one-fifth the weight of her body. She was ripe, ready to drop her eggs. Three male fish, knowing this, were near her, waiting to shed their milt on the eggs. One of them was Salar.

Behind the three cock-fish lay Garroo the cannibal trout. Behind Garroo lay two smaller trout who had tasted salmon eggs before. And lying close beside Gralaks was Grai, a salmon parr weighing two ounces, who had fallen in love with Gralaks with all the volume of his milt, which weighed one-tenth of an ounce. Gralaks was aware of Grai; indeed she was pleased by his nearness. Grai knew the other fish were there because of Gralaks, but his feeling for her, especially when she lay and hid him, was stronger than his fear. Grai was determined that no other cock-fish should lie beside Gralaks.

No other cock-fish had yet noticed Grai.

At nightfall Gralaks moved slowly forward on the level shallows above the throat of the pool. At once Salar and his two rivals moved behind her. She turned on her right side and sinuated in an arrested swimming motion, lifting by suction a few stones, which fell back with the stream. Watched by Salar and the other cock-fish, Gralaks settled into the slight furrow and thrust herself into it, to widen it.

During a pause in the digging Grai darted forward from beside Salar's left pectoral fin and took up his rightful place beside the mighty mistress of all sensation. The swift movement loosened a mistiness into the water behind the parr's tail.

The effect of this milt passing by the gills of the cock-fish was one of action and turmoil. One turned and slipped over Salar, and with open mouth made as if to bite the salmon on the other side of Salar, who drove at him, also with open mouth. The three-sided chase rocked the water of the Fireplay.

All during the night, at intervals, Gralaks was digging the redd for spawning—sweeping the gravel sideways and scooping a pit in which she lay. Another hen-fish was doing the same thing ten yards above her, and two more, each attended by one or more males, were working in the fast water between the tail of the Fireplay and a larger and deeper pool below. This was the Wheel Pool. It was wide and round. The stream entering it divided into two streams, one turning left-handed and continuing the main course of the river under overhanging oaks and past sombre yews, the other turning to the right and running back under alders until it was slowed by meeting the main run again. Sticks borne on this flattened circle rode round and round sometimes for months, shut within the backwater.

A ridge of rock lay across the middle of the Wheel Pool, and under this rock, with other quiet fish, Trutta was lying. The quiet fish were salmon new from the sea, and unaffected by the movements of the red fish, which had come into the river months before. Their greenish coats were still untarnished; they would not spawn until the end of January, when the redds of the spring fish which had spawned would be cut up again, and the eggs, dark-spotted with eyes, swept away.

The Wheel Pool was Trutta's pool. He had spawned in the run between the Wheel and the Fireplay seven times. On this his eighth visit from the sea, however, Trutta had not yet begun to share the general excitement. There was still a dark ring round his neck, although the black collar had gone. His kype, which was immense, had grown sideways, and looked to Shiner, who at noon climbed one of the oaks to look down into the pool, like a reversed clay-pipe held in the pug's jaws.

At night the stars were clear and large, frost-sharpened. Tufts of withering rushes and grasses and thistles were rimed with hoar-frost in the morning. Sunrise over the hill of fir plantations was a flush of pink and gold; a clear sky all day. Again night glowed with stars above a mist of frost settling on bracken and grass and branch. The water was colder, and fish did not move much.

Salar, lying behind Gralaks, saw the stars above him with the quietness of his other self. He became alert with the rumbling in the rock under him; and saw the water in front of him glow with fire, which gleamed on the back of Gralaks. **High** over the valley the train passed, puffing on the upgrade, dense steam hanging over its length, and the play of flames reflected from its engine cab.

For nearly a week the water ran colder, slower, clearer. On the first evening of December the wind went round to the west, the water became warmer, and fish became active. Gralaks was now ready to lay her eggs. Nearly five thousand were in the cavity beside her shrunken stomach. Spawning began towards the end of the night. During the darkness Salar had been roving round the pools, swimming from Fire-play down the run into Wheel, questing under the ledge of rock and hollows under the bank of alders. But always he had returned in haste, to move behind the trough where Gralaks lay, beside one or another of his waiting rivals. Both pools were astir with restless fish.

At last the tail of Gralaks began to work more quickly, and immediately one of the cock-fish moved up beside her and shouldered her from the pit she had dug. Grai the parr pressed himself beside a large flat yellow stone which had been exposed by the digging. So tiny was Grai, that the cock-fish did not even know he was there. Thrust off the redd, Gralaks swam forward her own length, and lay still, while Salar moved in beside the cock-fish. Immediately this fish turned with a sweep of its porpoise-bitten tail and came at Salar with open mouth. Salar swung round to avoid the lunge and also to grip his rival across the wrist. The swirl lifted **Grai** and scattered gravel. Grai recovered and darted to the trough again, to be behind the tail of Gralaks.

Heedless of the turmoil behind her, but thereby excited, Gralaks had turned on her right side, to-bend head and body backwards until her belly was curved palely like a water-sunk reflection of the young moon. She jerked and shook on her side, as though trying to touch the back of her neck with her tail. Eggs dribbled quickly from her, sinking with the current amidst gravel and sand and rolling into the trough.

The sight of the eggs and the taste of the water made Salar quiver; and as Gralaks moved backwards he moved forward, feeling as though he were being drawn from underneath by a lamprey of sweeter and sweeter sensation. His milt flowed from him in a mist, millions of invisible organisms wriggling in the water. Some of them found eggs, into the skins of which they bored, desperate for security. Those which were successful in finding the liquid within were lost in the creation of new life; the rest drifted away, to perish in water palely lighted by the star-galaxy of night, whose mirrored fate was their own.

For a few moments Salar lay in ecstasy on the redd, but his larger rival seized him by the tail and held him despite his violent lashings. Salar's head swung downstream; water was opening his gills, he could not breathe. The big fish swam upstream to drown him. The water was beaten and the two bodies rolled over. The other fish which was attending Gralaks was a grilse of her own school, which she had led from the Island Race; and this fish, whose back was a marbled pattern of green and pink, followed the struggle and in his excitement bit the larger salmon across the tail. This made it lose its hold of Salar, and dash downstream after the male grilse, abandon the chase and swing up again below the redd and lie there. Salar returned more slowly and lay behind it, and to one side. The grilse also returned, and the three fish lay there, at rest for the moment.

During the struggle and chase, Gralaks had laid again, and Grai had covered the eggs. He lay beside Gralaks, by her right pectoral fin which was wider than his own width. He was fatigued. Unknowingly he had given fertility to nine of the two hundred and thirty eggs which had trickled from Gralaks like a necklace of small amber beads strung on water.

After a rest Grai moved away to the shelter of a stone. From the stone he moved to his lie under the bank, his spawning done for that year. Most of his milt had been lost six weeks before, when he had been caught on an artificial fly during the last day of the fishing season. The angler had held Grai in his hand, and the touch of unwetted palm and fingers had been a scalding agony to the little fish writhing to escape. The fisherman had held the parr after he had worked the barb of the hook from the corner of Grai's mouth, to illustrate to his son carrying the net the difference in strength between a small trout and a parr of equal size and almost equal appearance. Holding Grai in his fist, he told the boy to observe the muscular strength. It was during that agony that Grai had shed most of his milt. It wetted the angler's hand, a chalk-white liquid, after the parr's release. That was in October; now it was three weeks before Christmas.

During the day following his first spawning, Grai rested himself; but the next night he was back again at the redd, lying behind the three great fish of whom now he was wary and afraid. But when Garroo the cannibal trout moved up beside him, Grai left the Fireplay and went down to other redds below the Wheel Pool and the yew-trees and waited behind a pair of sea-trout spawning in fast water there. Grai was hungry. Scores of eggs he swallowed as they rolled down between the stones.

All the other parr and trout of the river were feeding on eggs, too. Biggest of the berry-gatherers, as Shiner called them, was Garroo. Salar drove him many times from the redd of Gralaks. Shiner used to climb an alder beside the Fireplay, and in the clear water of sunlit noon he saw the fish there. Gralaks was almost hidden in the blur of the deeper water; behind her lay Salar, his red coat looking browny-purple under water, then the larger and darker fish, with the bite out of its tail-fin, and the smaller form of the male grilse. Behind the trio of square tails lay a big-headed black fish which was Garroo.

When the two larger cock-fish turned inwards to menace one another, Shiner knew the hen-fish was about to lay again. While the two big salmon were chasing and counter-chasing, the smaller fish moved up on to the redd; and at the same time Garroo thrust forward and turned on his side to suck the eggs into his mouth. Then the grilse would chase Garroo away, and move up again to the redd. But Salar or the other cock-fish, whichever returned first, drove the grilse off, and followed him downstream, while Garroo fled before the grilse. Shiner would see the waves of pursuit going round the bend.

A few moments later they would come back. The wan winter sunlight revealed every white and yellow and brown stone of the gravel over which Salar moved. Just behind him was the male grilse, and just behind the grilse was Garroo, his black jaw, scarred and misshapen, protruding as though with a leer at all such foolishness as spawning. Garroo's milt glands had long since shrunken in wicked old age.

A fortnight before Christmas the weather became cold again. The river was running low, many of its feeders on the moor being fringed with ice. The larger cock-fish with the bitten tail could no longer get on to the redd. Salar had to go past the stones and drift down to settle in the trough by the side of Gralaks. Even then his back and tail-fin were out of water. While he was coming back tail-first, the smaller grilse usually slithered over the heaped gravel and bit him across the wrist. Salar slashed the grilse away, and the movement scattered some of the eggs, which Garroo caught on the end of his kype. Shiner, watching from the tree, heard a distinct snapping noise as each egg was sucked into the trout's mouth.

Another time Shiner saw Salar chase Garroo round the pool, down the run into the Wheel Pool, and up again to the Fireplay, where the salmon caught the trout across the back and shook it, his head out of water. "'Twas just like a terrier shaking an ould black rat," said Shiner.

As the days went on Salar became heavy with weariness. Most of his milt was shed: in slow pulse after slow pulse his life's sweetness had been drawn from him, leaving with each emptiness a greater inflaming desire, which during the day lapped about the wasted body with dreams of an everlasting sea of rest; but when darkness came, and the water was ashine with stars, he felt himself running bright with the river, and sweetness returned to him on the redd beside Gralaks.

The time came when the last of the eggs were spawned, and Gralaks was gone, dropping back to the Wheel Pool, where Trutta was lying.

Trutta was dark brown, and thin. He had fought to cover the eggs of a clove-spotted sea-trout, a handsome hen-fish nearly as long as himself, but slimmer and younger, most pleasant to see and be near to; yet no milt had come from him. He had driven away all other sea-trout; and had it not been for the little peal which were ever ready to shed their milt, none of the eggs of that female would have hatched ninety days later.

Trutta remained on guard, never sleeping; and no salmon, even the forty-three-pounder who had arrived, a clean-run fish, in the last week of December, was allowed to approach his mate—as Trutta considered her. The hen-fish laid her eggs, indifferent to the clashes about her: the nearness of the little peal, with their dark mother-of-pearl hues, gave her contentment.

When the last egg was gone from her, hidden under the stones of the redd, she drifted down the river, and came to the shelter of the alder roots above Humpy Bridge.

She lay there, day after day, night after night, waiting for the rain and the spate which would take her down to the sea. Near her lay Gralaks. Kelt and graveling rested side by side, thin, discoloured, empty of all feeling, patiently awaiting the rain.

25

The colder the water, the greater its density. In the frosty nights of the year's end fish sank close to the rock and gravel of the pools, hardly moving. Those late-running salmon which had paired, and had not yet spawned, lay side by side in the fast water, which hid them although their back-fins were above a broken and uneven surface. The fever smouldered in them, as they waited for the frost to go.

Sticks and ferns near the waterfalls and fast glides around rocks which were wetted by spray slowly became coated with ice. Under many of the alders long stems of brambles were trailing in the water. These were cadets of the main root which during the past summer had set out to make their own lives. The exploring heads had put forth roots on finding water; these roots were spread long and white on the surface. As the water lipped them, so frost made a layer of ice on them. Soon the brambles were stretched straight, downstream, with a weight of ice on the ineffectual roots. When the ice-club became too heavy, the bramble broke and was dragged away. Ice began to dull the sight of the river where it was least alive: at the edges of pools and by the bays in the bank trodden by cattle. The frost had brought down the last leaves of waterside trees, and these had caught, one behind another, against outstanding stones of the shallows. The waterflow pressed them together in the shape of fir-cones, scores and even hundreds of leaves wadded together, and beginning to decompose on their undersides. This gave a little warmth, which was sought by snails and shrimps. Frost put its blind grey seal around the cones of leaves; frost bound together the roots of rushes; frost sealed the trickling places of the river, and thickened the icicles under the falls. Water found new trickling places; these too were sealed. Rocks and snags lipped by water were given brittle grey collars, which became wider until they broke off and floated into eddies and were welded into the local ice, strengthening it.

The slow solidification of eddies and still stretches by the shallows made the runs faster. New eddies were formed in reaction, new ice affirmed their stillness.

Towards noon the sun in a clear sky melted the rime on bracken and grasses, and in the straying hoofmarks of cattle and deer. Some of the grey sheets of ice cracked, and were borne down, making the water colder. No fly hatched, no fish moved. The larger eels were in the Atlantic, journeying under the Gulf Stream, seeking by instinct the weed-beds of the Sargasso. Smaller eels, the survivors of which would set forth the next autumn, were torpescent in holes and under stones. A large sheet of ice covering the stiller water of the Wheel Pool suddenly whimpered and cracked and tilted, then settled again on the slowly turning water.

The little heat of the sun was soon lost in a frost of gold and lengthening shadows. Ice floes which had stopped by the piers of Humpy Bridge were sealed to the stonework. The sun went down behind the trees, grass drooped again as rime grew white on its blades. Thin layers of water stroked the floes, thickening them. Gralaks lay in the deepest water, never moving.

Up in the Fireplay Pool Salar lay below the redd, as though guarding it. Clots of semi-opaque, jelly-like water passed him: a slush of ice. Rapidly within his body the germs of salmon-pest were multiplying; and as they conquered the living tissue weakened by the long strain of waiting stagnant in the river, so the vegetable fungus strengthened its hold on that tissue. Other forms of life were claiming that which in Salar had been assembled and used for a racial purpose of which he knew nothing. Salar was nearly emptied of self. He lay behind the redd, awaiting the rhythm of desire and all pleasure, seeing the stars wavery bright as he had seen them in the lustihood of Atlantic nights.

The fungus grew rapidly in the cold water. Soon Salar's jaw was covered with cream-coloured ruffs. The edges and centre of his tail-fin were corroded, too, and his skin, which had thickened and caused the scales to shrink since his return from the sea, was also patched with fungus where it had been bruised on the weirs, and by fighting.

One night when the Fireplay was covered with ice except for a narrow canal Salar saw many fish moving before him. One of them was Gralaks, leaping with silver coat, and returning to lie beside him. Salar drove at the other fish, for they would lure Gralaks from him. They fled from him, and vanished beyond the redd. Gralaks moved to the redd, and grew larger, until she was all the river which was streaming with stars along her flanks: she covered Salar, and was the river in spate and all the shining strength of ocean. But the fish came back, and were black, opening monstrous grampus-mouths to crush him, and Salar fled down the river which now was all broken water to bruise him and a weir which was high as the stars. The weir was a flood of red water, and thundering about him; then it was gone, and he saw the redd before him.

It was a goods train passing over the viaduct.

Salar had hardly moved, except to roll over in the delirium of his sickness.

The ice began to thaw the next day, with the coming of the south-west wind. Its melting released oxygen into the water, and Salar was stimulated to leap from the pool, falling back

367

in a formless splash. Shiner saw the leap: he saw the lean rusty-brown body, the prolonged misshapen head covered with creamy fungus, green slime on the gill-covers and the blackened jaw with its great white hook twisted and tipped with yellow. Edges of all the fins were yellow, too, while a rosette was fixed to the side, spreading out from the scar of the lamprey-wound.

"Poor old chap," said Shiner. "What you needs now is a nice li'l fresh, to take you down to the sea, to clean yourself."

The south-west was blowing, but it brought no rain. By the beginning of February the river was at low summer level again. The phantom of spent passion for which Salar had remained by the redd was gone from him; he lay now in the deeper Wheel Pool, under the shelf of rock beside Trutta. At night the two kelts moved up to the edge of the run where it broke over the shallow. Warmer water had delayed the growth of fungus, but the pest bacillus had spread through his body, heart, liver, and gut. Strips of his skin, which fungus had covered, had broken away, and the spent body had no strength for regrowth.

In the still deeps of the pool a dim blue-grey length lay, the rival of Salar. Two more dead cock-fish lay on their backs in the Fireplay. They had died while waiting by redds in the shallows above, and the stream had brought them down. Every pool in the Two Rivers held dead or dying male fish. The wind was now from the north-east, a barren wind of drouth, a dry cutting wind which made lambs on the moor huddle into their ewes, and drove all birds into the lower valleys and the estuary.

When Shiner next saw Salar the kelt was lying at the edge of the Fireplay, in still water, over a silt of mud and buried sticks. Salar did not move as Shiner knelt down and stared at him. He did not see the man above him. Even when Shiner put a hand out and curved it under the kelt's body, as though to support it, there was no movement. Only when he lifted it did Salar come back from his farawayness of self, and feel a shock, and move off slowly into deep water.

"You mustn't bide by the bank, midear," said Shiner. "That ould crane ban't like Shiner, you know. He'll give 'ee a dapp that won't do no one no good." Old Nog, passing in the sky, uttered a screech. "You bestways must wait where you be now, until the rain cometh, midear." The pale mask in the water moved forward. "That's right, midear. Shiner knoweth." And talking to himself, the old man ambled away along the river bank, peering into the water, seeing almost everything that happened.

Night after night was starless. Clouds passed over the valley from the west, driven by a high salt wind which ruffled the pools and scattered the packs of leaves on stones of the shallows. Plants of hornwort and celery began to spread on the gravel their first leaves of the year, and the crowsfoot was lengthening green near them. The dipper sang its soliloquy of stones-and-water; the kingfisher lanced its cry under the leafless alders. On the top of a spruce higher than the railway viaduct a missel-thrush sang to the flaming purple sunset.

With the last of the winter's night, snow began to fall on the moor, moulding itself thinly on the windward side of writhen beeches and thorns, falling thin and pale and shrinking to beads of water, but always falling, until the black places where turf had been cut were white, and clumps of moor-grass were cowled in white with flakes falling thicker until all save water was white. In the morning it was a new world upon which the sun looked briefly before clouds hid it again in snow with which the wind whitely streamlined all things standing from the earth—pillars of the viaduct, trunks of trees, felled timber, ploughshare left in an unfinished furrow, abandoned motor-cars, and sheep huddled under the hedges. Through the snow the otters romped, making a slide down the cattle-break in the bank by the yew-trees, whose portent dark loomed through night's glimmer.

When the moon rose in a clear sky the otters remained by their slide of trodden snow, sliding together and singly, violently and easily, into the water, whistling and talking and wrostling and splashing until sharp heads pointed up the pool, to the noise of a jumping fish. Salar had leapt, the second time in the New Year. A wild hope of a spate and the sea had stirred in him. Together the otters slipped into the water.

Trutta lay beside Salar. Wherever Salar had gone during the past month, Trutta had gone too, following the phosphoric gleam of the kelt's head and flank and tail. When Salar saw the swimming shapes of otters above him, he went wildly away downstream; but Trutta, sure of the deep water, turned with open mouth and swam up hard and bumped the larger otter. Then Trutta, his mouth still open, swam down and swam up again to bump the other otter. He did this again and again, followed them round the pool. Shiner was hidden behind the oak-tree, and saw what happened. The big pug bumped the otters again and again, until they were growling with rage and one of them ran out on the bank, standing up on its hind-legs and "chittering". Then it either saw or smelled Shiner, for after that he neither heard nor saw them more.

But when Shiner returned the next day he saw, lying on the gravel edge above the Fireplay, lapped by rising coloured water of the thaw, a great head with twisted kype joined to a backbone from which the flesh had been stripped, and a large tail-fin frayed convex at the edges. The otters had returned, and driven Trutta into thin water where he was helpless; and when they had killed and left him, a fox, who while passing over the viaduct had heard the noises of splashing and growling, had crept down to the river with his vixen.

And a hundred yards below the Fireplay Shiner found a kelt with fungus on its head and tail and flank, lying on its side in water not deep enough to cover it. Salar had got so far with the last of his strength, and had died in the darkness.

The spate rose rapidly and washed all away, to the sea which gives absolution alike to the living and the dead.

In the gravel of the moorland stream the eggs were hatching, little fish breaking from confining skins to seek life, each one alone, save for the friend of all, the Spirit of the waters. And the star-stream of heaven flowed westward, to far beyond the ocean where salmon, moving from deep water to the shallows of the islands, leapt—eager for immortality.

EPIGRAPH TO SALAR THE SALMON

A PERSONAL NOTE

The author has already told, in part, how *Tarka* was written; and so a few words on the "salmon book", as it was thought of during the five years at Shallowfood—the cottage just outside the Deer Park of the story—may not be out of place here.

While reading the proofs of this new edition in 1959, nearly a quarter of a century after *Salar* was first published (October 1935) I can feel again, behind the words, the difficulties of composition in the spring and summer of that year—the effect of which surely will be apparent to the reader. *Salar* is not easy to read, the book was hard to write. The publishers had advanced a sum of money on signing the contract: months passed, while I flinched from starting. Where, and how, should one begin?

I knew a small stretch of the river, I had watched salmon from Humpy Bridge to the Viaduct Pool (which I thought of as The Fireplay, a name still used by fishermen on the banks of the Bray below the old G.W.R. viaduct). I had spent thousands of hours up trees, on shillet banks, beside fast runs—"jabbles" as they are called in Canada. I had walked innumerable times along the banks of the Bray, down to its junction with the Mole; and thence through the valley of the Taw to Barnstaple and the estuary. There I had a sailing boat, *Pinta*, moored off the White House, a cottage on the sea-wall opposite the North Devon Cricket Club ground. Weeds hung on the bottom of that half-decked, 18-foot yacht; there had been no time for sailing.

On my shelves was a set of *The Salmon and Trout Magazine*, beginning with the first quarterly number published in December 1910, and continuing until the spring of 1930, my first season at Shallowford. Thereafter I was a member of The

Salmon & Trout Association, with its headquarters at Fish-mongers' Hall. I read all the back numbers, previously owned by Dr. T. E. Pryce-Tannatt, one of many scientific contributors to the magazine, together with such famous authorities as Dr. W. Rushton, Professor Knut Dahl, G. E. M. Skues, H. D. Turing, J. C. Mottram, Arthur Wanless, and others whose knowledge made me feel that what I had seen and stored in my mind was but the superficial observations of an amateur. How then dare I write about salmon? A natural diffidence, which had always been a barrier between myself and single-minded men, held me back from my project. Daring one day to speak of my doubts and hopes to an Edwardian cavalry officer, who, born in Devon, had fished all his life in the major West Country rivers, I received the bluff reply, "You may know about otters, but what do you know about salmon, that I should want to read such a book as you propose?"

Before this, he had told me that he got little fishing nowadays, whereupon I had ventured to invite the Major to fish my water, to be dismissed with, "Much too far to go!"

The writing of *Salar* was put off, month after month, while the proverb of William Blake, "He who desires, but acts not, breeds pestilence", ran through my days, like fungus growing on a drought-locked salmon. At last, returning one late afternoon in winter, having seen the wreckage of many spawned-out fish lying at the margins of the river, I sat before a wood fire in the sitting room at Shallowford and tremulously began to write. The first page came slowly, about a sentence a minute. Thereafter the work was continued, beginning each morning at 9.30 a.m. and the pen laid down any time between 5 p.m. and midnight. The words of Arnold Bennett, who once said to me, "I don't write so much as they think, but I write *regularly*", had replaced Blake's proverb.

The writing continued, with some enforced breaks (which were painful) until the early summer. During June and July of that year I sat on the lawn, wearing only shorts and smoked glasses, and typing because of cramps in my right hand. I had to set aside, every minute, persistent thoughts that the work was dull, commonplace, and unreadable.

At last I went to my field below the beech plantation at Windwhistle Cross, overlooking Barnstaple Bay, and stayed in my hut. It was a hot summer. Day after day I sat half-naked in the sun, beside a young pine tree, tapping intermittently, while overhead a biplane towed a long piece of cloth with the inscription BILE BEANS ARE GOOD FOR YOU. I cursed it, cold from the feet upwards, making every excuse to get up from the chair, wander round the field, sit in the grass and watch spiders, stare at lizards on the elm-boards of the hut, hoe my small lettuce patch—thus, it seemed, putting back enough energy to be transmuted into that imaginary life. By now one was writing against time, for the book was already announced for the early autumn.

Chapters were sent off, without being read through, as soon as they were completed. There was no time for galleys, those long paper strips of cased print, by which one might make excisions or add sentences before the type was formed into pages. As the publisher received the chapters, they were sent unread to the printer.

At last, towards the end of summer, the feeling was that if the salmon did not die, the author would: the story was brought to a quick ending, then I sat by the green baize table, bewildered and vacant, trying to force myself to get up, shut typewriter, gather last sheets together, and post them away. Then to pick some unwanted lettuces and eat them with hard lumps of bread and cheese remaining in the food box.

From that experience, one realised, later, that much of T. E. Lawrence's desperate, nihilistic feelings before he joined the R.A.F. were due to under-feeding and over-cerebration.

The book was published in time, with almost no corrections, and to my surprise the publisher told me just before Christmas that it had beaten all day-sale records for his firm, selling 3,000 copies in one day, making a total of 10,000; and thereby earning the sum paid (£750) for advanced royalties in the previous year.

So the style is that of one self-compelled to complete a work before the subject could be seen in detachment, one result of being confined to a narrow valley for several years, and dominated by ambition to bring the sight of water, tree, fish, sky, and other life upon paper.

In reaction to such a life, I thought to escape from self-imposed literary servitude, to become a farmer in another part of England; rods were put away, the seven-year cycle was over. I had no desire to fish again, at least for many years, and then only very occasionally.

Some readers found the book unreadable, including the Edwardian cavalryman, Major Instow; while in London the book was awarded, according to a report in a newspaper, "The Sitwell Prize for the Worst Novel of the Year" (1935). The Prize was a large stuffed bream in a glass case. I was not invited to receive this award, to my regret, for I admired the creative work of Miss Edith, Mr. Osbert, and Mr. Sacheverell Sitwell, and would have welcomed the opportunity to say to them, "I agree with you about *Salar*; I wrote it; but what are we four against so many?"

Now to easier pages, written soon after the war, in the carefree days of 1921 and 1922, when a little knowledge was not a dangerous thing.

THE EPIC OF
BROCK THE BADGER

THE EPIC OF BROCK THE BADGER

Bill Brock the badger was a real beast. He lived and died much as I have described in the following pages, which are told with some comic relief, and a little satire here and there. It was one of the first stories I wrote, a year or two before *Tarka*. My young self felt anger at the ruin of an animal faced with so many odds; but I hid my feelings, for having been through a war I had learned something, at least, of the many opposing faces of life.

I heard first of Brock in the village inns of long ago, before the motor-car raised the ruddle dust of the ironstone roads and gave a bloom of pale pink to the lime-washed cottage walls. I must admit responsibility for raising some of the dust during my journeys, usually at night, from village inn to town tavern, wherein to listen and learn and drink a little beer. Sometimes I was accompanied by my dog, squatting on the tank of the motor-bike between my arms. The Norton had no lights, the moon was my lantern. Sometimes on returning to Skirr cottage we passed a dark figure in the shadow cast by an outside chimney breast, and saluted the law by opening throttle and valve-lifter, to make flashing reports in the open nickel-plated exhaust pipe. The loud reports made no difference, the shadow never moved.

Perhaps the village constable regarded the passing scene as a diversion in a dull life; more probably, he wanted to remain unseen, for it was his habit at night to slip through the yard of the Lower House and sit in the kitchen, drinking beer with the widow and her daughters. The tenant of the pub had recently cut his throat in despair of making a living. Few came to his house, and a barrel of beer going sour was a disaster for one whose cobbling of village boots was not enough to provide a bare living. For times were changing, the village crafts were going. A char-a-banc of sorts now ran once a

379

week, on market day, between village and "Town", and more people went to shop there.

The constable was often in the kitchen of the Lower House after closing time, sitting there until midnight and sometimes into the small hours. By then the widow had long exhausted her small store of energy, she wept at the memory of her "good man" having done what he had done, and all because, she moaned, she had been sharp with her tongue. The suicide was a soldier returned from the war, to find a changed world.

The new owner of the Lower House was a badger digger, owning a famous terrier called The Mad Mullah. I wrote the first story of Bloody Bill Brock in 1921, and transferred the scene to another part of the West Country. It appeared in *Pearson's Magazine*, the editor of which paid £18, quite a lot of money for a morning's work: over three years' rent of my cottage!

Later, I wrote other stories of the series. The incident of the badger coming out to "cripple" hounds, after a fox had gone to earth in its sett, is founded on fact; also that of the big boar's last appearance.

1

Summer visitors to the west country town of Colham, hatless and carrying haversacks, strolling about noon in what is called Old Town, and gazing at the ancient timbered buildings of the narrow streets down by the river, sometimes hesitate in front of the latticed casements of the inn called The Rising Sun. The hesitation of these visitors, with their sunburned faces and shoes dusty from tramping the chalky tracks of the downs, may be caused by the modern signboard that proclaims in large purple letters on a red background:

THE RISING SUN HOTEL
ROBT. E. TINKER,
Managing Proprietor.

Those who overcome doubt and decide to enter and ask for bread-and-cheese and ale, are usually interested in the dog-like heads, mounted on small wooden shields, which are fixed round the varnished walls of the saloon bar. These heads, about a dozen of them, appear to be exactly alike; each one being about the size of a small fox terrier's head, and black, with a white broad-arrow running from the tip of the nose along the cheeks and over the pate. Each shield bears the name of a place, a date, a weight in pounds, and either the word *Sow* or *Boar*, in white painted letters.

Over the lintel of the doorway leading into the barrel room is a straight copper horn, resting on nails, and beside it a sheath and a knife with a six-inch pointed blade—a little dagger. Above them is a pair of long-handled iron tongs, crossed like pincers, and closing on an iron collar slightly wider than the necks of the arrowed heads.

Observing a glance at these objects, the Managing Proprietor

of The Rising Sun Hotel—the old inn has been "improved"—
fourteenth-century oak beams and joists hidden behind wood-
pulp ceiling boards; smoke-blackened oak-panelling painted
and varnished in "oak-grain" pattern; open hearth bricked
in and set with glazed reddish-purple tiles and cast-iron grate
—observing that his trophies are the object of curiosity, Mr.
Tinker is liable to pour out a whisky for himself, and regard
the masks complacently, while waiting to have his say about his
part in the old English sport of badger-digging.

Mr. Tinker tells how he carried the horn for over twenty
years, as Master of the Colham Badger-digging Club; how he
has dug out more than twenty-five score of badgers, "totalling
over seven tons of badger flesh, excluding cubs"; of the prowess
of his many terriers in going to earth and staying there, holding
the badgers from digging, while with two-bill, mattock, bar,
spade, and pick, the diggers follow them up the "pipes."

In answer to the invariable guileless question why badgers
—or brocks as he usually calls them—are dug out, Mr. Tinker
answers that the farmers like them killed, not that they do
much harm, he admits. Badger-digging, he explains, is a sport,
just like fox-hunting or coursing or ferreting or otter-hunting;
and while he carried the horn he found that most of the farmers
were a sporting lot, and allowed the Club to dig on their farms.
There was the beer, too, of course; they always took beer out
to a badger-dig, for the farmers!

Dogs get hurt? Not very often, although he had seen a dog
cut up proper! Well, yes, thank you very much, gentlemen;
he will have a drop of whisky. When he has poured himself a
drink, and given the change, Mr. Tinker retires for his demonstration skull, which, he says, ants cleaned for him—he put it
near a nest of the big wood-ants, and at the end of a week it
was as sweet as an empty whisky cask. Placing the skull on the
mahogany-varnished counter, he lifts the upper jaws, revealing
the cutting edge of grinder teeth, the sharp canines, the massive
bone of the brow. Then he lifts a pad off a nail in the wall, and
shows the black claws broken by digging in the last hours of
life, before tongs fastened round the brock's neck, and he was
drawn out to be killed.

Sometimes Mr. Tinker will lead his guests into his parlour beyond the barrel room, and show them one of his treasured possessions—a painting of Bloody Bill Brock, the 42 lb. boar-badger whose fame he has appropriated for himself, since he was the Master, for twenty years, of the Colham Badger-digging Club.

Some of the visitors may imagine from this painting that the pictures of animals in the coloured comic papers they had enjoyed in childhood were not so preposterous after all; while one, at least, decided that the artist must have learned his natural history entirely from his childish impressions of such papers. The boar-badger of the incredible portrait has four legs, apparently one set behind the other under its body. A mild and simple expression lies in the human eyes of its over-sized head, and its hair is uniformly the colour of a battleship.

"My son did that," Mr. Tinker is wont to declare, proudly. "My son was at the art school in High Street for two years. Don't look at that, that's nothing."

The "nothing" refers to the old sign on the reverse side of the badger portrait, which was painted on the back of the sign-board that used to hang outside the inn before the Great War increased Mr. Tinker's savings, enabling him to buy The Rising Sun, which is a free house. The flames of the sun are dis-lustred, the paint cracked with age, yet its beauty still rests on the wood. A poor artist painted it years ago, in exchange for a night's lodging.

"Good health, gentlemen! Many's the time we tried to dig out that badger, and couldn't get deep enough into the pipes. Once he crippled a pack of foxhounds, but it was pure luck that he got away from them. Nipped them all in the pads, he did; but we got him at last. The day after Christmas Day it was. He had six toes on his near fore-pad, and that's how we knew it was Bloody Bill Brock, as we called him.

"And when at last I did get his mask," says Mr. Tinker dramatically, "shall I tell you what I saw?" He leans over the counter, and points his pipe stem at the patient but expect-ant listener. "Never have I seen the like of it—no, sir, never before in my life!—and I've dug out scores and scores of badgers, scores and scores I've dug out—over seven tons of 'em! Wait a moment, please; I'll show you!"

But what Mr. Tinker shows his visitors belongs to the climax of the great boar's life, which was the manner of his death. Before that is told, these are the stories of Brock's Terror, and the fight with the d'Essantville foxhounds. . . . Away from the modernised, suburban inn: let the imagination arise into the air, beyond streets and houses, and stray away over the downs, to the forest home of the badgers, centuries old, many of the tunnels fallen in, for badgers are always digging. It is the month of May, and the little badger cub, later to be called Bloody Bill Brock, is three months old.

He was lying asleep with the other two cubs, snuggled into the sow-badger's side, when his mother uncurled herself, flung them off, and stiffened.

The cub smelt a strange smell, and kept still. The three cubs peered into the gloom, and then a ghastly roar filled the cave. They crouched very still at the unknown terror. The roar came again. His mother crept forward, and the cubs lay together.

A series of roars shook the darkness, following the sound of a hunting horn. The roars ceased abruptly. Something howled, and the roaring smell went away.

The earth trembled above them, and a flint fell on the cub's head. He could hear feet thumping and strange, terrifying shouts and notes of a hunting horn.

"Fetch 'un, Jenny, fetch 'un out!"

The sound seemed to whisper in the darkness, and the cub heard something creeping near him. He squeaked his terror, heard a guttural growl, and snapped at the hideous face. The apparition seized his sister and shook her, then dropped her limp and unmoving.

The cub whimpered for his mother, who rushed back from the other side, and to his joy, she bit the apparition three times —*click, click, click!* The thing let out a howl and fled the way it had come, taking its smell with it, but leaving behind a different scent that came from the ground. The cub sniffed the wet patch, and crouched into his mother again.

The boar-badger came suddenly to them, and the sow rubbed her nose against his in joy.

Outside the two holes in the hillside, about twenty people were grouped. One of them was kneeling down and listening. He was the Master of the Colham Badger-digging Club. To his belt hung a hunting knife, a copper horn, and a whistle. He thrust his ear down the hole as far as possible, and the effort caused him to show his beaver-like teeth.

Nearly all the spectators were men. Big Will'um, the bailiff of Skirr Farm, and a bearded crowstarver who lived alone in the spinney of the big wheatfield, held spades. Two very small boys standing near, Jack, the farmer's son, and his friend Willie, hoped they would be allowed to dig. They had rolled their sleeves up in anticipation, and Willie was moistening his palms for the third time. Jack was conserving his spittle. It was the first time they had seen a badger-dig. They were awfully excited, and so was Elsie, a slim girl with a plait of hair like a golden ear of wheat. Sometimes she gave Willie a sidelong glance, and he spat on his hands.

"Coolord!" said Willie, pointing.

Jenny crept out of the hole, and at sight of her a dozen dogs began to bark. Her tail was down and she trembled, lifting a paw. She had two red gashes in her shoulder, and her leg-bone was cracked. The Master swore and sent down another bitch. A dog and a bitch never quarrelled, but two bitches together often argued while Brock escaped. Two dogs together were quarrelsome, as well.

Clara came back, with a savage bite in her lower jaw.

"Coolord, I bet it's a big brock, man!" whispered Willie.

"Not half, I bet, man," agreed his friend.

After ten minutes they put down a fresh couple of dogs. A muffled barking sounded in the earth, and the listening Master pronounced his opinion that they were galloping. Willie asked Big Will'um where they were galloping to, and the bailiff replied that it meant fighting.

"Coolord!" said Jack and Willie together.

The men started to dig, following the instructions of the Master. Soon they stopped to remove their coats. It was hard

385

work, and frequently roots of the beech-tree had to be stubbed with the grubbing axe. And every respite meant that the badger might be digging farther into the earth.

Two hours passed, and they reached a hollow chamber that was odorous of past meals and partially filled with grass and bracken.

"Cubs," snorted the Master.

An insistent undertone of growling came from the dark hole. In silence they listened.

"Bob, fetch 'un, Bob! Gude boy, Bob, us be coming!" encouraged the Master. The undertone of surly discontent went on.

"Please, may we dig?" said Willie.

The Master looked at his thin arms.

"You might vall in, and then Brock would crack your arms," he said.

Several men laughed. Willie went red with vexation, and his eyes brimmed. But he blinked quickly, let a tear fall. He thought of blowing his nose, as it was possible to divert tears down the nose, but he had not a handkerchief. Elsie was looking, so he must not use the back of his hand. For a little while he sniffed, endeavouring to obliterate the unpleasant noises by discreet coughing.

Soon they reached the dogs, who held at bay a squat animal with a face like a small bear, and marked with black and white bars. Everyone cried: "There he is!" The dogs were smeared with earth and blood. Boldly the Master called for his tongs, and the moucher handed them to him, while Big Will'um murmured: "Tail un wi' your hand, measter."

"Not me," muttered the Master, red in the face, and his neck seeming to swell against his greasy stock-tie.

Willie and Jack peered under the legs of Big Will'um. The Master plunged the long iron tongs into the heaped earth and gripped the badger round the neck.

"Mind 'e don't bite ee, Mis'r Tinker," shrilly yelled a minute urchin with a head of drab hair. "Brock be a girt biter, ah seed un eat an ould ooman one night."

"Be off, Bill Nye!" ordered Big Will'um, amid the laughter.

386

"Ah wisht Brock wud eat my granmer," continued the midget. They laughed again, as his great-grandmother, Aholibah Nye, was known to be rough with him.

The Master gripped the badger and handed the tongs to Big Will'um. A sack was brought and its mouth held open.

"One, two, dree, and up he comes," said the Master, gripping the animal's tail and heaving it up. The dogs snapped and tried to worry it, the badger snarled and showed white teeth, and then it was dropped into the sack. The Master took the tongs and gave the heaving animal a scat on its head: it lay still. Swiftly it was turned out: the Master drew his hunting knife, stabbed the beast's neck, and one was dead.

Willie pitied the poor dead brock. All the dogs tied to trees mouthed their rage and strained towards the stricken thing.

"Now for Mrs. Brock and the cubs," grimly announced the Master. Willie stared at him and hated him.

The Master dug stolidly, pausing to swallow whisky from a flask. Sometimes, to encourage the dogs underground, he wound the little copper horn. Always a renewed galloping was heard when the piercing blasts were over.

The afternoon wore on. Elsie went home. The Master sweated and dug. Triumphantly he tore out the dining chamber and flung the limp little cub to the dogs. Willie tried to get it, hoping a spark of life remained, so that he could nurse it and have it as a pet about the house. There was little chance of the tiny thing being alive after six dogs had worried it. Willie began to think that badger-digging wasn't such fine sport as he had thought. While he was thinking this the moucher threw down his spade and, without a word, slouched away.

"Jim Holloman be mazed," laughed a labourer.

"You can have a turn now if you like," conceded the Master, who was weary, to the boys, just as the sun was going down and the beechwood was soft with golden light.

"I'm jolly glad you haven't cotched 'em," jeered Willie, running away. "Old Mrs. Brock's a better digger'n you, old Mister Tinker."

"Tails a badger with a coal-fork," chanted Jack.

The Master shouted that he would throw them to the badger.

Thus was little Bill Brock, who had been helping his mother to dig, and bitten her leg by mistake in his excitement, given a first experience of hereditary enemies.

One night, two years later, the moucher was lying by a fire in the spinney, listening to the nightingales which every spring-time sang in the hazel coverts. The sound of their deep notes was distinct in the night air, although the woods were half a mile away. Lying by the fire in an attitude of reverie, he listened to the silver birdsong. It floated over the green wheat with the night breeze; and suddenly he sat up, harking to a strange noise. In the spinney there was the shaking of a chain, the clank of iron on flint, a gruff cough. Jim lay still, waiting. The moon was behind him.

The clanking ceased, but the chain still rattled. Then a squat animal passed near him, a grey shadow in the moonlight. He knew that it was a badger and shouted. The animal ran away swiftly, Jim pursuing warily, a stick in his hand. Across the silver wheat-flags they rushed, but the badger was quicker, and Jim lost the rabbit and his trap as well. He never saw the trap again.

During that summer Farmer Temperley missed five sucking pigs. They were taken on five consecutive nights. On the fifth night it rained; and in the morning the six-toed mark was seen in the mud outside the shed. Big Will'um waited up the sixth night with his duck gun, but never saw a brock.

In the Cat and Gnatfly the matter was discussed. Old Granfer Will'um, who sat outside the inn all day in summer, held the opinion that it was no brock, but a master girt grawbey animal escaped from the Colham Fair. In fact, after two pints of Goliath XXX ale, he was wont to declare that it came knocking at his door at midnight. But Granfer Will'um was garrulous and very old, so no one heeded his theories.

The Master of the Colham Badger-digging Club came out several times to Rookhurst. That season he killed eleven badgers. But always Bill Brock, secure in his deep holt, bit harder than any of the dogs that crept underground to corner him. Still the raids upon fowl-houses went on. Once Brock met a fox by Farmer Turney's yard and fought with him, a most unusual thing to do. The farmer knew that the fox had been killed by a badger, because some long grey hairs were found in the fox's teeth. The head of the fox was nearly severed from its body. Willie skinned it, and Biddy his foster-mother made him a little waistcoat, of which he was very proud, until Bob the terrier found it and in a frenzy of joy tore it to pieces.

Although many attempts were made to dig him out, Bill Brock for some reason remained in his ancestral holt, which resembled from repeated excavations a series of small quarries. In the fourth year of his life he gained his cognomen of Bloody, becoming Bloody Bill Brock. This was given him because invariably he mauled the dogs who crept to ground after him. His favourite place to snap was in the lower jaw. He had a double bite, one with his back teeth that broke a dog's bone as a nutcracker breaks a nut, and the second one with his short front teeth that snapped like a trap.

All day long he slept and dozed (when he was not engaged with the Master of the Colham Club) and all night he prowled and hunted. He ate fruit fallen from trees; he dug out wasps' nests and the combs of wild bees; he dug up turnips, potatoes, carrots and roots; he caught mice and rats, small birds; he rolled hedgehogs into water to make them uncurl and then he ate them; he sucked the eggs of plover, pheasant and partridge; he fought with other boar-badgers and routed them, and he dug and dug and dug, making new homes in the hillside for his several mates, whom he visited in turn and treated with the same tenderness, playing with the cubs of each litter, and bringing in food and bedding for them.

Traps and gins were tilled for him, but he avoided them. He grew tired of dropping dead branches on the iron plates, and learned to spring them by rolling on them. Wild flowers he liked, frequently bringing them to his various families. And, although the situation of the great badger-earth was known, the badgers continued to roll the excavated earth away from the tunnel-mouth in order to conceal it.

Periodically correspondents in the *Colham and District Times* wrote to the editor and protested that badger-digging was a brutal and degrading sport. They stated that the badger did very little harm, and that any harm he might do was outweighed by the good he did. On these occasions the Master, then the tenant of The Rising Sun Inn, suggested that the farmers wrote in reply what damage Bloody Bill Brock had been known to do. At the same time he warned them not to say that three terriers had been chewed to a mass of splintered bones and punctured skin by him.

The Master swore that he would get him or die. One day in February he set out to get him. From another district had come Brock's Terror, a bitch that was fearless and a magnificent fighter, one so experienced and so battle-scarred that her lower jaw was hairless and pink from a hundred bites. In the tap-room of The Rising Sun she saw a grinning badger mask mounted on wood. She barked and sprang up, trying to get at it.

"Down, Terror, midear," ordered her master, but she who was usually obedient could not be restrained.

Willie and Jack heard of the expedition, and were present at the meet in Farmer Turney's yard. Fifty people came from round about to watch. Never were so many dogs grouped together, barking and leaping up at their masters, all eager for the blood of a brock.

The Master was dressed in a suit of rough tweed with cord breeches, stockings, and leather ankle protectors. On his large head he wore an old fishing cap stuck with trout flies. A tiepin made out of a badger's bone was fastened diagonally across his stock.

George Davidson, mazed-drunk and with his drooping moustache-ends brown with beer, carried the tongs and the shovels. The Master, at the centre of a group of sportsmen, was telling them that he would slit Bloody Bill's throat, even if he had to go down the pipes himself.

"Doan't ee worry, measter," said the owner of Brock's

Terror. "Her'll have 'un owt. Her's killed voorty brocks. Ban't ee, Terror, midear?" At the mention of brock, the terrier sprang into the air and screamed. Immediately the other dogs howled in reply, and the hunt set out for the beechwood.

They did not send Terror into the pipes immediately. They tried other dogs, who came back cowed and dejected, all except a sprightly dog who remained underground for an hour. The Master was most pleased with this beast's courage, until he discovered that it was barking at nothing and pretending to fight an imaginary badger. All the while Bloody Bill was ten yards away, waiting for the enemy to come nearer.

The Master could not have chosen a better time for his operations. The opportune choice was accidental, for he could not possibly have known that the sow-badger had given birth to a whelp just as the hunt arrived outside. Had the hunt arrived an hour earlier, the whelp would not have been born, because its mother had, like all sow-badgers, the power to postpone the birth of her offspring for several days, if need be.

The sow-badger, alarmed by the noise, turned to the wet squeaking thing and devoured it. To a human being ignorant of wild birds and animals and of their beautiful evolution of uncorrupted instinct this may cause a shudder of repulsion. There was no sentiment in the distressed animal's action; she did not caress her whelp, she made no moan over it. She ate it completely, because another terrible time was about to begin. Perhaps she thought that the small mewling thing would, if she ate it, be given back to her at a happier time. The sow-badger lay still for a few minutes, because the postponement of the litter gave her pain.

All that morning and afternoon the digging was unceasing. Bloody Bill was eventually separated from his mate, and three dogs barred the way to her. He heard her fierce snarling, and made a rush at the dogs, who gave way. Repeated piercing blasts upon the horn rang in the tunnel where he waited, while dull thuds and scrapings shook the earth. He dug with his black claws, and tore at the flint that was in his way. He endeavoured to dig downwards, but made small progress owing to the dogs. Weariness overcame him. Once he heard a roar

391

and a shouting, but he did not know that it was for the capture of his mate.

The Master grunted with satisfaction as he dropped the sow into the sack, and tapped her on the skull with his iron tongs.

"Now for the boar," he grinned. "Fetch Terror."

The three dogs were recalled from the tunnel, and Terror was loosened. Immediately she slipped into the hole, and the Master, on his knees and listening, said that they were galloping.

Inside dog and badger were facing one another, the dog being at a disadvantage because it had to attack and because the badger's skin gave a bad tooth-hold, the hide being so tough. Brock came forward with a swift movement and snapped, and any other dog would have been bitten through the nose. Terror, however, was a tried fighter, and quite as quick as Brock. She had perfected a way of avoiding the sudden forward lunge by twisting her head so that the blow glided off, and snapping at the badger's throat. Several times Bloody Bill was ripped in the throat, and he began to bleed. Once his teeth gashed Terror's shoulder, but the bitch did not heed the pain. Tirelessly she fought, striving for a grip on his jowl where she could hold till the diggers came.

Without warning Bill darted forward again; Terror timed the snap of his blood-frothed jaws, but did not allow for the continued rush. *Crack!*—he had broken her paw; *cruch, cruch!*—and torn her left shoulder muscle away. Terror howled. Bloody Bill seized her in his jaws—she was less than a third his weight—and carried her to the opening of the hole, just as George Davidson was about to stab the sow-badger.

The Master leapt out of the way, and George Davidson fell over. Bloody Bill went to his mate, and she began to move. *Crash!*—the tongs hit the earth beside Bloody Bill. Dogs ran at him, to be met with a black white-arrowed face that gave them nightmares for a long time to come. Willie and Jack ran like hares.

Bill Brock stood by his mate, blinking, apparently unconcerned. *Clank!* went a spade on the chalky soil, but they missed him. He scratched his mate with his paw, and grunted to her as she struggled to her feet. Together they waddled up the slope of the beechwood. Dogs screamed and followed, all the hunt scrambled up in their wake. Repeatedly Bill turned to meet them, but none would face him.

"Quick!" yelled the Master. "If they gets into the fox's earth us 'v losted 'em!"

Willie and Jack were now in front of the pursuers. Straight up the hill went Bill Brock and his mate, bleeding from their wounds. Terror was dying near that ruined holt, dying in the arms of her master; she was whimpering her last affectionate thoughts to him as she licked feebly the tears on his cheek.

Bloody Bill Brock went to earth in the covert with his mate. It was not his earth, but he did not care. It was a cunning move. For he turned out Fang-over-lip the fox who blundered down wind into the dogs and led them away over the fields. In the darkness they lay, breathing heavily. They discovered a pheasant half eaten in the earth, and rendered it completely eaten.

That night the Master swore that the boar must have died from his hurts, and included his demise in the Colham Badger-digging Club records, guessing his weight at forty pounds. He also entered up *One sow-badger taken and released*. He also got very drunk, celebrating the good day's sport with the other sportsmen.

2

In those days before the Great War there were trees in Rook-hurst Forest; there are none now. Autumn rains bring scarlet, buff and orange fungi on the rotten stump-circles of the felled beeches. The Brock holt, with its maze of corridors, kitchens and sleeping chambers tunnelled into the hillside—the work of centuries—is green with moss. In summer the entrances are hidden by the pink spires of foxgloves which have risen where the autumn beechmast crackled under the feet of swine. Rabbits burrow where once Fang-over-lip the fox crept for sanctuary; thistle and bramble cover the approaches trodden by the five-clawed pads of the badgers. There the huntsman listened to the sharp bell-like tang of Clarion, Conqueror, and Firefly: to the mellow and clamorous notes of thirteen couples so identical in pitch and quality; to the deep tongues of Nimrod and Solway, Thunderer and Doomsday. Nimrod the faultless! How his baying used to roll back from the wooded hillside of Rookhurst when he spoke to the scent of Fang-over-lip, his quarry of many seasons!

One winter morning Fang-over-lip lay out in the middle of the Big Wheatfield, which was ridged with furrows, and dry only in the centre. His chin rested on his paws, his eyes were shut, he was sleeping, and his nose was stroked by the wind that passed up the field to Crowstarvers Spinney in the middle. The sun was on his left. It was nearly noon, and the cold air was quiet.

Suddenly his ears were cocked, and his eyes were open, but he did not move otherwise. He heard a sound of rattled iron, the sound of a distant gate-fastener being lifted by the huntsman's whip-handle. He heard the voice of the whipper-in as in sharp authority he bade one of the hounds drop a rabbit-skin he had found in a ditch—*'Ware riot, Baronet!* He heard the jingle of bits and the soft thuds of hooves on furrows. The pack, led by Nimrod the faultless, the true fox-teller, had entered the north side of the Big Wheatfield, and was spreading to the huntsman's cast, noses to ground and sterns a-waver. Fang-over-lip waited for the voice of Nimrod, and as he waited a flea bit him under the ear. He scratched with a hind foot, and shook his head. He was concerned more with the flea than with Nimrod at that moment.

After a second of stillness he felt it moving down his neck, so he scratched again, balancing himself on the thigh of the other hind leg. He was still scratching when he heard a whimper, and then another whimper. The hounds were pressing round Nimrod, and their sterns were feathering. Before sunrise that morning Fang-over-lip had walked that way to his sleeping place among the furrows; hounds were three hundred yards away. He scratched no more. Nimrod was running towards him, the pack following. Fang-over-lip waited, for that morning he had not run straight to his bed, but down the wind, along the western hedge, and after a drink in the brook he had gone towards the eastern hedge, changed direction, and run diagonally across the wind until he reached his dry kennel.

He waited, and Nimrod turned, feathering. The hound was mute and his jealous rival, Bandit the babbler, threw his tongue and bounded before Nimrod.

Horses tossed their heads and opened their nostrils; some were impatient, and fought against curbs, plunging into the crusty furrows. The huntsman took his horn from where it was between the second and third brass buttons of his red coat; the pack loped down the field.

Seeing them, Fang-over-lip knew that it was time to go, and he stole up a furrow, brush low and ears laid back; but no hound or horseman saw Fang-over-lip. He heard the tongue of Bandit the babbler, and knew that he was not speaking to his scent; the note that came from his throat was not full and mellow; he was telling lies, and the huntsman knew it too, but he trusted Nimrod, and said nothing.

The Master halted, and the field of about forty riders waited behind him, the old hands remaining by the gate to see which way the fox would run. Further down the slope went red-coated huntsman and whipper-in, but still Nimrod did not speak. He worked steadily along the western hedge. The dew had dried off the earth, and scent was weak. Bandit had turned north, and the young hounds straggled after him; Bandit threw his tongue again, that lying tongue, and several hounds whimpered. Lying among young hounds is infectious. The huntsman watched Nimrod when he came to a shallow in the brook, and seeing his stern furiously a-feather he knew that he was working true. Still and upright on his bay mare he sat, horn in whip-hand.

By the pebbly shallow Nimrod whimpered, and leaping up the bank he ran straight and true the line that Fang-over-lip had travelled that morning. He threw a deep, hollow note. The huntsman cried: *"Hark to Nimrod! Leu-leu-leu!"* The young hounds deserted Bandit and followed Nimrod as he loped along a furrow. Bandit gave tongue and followed as well. At that moment a farmer on an old black cob by the gate stood up in his stirrups, took off his hat, roared out: "*Tally yo, maister!*" and holding it aloft pointed to Crowstarvers Spinney. He had seen the fox as it stole through the clump of hornbeam and fir. Immediately the horn of the huntsman sounded short and urgent notes, followed by little sharp ones that were like small beads of sound threaded on the morning air. The pack responded to the *Gone Away*, the light notes of Clarion, Conqueror and Firefly seemed to rebound from the solid clamour of the matched twenty-six; the tongues of Thunderer and Doomsday and Solway smote out their triple peal behind Nimrod, now mute and earnest.

They stopped at the bed of Fang-over-lip, a solid wheel of black and white and tan, nose-hubbed and compact; the wheel broke and became hounds that streamed up to the spinney and through the trees, past the dug-out of the crowstarver and through the eastern hedge to the ridge and furrow again.

A quarter of a mile below Fang-over-lip had crept through a thorn hedge, jumped a ditch, and run across two meadows. He was making for a distant earth that he had adapted for himself years ago from the ruinous earth of a vixen who had been killed. The earth was in a lychet, or hollow, in the southern slope of the downs. Fang-over-lip knew that he could reach it in safety, so he did not run his fastest. Frequently he sat down and listened with ears pricked, with red tongue dripping sweat, and brush swishing the grass. His upper canine teeth were long, yellow, and when he shut his mouth to listen they pressed on his lower lip. When he opened his mouth he seemed to grin. He was in no hurry, he knew that scent was weak; seasons ago he had overcome the fear of being hunted; he knew that another fox was in the habit of lying out in a field near him, and he wanted to be certain before the long run to the downs that the pack was hunting him. But the voice of Nimrod speaking at the hedge through which he had crept made him get on his four pads and run straight for the earth four miles away.

He crossed stubble and ploughlands, sending up partridge and pigeon, plover, finch and rook. To delay the pursuit he ran among a drove of bullocks, driving them to splash and wallow among the rushes and water-grasses in the boggy land beside the brook. He stopped suddenly and rolled, while they trotted near him, snuffling and with horns held low, ready to back and bound away. He sat up, stretched himself and walked on slowly, the bullocks following and stamping out his tracks. Fang-over-lip had rolled and made them timidly curious to follow him because he knew that they would trample out his scent. He led them thus to the hedge, and selecting the thickest thorns he crept through and crossed other fields and lanes before reaching the short turf of the downs. There was a thick patch of dead thistles in a lychet at the base of the hill, and through this he leapt; hounds would have to follow nose-to-line and would prick their muzzles. Fang-over-lip knew many more ways of hindering and baffling a pack, but at present there was no need to exert either himself or his wits.

He lay down on a chalky cattle patch a few paces above the thistle patch, and watched hounds a mile away. He saw the riders behind, some taking the fences and others going through the gates. He heard the thin twang of the huntsman's horn and the answering bay of a hound. He waited and rested while they came nearer, and the cattle in the water-meadow blundered round their rushy field. He listened to the voice of Bandit declaring that Fang-over-lip had turned left-handed and run down the vale which led to Colham. He grinned a foxy grin, and rolled with pleasure. But the anxiety he felt under his self-confidence made him sit up immediately. He saw the first-flighters of the field wait behind the pink-coated Master, while the young hounds followed the babbler. But Nimrod, Doomsday, Solway, and Thunderer made wide casts round the field, running the hedges to find the broken line of scent.

Fang-over-lip dallied no more. He heard Nimrod baying and knew that he had found his line. The full clangour of the pack floated up to him with the jubilant notes of the horn, and Fang-over-lip fled. His brush was straight behind, pads crushing the little empty shells of snails that strewed the turf. High overhead a mouse hawk watched silently, fluttering brown wings into the wind that buoyed its flight. In a groove of the downs where the plough never scarred the sward was the brake of furze and thorn under the roots of which he, and the vixen now dead, had scratched out the tunnel. Fang-over-lip ran straight for the earth where he might hide deep and defy his old enemy, Daisy the terrier. By the hoarse cries of the men in the field beneath him he knew that he was seen; the hound-chorus swelled louder. He ran swiftly over the sward which rose steeply before the lychet; he climbed the hump before the thorny hollow, to see two men with spades in their hands standing by the earth, which they had just filled in. Like a menace of certain death the deep voice of Nimrod, terrible and relentless, filled the hollow in the downs.

Fang-over-lip looked at the men during the space of five heart-beats. He thought of the other earth in a gravel pit he had been working on at night: he thought of running up the hill and over the downs to the plain beyond—a journey he had made the winter before, during the great snow famine. He knew of the badgers' holt in Rookhurst Forest. For this he decided to make. His heart contracted for the sixth pulse of blood as he turned his face to the sun and ran downhill. The huntsman saw him as he put his mare at the last hedge, and instinctively checked her. The slight check caused the sensitive animal to hesitate, but answering the pressure of his legs upon her ribs, she gathered her hocks under her and sprang at the tall fence. Originally it had been a wire-and-post fence, but field-fares and other birds perching on it in winter had dropped peggles and sown a hedge of hawthorn, which under the wind had grown straight and thick. Her forefoot caught in the rusty top-strand of the wire fence; she fell on her neck, and the huntsman took a toss. He fell clear, however, with muscles relaxed and head tucked in, and so he did not hurt himself. By the time he had picked himself up hounds were too far to be urged by horn and cap to where Fang-over-lip had doubled. After Nimrod they lolloped uphill to the lychet, and led by that faultless eight-year-old they streamed downhill to the plain.

Fang-over-lip was no longer cool. He ran with tongue quivering and slavering over his grinder-teeth. Over plough-land and stubble, water-meadow and winter-wheatfield he ran, creeping under hedge and gate. When half an hour later he came to Skirr Farm, and ran through the farmyard, in a red rage against mankind that was hunting him he chased and captured one of man's tamed creatures, a turkey, and dragged it over fifty yards. Two small boys rushed out of the house and pursued him with wild excited cries; a sheepdog followed, soon outstripping them. Three hundred yards behind Nimrod ran with Solway and Doomsday, the pack just behind them. Fang-over-lip hung on to the turkey until the sheepdog snarling by his brush made him loosen his jaws and drop it. Seeing the base dog Nimrod bayed in a tongue so savage that the sheep-dog immediately turned and fled away with long tail tucked under his hindquarters like a hairy letter S.

The hounds passed the boys, and after them came the hunts-man, who had a thorn-tear across his forehead, the whipper-in, two men and a young lady; behind, for nearly two miles, other riders were following. Fang-over-lip was sinking, and seeing him lie down three hundred yards in front of Nimrod, the huntsman urged them with voice and cap to a final burst. Four fields ahead the first beeches of the forest had their roots in the slope of the hillside, and he wanted to kill his fox in the open.

Fang-over-lip was in distress. His brush drooped with the weight of mud clinging to the underhairs in a lump that grew bigger over every ploughfield. His pads were hot; his heart slogging blood in thickening pain against the base of his skull. Nimrod was two hundred yards behind him. He fell into a ditch half-filled with water, and found it difficult to climb up the bank; his claws tore long smooth scars in the clay, but he managed to bite on a root and haul himself up. He shook the water from his coat, and turned to see Nimrod less than a hundred yards away, with three hounds at his heels, running at him. Fang-over-lip stood still with lowered head and mouth open in a grin; head, back, and brush made a curve of snarling defiance. But the water had refreshed him, and he thought he could reach the Brock's holt. So he turned again and ran away from Nimrod with all his strength, gaining distance because the slippery clay bank baulked hounds. He heard them splashing; he heard their short cries of excitement and rage. Then Nimrod was through the hedge, and gaining with long strides of heavy legs swiftly upon him. One more hedge to scramble under, a brook to leap, and he would be in the forest. Fang-over-lip lapped stiffly, and fell into the water. He paddled against its flow a few strokes, then gave up and drifted with the current. It bore him downstream; he lapped as he floated. Soon he heard the whimper of Nimrod at the place where he had leapt; he listened to the puzzled note. In his fatigue he had a desire to run no more, but to let hounds tear him and eat him, so that he could drift forever in cool waters; but the touch of gravel on his pads made him fully awake, and fear came back with refreshment and the will to live. He paddled to the left bank of the stream, where it was deeper; softly and slowly he drifted. Then he heard, with joy, the voice of Bandit telling lies upstream: the full, savage, joyful tongues of the pack, and the harsh *Leu-leu-leu, get-on-to-'im! Get-on-to-'im!* of the huntsman. Fang-over-lip crept out of the water, and walked stiffly uphill to the holt among the crisp brown beech leaves. He did not shake himself; he left a line of water behind him, dripping from the hairs of his belly.

While he was walking among the trees, Bandit had returned in silence from the false line. In the heat of the chase he never lied deliberately—his roused hunting instincts were too firm and true. During his first season he had been eager and impetuous: the huntsman had seen in him then the makings of a first-class fox-catcher. But from these very qualities of zeal and keenness had come an arrogancy, a desire to be foremost, and the elder hounds liked him not. They had already their special friends and followers: yet Bandit's voice had a certain authority among the young entry of the kennels. He had led the pack astray at the stream, not deliberately as he had in the Big Wheatfield, but because his quality of imaginativeness and the keenness of his desire laid the scent upstream, and he believed it was there. He led the pack fifty yards, then returned in silence.

Meanwhile Nimrod had run the bank downstream, and finding no scent he had leapt into the water and crossed to the opposite bank. He climbed out and immediately spoke to the scent of Fang-over-lip. Hunting cries came from thirty-five hasty-breathing throats: with plunging leaps hounds blundered into the stream: a thousand rooks rose from the treetops, and the wind from black wings scattered the brown leaves on the path below. Nimrod leapt up the mossy slope; Fang-over-lip staggered in front of him. The lemon-and-white hound gained two yards to the fox's one yard, and with head thrust forward and stern thrust back he bared his teeth to chop. But as Fang-over-lip struggled on he saw before him the entrance of the badger's holt and the path leading to it. His brush, so heavy with mud, seemed to drag him back. He heard the throaty breath of Nimrod as the hound flung himself forward in the last burst of speed. The hound leapt at the brush: the polished hardness of his teeth snapped the air. The sudden stop flung him on his back. He turned, but the fox had vanished, where Nimrod could not follow.

A big boar-badger was sleeping in his kitchen, curled in a fresh bed of grass, bracken, moss and bark-fibres, all bitten into small, soft fragments. This oval chamber—which was a little over three feet wide and about two feet high—in one direction led along eight feet of pipe to the open air. Many diggings by man had brought it near the light; but there were other chambers deep under the hill. A corridor led to the second chamber five feet deeper; beyond this were three more. From the last two the pipe branched. One corridor led to disused kitchens, and the other led to the exit beside a tindery beech, one hundred and nine feet from the entrance. Two feet outside the entrance were dug the latrines, for the tribe had a regard for cleanliness and health.

The badger's sleep ended. He lifted his head, sharp-nosed and small and black, marked with a white broad-arrow from brown weasel nose along cheeks and over forehead. His little eyes peered at the entrance, and he sniffed. He felt the shake of the ground, he heard in the tunnel the dull, faraway bay of hounds. He heard the thin twang of the horn; the badger-diggers used an identical horn and notes to speak to the terriers underground. He knew what it meant. He waited.

The white dimness in the tunnel was darkened. Two eyes, pale green and bleared with breath, came woefully to him. He smelt Fang-over-lip. Fang-over-lip's distressful panting filled the kitchen. He came to the badger in utter dejection. His mud-balled brush dragged on the dry crumbled earth. The badger did not bite him. He had bitten other foxes, but not Fang-over-lip. He let him pass into the kitchen, although he liked not very much the smell of his pads and his breath. Fang-over-lip dragged himself deeper and deeper into the holt, passing various kitchens where other badgers were curled, but none of them were so big as the one on guard. They were the growing children of the big boar, and he loved them all; his mates would give him other farrows during the next month, which would be February; there was never a whelp born to the Rookhurst Forest holt in any other month. Fang-over-lip was neither welcome nor resented by the growing cubs; he had the freedom of the holt; he crept to sanctuary deep and dark, and collapsed in a damp kitchen beside a heap of rusty gins.

The sentinel boar remained where he was. He waited in the first kitchen, and during the wait he curled himself and rested. He knew by the noise outside that a troubled time was coming. His eyes, the size of ripe hawthorn peggles, but black, blinked towards the light and his nostrils worked. Suddenly the ground shook and the baying of hounds roared down the pipe. He heard the scratching of heavy feet and the shrill furious whimper of Bandit. Minute after minute the rough roaring boomed in the tunnel air, until a long keen note of the horn and the voice of man and the cracks of a lash drove the hounds back. Still they bayed, and still the voices of huntsman and whip urged them down the hill. Slowly the sounds drew away, and then a single voice was heard speaking softly, *Goo' girl, Daisy, fetch 'un out, Goo' girl, Daisy,* and the patting of the hunt terrier's neck. She was short on the leg and experienced with foxes; her yapping had driven many from earth and drain. Daisy had been riding in a leather satchel slung across a groom's chest during the chase, and she was fresh. Eager for a fight she crept gamely down the pipe, and came to the kitchen where the badger, the fiercest boar-badger in the West Country, was awaiting her.

The Master, in his cap of blue velvet, pink coat, white breeches, and black hunting boots, stood upright and held up his hand. He wanted the fox to have a real sporting chance when it bolted from the sturdy terrier. The hounds were in a leaf-filled hollow fifty yards below the entrance. They could not see the earth. They sat on their haunches, alert and anxious, watching the huntsman's face and awaiting the sign of the lifted cap.

"Let no one tally, please!" the Master urged in a loud confidential whisper to the dismounted horsemen standing near. "Let no one tally when he slips out! Give him a sporting chance. No tally, gentlemen, please!"

Their voices murmured in respectful obedience. They could hear the yapping of Daisy under the ground. The sharpness of the noise was blunted by the earth, but it was regular and unceasing. Horses in the field across the stream shook bit and bridle and pawed the ground; a mist of sweat rose from their lathered flanks. The cawing of the rooks ceased as the birds drifted away; again, the Master, on hearing a sudden increased yapping of Daisy, whispered urgently, in a hoarse, sweet, burring voice:

"No tally, please! No tally, gentlemen! No tally!"

The yapping rose to a frenzy of snarling. The white-haired Master, immensely apprehensive lest an accident unworthy of the Hunt's sporting reputation should hap, whispered, "He's coming out! No tally! No tally! No tally!" with beseeching eyes and a finger of warning that trembled.

All stood still. The white-haired Master glanced round at the pack; he could see the heads only of the front hounds. His big blue eyes in his round red face were wide with the important moment.

But curiously his expression changed. The Master frowned. For the buried snarling of Daisy had risen to a shrill howling, telling of pain and fear, which had ended most unexpectedly in absolute silence. Not a sound came from the earth. The Master looked at his huntsman. He said some words to him, and stared anxiously at the hole. It was a circular hole, about a foot in diameter. The earth scratched out of the pipe had long ago been thrown by badgers' hind legs down the slope, and trodden hard and flat.

"Charlie, there must be badgers in the earth," said the Master, tapping boot with the handle of his whip.

"Big boar inside, my lord," replied the huntsman. "Never been able to dig 'm out. Known as Bloody Bill Brock, my lord. Once killed a fox at Skirr Farm."

The huntsman beckoned his second horseman, who came forward smartly.

"Go and get a couple of men with spades from the farm, Jack."

While they were waiting for the diggers, Nimrod stole up to the earth, and Captain crept behind him, with Solway and Queenie, Thunderer, Firefly and Starlight. Other hounds followed, squatting on haunches, while with breath-flacking tongues they looked from earth to huntsman's face, to whip's face, to earth again, hearkening for the voice of Daisy. It came no more.

The huntsman kneeled at the hole and turned his head sideways to listen. A few grains of earth trickled on the riband-bow at the back of his blue velvet cap. He got up suddenly, and jumped away from the hole. Bloody Bill Brock stood there looking at him. With four lumbering steps he was outside the hole. He scrutinised the Master's features, and then turned his gaze to the pack. He neither grunted nor snarled; he showed no sign of annoyance. He did not even sniff.

The tongues ceased to flack. They remained in whatever position they were in when the white-striped face appeared— tongues hanging out; tongues, whose tips showed between teeth; no tongues at all. The hounds had arranged themselves in three tiers before the hole, and Nimrod, the largest hound, sat behind, in the centre. When the face appeared he was swallowing. He sucked in his tongue and closed his jaws with a click and fixed the small face at the hole with an intent stare. The red haws below his eyes became more sunken. Standing motionless except for distinct but minute movements of the head each time his gaze shifted, Bloody Bill Brock looked deliberately at every hound. From Dewdrop on the left to Dragon on the right a slow scrutiny was made, and back again, as though he were estimating the strength of the pack. When his gaze returned to Nimrod, it remained there; he yawned; and then came forward, his grey squat body low on the ground. He ran straight at Nimrod, pushing through hounds in the first and second row; he looked up into the face of Nimrod, at his bared yellow teeth and red haws of his eyes. He snapped at his paw and sunk his teeth into tendons and bones; he twisted his thick neck so firmly on his immense shoulders, and threw the hound on his back.

Without pausing he turned to Firefly and threw her over. Immediately he was enclosed by a hot and solid wheel of hound flesh, a wheel of black and white and brown patches, a wheel head-hubbed and snarling. Teeth found nothing to bite on the thick hide; there was no hold on the long hair. Solway tried to seize Bill's off-forepaw; he crippled Solway. Then Tunable, mother of many puppies, seized his yellow, goat-like scut, or tail; he turned and nipped her through the nose. He knew that they would try and hold him by his pads; then it would be over, and they would send him where he had sent Daisy. So he ran under Guardsman and quickly under the bellies of Grappler, Pealer, Voluble, Singwell, Vagabond and Castaway. He got clear, and waddled on as though indifferently. It was his way of fighting in the open.

The pack got angry. He went downhill, hounds behind him and on both flanks of him, chopping at his head, at his neck, at his back, at his pads.

Nimrod in fang-frothed rage limped to him; with a movement like the awkward bobbing bow of someone self-conscious of his stumpy fat legs among so many of the kennel quality,

405

Bill turned and bit through his other forepaw. Then he blinked his ugly little pig-eyes like someone snubbed, and bit the paw of Prudence; and turning again, he bit Choirboy, a young hound who immediately lifted up his muzzle and sang. And all the way to the brook the rough fellow lumbered, bobbing left and right and blinking as though ill-at-ease among the great ones; but he bit a paw every time. At the bottom of the hill his action was neither so swift nor so smart as it had been at the beginning of the fight. His face was smeared with red, and not all of it was hound blood. He coughed crimson froth from his mouth, for his tongue was broken by many bites. Sometimes he turned and ran among them, his little fierce eyes blinking; but it seemed that they were not quite so eager as they had been to punish him for his bad form in considering himself worthy of being hunted by foxhounds. By its smell they knew not the strange beast, and neither Bandit nor Nimrod remained to lead them. So the fight went on, up and down the hill.

The huntsman was agitated and cursing, because his hounds were being hurt. He ran down to the stream, where the kennel-boy was holding his horse's head, meaning to flick a stirrup-iron and leather from bar under saddle-flap, and to kill the badger with a blow on the nose. But the badger was down-hill first, and the huntsman's mare, who loathed the smell of blood as do most hunters, plunged with a terrified snort into the brook and dragged in the plucky kennel-boy after her. Another horse, a vicious black gelding with a red riband on its tail, reared and lashed out at Baronet the rabbit-chaser, who howled so painfully that he started off another horse, which bolted among the trees and caused the pack to scatter.

But half-a-dozen couple of hounds, led by Thunderer, had not finished with him. Among themselves they swore a hound oath of vengeance; they heeded neither the notes of the horn nor the lash of the whipper-in. A hound called Mutinous bit the hunt servant in the whip-hand, and returned to the worry. Bloody Bill crippled Mutinous ten minutes later, after staving off their rushes for three hundred yards up the hill. He was making for the holt again, but his progress was slow as he left red drops on the leaves and mosses wherever his broken pads pressed. By the big heap of chalk before the entrance they got him, shaking, tearing, worrying; but he worked himself through the press of legs and muzzles, and at last was creeping down the tunnel away from them.

This is the story they tell in the village inn at night, of how Bloody Bill Brock took on thirty-five hounds and one fox terrier, in the forest of Rookhurst, and how he vanquished them. They tell also how the pack went home to kennels that winter afternoon, as though on crutches. But only the Brocks know why the great boar went out to fight the enemies of Fang-over-lip; whom he found on his return, slumbering in a kitchen beside a heap of rusty iron gins—two of which, Tom Cocker-legg, that old liar, declares, the fox had dug up when one night he had found the badger helplessly trapped by fore and hind paws.

3

Silence is never of earth or sky—even under the hills when day and night are balanced in the still air, and blackbirds roosting in the hollies have ceased shrill cries at the passing shadowy owls; when the wintry moon is too wan for shining, and the chalk quarries grow grey in the dusk.

Always there is sound and movement. Worms are pushing out of their galleries, seizing fragments of dead leaves, and drawing them to their holes before roving again for others—always with their tails in their holes, for an instant return; slugs and beetles are abroad in the dewfall; sleepy birds breathing softly through puffed feathers; rabbits lolloping along their runs in the stubble, pausing to nibble the young clover leaves; partridges, their wheezy dimmit-calling over, settling closer in mid-field; mice claws pattering on twigs and leaf-mould; slow sappy pulses of the still trees rising and falling along their cold grey boles. And from the tunnels of the badgers' earth come muffled sounds, and grunts, and the nearer noise of a mouth stretching. Quietness again, while a last leaf falls among the wandering mice, and the edges of black boughs begin to glisten. The wan air of dusk deepens into night, with star points flickering, and the moon lays the pale shadows of trunks and branches. All the while, by the glimmering badgers' earth, a nose is working at the smells of the air, and ears are harkening.

For a hundred and twenty yards along the top of the beech wood the ground was pressed into paths, and heaped in nine places with soil, as though cartloads had been tipped there. Some gleamed white, where tons of chalk had been thrown out. Tree trunks were buried five and six feet deep in the heaps, which were the mine-heads of the badgers' holt. They were always digging to extend their galleries among the roots, and carry their kitchens deeper into the chalk, which was dry.

An owl flew through the wood, alighting on a branch above the main opening. It listened and peered for a minute and a half, hearing the breathing of the badger, but unable to see its head. The moonlight made a blur of the trodden heap before the hole, with its scatter of chalk, and the white-arrowed head in the tunnel's dark opening was part of the blur. The owl flew on to its next perching place, and soon after it had gone the head withdrew, a grunt sounded down the tunnel, followed by the muffled thumping of broad paws.

The hole, ragged with broken roots and hanging rootlets, was wider than the badger, yet he came out laboriously, with much scraping and grunting. He did not tread on his pads, but heaved himself along by the blunt black claws of his fore-paws against the side of the tunnel. He moved like an immense mole. When his head and shoulders were outside he remained in his awkward position, his sharp nose pointing at the heap of earth. Then putting his nose between his paws he bent his thick neck and turned head over heels. Remaining on his back, he rolled until he had covered the area of the heap. Afterwards he got on his short legs and shook himself.

Every night he rolled like this, in case gins had been tilled there by day to catch him by the paw.

Four other badgers followed the old boar, rolling in the same manner. They followed him down a trodden path among the trees, indistinct in moonlight and shadow, one behind the other, and came to the streamlet at the bottom of the wood, where they drank.

The water was cold. The four smaller badgers lapped steadily, but the old boar drank with many pauses. He stood by the streamlet, lapping and pausing, nearly a minute after the others had gone to their prowling, one along a fox-path which lay straitly down the stubble field, another following up the water by its edge, a third going down the stream, the fourth returning into the wood. Thus they set about their night's work, each badger having its own ways.

The old boar lumbered after the badger in the wood, following by scent. He hastened in his waddling run, being hungry. He was always hungry.

The boar was many years older than the badger he followed. She and the other three had been born in the same farrow seven months before. During the summer her parents had been dug out by the badger-diggers, dropped into canvas bags, taken away, hit on the nose with spades, turned out, and stabbed. The old boar had followed the cubs home one morning, and curled up with them in their kitchen. Since he preferred to sleep warm, with much food inside him, he had remained there. From him the growing cubs had learned, unconsciously, by imitating his tumble, the way to spring gins, which the earth-stopper of the d'Essantville Foxhounds sometimes tilled outside the badger earths. The Hunt wished badgers destroyed, because their deep tunnels gave shelter to hunted foxes, and so spoiled many kills in the open.

Bloody Bill Brock waddled after the young badger among the trees, moving off her trail to gobble a big black slug he smelt two yards away. Then he picked up a couple of worms, rubbed his head against the trunk of a tree, and returned to the trail. He breathed heavily, grunting with exertion.

When he came upon the young badger, she was eating a dead wood-pigeon, one that had been shot in flight, its hard feathers having stopped the lead pellets; but a mile away it had fallen dead of the blow on the breast. The young badger's teeth, which could have bitten through a man's wrist, cracked the bones as though they were straw. Bill Brock, whose jaws were twice the size of her own, tried to pull the food from her mouth, and she let him have the wings and feet. He swallowed the reddish legs with wheezy gulps, while she was finishing the rest of the bird.

The two wandered over ten miles that night. Beside a hawthorn hedge the boar found a rabbit in a wire snare, set by the lime-burner who lived in the quarry beside the Colham road; and although he was hungry the smaller badger, who hurried round from the other side of the quarry when she heard the rabbit's last throttled cries, ate most of it.

The same thing happened with the next large meal he discovered. Thrusting his snout into a leaf-choked hole under a furze bush, the boar blew and sniffed, and then withdrew his snout, and began to dig. Earth, stones, rootlets, all were thrust behind him. At the end of the hole he found a heavy ball of dry leaves. Some of them were holly leaves, but more prickly than ever they had been when guarding the lower branches of their parent trees. Every leaf now bristled with spikes. Bill Brock grunted with pleasure, and rolled the leaf-ball into the open.

Turning it with snout and paws until he had determined, as it were, the axis on which the hedgehog had rolled itself, he then trod on it with a paw, using the paw as a wedge. His weight forced the ball open, and he bit its neck. He dropped it immediately.

When the young badger came she bared her teeth, drew back her tongue—as a horse crops furze—and bit through leaves, spines, and skin; and the hedgehog, which had slept through it all, died in a strange dream.

The young badger ate most of the hedgehog, and all the boar got was some of the skin.

Just before sunrise he followed the young badger into the holt in Rookhurst forest, not exactly famished, but hungry enough. Mice, worms, snails, slugs, pigeons' feet and feathers, dead leaves, hedgehog skin, rabbits' paws and pieces of fur, the core of an apple—poor fare with which to stay strength for the onslaught of seventeen dogs in the open.

Already in the barrel room of The Rising Sun, five miles away, the foam of Mr. Tinker's second-best ale was rising to the top of the first wicker-covered earthenware jars, and the servant-wench in the kitchen was cutting loaves and cheese into hunks and wedges, for the day's sport. Mr. Tinker was snoring in bed, the water in his bedroom ewer as yet ungulped—for he had celebrated Christmas in proper style.

At the very moment that Mr. Tinker became aware of daylight and an aching head, Bill Brock began to snore. He lay curled on top of two young boar badgers, who were sleeping in the main kitchen when he returned. By his side his young companion was curled, and the four were drowsing off when the fifth badger returned, and, after wiping his pads against a flint to get the mud off them, waddled down the tunnel and scrambled on their backs. Weary grunts greeted him, and then the five settled down, snug and warm, and fell asleep.

The annual badger-dig on "the Day after Christmas Day," as that national holiday was always called by the inhabitants of Colham Old Town, was the biggest of the year. Badgers were always taken, owing to the numbers of labourers who came out to dig—and to get the free beer and food—bringing either pick or shovel or two-bill, and hoping for a large attendance of "gentry" (a comprehensive term, including, for the occasion, all in brown boots) to swell the collection for diggers at the end of the day's sport.

They began digging at nine o'clock in the morning, after thrusting down slender sticks to discover the direction of the pipe, and encouraging, with horn and voice and patting, a couple of terriers into the tunnel. At one o'clock, the terriers still being underground, they stopped for lunch. For the sportsmen ("Messrs. Tinker, Swidge, Potstacker, Corney, Dellbridge, Gammon, Ovey, and Krumm, no tyros at the game,"

as the local paper described them) there was whisky. Mr.
Tinker's headache had gone, after an hour's strenuous digging;
it would no doubt return before closing time that night.

At three o'clock in the afternoon—by which time six terriers
had been put to ground, four of them creeping back bitten about
the shoulders and jaws—Mr. Tinker, kneeling at the main
breach in the chalk, declared that another ten minutes would
do it. He had already identified Bloody Bill Brock by the
six-toed pad leading into the tunnel. The Master's teeth
(made up by Mr. Swidge, the quack dentist) dropped out in
his excitement. They all laughed.

"Lucky for me Bloody Bill wasn't nearby!" said Mr.
Tinker jokingly. "Well, gentlemen, I've carried the horn for
eighteen year, and it looks as though we're going to get the
old boar at last."

He seized a pick from a labourer, and struck at the chalk.
Five minutes of work made him wet and breathless, and he
stood back, saying: "To h-ll with that! Here, Jan, take a turn."

Half an hour later the sportsmen, sitting or standing around
and above the miniature quarry, saw a short tail poke out and
disappear again.

"The Mullah!" they cried.

"I told you The Mullah'd hold'n," said Mr. Corney, a short
man in clothes that looked and smelled as though they had
been slept in for weeks. The pawnbroker rapidly brushed his
drooping damp moustache with the back of one hand. "I told
you The Mullah'd have'n."

The Mad Mullah was his terrier.

The tunnel had already been broken in two places, and
dim daylight either way barred the escape. Colham Belle held
the right entrance, Mad Mullah the left. Mr. Tinker edged
out of the group, got his badger-tongs, and asked them to stand
back.

"As fine a bit of terrier work as I've seen in all the eighteen—
yic—years I've carried the—yic—horn," he announced.

"I'm sure of it," exclaimed Mr. Corney, spitting, or rather
squirting tobacco juice and saliva accurately between his
boots. "I told you the Mullah'd have'n."

The Mad Mullah hastily backed out of the tunnel, as though pushed by a narrow black pointed head, set with a white arrow. The small expressionless eyes glanced about, and the head retired, followed by the terrier, whose tail and hindquarters stuck out of the hole.

"They'm very near. Goo' boy, Mullah!" cried the Master.

"Don't forget Colham Belle," suggested a voice.

"I'm not forgetting nothing," replied the Master, shortly.

Mr. Corney relit his pipe for the twentieth time, puffing out vast cheekfuls of rank smoke with immense satisfaction.

"Mullah's the boy," he said. "I wouldn't part with that dog for something. Noomye! Not if you was to offer me——"

The terrier backed again, and another face poked out. It was twice the size of the first white-arrowed head, and the short hair of the cheeks was grey instead of black. The Master said afterwards that he knew it was Bill, for the badger did what he had never known any other brock do during the eighteen years he had carried the horn—the badger came out to fight.

The sportsmen had been pressed tightly round the cavity. They scrambled back, pushing and pulling in their haste. The Master was unable to open the tongs in time to collar the boar as he waddled between his legs.

"Look out!" yelled Mr. Corney. "The b——'s loose!"

Bill Brock waddled on, the Mad Mullah retreating before him and making sudden rushes forward, but every time the terrier got within snapping distance the arrowed head turned at him and pierced his courage. Then, curiously, when he was about three yards outside the hole, the boar stopped, opened his mouth as though in a yawn, and gave a prolonged groan. His tail stiffened and trembled. He stood there, with nose pointing to the ground, still except for the shudders that ran along his curved back. The Mad Mullah snarled at the air before him.

"Get the tongs round his neck—quick!" said the Master in a grating voice, as he pushed forward the long iron instrument. "Quick—yic—get th' tongs round neck."

Mr. Swidge took them.

"Hold on to him tight," said the Master, in glee, when this had been done easily. "Hold his head down. Hold'm tight. Don't let'm get away, for God's sake. Gennulmen, I've carried the horn for—yic—eighteen year, and I've never seen a smarter bit of work."

"Th' Mullah'd'v 'ad'n without the tongs," grumbled Mr. Corney.

"Not likely!" replied Mr. Swidge, the owner of Colham Belle, promptly.

Bill Brock groaned.

While Mr. Swidge gripped the handles of the tongs with unnecessary strength, the potman called Jan fetched the bag. It was the size of a mail-bag, and the canvas was so stout that no badger teeth could bite through it. Many a badger, curled still in the bottom of that bag, had been bashed on the snout with a spade, and known nothing more.

The Master stooped down and gripped the trembling tail, and, holding his breath, lifted the boar up and dropped him into the bag.

"There," he said. "Bliddy William tailed at last!"

Several hands courageously helped to hold open the top of the bag, while peering heads craned over and bumped each other. The top of the bag was twisted, and fastened with cord. With slightly shaking hands the Master unhooked a spring-balance from his belt, where his hunting-knife hung, and hitched the cord to it.

"Two score and two pounds, gentlemen. The biggest brock I've ever dug out in all the eighteen—yic——"

"And yer woudden'v done that wi'out th' Mullah, noomye!" Mr. Corney put in, kicking a piece of chalk violently with his boot. "No other dog'd'v keppim from diggin' away, and I don't care who hears me say it!"

"No one's saying anything dissenting," declared the Master. "I think we're all sportsmen here, gentle—yic——"

All agreed to this immediately. Mr. Corney muttered something, and looked surly as before.

While the boar lay still in the bag they had drinks all round.

Afterwards they opened the bag, thrust in the tongs, encircled his neck with the iron collar, and drew him out. Then, while the Master pressed his weight on the handles so that the boar's chin was fixed on the ground, a young terrier was led forward and urged to attack the head. It whined and growled and snarled, but would not go near the white arrow and the small blinking eyes. Others were brought, and they all refused.

"I'll tell you what, gentlemen," said the Master, looking over first one shoulder then the other. His voice became low. "Yic", he said, beckoning generally with his nose. "We're all sports here, I think, gentlemen, and this won't go further, I'm sure. I've always tried to show good sport to the field. How about taking the boar down to the cover, and trying the terriers on him loose, a brace at a time?" This was badger-baiting, and illegal.

"Mullah'll 'ave'n, don't you worry," muttered Mr. Corney, looking at the ground and puffing out smoke violently.

The Master looked at the others, and winked.

So the boar was dropped in the bag again, and they took him down to the field. Here they spread out into a circle, holding their dogs on leash. The Master and the huntsman (Jan the potman) untied the bag, dropped it, and ran back. It heaved, and after a while the dreaded head poked out, sniffing the air. Two terriers were released. They ran at the badger, while every leashed dog sprang up and began to howl.

Slowly Bloody Bill Brock waddled out of the bag, and looked about him. When the two terriers were about a foot away he glanced at them, and did not otherwise appear to regard them; but when one of them came near enough to snap, he made a quick turn of his head; and its will broke.

"Try The Mullah," shouted Mr. Corney irritably. Without waiting for permission, he unleashed his terrier, but the dog would not, or could not, get within gripping distance of the boar's head. Mr. Corney yelled at it in a bloodthirsty (whisky variety) voice.

Bloody Bill Brock walked over the stubble and the clover, while the circle of men moved with him. Whenever he approached the shifting human group he was driven back with shouts and the banging of spades and picks. Up and down the field he walked, his head turning with instant swiftness at any terrier that dashed at him. He walked very slowly. The Master became impatient.

He blew his horn. "Let every terrier loose!" he shouted, and waved the tongs in a semicircle.

Two of the labourers had brought their lurchers with them— long-legged hairy dogs, of mongrel greyhound strain, used for silent poaching—and these were loosed with the terriers.

"Get back!" yelled the Master, red in the face, to Mr. Corney, who was running forward with raised pick. "Let the terriers tackle him! We're all sports here, not—yic—bliddy rat-catchers!"

The terriers snarled and scrambled and screamed in a tusselling heap around the badger. Four of them—a Parson Jack Russell, two Sealyhams, and a Bedlington—got a grip on each other, and hung on grimly. A long-legged neurotic animal resembling a diminutive elderly sheep, called Trixie, who had been shrieking almost incessantly since the meet in the farmyard that morning, began a fight with one of the lurchers, and the fight spread to their respective owners, when Mr. Potstacker kicked the lurcher in the ribs and was himself thumped on the ear by an enraged labourer. Shouts, oaths, drunken laughter, yelps, barks, growls; and in the centre of the confusion walked the old, old badger, opening his jaws slightly and thrusting his head at every snarling dog face. None dared to encounter the bite of the terrible boar.

At last the Master, having told anyone he could get to listen to him what he thought of the whole lot of dogs (he had no terrier of his own), decided to end it. He blew the recall on his horn, and bawled at them, asking if they knew what he was blowing?

One by one the dogs were gripped by their scruffs, and lugged away, collared, and held back on leashes. All became extremely bloodthirsty, and leapt up to get at the boar again.

The boar was standing still, shuddering. The Master approached him from behind, and gripped his neck without the least difficulty.

"Keep terriers back! Jan, bring a spade!"

While the huntsman was bringing the spade, the Master said: "Us'll make sure of ye this time, ye old——!" and with his right hand fumbled round his belt for his hunting knife.

A strange creaking noise was coming from the badger's throat. He gave a prolonged shudder, a feeble groan, and fell on his side. The Master pushed the limp body with his foot, and the head, with its filmy eyes, rolled loosely.

"Darn me if he isn't dead," said the Master.

When the business of taking the trophies—the sporting term for hacking off head and pads—was done, Mr. Tinker, before throwing the trunk to the terriers, thought he would try and find out what had caused the badger's death. He found, among other things, a piece of hedgehog skin with the prickles on it, the feet of a wood pigeon, and the core of an apple, all unchewed and undigested.

"Colic," he said.

And when he opened the mouth of Bloody Bill Brock, the unconquerable, whose bite all his enemies had feared, he saw the reason of death: for not a tooth was left in the old jaws, but only brown stumps level with the gums.

CHAKCHEK
THE PEREGRINE

CHAKCHEK THE PEREGRINE

The series of stories about the Peregrine falcons which I named, from their alarm cry, *Chak-chek*, was written in the early 'twenties. In those days I was continually surprising myself by what flowed from my pen in a spate of ink. For a story appeared to write itself, I had but a general idea of what it would be about, and how it would end. Usually I did not know, beyond the sentence I was writing, what lay ahead. Perhaps all writers get their stories done like this, unless the scenes are first composed in the head, as Arnold Bennett declared to be his method. (And very nervous he was, before the start and during the mental cogitation and arrangement, so nervous that if a pen or pencil on his desk had been put by someone, tidying in the morning, an inch or two out of place, it was almost a disaster.)

In Bennett's case, judging by the manuscripts, he seldom altered a word. I envied those bound books, beautifully scripted; but then my first drafts were too often only quarried material which later had to be built into a story, with a beginning, a middle, and an end.

It was the publican of the Lower House, the badger-digging gent, who first told me of the methods in use in the town to destroy peregrine falcons when they flew from their eyries on Lundy, Hartland Point, Baggy Point, Lee Bay, and Lynton to take pigeons flying in kits or flights over the town in the early summer. The pigeon fanciers got together to arrange decoy kits. The pigeons chosen for this purpose were of inferior powers, and at first were sent up with strips of liver, rubbed with strychnine, tied to their breasts. This proving ineffectual, a mixture of lard and strychnine was used. From what I was told, while knowing little about either racing or high-flying pigeons, the first story was dashed off one morning; and to my delight it was sold in New York for $500, a great sum for me in those days. At the same time it found a home in one of the many monthly family magazines published in London. More short stories, in similar romantic style, were printed in *The Saturday Evening Post, Collier's, Pictorial Review,* and other magazines, all of which paid $500. On this success I got married. Then, when my knowledge of wild life was a little less confined to inexperience, I wrote other stories which were consistently rejected, one agent in Manhattan writing to say, "Please do not be so selfish." Three of these stories are included in the pages which follow this bibliographical note; the discerning reader will spot them at once.

One of the first stories which were sold contained a fictitious character called Sir Godfrey Crawdelhook. Within a year I was ashamed of that bit of "characterisation", which was unknowledgeable and in one dimension: a villain of commonplace fiction of the period before I had outgrown the contemporary idiom of fiction-for-the-masses, and all else from which it arose.

My story of the peregrines, then, is a mixed affair, belonging partly to the days of unsophisticated youth; it ends with the Vigil of Mousing Keekee, a kestrel which I saw feeding young peregrine eyesses when their parents had failed to return; and with the scene on Bone Ledge the saga of an early writing period is ended.

1

The eyesses had slept and awakened over a hundred times during the night as the mail train took them eastwards towards London. Although they were starving, they would not tear the two plucked pigeons lying beside them. They had no hunger. At Paddington they were taken out of the guard's van, and many people waiting in the vast and gloomy station wondered what made the shrill chattering inside the basket. In the luggage room, where they remained awhile, they fell asleep, to awake when the lid was lifted.

The man looking at them was a colonel of cavalry with grey moustache and sunburnt skin. With the eye of an experienced falconer he examined the plumage, to see whether the eyesses, or young peregrine falcons, had been taken too early from the eyrie on Lundy. Every season from time immemorial fishermen had scaled the cliff for the peregrine's young, receiving five pounds every midsummer for a cast of three. There were two eyries on the island, and the right to take the young falcons had been leased by the owner for many years: the subject of a legal contract.

The wildness of the three young birds in the basket assured the new owner that they were fresh taken; and signing the receipt form, he carried them to a car outside and drove through London and down the Old Kent Road into Kent, and to his home at the foot of the downs overlooking the English Channel.

Up the straight wooden wall-ladder to the loft over the coach-house he took the basket, gently turning the trembling birds out on the straw, and leaving them with a bowl of water.

When the next morning came they were still crouched there. He picked them up in thick leather gauntlets, into which they stuck their talons, not with intent to wound, but because their tense nervous systems were shocked into a world without coherence or meaning.

Upon the leg of each bird he fixed two small Lahore bells, and a jess, or strip of soft greased hide of the white whale, a swivel attached to it. The agony of his touch did not last long, for the falconer had brought a hack-board, whereon was placed food for them—three heaps of beef chopped up with hard-boiled eggs. He put it on the floor, and left them. They did not feed.

At five o'clock in the afternoon he returned, and without showing head or body, stretched up an arm, removed the hack-board, cleaned it under a tap in the stable wall, made three fresh heaps of the same food, mixed with rabbits' fur and pigeons' feathers. Quietly he placed the evening meal before them; and when he had gone they fed ravenously.

Twice a day for the next fortnight the hack-board was put over the edge of the trap-door, sometimes with strips of raw beef and dead rabbits tied to it. The eyesses became used to their food arriving, as it were, by itself. The falconer did not show himself with the food because he did not want them to associate the ideas of food-arrival with man-arrival; he wanted to train them, when they were older, to fly at rooks and magpies, and possibly herons, on the downs; and a hawk that would scream, or cry out to him when unhooded, would be useless.

It was warm sunny weather, with wild doves nesting in the larches around the house, and oak-leaves green and rustling outside the open window. The eyesses taught themselves to fly from beam to beam of the loft. Nearly all the baby fluff had gone when the largest, a female bird, called falcon, after three days of indecision on the ivy-grown sill launched herself into the air and, flapping wildly, clung to a lichened branch. One of her brothers, a male bird, called tiercel, followed her after half an hour of shrill chattering.

At the end of another week nearly every branch of the tree had been perched upon. For the first two evenings they returned to roost in the loft, but when the oak was familiar, they slept there. The hack-board was now placed outside the loft, on a strip of grass, for they would not return under a roof once they were free. As soon as they saw it, they jumped upon the hack-board and tore off their breakfast. Afterwards they returned to the tree, preening flight feathers and nibbling dry skin fragments off legs and toes.

The falcon, larger than her brothers, was the first to venture forth from the oak. She flew across the rose garden of the house, over a tennis lawn, and perched on an elm that overlooked a walled-in kitchen garden. Swifts, with their black curved wings that made a sound like *frer* as they tore through the wind, screamed their puny screams as they saw her, and her full liquid brown eyes watched them. She rested for nearly an hour, snapping at bluebottles buzzing about her, watching the flight of birds and insects. She began to chatter as she dipped, preparatory to flight, for she was not yet confident of her wing-power.

The falconer, watching her, saw her suddenly cock her eye at the sky. He uttered an exclamation, for, wheeling overhead, was a wild peregrine. Its flight was like a swift's, but its wings were broader at the elbow, whence to the tips they narrowed to sharp points.

He watched the young falcon glide off the branch, and begin to ring above the kitchen garden with a series of sharp flaps followed by glides on level pinions. At every glide she depressed her tail and rose higher, and at the curves she gained speed again. When she had climbed five hundred feet the stranger, who had swung round and was now hung head-to-wind, closed his pinions and stooped upon her. She saw him and cried out in fear, but he swerved and passed her, to turn under her and make his point above her again. His breast was a creamy white, barred with thin black lines, and two black moustachial patches on his cheeks gave him a fierce and beautiful appearance. Like the falcon, he had yellow legs; but his back was not brown, like hers, but a grey blue.

He flew beside her, and she chattered at him, still being afraid. He was a wild tiercel, in his first mature plumage, which he wore with dashing pride. Suddenly he fell, and watching his stoop with thrilling delight, the falconer saw him miss a swift, immediately to make his point in a perfect sweep upwards and rejoin her.

Unknown to the colonel, the wild tiercel was Chakchek the Backbreaker, escaped from a mews on Salisbury Plain, where among falconers he was famed for his skill in swiftly man-œuvring a rook into position to receive the grand stoop, and also for his courage and prowess in attacking herons.

The next day the wild tiercel joined the three eyesses in the elm. He bore a starling in his talons. He plucked, skinned, and ate it as he stood on a bough, while they watched every beak-stroke, every rip, every gulp, with the most eager curiosity. Someone else was watching too, for in the falconer's mind were plans for its capture.

The previous autumn he had been in Holland to examine the hawk traps on the great plain of Walkenswaard, where for centuries a family of Dutchmen had taken migrating, or passage, hawks. It was the colonel's ambition to reclaim an adult wild peregrine and train it to be as good a bird as the most famous hawks of olden time; a tiercel taken mature would be more dashing than an eyess that had never killed its own prey before being reclaimed.

The eyesses grew strong of wing, and after breakfast every morning at sunrise they set their feathers straight and cleaned their talons, and then—away into the sky! The colonel, who was a lonely widower since his only daughter's recent marriage, had learned a little about the training of falcons during his service on Indian plains, where the larger sacer falcons were flown as kites and gamebirds by native officers.

The young peregrines enjoyed their play in the air, chasing and stooping at one another through the sunlit wind. The wild tiercel came every day, joining in their games, and playing with the falcon more than with her brothers. Often they dashed down the wind, seen as specks from below, to swing round and be thrown up by the impetus of the swerve.

The colonel used to lie in a deck-chair in the sun and watch them through glasses until they were beyond sight, where for an hour and more they tumbled and swooped and rejoiced in the cold untrodden ways of the lofty summer sky. Although they were beyond human sight aided by lenses and prisms, yet the movements of the man below were visible to four pairs of eyes whenever he crossed one leg over another or put his arms behind his white panama hat.

One day as he was lounging there, listening to the sea's continuous *ah-ah's* on the distant shore, he heard a hissing noise above, and looked up in time to see the wild tiercel stoop upon a carrion crow which had been stealing squabs, or nestling pigeons, from the larch wood. The carrion crow cawed harshly, and flew back towards the trees; but before it could reach cover and hide in the maze of branches, the tiercel in a magnificent stoop had hit it so accurately that it was instantly killed. Its mate appeared out of the wood a few seconds later in answer to its cawing, and The Backbreaker, who had shot up to a pitch three hundred feet above the striking place, stooped upon her. She avoided his line of stoop by a violent shift, and the falconer heard the swishing as the tiercel turned on his back, making the figure 6, and ripped with his talons as he passed under her. She fell mortally wounded, her crop torn open, in the rose garden; and running to her, the colonel killed her with a blow of a stick.

Three squabs were in the crop, and to his surprise one of them, about three days old, was alive. He carried it away and put it in a dovecot beside a tippler squab whose mother nourished it thenceforward as her own offspring. It was uninjured, having been swallowed whole by the crow. Eventually it grew to be a fine bird.

The falconer, filled with admiration for the prowess and skill of the wild tiercel, visited a cobbler in the village who trapped skylarks during the autumn migration across the downs. This man made him a bow-net after the pattern of the Dutch nets. Together they fixed it in the paddock adjoining the stables.

For several days The Backbreaker had been coming morning and evening to the hack-board, and feeding with the eyesses, who never failed to return at meal-times, crying *Way-ee, Way-ee* and shivering their wings when they saw him—a happy sign that they had not learnt to kill for themselves. Although they wailed to him, and showed no fear of him, they would not allow him to approach within a yard of them. The falconer was astonished at the wild bird's tameness until he saw a bell on its leg, and then realised that it must have escaped. He was the more determined to recapture this haggard tiercel— *haggard* being the term applied to a falcon which, having been trained, had gone wild again.

Very soon, he thought, he would have to begin to break-in the eyesses. Within a week they must be caught, hooded, and each lashed to its wooden block driven into the lawn. After an hour or two of quiet perching, one would be taken on his wrist and carried about, stroked with a feather, and fed through the hood. The hood would be removed inside the shuttered coach-house, by candlelight, quietly, during a meal, and put on again but before the meal's end—lest the idea of hooding and termination of a meal be associated in their minds. The next stage would be to feed them in daylight, and to break them in quietly to the putting on of the hood, for when hooded they could rest and grow calm. Afterwards would begin the training proper, a very patient work, to make them return to the lure—wings of a duck tied to a pad and swung on a string for the recall.

For the haggard tiercel, however, the reclaiming would be more severe. For two days and nights, by sunlight and candlelight, it would be stroked with a feather, handled gently, and prevented from sleeping. Then it would be starved. At the end of forty-eight hours, if all went well, its fierce and haughty spirit would be subdued, its sense of lordship in the open sky be dulled, its resentment of captivity gone, and patiently it would submit to a hood and take food from its captor's hand.

The falconer bided his time. The bow-net was made, and fixed in the paddock. The squab that had escaped death in the crow's crop, and whose life was owed to The Backbreaker, was fully fledged when the day planned for the taking of the four peregrines arrived. Recently the wild tiercel had been roosting on the tower of the Norman church in the village near by, and frequently the three slept with him. He was their protector. Once seventeen magpies had found one of the young male eyesses resting on a downland thorn, perched insecurely on a top spray in the sea-breeze, and had mobbed him. They had pecked at him, knowing he was little, and tried to pull out his tail and flight feathers. The Backbreaker had seen them as he swooped in play at his favourite falcon; he had swept up with the wind two thousand feet above, he had poised for the grand stoop; he had tipped up, beating wings to increase the shear of his dive head first—faster, faster, the wind screaming against his barbed strength—seventeen magpies were scattered like pieces of half-burnt paper, except one whose head spun away from its flattened body and fell seventy feet distant from the thorn bush.

Sixteen magpies fought for the body two minutes afterwards, but ants had the head, leaving horn and bone clean a day later.

Now the falconer was waiting to take the four friends.

The net was circular, a yard across, with a pliant hazel-rod bent like a bow and tied to half the net's circumference. To the bow-net was attached fifty yards of line. The unattached half of the net was pegged to the ground, and the loose folds tucked under the hazel bow. Beside the bow was placed the hack-board, with dead rats and rabbits tied to it. Fifty yards away the falconer squatted in the grass, the smoke of his pipe straying into the quiet evening air among the gnats which rose and fell in dance over his head.

Seven was the usual feeding time, and the stable clock had hardly struck the hour when a speck appeared over the downs, and grew rapidly into the barb-shape of a swooping eyess. He fell like an arrowhead to the hack-board, where he was joined by the other eyess tiercel two minutes later. The falconer waited for the falcon eyess and the wild tiercel, but when at a quarter past seven they were still absent, he jerked the line so that the bow rose over the eyesses and they were caught in the spread circle of the net. How they chattered and struggled! Gently the hand-in-gauntlet held wings against sides. They were drawn out one at a time, and rufter hoods slipped over their heads and fastened with straps round their necks. Good-bye to freedom, little Lundy tiercels! The light caps of leather, which were open to permit feeding, blindfolded them; they ceased to struggle; swivels and leashes were attached to the jesses on their legs; the leashes tied to the larchwood blocks a hundred yards away in the grass.

The other peregrines did not return to the hack-board, and the falconer concluded that the wild tiercel had killed for the falcon eyess. At sunset the pair returned to the church tower, where they slept. Before dawn the next morning the falconer arose and prepared fresh food on the hack-board, which he then took to the dewy grass of the paddock. He waited for half an hour, while the stars paled in the steely glow above him and the line of the downs grew dark as light showed up to the zenith. Larks were already singing when a thrush flew to the elm and its bold ringing notes awoke the drowsiest birds. Swallows flew round him and a cohort of swifts seemed to descend from the stars as though poured out of an unseen pitcher.

The last star was dimmed when the eyess falcon suddenly appeared, The Backbreaker behind her. She was about to alight upon the hack-board when the tiercel cried *chak-chek-chek!* She swerved away, to make her point above the net and complain in a baby wail to the falconer. *Way-ee, way-ee,* she wailed, but the tiercel swooped at her and drove her off. Once netted, twice shy, thought the falconer.

The cries were heard by the eyesses hooded and leashed in a disused chickenhouse, and they too cried *way-ee, way-ee.* Every time the eyess swooped down to the hack-board the tiercel drove her up and *way-ee, way-ee,* she complained to the falconer, flying round his head, her bell tinkling, and crying *way-ee, way-ee, way-ee!*

To the colonel, a sensitive and thoughtful man, the eyess seemed like a young bride, reluctant to leave a loved home, yet eager for love and life. The Backbreaker chattered and called her, her brothers wailed as she circled above the paddock, crying to the one whom she knew as parent and guardian. A feeling of sadness came over him, as he stood and watched, the cord loose in his hand, for in that moment he realised how near to men were animals and birds, in their desires and aspirations. "We're all the same," he murmured to himself.

He dropped the cord. He would try no further to net them. He walked to the house, followed by the young eyess. He was moved by her cries to him, remembering his daughter on her wedding eve.

"Go your ways, little falcon," he said. "That handsome fellow has first claim on you."

Then he stood still in amazement; for even as he spoke, the falcon dashed upwards to The Backbreaker, and together they flew into the sky.

The eyess tiercels were trained, and accounted for many thieving crows and magpies during happy hours of wandering with the falconer and a spaniel on the downs. Buccaneer and Belfry they were called, and lived to be old birds; but they never saw The Backbreaker or his mate again.

Far away over the North Devon seaboard the pair ranged, from their eyrie on Bone Ledge where The Backbreaker had been born—he the heir of more than a hundred thousand years of fearlessness.

2

On a certain afternoon in the early spring a solitary heron was standing on an islet in the estuary, near the overturned hulk of a gravel barge. The islet was formed of sand lodging against a tree uprooted in winter floods and partly reburied by the lapse and flow of a hundred salt-water tides. He had flown there from the heronry in the oakwood four miles away. and a strong east wind had swept him forward with hardly a thrust of his broad vanes. He was Old Nog, and for a living he speared fish with a long sharp beak. The old bird was working very hard just now. Gone were the easy days when with a full crop the grey fisher used to walk on his lanky legs to the middle of the sandbank, draw up one foot, lay his head in the middle of his back, and sleep, motionless as grey, dry seaweed on two sticks. No naps for Nog nowadays. He'd got two growing young 'uns, old enough, thought Nog, to leave the treetop nest and learn to fish for themselves. As, however, they wouldn't leave, Old Nog had to work thrice as hard, for unknown to him his mate had been struck down and killed by peregrine falcons a week ago as she was spearing her seven-hundredth yearling in a trout farm. He missed her very much, and since the moon had grown bright he had fished all night, being so hungry.

The tide on this afternoon was nearly slack, and he peered keenly at the water in which he was wading to his knee-joints. The little light-coloured eyes saw a disturbance of sand-grains, the narrow head peered forward, while the wind stirred black plumes on the long neck that was scarcely thicker than his spindle-shanks. Many times he had been angered to see a wriggling and doleful specimen of a heron looking at himself out of the water. It had blue-grey plumage, streaked with black, and white in parts. Old Nog threatened it many times a day for coming where he was. It threatened him, too, holding out its ragged wings, dancing on tottery legs, and opening its beak. Fancy not knowing himself! A dull old bird, a silly old bird, so thought the carrion crows of the higher reaches of the estuary. They knew why his mate had not returned. But Old Nog was not so dull or silly as they thought, for on this particular afternoon . . . but as yet no bird of the estuary had seen the specks of death waiting on in the sky, waiting on . . .

Old Nog continued to peer. The movement of sand was made by a dab, or small flatfish, rising off the bed of the estuary where it had been lying invisible owing to a back speckled and dotted like sand. Old Nog darted at the movement, transfixing the dab with the two tips of his beak just opened. Lifting it, he threw it on his tongue, and swallowed with a shake of his head that scattered the water out of his eyes. Another movement, in water deeper by two inches. He waded on legs like stilts, and green as rushes, peered low, struck with hardly a splash, and swallowed a shrimp. Thus he fished for several minutes, taking many dabs and shrimps, until five herring gulls which had been patrolling the tide-line looking for carrion or fish, alighted on the water near the heron and paddled around the tree. None dared to swim near that spear of a beak.

Old Nog had many fishing places in the muddy creeks and dykes of the low marshland country of the Two Rivers' estuary. He visited them one after another, beginning at dawn, and going on all day, from drain to mill-leat, from mill-leat to brook, from brook to creek, and, at low tide, to the estuary islet. This afternoon he had just flown from the duck-ponds a mile away, after taking a rainbow-trout, a frog, a rat, a beetle, and a duckling. The keeper had tried to stalk him, but the old heron had been standing where he could see the approach of man beyond gunshot range.

The gulls paddled around the islet, ignored by Old Nog. At the tide-line of the muddy shore four yards away a curlew was walking, thrusting a curved delicate bill into craters small as pennies, drawing out worms that lay beneath, and swallowing them without a jerk, with head still lowered. Neither gull nor heron, with their proportionately shorter beaks, could suck up the food like this. The gulls watched both feeding birds. Every time the heron struck and withdrew with a headshake the gulls screamed, lest the beak lose its grip and fling its prey aside. Every time the curlew bowed, keen and pale eyes watched for sight of wriggling worm. A blackpoll gull was near her when this happened, and ran to steal it; the curlew lifted her brown freckled wings and ran, uttering a trill of notes ascending in scale. From the beak of the gull a raucous scream came, and he ran after the curlew, but when he reached her the worm was swallowed. His ferocious attitude fell from him, and both birds went on with the intent search for food.

A small bird piped a shrill *peet-peet* as it flew across the river to the islet. It was the size of a sparrow, but sturdier, with white throat, black beak, rich auburn breast, wings and back a greenish-blue, the head and neck being barred with brilliant azure. To the tree it flew straight and swift, perching with pink feet on a weed-hung twig. It gazed at the water, being a kingfisher; it patrolled the higher reaches of the estuary every day,

433

as regularly as the heron, flying zigzag from bank to bank, from one perching rock to another. It saw nothing, and restlessly piping *peet-peet* it flew away, and had gone less than fifty yards when it saw a little fish and splashed into the water, returning to the tree to kill and swallow its catch.

Another bird was fishing near, like a large scarecrow of a duck turned pirate, black as coal with a greenish sheen on its oily feathers. His beak was as long as the beak of Old Nog, only black, and hooked at the tip. He was Oylegrin the shag, one of the Pelican family, but, unlike his large relative, his beak had not the capacity of his belly. He paddled with black webbed feet in deeper water, and every minute he bobbed his head, tipped up and swam to the river-bed. Looking up with his green eyes he could see any fish swimming over him as a shape shown up by the quicksilvery surface. In one of his underwater swims, as he thrust along with strong pushes, his neck stretched out, he espied an eel, and opened his beak. The eel was near the islet, and as Oylegrin snapped at its tail, Old Nog, who had suddenly waded into deeper water, darted his neck forward and speared. So swift the judgment, so precise the angle of striking, that the mandibles held the slimy skin of the eel and drew it curling and lashing from the water.

Observing the eel the five herring gulls screamed, and beat their wings to arise and fly about the heron. Out of the water bobbed the head of the shag, and the eel's tail was seized in the hook-tip. The kingfisher flew up-estuary, the curlew walked away, for she was a gentle bird, a lover of water-murmurous solitude, and disliked the wrangling of gulls. From the spear-tip of heron's beak the eel was pulled by Oylegrin, and it dropped into six inches of water, to be gripped by the sharp edge of the shag's mandibles before it had time to writhe in one curl. Spray was beaten by the big black wings immediately, for Nog speared the eel again. Shag tried to swallow it, his green eye fierce, and the crest of feathers on his head risen with fury. He threatened with a greasy mutter in his throat, while two beachcombing crows flew from over the water to see what might be doing for themselves. They perched on the hulk and waited; eel, wounded heron, maimed shag—and what might be in their crops—anything and everything, dead or alive, was food for crows.

Old Nog got the eel again, but before he could throw it up and gulp it into a crop already laden, Oylegrin the shag had gripped the tail end. The spearing and buffeting and nipping soon killed the eel, although its nerves continued to twitch and flick in death.

While the birds were struggling, neither managing to swallow the eel, something was seen by the gulls and crows. The effect was immediate. *Krok-Krok-Krok* said one of the crows, and they were gone from the hulk, beating wings faster than usual as they fled silently over the water to the oak trees on the bank. With a gabbling cry one of the herring gulls made off, followed by four others and the smaller blackpoll. Oylegrin the shag, at the verge of the scratched and spurred sand of the islet, wary for the stroke of the heron's spear-tip, suddenly turned away and vanished under a bulging water-ring. From this ring ripples spread out and disappeared in the frothy tops of wave-lets. Oylegrin bobbed up fifty yards away, breathed, took a glance skywards, bobbed under. Beside a stone crouched the curlew, head to wind, immobile and coloured as the stone. Only the heron had not seen what the others had seen.

Squark! cried Old Nog, very satisfied, as he picked up the eel. After many tosses and jerks it joined the duckling, the beetle, the rainbow trout, the frog, and the rat. Then leisurely spreading his grey vanes he jumped into the wind, tucked a scraggy neck between shoulders, stretched out his long thin legs behind him, and beat towards the heronry, four miles away.

Half a mile above him, steady on pitches in the wind, three birds, sharp in outline like specks of slate, were watching him, and—in an ancient term of falconry—were waiting on.

They were peregrine falcons of the ancient and noble house of Chakchek. A Chakchek was famous among falconers through-out Europe during the reign of Queen Elizabeth. A Chakchek founded the northern eyrie upon the Atlantic isle called Lundy five thousand years before the earliest chapters of the Bible were composed. The Lundy cream-breasted peregrines are still considered among falconers to be the finest in Europe. A Chakchek surveyed the battle of Trafalgar. Another slew the Frenchman's message pigeons before Sedan. One, called Chakchek the One-Eyed, was in Ypres during the first bombardment. A Chakchek was hunting the airways of the Two Rivers' estuary as the ships went over the bar to join Drake's fleet; centuries before, when Phoenicians first came to trade; long, long before, when moose roamed in the forest which stood where the Pebble Ridge of Westward Ho! now lies—the trees are long since gone under the sand, drowned by the sea.

They were Chakcheks, father and mother and son—tiercel and falcon, and a young male bird of immature plumage, an eyess hatched and reared less than a year before, in the month of May. There had been two daughters. One hunted in Scotland with a mate; the other had been shot off the coasts of Florida. Chakcheks have wandered from Spitzbergen to Samoa; they are free of the winds of the world. They attack and drive eagles. No man knows where the old birds go to die; for there are no old Chakcheks. They die young, beloved of their god. Noble they are, of lineage as ancient as the first gods of man, and their god is older, being Altair in the constellation of Aquila, a night-sun with gold-flickering wings.

The wind of early spring blew cold at two thousand feet, but the peregrines, one above and beyond the other, felt neither heat nor cold. Their feathers were tight against bodies. The parent birds were slatey-blue of back and creamy of breast, which was thinly barred in black. The eyess had a dark brown back and dingy white breast, draggled brown. He was the heir to the eyrie of Bone Ledge. Their beaks were short and curved, with yellow skin round the base, and their eyes were full, liquid, and dark, steadfast with an untameable hauteur, eyes which saw many times as keenly as man.

The wind did not rock them. They were as though fixed in the sky. They waited on. The leader, the tiercel, was The Backbreaker. They saw the gulls, the shag, the crows. These slunk away, and the lank grey bird launched himself. He had gone two hundred vane-flaps when the tiercel cried "*Chak-*

chek-chek!" turned on his side and slipped from his pitch. With beak to earth he beat his wings ten times, then closed them. The falcon followed, and the eyess. The triple-cut air whined as though in complaint.

Old Nog saw the tiercel falling upon him, and shifted with violent flaps. The Backbreaker dropped below him. Two seconds later the falcon swished past him, and the eyess followed so quickly that he was struck at an elbow joint, and feathers were knocked away. He cried *Krark!*

As the three made their points—shooting up perpendicularly with the impetus of their stoops—the heron climbed, swinging round with the wind and making ring after ring. In long spiral curves he mounted towards the clouds, but ring after ring the peregrines made also, rushing downward for half a mile and tearing round in a great banking circle that shot them up hundreds of feet. The Backbreaker mounted to his pitch above, at such a height that a man watching below could not see him. Again the grand stoop, again the tiercel fell past the heron four hundred feet before he could make another point. Old Nog tried desperately to climb. He was too weary. He opened his beak and the eel fell out.

Down came the falcon—than whom the tiercel was smaller by a tierce, or third—driving at him with yellow feet spread, black sickle-claws open to rip up his back. Old Nog rocked, and nearly overturned. He could see the leafless oak trees of the heronry, and young birds standing in the topmost branches, beyond the winding of the river and its sandy wastes. The clouds were high above him, but reach them he must. He cried out in his fear as the eyess fell upon him. The dabs, the rat, and the rainbow trout followed the eel.

The tiercel was ringing again, climbing three yards to the heron's one, level but distant half a mile upwind at one moment, two hundred yards over and passing downwind at a hundred miles an hour a few seconds afterwards, and three minutes later almost out of sight. *Krark! Krark!!* cried Old Nog dolefully, and breathing fast with his efforts. Tiercel poised in his pitch for a grand stoop, his eyes fixed on the labouring expanse of wings, every nerve and sinew tightened for the downward drive at two hundred miles an hour. He waited, his pinions crooking back with nervous false starts many times in the ten seconds during which he was poised. *Chak-chek-chek!* He saw the line, tipped up sideways, beat a dozen swift strokes, closed pinions, pressed every feather, into a taut and quivering body, and stooped. The rush of air against his eyes was so keen and hard that he blinked the third eyelid over the dark orbs, so that he saw but dimly. Larger and larger grew the heron, and The Backbreaker's eyes became clear and brown; he held his breath for the impact and spread his talons—*whish!* he had passed Old Nog. The heron escaped by a falling spin, losing in ten seconds the height he had gained by two minutes' ringing. Down fell duckling, frog, and beetle.

He recovered his balance in time to avoid the falcon's stoop, but the eyess, pressing hard behind his mother, hit him between the shoulders. Old Nog tumbled, and abandoned hope of climbing above his enemies. He was flustered and shaken. He began to flap wildly in the direction of the heronry. No other birds were visible in the air. He cried out in his helplessness, and the third *Krark!* ended abruptly, for Chakchek had made his point above him and stooped so surely that he struck him and bound to the grey back with his claws. Down came falcon and eyess, giving him two more tremendous jolts, and Old Nog sank down under the weight, crying for help.

All four fell on a mudbank, near the eel, and the blow knocked the heron feeble. Immediately falcon and tiercel began to rip with their beaks, and the eyess flew arrogantly at the head. Old Nog lifted a muddy spear and stabbed so swift and true that he shattered an eye of the young peregrine. Chattering with pain he flew up, as Old Nog feeling stronger jumped up on tottery legs and faced the pair with vanes held around him like shields. The feathers of his throat and breast were muddy, and a froth of blood was on his beak. In the ragged tent of his wings he stood grey and anxious and lank, holding up a crimsoning spear. The tiercel uttered the ringing cry of his race, *Chak-chek-chek!*, and dashed at him, to swerve as the spear flashed at his throat. Upwind flew the falcon, and cut at Nog, followed

438

by the wounded eyess, whose hind claws nearly ripped open the narrow skull. Swoop after swoop Old Nog met with a stab; and then they flew away.

But the heron did not move. He crouched in the mud, his head trembling between narrow shoulders, gazing fixedly at the sky. He watched the three birds cutting circles higher and higher, farther and farther away, where the wind had torn wisps of mist from the cloud-laden wains of sky. The heron watched the specks slipping downwind, swing round, and the specks gave out a minute flickering as the peregrines climbed up against the wind. Minute after minute Old Nog stood in his tent, taking counsel with himself, his spear upright. The specks vanished in a cloud.

Old Nog flapped his vanes, and cried *Squark!* He preened his flight-quills by drawing them through his beak, and looked about him. He took several steps forward, then sideways, then round. Again he shook himself, and flapped his vanes. *Squark!* a cry of satisfaction. A scrutiny of the sky revealed nothing of his enemies, so he gazed around, to see the eel lying not far off. Gravely he walked over to it, leaving the spurs of his three big toes on the mud among worm-castings and empty mussel shells. Picking it up in his beak he tossed it until the head was on his tongue, and with shake and gulp it disappeared into his crop. Forthwith he looked around for the duckling. He found it. And the rat. *Squark!* said Old Nog, stalking on stilty legs after the rainbow trout. Afterwards he stood on one leg and tried to scratch mud off his plume. Thence an amble to a water-filled creek, where he watched for dab and shrimp. They had ceased feeding, and were invisible. He climbed out of the creek, and launched himself homeward.

He had flown, stiffly and laboriously, about half the way to the heronry when the three Chakcheks, who from pitches two miles away had watched him picking up the eel, half closed their pinions, and shot down an incline at nearly twice flying speed. Their wings made the shape of an anchor-head with shortened shank and crooked flukes. The pain of a shattered eye went from the eyess in jubilation as he felt his tail thrumming, his pinions hissing. He opened the toes of his feet pressed into his feathers, and the air whined as the claws scratched eight unseen lines in the sky. Behind his parents he stooped, and when the heron saw them he cried aloud in distress.

A hundred pairs of pale yellow eyes were watching them from the heronry. They saw Old Nog shift as the falcon stooped, but he was tired, and his broad vanes too clumsy for so light a body. He tried to stab her, she crashed into the long black flight-quills, passed behind him, turned in a short swishing curve and passed under his breast, on her back, bursting away scores of feathers. Seven seconds later she was bound to his back, sinking with him. The tiercel joined her. They bore the old bird down, and Old Nog ceased to struggle, and closed his vanes. But seeing below him the river, which was tidal for three miles beyond the heronry, he gave a cry and opened them in order to beat into a position for diving. With two of his enemies on his back, and a third chattering around him, Old Nog plunged headfirst into the river.

Not long afterwards nearly a hundred young herons dozing on flat piles of sticks in the tree tops, while waiting for food, poked up their heads again.

The arrival of Old Nog, bedraggled, dripping wet, with skinny breast unfeathered, frayed vanes, and red beak, was welcomed by a hubbub of guttural squawks. Slowly and heavily he sailed nearer to the uproar of flapping wings, stretching necks, and opening beaks. Was this a demonstration of victory, of greeting the conquering hero? Oh, no, for the fight was already forgotten and Old Nog was merely a parent bird coming with food, a parent claimed by every youngster, frenziedly implored to alight at every nest and to give up what he had got. Old Nog flapped over the heronry, sailed to a branch near his nest, closed his tattered vanes, and perched swaying six feet away from his noisy sons. He hunched up his shoulders and sank his head between them, desiring only to rest after the contest, and digest his meal. Far away a young peregrine was flying alone—his parents drowned. Chakchek the Backbreaker is dead—long live Chakchek the One-Eyed!

Seeing him huddled on the tree, the sons of Nog, who had

learned during the past few days to walk on branches, went foot
by foot to where he was perched, and yelled *Pa! Pa!* so loudly
that Old Nog opened his eyes. Seeing he was awake they
flapped their vanes and pulled down his head. Old Nog pulled
it up again; but one or the other got hold of it, and pulled it
down again. *Krark!* said Old Nog, but the two grawbeys would
not be quiet. Old Nog yawned, and bending down, yielded
trout and rat to one, and duckling and eel to the other. Such
robbery had happened to Old Nog for over twenty years—
every spring he fished and toiled all day and half the night,
and whenever he flew home for rest and quiet, the nestlings
not only pestered him with their noisiness, but took away his
food. With a melancholy *Krark!* Old Nog flapped away from
the heronry, and after filling himself with dabs, walked wearily
and stiffly to the middle of a sandbank, secure from man and
nestlings, and slept until the tide wetted him four hours afterwards. Then, fishing for half an hour, he filled his crop, and
went back to the heronry to see how the young 'uns were
getting on.

3

Again the dark sharp-winged bird cut a swift air-circle round
the petrified figure standing on the column one hundred
and forty-five feet above the earth. The figure was eighteen
feet tall, and wore cocked hat, coat, knee-breeches, and shoes,
all of stone. Sightlessly it stared, fixed and immobile, alone in
the sky, the southern sun shining on its smoke-dark face. Thus
had it been staring many years over the highway, on which
proceeded perpetual lines of horse and motor traffic. Below
the column were four bronze lions. Two fountains were
playing. A dissonant hum of engines arose from the highway,
up and down which thousands of men and women were
hurrying.

Not one of the hurrying men and women looked up at the
statue or saw the sharp speck flying in a circle above the monu-
ment to a dead admiral. The gaze of the people was on the

pavements and no higher than omnibus driver or pedestrian immediately approximate. And at the moment most of them thought hatefully and scornfully of another nation, as that nation thought hatefully and scornfully of them. Among these people, determined in a conviction of their national righteousness, were many civil servants from the War and Admiralty Offices going to lunch in restaurants in the Strand, and old men wearing uniforms, whose heels flashed.

The agitated streams of moving hats on the pavements, the dark dots passing through the traffic, the coloured motor-buses and cabs, were ignored by the bird above. The hum and shimmer and shuffle uprising in a hundred confused echoes smote continuously upon his senses of sight and sound, but he accepted them calmly as he had accepted the rivers and woods and towns over which he had passed since the death of his parents several weeks before. More than two centuries before, one of his ancestors had killed rooks which lived in the trees whose roots now rotted under the asphalt walks of Trafalgar Square, which was then called Porridge Island in the village of Charing.

He flew with quick flickerings of pointed wings, followed by short level glides. His scaly yellow legs, with their four toes and black sickle-claws, were pressed into the brownish-white plumage of his belly. His beak was blue and pointed. He had black patches on his cheeks. His eye showed him to be noble; indeed, an English king had once conferred an earldom on one of his ancestors; his eye was large and fierce and proud, of a beautiful brown, with liquid blue-black pupil. The other eye-socket was empty. He was Chakchek the One-Eyed.

He flew seven hundred feet above Whitehall, seeing below him an immense wilderness of buildings, an immense spreading patch whose edges were lost in grey smoke rising in the windless air from a million chimney-pots. He saw the river crossed by many bridges, its wide and silver flowing broken by tugs and barges, and its banks overcrowded with wharves and cranes, and tangled with spars and rigging. He climbed to a thousand feet, flying at sixty miles an hour, and turned suddenly by opening and depressing the stiff feathers of his tail, so that with a hissing of air he was flung up in a loop, at the top of which he rolled over, facing Trafalgar Square, and pointing at the figure on the top of the column. With wings half closed the tiercel slanted down from the sky at a hundred miles an hour, breaking his point just before the statue by using wings and tail as brakes, thrusting out spread yellow feet, and alighting on the admiral's cocked hat with scratch of claws. He preened the long flight quills of his wings, drawing them through his beak and smoothing the ruffled filaments. When he had made those airworthy he preened his tail feathers in the same way, and cleaned his breast and toes. Afterwards he shook himself, stretched pinions and legs, and looked at the strangers around and under him.

Immediately below the statue was a wide ledge, and on this were lying hundreds of skeletons and claws and scattered bones. And there were skulls, most of them about an inch and a half long, but there were smaller, blunter skulls as well. For this was a dying-place of London's birds. It was nearest the sky, and no bird likes to die on the ground. Here pigeons and sparrows who found their food in the Square flew with last wingbeats when they felt the world they knew passing away from them. There was the body of a humble-bee lying on its side by a sparrow skull, with frayed vanes folded tranquilly over its black and gold body. It had died that morning, having come to London in a Kentish flower waggon, wearily clinging in the starlit frosty night to an aster flower. The beams of the sun had given it enough strength to fly up, but its spirit had gone back to the happy meadows as its body dropped on the ledge.

Suddenly the perching bird stiffened. A flock of pigeons had flown up from somewhere behind the Admiralty Arch. He was not hungry, having gorged himself on a chicken taken from a garden in Woking half an hour previously. In the arrogancy of his young life he stared at them. They floated to the Square, with wings held at a high angle. He watched with fierce eye all their movements. They fluttered round a woman who held a paper bag, from which she took handfuls of maize to scatter

443

for them. The pigeons walked quickly on the asphalt, picking up the grains and having no fear of the idlers. She held out a palmful and two birds perched on her wrist. Then something little, which had been standing like a tree-stump rooted in the pavement, with a paper-bill stuck to it, became alive, and slouched big-booted to her. It wore a dinted bowler hat with a brass band shining with the letters STAR round the crown. It had fed many generations of pigeons with corn on the brim of that official hat. The woman dropped a trickle of maize over it. Three birds fluttered round it. One perched on the crown. The tree-stump became human. It smiled. It held newspapers under one arm, and cried *Brisharmgravictryspeshl.*

The peregrine fixed the pigeon on the hat with his eye, leaned forward, and slipped off his perch. He fell almost perpendicularly, with wings arched back sharply.

He fell thus half the height of the Nelson Column, and then he opened and beat his wings, swooping low and fast just above the heads of two uniformed Eastern Telegraph boys. A sparrow sipping water on the stone edge of the fountain basin saw him, and fell into the water with fright. The newspaper seller, faithful purveyor of racing selections during thousands of lunch-hours, patron of pigeons and worthy citizen, was offering his double news-sheet which told of the *British Army's Great Victory—Special*—to a pale-faced shipping clerk, when the bird on his hat was knocked three yards in a horizontal direction towards Cockspur Street, and half a hundred pigeons and a dozen sparrows on the ground scattered like spoke-splinters and felloes of a grey limber-wheel struck by a noiseless shell.

No one with human intelligence knew what had happened. The pigeon was picked up in one place, and its head several paces beyond, where it had rolled. Its crop was ripped open, and maize-berries fell out. The shipping clerk asked if it were dead.

"Dead?" replied one of the cheeky Telegraph boys, "what yer fink 'e is? Springcleaning 'isself?"

A tall policeman strolled over with noiseless tread, controlled and immaculate. The newspaper man held out the decapitated

pigeon, an appealing look on his barky face. A dozen voices
tried to tell the policeman what had happened. Someone
suggested it must have been shot. Someone else said a stone
must have been thrown at it. An office boy munching a beef
sandwich tried to assume a knowing expression, as though to
direct upon himself the prominence of suspicion. He was an
opportunist with imagination, as yet undeveloped, and he
was being wasted as an envelope flap-licker and stamp-
thumper.

Another individual suggested that a German spy was concealed among the chimney-pots, sniping with an air-gun the
military staff of the War Office. Hearing this, a territorial
rifleman with blistered feet, recruit of three days' training
(it was September of Nineteen Fourteen), looked alarmed, and
the policeman produced his note-book. A crowd of several
hundreds had been formed. The policeman ordered people
to move on, and they shuffled a few feet. The crowd blocked
the road, and immediately the fluid traffic lines began to
coagulate. The word *Germans* made a sibilance on the tongues
of the people.

Soon the people wandered away, the traffic pulsed again up
and down Whitehall, Cockspur Street, and the Strand; back
went the note-book into the policeman's breast pocket. The
paper "boy" rolled the body of the pigeon in one of the news-
bills of the lunch edition of the *Star*, and put it in his pocket,
muttering "Lor, won't it be loverly in a poi for Sunday's dinner!
lor, won't it taste loverly!" Sparrows and pigeons came back
to the Square, and the fountains splashed in the great stone
basins, casting sun-dogs out of the rising waterspray which
the passers-by did not see.

That afternoon The One-Eyed stooped at three pigeons from
the gilt cross on the dome of St. Paul's Cathedral, losing the
first bird, striking the second above an omnibus but missing
a clutch, so that it hit the wooden surface of the street with
such force that it bounced a yard. The third he missed in his
first plunge, but recovering immediately he circled under it
and drove it up to an altitude about thrice the height of the

cathedral. Then his relentless round-and-round tactics changed; the steady beating of his wings became agitated; with a burst of speed he dashed at the tail of the dingy pigeon, who towered and escaped, to fall towards a retreat below the lead dome where scores of its brethren were crouching. The One-Eyed fell upon it before it had dropped two hundred feet, and the people watching below saw the two birds meet and become one which faded into the dome, leaving feathers only in the air where they had apparently joined.

The One-Eyed stood on the small pigeon, descendant of a stock dove, and plucked and tore the flesh from the frame, often pausing to peer from the ledge as though fearing disturbance. What he left ten minutes later weighed about an ounce— tail and pinion feathers, part of the breast-bone, mandibles and part of the skull-bone, legbones, feet, and gizzard.

For two days he harried the pigeons of St. Paul's Cathedral, and then he left, making a temporary roost in one of the elms of Hyde Park. He killed a green woodpecker as it was pushing itself up a trunk with its pointed tail feathers, to the excitement of a falcon-eyed, white-bearded man who had been watching it through glasses; for the old gentleman had been observing birds in Hyde Park for many years, and he knew that the peregrine falcon was a rare visitor.[1]

In this pleasaunce a grey American squirrel ceased to live, after a chase among yellowing leaf-patches and a bounding run among the grasses that ended in sharp death for one of the invading tribe which had helped decimate the brown English squirrel.

Other strange things happened. The sexton of a church at Hampstead was surprised one morning to find the remains of a bantam cock lying on one of his tombs; but he was not more surprised than the gunner subaltern at the R.A. mess, Woolwich, whose horse shied and threw him during a canter round Blackheath when a rook sprawled through the air, broken backed, and fell just before its nose. The striking-down of the rook from eleven hundred feet took place less than eight minutes after The One-Eyed had flown up from the

[1] This old gentleman bore a resemblance to the late W. H. Hudson.

cockerel, and as Hampstead to Blackheath is about ten miles, one may estimate his roving pace.

For a few weeks he hunted in Greater London, and many adventures he had, including a terrible minute when near Eltham he stooped at the decoy-bird of a netter, tied to a post in a waste land to attract passing finches. For the netter concealed behind a bush jerked the cord to release the clap net, which held him captive. The One-Eyed's hind claw missed the decoy-bird, a bullfinch, but so great was the terror of the little bird that it fell into a swoon, and hung by one frail leg from its foul perch. The netter, an unshaven and insignificant individual, who worked for a maculate Yiddish "birdfancier" in Whitechapel, ran forward to see what strange thing was struggling in his net. It was a bird with a single eye, fiercer than any he had seen before, with yellow legs trousered with feathers, gripping the meshes by sharp black claws. The sight made him imagine that it was a rare kind of parrot escaped from a cage, and he thought of a reward.

He was afraid to take it in his hand, and went back to his hiding-place behind a willow stole to fetch the sacking with which he covered the cages when he travelled—for magistrates had been known to fine trappers the sum of half a crown for breaking the law that protected the nation's wild songsters from ravagement by mercenary wretches.

He had two cages, of wood and iron wire, nine inches long, five inches wide, and eight inches high. He had twelve linnets and two goldfinches in one and nine chaffinches in the other, all struggling to escape, clawing one another, beating wings and pushing bloodied beaks through the bars to find a way to the wandering air and the thistleheads.

He knelt by the net through which the falcon was trying to thrust himself with foot and pinion. He smothered him with the sacking, and lifted the cane hoop of the net. The talons of one foot pierced the sacking and the skin of the thumb of the dirty hand pressing upon it, but the netter, thinking of his luck and determined not to lose the "parrot," held on. The thorn-prick tightened, and was as the piercing of steel fish-hooks. He threw the other piece of sacking over the head, grasped it firmly, released the hold of his other hand, and sought to draw the bird from the net.

But The One-Eyed was held to the net by his clutch on the sacking through the meshes. He threshed so powerfully with his wings that the netter became afraid and tried to smother him in the covering by which he held his head. To do this he had to shift his hold, and immediately he did so The One-Eyed bit him in the index finger, breaking the nail. In pain the man snatched away his hand, bringing the beak near his face. The One-Eyed struck with a taloned foot at his ear, and clenched; at the same time he nicked with his beak and ripped the flesh under the cheekbone. The man shut his eyes, threw away the bird, and hid his face in his arms; then blundering to his feet he ran to his hiding-place, his boots snapping and tearing the meshes of his net. He kicked over one of the cages, and the door opened, releasing linnets and goldfinches, which fluttered away with sweet twitters of joy. The chaffinches remained, however, and eventually they were taken to an East-end slum, where some were blinded with red-hot needles to make their song brighter, where their feather-colours faded, and where those that did not die of a broken heart (being older birds) lived in tiny cages and ate seed and sang and sang and sang to blackened heaven.

For a week more The One-Eyed remained near London, and during that time he hunted a stretch of the Thames some miles above Richmond, where among the reeds of the eyots thousands of swallows were gathered for the autumnal migration. There was another bird preying upon the pilgrims, a bird swift as the peregrine, and very much like him in shape, but smaller. He weighed nine ounces. The stranger was about twelve inches long, with white neck and chin and black cheeks; he had a yellowish-white breast streaked broadly with brown, and his back was the colour of dark slate. He had the magnificent eyes of the noble falcons, the bluish curved beak with the notch, and yellow skin, or cere, round its base. He used to dash into the twittering clouds of swallows and seize one. Sometimes the chosen bird dodged him, but the little pirate, who was one of

448

the rare hobby falcons, would follow its every twist and turn and tumble until with a sudden stroke he caught it. The peregrine's way was not the hobby's way, for when he missed his swallow in the first swoop he used to leave it, and pursue another.

One afternoon as he was flying over Richmond Bridge he saw a long formation of birds in the air about a mile from him. The formation was constantly changing. As the birds wheeled in unison their broad wings made the flight like an eyebrow above the horizon; but after the turning movement it became as a string of dust. They were peewits, or green plover, which had come from the snows of Scandinavia to the English autumn ploughlands so rich with worm and grub. The leaders dived soughing over a field, and the birds sank down together. Their plumage was a harmony of tarnished green, black, white, and brown, and each bird had a plume on its poll. They ran to their feeding, all running one way, and suddenly the thousand birds ceased movement, for The One-Eyed was above them.

He stooped, and they took the air. He cut in among them, and missed his bird, for it tumbled out of the air-path of his swoop. He looped and cut at it again, and it fled before him, twisting and tumbling, the spread tips of its flight quills making a gruff noise. Four times the peregrine slid down in his half-point at the plover, and then he gave up the chase and followed another bird. This was one of the season's youngsters, and it was not so quick at twisting as an old bird. It was struck underneath by the tiercel who had turned on his back, and the two hind-talons ripped half the feathers from its breast. The wings became workless, and as it dropped limp it was clutched and borne to the middle of the field, and eaten.

For several days the swallows, gathered in the river eyots, made their false starts in migration, and every hour new wanderers from the north joined the excited throng. The red sun going down in the west made them strangely agitated, and one morning when the life-giver came up beyond the sea at the Thames mouth they were gone.

The One-Eyed had set out on a journey before them—over

the sea, over land and air which was lit and buffeted down one corridor of its breadth by immense concussions, filled with strange hissings and whinings, and glowing at night, a livid wound—the trench line between the Belgian coast and the Swiss mountains. Flying South, the tiercel entered the valley of a great river, ending in hundreds of square miles of reeds, waterways, and marshes, where flamingoes stood—over another sea, and strange forests and mountains and rivers—deserts of ribbed sand and strange brown birds difficult to see until his eye became used to the bright light—south he flew over Africa, and onwards over the lonely seas, scanning the sky for a wing-flicker like his own. He did not return to the Devon headland of his birth until he had girdled the earth in flight.

One night, when out of the brands on the hearth arise antlers and wings and talons of flame, and the roar of the Atlantic is carried up the valley by the wind mumbling in the chimney, and the pots of ale are warm by the fire, I will tell you of what befell his home-coming.

4

A roaring westerly wind came over the Atlantic, scattering a spray from the crests of the green rollers and rushing up the face of the precipice. Gulls perched on the ledges of the cliff had only to launch themselves forward into the uptrend in order to reach the swarded lip above, but their movements were clumsy. Usually they were masters of wind, but to-day a gale was blowing, and they were whirled and buffeted and tossed like the dry brown heads of old sea-pinks in the crevices around them.

But to the blast and rush of the gale Chakchek the One-Eyed was indifferent. Three thousand feet over the Devon promontory he hung, wings curved slightly backwards; sometimes those wings twinkled; he was a black star in the wind on which, six days before, he had swept from Labrador to England.

His eye regarded all below him: the three rabbits venturing forth from the bonded stone wall, the raven behind it standing in the furrows turned that morning, the finch striving vainly to fly into the wind, the yelping gulls, the oyster-catchers perched on the rocks. At three thousand feet he was anchored, this tiercel, or male peregrine falcon, contemptuous of the gusts, contemptuous of the raven, the gulls, the rabbits, scornful of every living thing: head of the ancient and noble house of Chakchek, haughtiest falcons in the West Country; the One-Eyed, who ranged the airways above Exmoor and the Severn Sea; who fled at will along the Atlantic seaboard from Skomer to Tintagel; who raced over to Lundy because he fancied the blood of a sea-parrot; Chakchek the unmated, Chakchek the outlaw. Hark to the Saga of Chakchek the One-Eyed!

In the wind was he fixed, watching the land far below, unmoving, his eye fiercely beautiful, his blue notched beak pointing downwards. The wind hummed past his taut pinions, thrummed in his stiff tail; there was he fixed—but now the wind shrieked by those compressed feathers, he was falling, falling; the greensward rushed upwards, and he cried out aloud for the very sweetness of life. The linnet that was struggling in the wind collapsed as the shrill cry dropped to a chromatic whine below it. The tiercel had missed by seven inches, and the linnet was saved; but so agitated was the tiny bird's heart that it fell quivering into a gorse bush, gaping and gasping. As for Chakchek, he was three thousand feet above the headland, having swooped up in a great curve.

The large sensitive eye responded to the slightest movement. Something Chakchek must have seen from the rear corner of it, for with racing sweeps he climbed to an altitude of six thousand feet—invisible from below. Once more he was anchored, then slipping across the blue sky in a slightly slanting line.

He had seen the pigeons wheeling above Scarnell Court, a white house ten miles away, and standing in a wood on the slope of the river. One hundred seconds passed, and he was

451

half-way over the lonely sandhills and the wastes of the Burrows. Above the ribs of wrecked boats embedded in the flats he passed, losing height as he swept downward like a hissing and shankless anchorhead of iron. One hundred and fifty seconds, and now he was passing a train and its tiny string of white steam, as it crawled beside the estuary and its fawn sandbanks. Two hundred and eighty seconds, and the pigeons saw what was hurtling upon them; they scattered like torn paper thrown to the wind; the terror was above them, and falling vertically in the grand stoop. The feather-scream of the tiercel rose in pitch; at over two hundred miles an hour he fell. Now the pigeons were dashing into the trees, all except one that was neck-limp and clutched in the tiercel's talons; now an old gentleman, dozing in a chair on the lawn below, was alarmed by the blood-splashes that appeared suddenly on his book.

The old man peered upwards, but saw nothing; for Chakchek was hidden by the gables of the house, upon the roof of which he plucked and ate the pigeon, leaving a complete skeleton near a skylight four minutes later. Then once more he was a speck in the sky, racing eastwards. Only when the red sun was sinking into a wild ocean that winter afternoon did he return to the headland, having arrived there after roving in a course of nearly four hundred miles; and he brought with him a mate to be mother of Chakcheks, having found her in the great forest of Savernake, near Marlborough. She was a daughter of that branch of the Chakcheks which had bred for centuries in the spire of Salisbury Cathedral, that glorious work of God in man.

Days of rain and frost passed away, the larks sang over the oat-blades growing on the stony fields of the headland, and The One-Eyed was happy. He and the mate, who was larger than himself, swept the sky from dawn till sunset, and when the evening star was silver in the west they returned to the precipice, closing their pinions and plunging past the gulls to Bone Ledge, the eyrie above the Cave of Seals.

One morning as they hung aloft a bird with broad brown wings sailed over their heads, and from it came a mewling cry.

Chakchek cocked his head, and the one eye glittered. The falcon appeared oblivious of the thing above—it was not her affair.

The buzzard belonged to the same family as the falcon, but the relationship was distant. He had no tooth, or notch, in his beak; an ignoble fellow that fed on the creeping things of the earth—beetles, rabbits, snakes, rats, mice, and even worms. In the lower air he was the sport of gulls, flapping like an owl with his clumsy wings. But in the high freeness his flight was superb; he could soar away tranquil hours without a wing-beat; not for him the fever and the restlessness of a peregrine's life. *Hissh*—he rocked on his back, striking upwards with heavy claws. The One-Eyed swerved in his stoop and shot a hundred feet below him; climbed again and dashed at the intruder. The buzzard, who had only been calling for his mate to join him in peaceful contemplation of the green sea and blue shadows, was sent into a terrified fluster. At every swoop he cried out, losing height all the time, until he was driven half-way to the mainland, where Kronk the raven usually made his nest. Here Chakchek left him, and before he went back he stooped at Kronk, but changed his mind abruptly and returned to the precipice.

The buzzard flapped away from the harsh oaths of Kronk and his wife, and when they were tired of trying to pull out his tail feathers, a dozen gulls took up the pursuit. Over the mainland they abandoned him, and a tomtit as big as a mouse pursued him; serenely the buzzard sailed down the valley to his treetop castle in the pinewood.

Chakchek glided a mile in thirty-eight seconds and found the mate still poised. He joined her, chattering shrilly a greeting. Suddenly she swung away, and commenced to climb. Chakchek followed. Into a cloud they flew, bursting through the vapour to see the blue sky above them. Higher and higher they mounted, Chakchek feeling the strings of his heart vibrating with a radiant warmness. Soon the headland lay below them very small, with brown and green patches, divided by dark stone walls, and edged with white foam. From this loftiness mortal eye could have perceived no life,

453

discerned no movement, but the one eye of Chakchek saw every gull, every jade-black shag squatting on their rock beneath the cliff; it saw the head of Jarrk the seal filling its lungs before diving again for conger eel, and the motionless humans lying at the precipice edge. Higher they climbed, till they could see the mountains of Wales across the Severn Sea, to the north, and southwards the tors of Dartmoor: beyond, to the English Channel and a blue line that might have been France.

The pinions of the mate ceased to strike the air. She drew them into her sides, and fell. Chakchek followed; she rolled over and faced him; he touched her beak with his, and they snapped together—never had there been such rapture in his heart. Madly towards the headland they dashed, kissing and chattering. The girl and her companion lying on the sward heard the hissing of their descent, and jumped up, shouting. Down, down, down the falcons whirled; every gull yelped and seemed to fade away into the rocky sides of the cliff; the girl clutched the boy, for surely the falcons were going to tear them: *hiss-s-h*, they swerved and with barred wings and blue backs flashed past, surely to be killed on the grey boulders below—but no, they were flying rapidly out to sea. Then they turned and rushed back, twirling round one another, and uttering all the time their sweet-shrill cries of love.

"There will be eggs in the nest before long," said the boy. "Do you remember how we climbed for that heron's nest last year?"

The girl nodded. She had long black hair, and her eyes were brown and gentle.

"But, Howard, by the time they lay, the hols. will be over, and I shall be back at the convent."

"Well, I'll watch them and guard it from collectors, and go down when they're hatched and bag one. Then when you come back I'll have it trained."

"How lovely!" cried the girl, her eyes in excitement suddenly auburn like the field behind the bonded stone wall. "Look, look!" she pointed.

An oyster-catcher—a creature with long crimson beak and pied wings—had been flying unconcernedly from Morte Point.

The falcons half a mile high were apparently annoyed, for both swept down: The One-Eyed arrived first, and the puff of feathers was hardly scattered before the broken thing was lying in the water, and they were gone. As the boy and the girl looked a fish rose and seized it and once more the ocean was calm under the April sun.

The sea-pinks came out, and the gulls too began to sit. Chakchek was happy. One late May morning, as he dropped from the sky to Bone Ledge with a rock-dove in his claws, he was amazed by the curious attitude of his mate. She was standing over the three reddish-brown eggs, her head turned to one side, very still. Chakchek ran to her, and listened. Faintly within one shell there was the sound of feeble tapping. He peered with his one eye. Tap-tip.

Chakchek had been born on Bone Ledge two years before, and this was his first mating. Rapture at the sound overcame him, and he danced. Then he went quite close to the mate and fondled her beak with his, and spoke to her tenderly. After kissing her several times—he did this by snapping the upper mandible of his bill with hers, inverting his head to do so—he fed her, as she nestled over the eggs, with morsels from the dead rock-dove. He displayed the same tenderness all the afternoon, and at six o'clock one nestling was free of the encumbering shell. In a frail voice it said its name was Wizzle.

To celebrate the wonder, Chakchek had a fight with Kronk, nearly impaling himself on the raven's beak in his jubilance. Then he dashed at the shags perched upon their family rock, causing them to dive into the water. Afterwards he brought many rock-pipits, finches, doves and little auks to Bone Ledge, to ensure that his first-born should not die of hunger.

The mate was several seasons old, and had had as many broods, although all of them had been destroyed. Chakchek had not had her experience, and only realised after tearing up seven birds that one nestling did not require so many, nor could it tear them itself, but required minute morsels. Chakchek was amused by the downy thing, and tried to squeak to it in return; at which the mate kissed him and preened his pinion

455

feathers, then shivered her own as though she too were little, and required feeding. Immediately Chakchek brought morsels for her, which she swallowed while rapturously kissing the squeaker. Oh, they loved each other, Chakchek the One-eyed and his mate; and they loved more than ever when another squeaker was out of a red-brown shell.

When they were three days old, the tiercel took over the duties of brooding, and the falcon brought plucked and skinned birds to him. Every evening the pair flew a mile above Baggy Point, to fall wing-tumbled and swooping. Once they saw two immense birds flying high over them with stretched necks and white wings. They were a mile higher than themselves, wild swans from whom came a flourish of silver-trumpet notes. Chakchek did not attack them; they were nowhere near Bone Ledge.

During June, and both birds were busy from dawn till sunset. The mate did the hunting, bringing birds and calling *way-ee* to Chakchek, who answered her and slipped off to take in mid-air the food she brought. The two eyesses had grown considerably, and their wing-feathers were sprouting from grey quills. Many times during the day The One-eyed called for food, *way-ee, way-ee*, just like a gull. When it came he yapped to the fledgelings to make them eat the faster.

Usually when the falcon uttered the food cry, he flew out and took the prey from her in the air; but sometimes she brought it, often headless—so terrible her kill—to the eyrie. Chakchek distributed mouthfuls of feathers first, then pieces of flesh. Large lumps he swallowed himself. The eyesses swallowed most of the bones, and the legs as well. They fought, and had many tugging matches for legs and feathers. When they were no longer hungry, their crops bulged. Wizzle, first-born and tiercel, was half the size of his sister. Bone Ledge became littered with wings of rock-doves and partridges, little auks, oyster-catchers, lapwing, kestrel, and wild duck. Besides these were dozens of small aluminium rings stamped with letters and numbers, of racing pigeons from the loft of Scarnell Court.

Sir Godfrey, first ("war mushroom") baronet, a retired profiteer, was not an amiable man even when he endeavoured to be specially pleasant to anyone, and it was often said in Barum that the only things he cared about were his pigeons. Day after day he waited with a twelve-bore gun in order to shoot the raiding falcon.

Day after day she mounted high above the headland, and saw the summer vapour lying over the Santon Burrows, and beyond, the Long Bridge of Bideford and its slow human traffic. But her interest lay eastwards, towards the hillside village of St. Brannocks, and miles onwards, the masts of ships on the stocks at the old port of Barum. The falcon would glide across the sky, so high as to be invisible from the earth, and fall with her shattering stoop. Regularly every morning she took a pigeon from Scarnell.

Sir Godfrey Crawdelhook talked with his head keeper, and asked him if he had any suggestions to make about the means of destroying the raider. The keeper mentioned gins; then said that the best way was to find the eyrie, wait above it, and shoot the old birds as they returned.

"And where is the eyrie?" demanded his master irritably.

"Maybe on Lundy, zur. They be master-birds fur roving!"

The attention of both men was drawn to the disturbance of the pigeons above them. They held their guns in readiness. Infinitely high in the sky a sharp black speck was seen. This time Chakchek was coming. With terrified wingbeats the racing pigeons made for the shelter of the trees; but Chakchek was a precise judge of movement. He was moving as well. At a steady ninety miles an hour he had flown downwind, over the Taw, then he closed wings and dropped head-first. From a height of ten thousand feet he fell to the treetops in a little over thirty-five seconds. He saw only the pigeon he had marked, and knew that he could get it—then the air rocked around him with four claps of thunder. Chakchek lost control, turned a somersault, and recovered, to see two men waving their arms and to hear them shouting. He saw the pigeon disappear into the house.

So he followed and snatched it as it bumped into a bookcase, smashing the glass. A cat leapt at him as he flew out of the door, and something was flung at him. Chakchek flew up with the pigeon, just as Sir Godfrey's gun was fired through Sir Godfrey's own window.

A week later Chakchek and the mate went together to Barum. For a while they hung over the Square, watching the horses, the motor-cars, and the people below. It was Friday, the market-day, and the town was crowded. Howard was there, and he saw them. He thought of going to the headland with The Tiger, an old fisherman who had known the cliffs from boyhood—a fearless climber. Howard desired a peregrine eyess for a pet. He would fly it at duck during the winter and train it to retrieve its kill. The sight of the birds watching the town thrilled him so that he determined to go with Tiger on the morrow. He would be going up to Oxford shortly; he would take the peregrine with him! Even as he watched the peregrines turned, and swept away westwards.

No pigeons were visible around the house of Sir Godfrey Crawdelhook. Falcon and tiercel dropped to a height of four hundred feet. Nothing stirred.

Half a minute later a pigeon started to run across the lawn. Chakchek scrutinised its peculiar movements. It flapped its wings, flew up clumsily, and the falcon stooped. Chakchek remained still, ready to stoop if the falcon missed. Now she was very small below him. The pigeon flapped desperately, and the falcon had caught it. Chakchek called to her, and dived to the house-roof, where she bore her catch, and commenced to tear it, standing on it to do so.

Inside the house, Sir Godfrey chuckled as he wound in the snapped thread of black cotton.

Upon the roof Chakchek contentedly watched the falcon. The sun was warm, and the sky was a royal blue. Three swifts passed with shrill cried by them, and he cocked his one eye at them. He began to preen his feathers.

The falcon stopped eating, and drew back from the dying pigeon. She turned her head towards Chakchek, and uttered a frail whisper. He went to her, distressed. Her beak opened, and she panted, her throat throbbing. Over her liquid eyes the nictitating membranes were repeatedly drawn. She walked backwards unsteadily, all the time whispering (she remembered her young), followed by the tiercel. Once she fell over, but struggled to her feet and walked on.

With cries of anguish Chakchek flew up, imploring her to follow. With violent wing-beats she managed to clear the coping of the building, but she flew in curious zig-zags, like one of the snipe that Chakchek had often seized along the shores of the estuary. He screamed as two men appeared below. The falcon was flapping wildly. Chakchek called to her, but she was unheeding. With a queer spinning movement she reached the lawn below, beating her wings.

For ten minutes they stood and watched her struggles, while from above Chakchek beseeched her to fly to him. She reared herself on her tail, and lay back on her wings, menacing the men with yellow feet ready to tear and blue beak ready to rend. She tried to answer Chakchek, but no sound would come.

"She'll die as soon as we give her water," said Sir Godfrey, "and it's the falcon, too. The tiercel will feed the youngsters, so we'll get him next."

The falcon was gasping, for she was getting feebler. A small chirruping came from her, and Chakchek heard. Round and round the lawn he flew, just out of gunshot, his flight no longer swift and dashing and proud, but laboured like that of a buzzard in distress.

The keeper went away, and returned with a shallow trough and a can of water. He filled it, placed it near the mother-bird, and withdrew. She flopped forward, and drank; wildly she beat her wings; she twitched and gaped; wildly she called to Chakchek; a convulsion passed over her, and she was dead.

Sir Godfrey picked her up and carried her into a greenhouse to put her on a shelf where she would be safe from blowflies until sent to the taxidermist.

The keeper got his gun, thinking that he would shoot the tiercel. He had hardly gone, leaving his master in the conservatory, when Chakchek, recovering his old dash, swept after the falcon. Seeing him, Sir Godfrey shouted, dropped the poisoned bird, and hid his face in his arms. Attracted by the shout, the keeper came back, entered, and shut the door. Chakchek was a prisoner.

"Mind your eyes, zur," he cried; "master bird fur clitching anyone. Come this way, zur. Us can slip out of the door and leave un trapped."

Chakchek flew agitatedly inside the greenhouse, knocking over several pots, and bumping into the glass. The falcon was lying on the concrete floor; he went to her, fondled her bill, but there was no response. In a little voice he spoke to her, caressing her, and making a pathetic attempt to preen her pinion feathers—as of old in the sunshine on Bone Ledge he had done.

The men returned, Sir Godfrey in a fencing mask and gauntlets, the other with a sack tied round his head and another in his hands. Sir Godfrey held a tennis racket, and with it he stunned Chakchek.

"He's got a blind eye," he said, holding the tiercel in his left hand. "Well, we'll soon even things up."

He took something from his pocket, laid the bird against his thigh, and bent over.

"Shall I wring his neck, zur?" asked the keeper a minute later, holding Chakchek, now a struggling bundle of sinews and piercing talons, in the sack.

Sir Godfrey laughed.

"It's only got a taste of what it's done to my pigeons. Besides," he laughed cynically, "it will be interesting from a scientific point of view to see how it gets on. Let it go."

So Chakchek was released, and he flew up into the sky. Higher and higher he towered, while the lark-song faded and the sounds below became murmurous and then silent—even the far wash of the sea that he loved so well. Perhaps he flew upwards because in his pain some dim instinct told him that he would find the falcon in the solitudes of heaven, near the life-giving sun, even beyond, where it was very quiet and peaceful. The air was chilly, and Chakchek flew above the airlines of migration, those uncharted tracks of the winged hosts passing in spring and autumn; up and up he flew. In the thin windless air his pinions beat faster, and then they ceased. His towering (which was the sunward flight of a dying bird) was ended. He gave a cry, and fell, but not in the old proud battle swoop.

Sometimes the head pointed to the earth, sometimes the feet, sometimes a swaying pinion—a scarecrow of a bird. Nothing heeded it as it neared the earth. Into the Santon Burrows the loose body flopped, and rolled down a sandhill, among the bleached skulls of rabbits from which spilled runlets of sand, coming to rest among the empty shells of snails. Whilom the proudest of all living creatures, swiftest rover of the airways, tender lover and faithful father—thus died Chakchek the Blind.

5

Far away over the western sea a star flickered, like a gold falcon flying in the dark. Perhaps it was the god of all the hawks, giving rest to the spirits broken from feathered bodies by men with shot, gin, and poisoned lure. Wizzle of the Chakcheks saw it—the nestling who at that hour should have been sleeping warm and hugged by brooding parent. His sister lay quiet beside him, her head resting on a rusty-brown egg.

The star hung over Lundy, midway between the two lighthouses. The flickering gold of its flashes seemed to tremble and beat like the wings of a faithful guardian watching in the night. A sound came from the fledgeling's throat, a sound between a chirrup and a whimper. He was crying to the star. The cry was no longer lusty, as it had been all the previous day, when he and his sister had waited for their parents to drop down the cliff face to Bone Ledge, bringing food. Neither falcon nor tiercel had come, although they had cried *way-ee, way-ee,* always *way-ee, way-ee.* Mewliboy the buzzard had flapped past quickly, Kronk the raven after him, but they had brought no food. Wizzle had opened his sharp beak and uttered his wailing cries; and now he chirruped to the star.

Two hundred feet below Bone Ledge, Atlantic waves slid over the black rocks and rolled the big pebbles of the cove with the roar of high tide. Wizzle's head drooped, and he lay in sleep on the neck of his sister. When he looked up the star was flown, and the sea was wan. Gulls were drifting by Bone Ledge, floating on the uptrends of wind. Their sad cries filled the air of the curved precipice. The nestling crouched lower, cold, shivering, uncomforted.

Jarrk the seal slipped from his rock in the cave, and swam to the open sea to dive for bass and conger. Oylegrin the shag began to preen green-black feathers with oil applied by the long hooked beak from the pouch on his back. The pale light grew paler, and a sailing ship was seen. Oylegrin flew across the waves, and with a splash settled on the water, presently bobbing under to chase a fish.

When the sun had climbed the hills of the mainland the sea was calm and smooth, but not so blue as the clear sky that seemed to join it beyond the sailing ship. The shag returned to his rock, no longer hungry, and squatted with four other shags and a cormorant. Kronk the raven flew inland to Deadsheep Gully, where he might glut himself and bring back a full beak and craw for his children who could not yet fly. Far away in the sandhills two sexton beetles were beginning their compassionate labours beneath the cold clay of the tiercel, and ants were exploring the empty orbits. And further still, a bluebottle, woken from its wall-sleep by the sun, was buzzing round the skinned corpse of the falcon.

Sea-pinks grew from a crack in Bone Ledge, stirred by the breeze. Wizzle looked up, but his larger sister lay quiet, her legs behind her. He saw a slim brown bird that passed two hundred yards away, its pointed wings throwing warm, yellow-ruddy colour back to the sun. Strengthened by the sight, Wizzle stood on weak legs and called the food cry, a plaintive and feeble *way-ee*, and began to rake over the picked skeletons of pigeons and rock-dove, oyster-catcher, pipit, and puffin. There were kestrel wings as well, joined by their bones, white and frayed and nicked, for most members of the Chakchek family kill the smaller brown mousing windhover, or kestrel.

One of the skeletons was a week old, all that remained of Mousing Keekee's mate.

It was Mousing Keekee who had just flown by Bone Ledge. She was sad, for she had lost mate and children. A week ago, crouching beside a gorse bush, she had heard his screams and watched his tumbles and wild wingbeats as Chakchek stooped at him. He had been struck down, the falling body had been clutched as it fell, and been taken away to the tiercel's plucking rock. Wizzle and his sister had swallowed many mouthfuls of his feathers and flesh. And when Keekee the widow returned to her young in the old lichen-grown magpie nest in the salt-blasted blackthorn brake, they were gone. She cried for them in her plaintive voice all the morning, but there was no answer. For that robber, Kronk, who had lived on the headland longer than any other living thing, had stolen them. He had seen them from the air as he returned from Deadsheep Gully. He cared nothing for any Chakchek, having fought with them many times each year for over a century.

Scores of Kronk's children had been poisoned, trapped, caged, and shot; the headland birds and beasts believed him to be immortal. He had declared himself to be god—the god of black magic, which nothing could poison, shoot or trap. He had sucked thousands of eggs, filched thousands of nestlings, picked out the eyes of hundreds of lambs, of rabbits in gins, of fat sheep on their woolly backs, of dead sailors left by the tide on the shore from Harty Light to the Morte. As a young bird, he had seen beacons kindled on all the hills when Napoleon was taken. His dirty old feathers were full of fleas, his eyes were gummy, he was partially bald, and his feet were knobbed with corns.

Once when a brood of his was taken by The Tiger, he followed with his wife to their cottage inland, and tore at the thatch, banged at the door, killed a tom-cat with a blow of his beak, and led the fledgelings away. It was after this encounter with man that he had declared himself to be mightier than death, that thing dealt by man, and therefore to be god.

Kronk was king of the Corvidæ—the Crow family—and the

original owners of the nest, a pair of cunning magpies, were relatives of his. Knowing his ways, these magpies had built the nest with a heap of thorns on top, to protect their eggs and young. But the storms of winter had blown the cover away, and when the following year the kestrel laid her eggs and hatched them there, Mousing Keekee's infants were exposed. So Mousing Keekee lost them, and all the morning flew about disconsolate, yelping for her little fluffy-white babes to answer her, and so to change the pain in her heart to warm joy. For three days she pined, once visiting the nest of Mewliboy the buzzard just to see a nestling. She perched on the edge of the mass of twigs, sheep's wool, green leaves and rotting rats' tails, and spoke to the nestlings. They were fighting over a young rabbit, and ignored her. She flew away, and hovered over a barley field for the sight of a field mouse, but, being restless, swept away with the warm upper wind blowing from the mainland.

Now Wizzle saw her as for a moment she floated past Bone Ledge, her wings flickering a brown-yellow as they caught the morning sun. His food cry, learned from the One-Eyed his father, who so often had called it to the falcon whenever she was late, trembled from Bone Ledge. On thin legs he tottered about, biting a pink flower of sea-thrift and swallowing it. *Way-ee, way-ee*, he wailed, and retched, ejecting the flower head. Slowly, with a peculiar flight that seemed almost laboured, Mousing Keekee flapped to the eyrie and hovered about three feet from it, her tail depressed and legs hanging loosely. She regarded the starving aristocrats. Wizzle and his sister swayed and beat fluffy wings, beaks wide open, eyes large and hunger-staring, chirruping for food. Mousing Keekee alighted on Bone Ledge timidly. Her back was a chestnut brown streaked with black. She had the tooth or notch in her beak—mark of the noble branch of the Falconidæ race, and distinguishing them from the baser hawks—and a yellow patch of bare skin round the lead-coloured beak. Her eyes were deep brown, with soft blue-black pupils.

She stood on Bone Ledge and stared nervously, then seized a wing of a skeleton in her left foot, and pulled at the feathers, as though she would feed them. She ceased, and with a dainty movement launched herself into the air, passing to her beak the wings so loosely joined, and dropped them. The remains of her mate—for his spirit used to animate and employ those bone-linked pinions—spun slowly and lightly to the sea, to be swallowed by Garbargee the conger eel.

Three minutes later Mousing Keekee was leaning her breast to the wind, which buoyed her up. Her tail, barred with black, was spread and depressed, catching the air; her wings were outspread, and in a steady wind they were adjusted by slight lift and drop to keep her always leaning forward. Sometimes in a moment's lull, they were beaten rapidly, not with the thrusting stroke of forward movement, but with a vertical fanning motion. Her head was bent downwards; her yellow feet tucked back; she was twenty yards above the green barley. She looked at nothing, because her sight was fixed to observe any movement. After several seconds, she swung round and glided downwind a hundred and fifty yards, luffing into the breeze again, adjusting her weight so that it was balanced by the wind on the exact centre of her breast; and watched. She was now poised above the long slope that led down to the cliff edge, sward broken by stunted furze, bracken and bramble, and scarred in long lines by sheep-paths.

Something moved in a patch of old brown bracken, and she slipped down to within seven feet of the ground. Rapid beat of wings; descending another foot; then a drop to the ground, and a baby rabbit seized in the black talons. It squealed, but the sharp, hooked beak broke into the base of the skull, and the head was limp. It was borne to Bone Ledge.

Wizzle screamed and staggered forward with his sister. Many flies were buzzing about Bone Ledge, attracted by smell to lay their eggs. The birds themselves did not possess any sense of smell. The sister grabbed the rabbit and hopped away with it, while Wizzle seized a foot in his beak and tugged. The sister lay back, and Keekee watched them, then flew away.

She glided a quarter of a mile towards the mainland, swung round, and luffed into the wind. A Greater Black-backed Gull, passing overhead, slid down with a hoarse cursing noise and stooped at her, his beak open to peck. She avoided him; he reversed and continued the bullying for three minutes, and at each rush Keekee moved sideways and he blundered below her. The gull's name was Nugg, and he swallowed young rabbits whole whenever he caught them. His spread wings spanned nearly six feet. Nugg was one of the four members of his species that nested on the headland; owing to egg-collectors, they did not increase. Nugg bullied all the Falconidæ he met —but he had never met anything larger than Mewliboy and Chakchek. Nugg and Kronk, the raven, ignored each other; Nugg claimed everything floating on water, and Kronk claimed everything on land. Only once had they fought, over the body of a whale left by the tide, but there had been enough for two, and after exchange of the vilest oaths, Kronk had begun at the head and Nugg at the tail.

During the next half hour Keekee took three sun beetles and a tiny mouse to Bone Ledge. Wizzle and his sister were still tugging at the rabbit; one hind leg was down Wizzle's throat. He disgorged it to take the mouse, and his sister began to tear the rabbit's skull, swallowing fur and bone. Screaming, Wizzle took the beetles from Keekee's beak, gulped them down, and then seized her shoulder. Keekee cried and flapped her wings, but the starving tiercel hung on, only letting go when he remembered the rabbit.

Two herring gulls deliberately went out of their course to harry Keekee some minutes later, but she patiently slipped from their rushes, and at last flew away, luffing into the wind a mile from Bone Ledge. She caught two more beetles—with shining blue-green shards, or wing covers—and swallowed them.

Clakkilad the little stonechat saw her, and after a wild alarm to his wife darted into the brambles where was their nest and never moved so much as an eye during the two hundred and eight seconds that Keekee hung four feet above, watching. Clakkilad's heart beat under his coppery feathers so fast that when the danger was over, he gaped for some seconds and could not move, and with dropped wings quivered among the brambles. But this happened a dozen times every day, and each time his mate—hidden deep in the bush—spoke tenderly to

466

the gallant Clakkilad, and comforted him. Always he recovered his nerve before the kestrel had swung up into her next wind-mooring; and, perched on a dead bramble, rattled defiance to everything—everything distant.

Every dawn the foster-mother appeared at the eyrie. She did not brood the eyesses or young peregrine falcons, because they were too big and fierce for her. They never received enough food, and so could never sleep the entire night. They swallowed about one quarter of the food they needed. Mice, beetles, and moths were the principal catch of the kestrel; and small birds and young rabbits were sometimes brought. Wizzle and his sister tore them up and ate every part—skull and feet, legs, feathers, fur, tail and entrails. Once Keekee brought a tailless lizard that had been sunning itself in the furze; the lizard shed its tail with fear; Wizzle gulped it down. On several occasions Keekee brought worms and butterflies. Everything was eaten. Keekee grew thinner; a strained look came on her face.

Scarl the Baseborn, the carrion crow, having had his mate shot way inland by a gamekeeper, and his young destroyed, came to the headland to see what he could sneak from any-thing or anybody, what smaller animal or bird he could pick or batter to death. Whenever Scarl the Baseborn saw Keekee, he called in his coarse bass voice, *krok-krok-krok-r*, and pestered her for long periods of time. He followed her to Bone Ledge and returned when she was away, alighting confidently on the rock and walking towards the eyesses. He was met with hisses of furious hate, and cursed with throat-noises like blunt metal drills turning on basalt. He was struck at by talons thrust forward by Wizzle and his sister lying back with wide beaks; so he hopped off, and joined seven herring gulls annoying Mewliboy the buzzard, who protested with usual wails.

Bone Ledge became foul, and restless flies pestered the eyesses, who learned to catch them by snapping. In their hunger they tore all the flowerheads of thrift, swallowing them only to disgorge immediately. Other things they disgorged—pellets about an inch long and a quarter of an inch wide, but the blowflies were not attracted by these strange things, because they were made of fur and feather, bones, skulls, and blue and green beetle shards—all clean and freed of flesh. A small kind of fly, however, used to lay her eggs on them, and soon afterwards little white maggots hatched in the sun and bored into the greyish mass. These pellets, or castings, were moist, easily crumbled, and sometimes shapeless; and this moistness was a sign of ill-health, for a strong tiercel throws up his castings dry and of regular size—which means proper and sufficient nourishment, and therefore full power of hunt.

The castings of Keekee changed; they became loose and moist. She had no time to preen herself, and became drab; her pinion feathers were frayed at the end, and lost their lustre. She grew thinner, and her eyes seemed to be more prominent. Many times a day she returned without food, so anxious was she about the welfare of the orphans. Wizzle had more vitality than his sister, who became languid and did not wail so loudly or so often for food. Never once did their crops bulge in their necks; never once during the whole ten days that Keekee hunted for them—the crops that should have bulged at least five times every day. Standing weakly on his feet, Wizzle looked like an ancient moulting bird that had lived for years in some town cage or zoo; like an old bird, pining, broken-hearted, ailing, soon to leave for that shining realm of which unhappy caged birds do dream, where one wing-beat suffices everlastingly for a glide in luminous air.

But Keekee never failed. She was female; she worked for little ones. When poising, the nervous flutter of her wings was required more often than before, because she was lighter on the wind, and her breast was no longer rounded.

Often she was to be seen hovering over a hedge. The hedges of the headland were made of flakes of rock builded up and bonded with earth, and she was watching for something to move again in the tall foxtail grasses and thistles that grew on top. She fluttered her wings more than usual, for she was weary and weak. Her travail had been long. Again she saw a movement, and dropped upon it, her feet spread. She clutched as they touched her prey, which was a rabbit, nearly full grown. The rabbit squealed, and instantly all along the hedge, dull thumpings came from the ground. These were the alarm signals of many rabbits, who thumped with their hind legs. Keekee's talons pierced the young rabbit's skin, and it struggled down the hedge. Bird and animal tumbled four feet together. But Keekee hung on. The rabbit dragged itself among the spare wind-bitten oats, where the first poppies were showing their scarlet spots of colour among the yellow charlock and mauve thistle cardoons.

Now the young rabbit had recently run across the other field, often stopping suddenly to crouch in a quivering silence of terror, although no hawk had been in the sky. This had been caused by the knowledge that Swagdagger was running him. Sometimes he screamed. Swagdagger would pass all other rabbits—he was following the scent of one rabbit.

Swagdagger was a dog stoat, a flat-headed, low-down animal that stank in life with the stinks of death. He was distant by less than a minute's gallop when Keekee's claws pierced the skin of his quarry, and the rabbit squealed in a different way. Swagdagger made a sharp, chattering stutter, and bounded forward, rippled up the wall, nosed around, and rippled down the other side of the wall. In a bare patch of the stony field— where the scythe of the wind had cleared all oaten stems, but not the thistles—he came upon Keekee, standing on the rabbit, beating her wings and pecking the soft base of the skull with black-tipped hook of beak. Swagdagger rushed at her, his sharp teeth bared, and chattering his fiercest battle cries about her blood, her cracked bones, and her death. Keekee flew up, or rather tried to; but she was held by a claw. She lay back, beak open, and grasped the face of Swagdagger in her foot. One black claw sank into the left eye of the stoat, who continued his chatter and bit the foot. He bit four times in less than two seconds, so that two toes were severed from the foot, and the grip on his face fell away. He scratched with his claws, and feathers rolled away from Keekee's breast, dancing lightly over the thistles and the weeds of charlock.

For a time bird and stoat rolled, screamed and chattered, and then they were apart; and Swagdagger was leaping about and trying to shake from his eye a thing that was like a black curved thorn. Keekee flew away with one leg hanging, and whimpering to herself.

Swagdagger's subsequent history may be of brief interest. He was met by Kronk in the neighbourhood of Dead-sheep Gully a week later, and the raven, who disliked all members of the weasel family, without the least hesitation punctured his skull, knocked his head off, and left him to ants and flies.

But all was not well with Keekee, the foster-mother. As she flew, she whimpered to herself, and the toes of her whole foot were drawn together. The other leg hung loosely. A strong breeze was flowing up the precipice, and hundreds of gulls were circling above, wailing their anger and alarm. A thousand feet above the cliff two dark specks moved slowly, while silver cloudlets passed above them to the mainland. Kronk and his wife were watching the work of the humans below. The wounded kestrel cried her anguish when she saw them, and slipped like a sere chestnut leaf-spray to Bone Ledge, where Wizzle sprang up and whimpered for food. His sister seemed to be sleeping, and did not move. Her neck rested on the rusty egg.

Three yards back from the lip of the hole a grey-haired man in a blue guernsey was driving a crowbar slantwise into the sward and the rock it covered. The thuds of the sled rang in the iron. The hammer swinger frowned at the blurred top with fierce and wild blue eyes—this was The Tiger, fisherman and blacksmith, who was born at the headland farm, and knew every ledge and hole of its cliffs. With him was a young man, tall and with broad shoulders, dressed in a white sweater, cord breeches, puttees, and stout nailed boots. Two ropes were coiled on the ground, and he was making the thinner rope fast round his chest with a bowline knot. The Tiger brought down the hammer head with steady force, and each time small empty shells and crab-claws on the sward at the base of the bar jumped and hopped. The men were near a rock pipit's nest, for the bird flitted round them, piping distress. Then Nugg, the Greater Black-backed Gull, swooped down at them, flattening about eight feet over their heads with a soughing of stiff feathers. He swooped again and again, making an angry throaty mutter. Keekee, her maimed leg hanging down, flapped round and round in the bowl of air above the sea, calling in her petulant voice, *kee kee kee kee kee*. Mewliboy soared nearly a mile above them, wailing in his sad tones, *Finish, Finish.*

When the bar was firm as the rock in which it was wedged, The Tiger tied one end of the thicker rope round its base in a bowline knot, and slogged the bar with the hammer to test its firmness. Then the youth slung a wicker fishing creel over his shoulders, and said with a smile,

"Ready?"

"Aiy, aiy, midear!" cried Tiger. "Now, don't ee worry about they old birds. They won't titch ee! They might dive to ee, but they won't clitch on to ee."

In his younger days he had gone down every season for the eyesses, for there was always a gentleman anxious to buy a cast for falconry. Once he had been attacked by a tiercel—it was Chakchek The Eagle-Smiter, Wizzle's great-great-grandfather —that had swooped at him, and every time Tiger watched the bird swooping down at any angle of thirty degrees, he had thought it would hit him and tear away his cheek.

Tiger flung the thick rope over the precipice. Its curls and loops straightened, and a tremor of the bar told that it hung straight. Howard picked it up, and leaning with his weight on his arms, stepped backwards till he came to the ragged lip. Then taking a deep breath and looking resolutely at the sky, he exchanged one handhold for another, and walked backwards into air. Three hundred and ten feet below the sea fretted blue boulders and black rocks, and to the yelps of hundreds of gulls, he started the first yards of his hundred-foot descent to the eyrie. Seabirds were scattered whitely above and below him, blaking in anger and in fear for their speckled young that crouched on nests of seaweed and fishy scales. Kronk dropped to earth, and from a spur of rock two hundred yards away watched the tiny human figure creeping so slowly down the cliff. Keekee fluttered near his head, and stared into his face with her large eyes, coming within five feet of him, and chattering her anguish.

The rock bulged twenty feet above Bone Ledge, and this made it easier for the climber, although the weight of his body was always on his wrists. His face was red and damp, and blood streamed down his left cheek from a gash on the temple. He made a grunting noise that caused Wizzle to lay on his back and to strike upwards with yellow feet and black talons, and to push closer to his sister. Below in the sea, his nose just above water, Jarrk the seal watched something spinning on a rope, slowly. It was seven minutes before Howard, trying to rock himself into a swing, snorting and a-run with sweat, was able to touch Bone Ledge with the toe of his boot.

Bone Ledge was about nine feet from the perpendicular of the rope. Soon the most difficult thing would have to be done— to hold the rope with one hand, and to clutch the ledge with the other; to remain thus; to loosen the handhold of the rope, grip the ledge with both hands, and to clamber on it. Weak fingers meant an awful crash to the boulders two hundred feet below.

Kronk the raven made a quiet, deep croak. He had seen a man fall from Bone Ledge before, and the brain of the man had been good. Kronk squatted on one leg, and with the claw of the other scratched some lice from his neck; he permitted very few sights to interfere with his routine, and he had outworn all excitements.

Hearing the cries of Keekee, he croaked again, and whetted his black four-inch murder-tool of a beak upon the rock. Keekee flew round and round, always crying her anguish, and going quite near to the man who meant harm to her little ones.

Wizzle drew himself up each time the figure grew large, and his fierce eyes blinked as the booted leg thrust away from the ledge. Continually stones and fragments hurled past. At last Howard held the ledge with his hand, hung outwards a minute, seeming to shudder, and quivered as he found himself a foothold below. His eyes were level with Bone Ledge, staring at Wizzle, three feet away. His other hand held the taut rope, which shook to the trembling of his arm. He did not move. Fear had come to him. *Kee kee kee kee kee kee* wailed the wounded kestrel in the sunlit air. *Kronk*, said the raven, serenely, and waited.

Howard heard the low croak, and wished that he had not climbed down the cliff. He knew that he had sufficient strength in reserve to enable him to regain the top, provided that he abandoned at once the idea of getting a young falcon. If he remained as he was, he knew that his reserve of strength would quickly go. His left hand gripped the ledge, or rather the top joints of the fingers of that hand. An insecure foothold relieved a little of the weight that his fingers bore; but the rope, held in his right hand, was pulling him outwards, since the cliff overhung the ledge. He dared not let go the rope; Tiger could not haul him up by the thin safety rope; even if he could, the rope would be frayed through before he reached the top.

He hung there, quivering, blood on his face and knuckles. Here was the longed-for eyrie, with the eyesses almost within reach. Something in the constitution of the youth made him determined to get a falcon, even if he died; and even as he hesitated he thrust the idea of death from his mind. To climb on Bone Ledge he would have to lose his hold of the main rope, which was now taut, and that might mean a swinging out on the thin guide rope tied round his chest, to get it again. That would be possible only if Tiger had made it fast to the crowbar. He drew in a breath, and feverishly thought the beginning of the Lord's Prayer. He was boiling hot. He loosened the hold of his right hand. This was not easy, since the palm was stuck to the rope. He forced his left fingers to cling. Then his right hand was free, and he hung to the ledge. Fortunately the main rope was kept from swinging out by his shoulder. With slow strain he drew himself up, shot forward the left hand, and found a finger-grip. Wizzle bit savagely his hand. Unheeding, he crawled on Bone Ledge, where he lay for five minutes, with shut eyes. Then he sat up, fumbled for his pipe, lit the old dottle therein, and looked around, feeling very happy.

Bone Ledge was about ten feet long, and nearly a yard wide. It sloped inwards at a slight angle. Deliberately he refrained from looking at the eyesses. So keen was his triumph, that he wanted to postpone it. He chuckled to himself; and then was amazed by the behaviour of the kestrel that, for some extraordinary reason, had been flying near his head during the period of the climb down.

The little mouse hawk, after hesitation, lit nervously on the ledge, and he saw that one leg was drawn up into her shabby feathers, that she seemed weak and bedraggled, and that there was bright blood on her neck. She regarded him fixedly, while her wings, dropped by her sides, shivered unceasingly. She made no attempt to fly away, and after some minutes of watching her, Howard turned to explore the eyrie. The kestrel seemed unafraid of him.

He saw pigeon-rings, light rings of aluminium stamped with letters and numbers, dozens of them. He saw also many skeleton feet of pigeons and other birds disgorged with the pellets of bones and feathers. Pink flowers of sea-thrift grew in the dusty crevices of the rock, and there were many carrion flies buzzing about the stench of bones and feathers. Stretching out his hand, he discovered in the heap the wing-bones and primaries of two kestrel hawks. Looking down at the sea, he saw a black shape whose outline grew black as it rose in the green waters. Jarrk broke the surface, stuck out his head, and refilled his lungs. Farther to the left, Howard saw four shags squatting on their favourite rock, never covered by the highest tide. One of them, Oylegrin, was holding out black wings to dry in the sun. He looked partially inebriated, like an old man, with two umbrellas inverted by wind, unable to stagger farther.

Having prolonged the exquisite pleasure of resting and smoking on Bone Ledge, Howard turned to see Keekee still standing there, very quiet, her gaze never moving from his face. He felt a queer sensation; the bird seemed to be suffering all the time; and somehow, he thought, to be asking him to do something for her. He looked at the nestlings. Wizzle stared haughtily; but his breastbone stuck out between meagre feathers. He snapped as Howard picked him up. The youth wondered why he was so light, so thin, and why he had such a

474

drawn look. At this moment, Keekee opened her beak, and screamed weakly at him, and shivered her wings like a little bird hungry. He wondered again at the extraordinary presence of the little falcon, so peculiar in stare, so unusually tame. But he would have to climb back, now that he was rested. He picked up the egg, and shook it, knowing by the sloppy sound that it was infertile, or addled. This he put in his pocket, first wrapping it round with his handkerchief. Then high in the sky he heard a plaintive cry, but it was only a buzzard; and tapping out his pipe, he put it in his pocket, and a set expression came on his face.

Into the creel he put the tiercel, deciding to leave the larger nestling for what he thought would be the distressed parents. Then he grasped the rope, took a deep breath, refrained from looking at the boulders below, and swung outwards. His last sight of the kestrel was of Keekee remaining where she stood. He waited till the length of his swings decreased, and began to climb. The worst part was at the commencement, where the rope lay pressed against the overjutting cliff. His hands were frequently cut. But his biceps were powerful, he had no fear, and soon this part was passed. For the rest, it was arduous work lifting oneself hand over hand, helped by occasional foot-holds; but it was twenty minutes before it was achieved, and the panting youth, with breeches torn, with wet hair and bloody face, flung himself on the sward, while the veteran fisherman in a blue guernsey shouted:

"A master climb! A master climb, midear!"

And *finish, finish*, wailed Mewliboy, long after the gulls were settled again, their young fed, and he was sailing alone in the sky. Wave and air were quiet. Kronk and his wife were gone inland somewhere, and neither Nugg nor Scarl nor herring gull chased Keekee, for she was far away, poised in the luminous air of a shining realm, where nothing bullied the gentlest of the falcons, or made frantic the little mother-spirit; and there no mice knew fear. Once again she was joyful, with the happiness that comes after fret and anxiety, and the fosterling was with her.

The sun dipped below the sea-line, leaving in the lake of the sky a scatter of little clouds like scarlet feathers from some heavenly bird. Mewliboy soared among them, wheeling in wide, calm circles before going home to his tree-top castle. He was serene at that height, and he needed not to beat his wings as he soared away the last of the day's light. The dusk stole over sea and land, silently, invisibly. Below him the bay was calm and glimmering, and above the scarlet feathers were scarlet no more, but grey, as though old. Tranquilly the buzzard surveyed the darkening fields of the earth. Warm air rose from the sea, and his broad sails were filled as he turned westwards. Whiter shone the white surge that edged the rocks of the headland, and the wind moved inland quickly. Then high in the west, a faint point of light, he saw the star of all the falcons. It became brighter, and beat sharp wings as it hovered, protecting, in the evening sky. Having seen the star come in the summer night, Mewliboy drifted homeward on the warm wind, passing over the coastline and above many dusky fields till he came to his pinewood.

The night passed, and steadfastly the star hovered, flickering gold wings in the west. It burned brighter as it swooped seawards, and settled, a shining glory, beyond the dark island. Its wings were poised to heaven, then slowly drawn down and folded round its immortal body.

It was very far away. The waves broke on the rocks, rushing in white foam, lapsing, and rushing again. The tide ebbed.

The tide flowed. Somewhere below Bone Ledge an oyster-catcher whistled, and a kittiwake cried in the cliffs. Above the mainland a dim light was spreading in the darkness, and the mists over the sea rolled cold and grey before the dawn wind. Bird after bird awoke and called in the first light of the east; gulls glided from their nests, ravens croaked, shags flapped their wings, rock pipits and stonechats called in the new day. Once again the search for food, for life, began. The mainland became outlined against the pale sky, and soon the sun would come. Larks sang above the fields of the headland.

Light, the master-builder of all things that are on the earth, sought every feather, every bone, every skull in the eyrie, and discovered the form of Keekee facing the west. Her wings were drooped and fallen by her side. Her head was bowed, her eyes were closed, as in humility of prayer, as in ecstasy of love. She brooded the fledgeling, whose head peeped from her dead breast. They were happy, they were flying, they were with the star!